REPUBLICAN VIETNAM, 1963–1975

A Study of the Weatherhead East Asian Institute, Columbia University, and the US-Vietnam Research Center, University of Oregon

The Studies of the Weatherhead East Asian Institute of Columbia University were inaugurated in 1962 to bring to a wider public the results of significant new research on modern and contemporary East Asia.

The US-Vietnam Research Center at the University of Oregon devotes our efforts to promote research and education on modern Vietnam and the Vietnamese American community.

REPUBLICAN VIETNAM, 1963–1975

War, Society, Diaspora

Edited by Trinh M. Luu
and Tuong Vu

University of Hawai'i Press
HONOLULU

© 2023 University of Hawai'i Press
All rights reserved
Paperback edition 2025
Printed in the United States of America

First printed 2023

Library of Congress Cataloging-in-Publication Data

Names: Luu, Trinh M., editor. | Vu, Tuong, editor.
Title: Republican Vietnam, 1963–1975 : war, society, diaspora / edited by Trinh M. Luu and Tuong Vu.
Other titles: Studies of the Weatherhead East Asian Institute, Columbia University.
Description: Honolulu : University of Hawai'i Press, [2023] | Series: Studies of the Weatherhead East Asian Institute, Columbia University | Includes bibliographical references and index.
Identifiers: LCCN 2023019308 | ISBN 9780824895181 (hardback) | ISBN 9780824896355 (epub) | ISBN 9780824896362 (kindle edition) | ISBN 9780824896348 (pdf)
Subjects: LCSH: Vietnamese diaspora. | Vietnamese—Foreign countries. | Republicanism. | Vietnam (Republic)—Civilization.
Classification: LCC DS556.9 .R473 2023 | DDC 959.704/3—dc23/eng/20230505
LC record available at https://lccn.loc.gov/2023019308

ISBN 9798880701698 (paperback)

University of Hawai'i Press books are printed on acid-free paper and meet the guidelines for permanence and durability of the Council on Library Resources.

Cover Art: Illustration to the song, "Nẻo đường kỷ niệm," best translated as "Memory's Backroads," written by Tuấn Khanh (1933–) and Hoài Linh (1920-1995). An imprint of Việt Nam Nhạc Tuyển, the publishing arm of Dĩa hát Việt Nam.

Contents

Acknowledgments ix

Abbreviations xi

INTRODUCTION
War, the Second Republic, and the Diaspora
Trinh M. Luu and Tuong Vu
1

CHAPTER ONE
**"Everything Depends on Us Alone":
President Nguyễn Văn Thiệu's Vietnamization Strategy**
David L. Prentice
21

CHAPTER TWO
"All the Communists Must Leave": The Origin, Evolution, and Failure of Saigon's Peace Demands, 1963–1973
George J. Veith
41

CHAPTER THREE
War, Nation-Building, and the Role of the Press in the Second Republic
Thanh Hoang and Tuong Vu
61

CHAPTER FOUR
Reconceptualizing Foreign Aid: The United States' Commercial Import Program for the Republic of Vietnam, 1954–1975
Phạm Thị Hồng Hà
83

CHAPTER FIVE
Building Higher Education during War: South Vietnam's Public Universities in the Second Republic, 1967–1975
Trương Thùy Dung
104

CHAPTER SIX
Buddhist Social Work in the Vietnam War: Thích Nhất Hạnh and the School of Youth for Social Service
Adrienne Minh-Châu Lê
124

CHAPTER SEVEN
Political Philology and Academic Freedom: A Defense of Thích Minh Châu
Wynn Gadkar-Wilcox
145

CHAPTER EIGHT
Songs of Sympathy in Time of War: Commercial Music in the Republic of Vietnam
Jason Gibbs
168

CHAPTER NINE
Pray the Rosary and Do Apostolic Work: The Modern Vietnamese Catholic Associational Culture
Tuan Hoang
189

CHAPTER TEN
Rhizomatic Transnationalism: Nhạc Vàng and the Legacy of Republicanism in Overseas Vietnamese Communities
Vinh Phu Pham
203

CHAPTER ELEVEN

Ethnic Buddhism and Women in Hoa Pham's
Lady of the Realm* and Chi Vu's *Anguli Ma: A Gothic Tale
Phạm Vũ Lan Anh
224

CHAPTER TWELVE

Vietism: Human Rights, Carl Jung, and the New Vietnamese
Trinh M. Luu
245

Bibliography 273

Contributors 295

Index 299

Acknowledgments

Like *Building a Republican Nation in Vietnam, 1920–1963*, this volume is a product of the international conference, "Studying Republican Vietnam: Issues, Challenges, and Prospects," held at the University of Oregon on October 14–15, 2019. We are grateful to the participants, especially Keith Taylor and Peter Zinoman, for sharing their deep knowledge and great enthusiasm. Until recently, the scholarship on modern Vietnamese history, the Vietnam War, and the Vietnamese diaspora have largely ignored republican Vietnam's perspectives. By focusing on the post-1963 period in this volume, we hope to introduce fresh research on the Second Republic, especially its wartime society and diasporic continuities.

The US-Vietnam Research Center, which organized the conference, is indebted to the University of Oregon, especially the Global Studies Institute, the Department of Political Science, the Program of Asian Studies, and the university's libraries, for their institutional and financial support. Holly Lakey, Cindy Nelson, Lori O'Hollaren, and Dennis Galvan made everything easy for us. Alex-Thai Vo, Nguyễn Lương Hải Khôi, and Nguyễn Thị Thủy provided much needed assistance.

The list of individuals who offered funding, advice, and inspiration for the conference is long: Mr. and Mrs. Nguyễn Đức Cường, Mr. Hoàng Đức Nhã, the late Phạm Kim Ngọc, Dr. Trần Quang Minh, Mr. and Mrs. Phan Lương Quang, Professor Nguyễn Mạnh Hùng, and Mr. and Mrs. Nguyễn Tường Thiết. Thanks are also due to Nancy Bui, Linda Ho Peche, Bùi Văn Phú, Nguyễn Đình Thắng, Ngô Văn, Hà Thúc Tiến, Bùi Đình Đại, Võ Thành Nhân, and Kính Hoà.

We also thank the participants and presenters at the conference whose insightful works are not part of either volume. They include Keith Taylor, Olga Dror, Christoph Giebel, Judith Henchy, Mark Sidel, Edward Miller, Nathalie Huynh Chau Nguyen, Alvin Bui, Nguyễn Đức Cường, Hoàng Đức Nhã, Nguyễn Thị Từ Huy, Sean Fear, and Hao Jun Tam.

The volume would not have been possible without the early support of Lien-Hang Nguyen and Columbia University's Weatherhead East Asian Institute. Masako Ikeda, our editor at the University of Hawai'i Press, deserves special thanks for her patience and encouragement. As we prepared the manuscript, Mark Sidel, Nu-Anh Tran, Marguerite Nguyen, Peter Zinoman, and Kevin Li read and commented on various chapters. We thank them for their many great suggestions.

Trinh Luu would like to dedicate this volume to her parents. Tuong Vu would like to dedicate this volume to his family.

Abbreviations

ARVN	Army of the Republic of Vietnam
CIP	Commercial Import Program
DRV	Democratic Republic of Vietnam
NLF	National Liberation Front
NSC	National Security Council
PRG	Provisional Revolutionary Government
RVN	Republic of Vietnam
RVNAF	Republic of Vietnam Armed Forces
SYSS	School of Youth for Social Service
SRV	Socialist Republic of Vietnam
UBC	Unified Buddhist Church

INTRODUCTION

War, the Second Republic, and the Diaspora

Trinh M. Luu and Tuong Vu

In some measure, the Republic of Vietnam (RVN) was born out of a street battle in April 1955—"the Battle of Saigon." In the thick of the fray, which lasted several days, the French-trained Vietnam National Army, under the newly appointed Premier Ngô Đình Diệm's leadership, defeated the Bình Xuyên militia for control of Saigon. The premier's victory at great odds helped persuade the Eisenhower administration to throw US support behind him, allowing him to prevail over other rivals and oust the chief of state, Bảo Đại. He founded the RVN in October 1955.[1]

That victory offered the newly established republic only a brief period of peace; war would soon resume. The RVN's demise was not predestined, but its survival was often under severe threat. As war escalated throughout the 1960s and 1970s, more than half a million allied troops fought alongside the republic's Armed Forces against large units of North Vietnamese fighters that had infiltrated the South—joined by many locals and backed logistically by Chinese and Soviet forces. Such circumstances triggered radical changes in South Vietnam as the government and most southerners sought to harness forces beyond their control, not only to survive but also to build the country and to live meaningful lives. The dynamism of such changes amid a devastating war and massive outside intervention is the focus of this book.

Like *Building a Republican Nation in Vietnam, 1920–1963,* this volume grew out of a conference on Vietnamese republicanism held at the University of Oregon in October 2019.[2] Both volumes break with most existing scholarship, reexamining the history of modern Vietnam, the Vietnam War, and the Vietnamese diaspora from the perspective of republican ideas and politics. Central to modern republicanism are beliefs in popular sovereignty, democratic government, the separation of church and state, and the rule of law.[3] Early twentieth-century Vietnamese intellectuals drew inspiration from French, American, Japanese, and Chinese thinkers to develop their own sense of a modern Vietnamese nation. As *Building a Republican Nation* shows, Vietnamese republicans bitterly fought for those ideals even as they collectively struggled against communism. Despite a hopeful beginning, the First Republic that came about under Ngô Đình Diệm was far from realizing such ideals. Authoritarian rather than democratic rule defined it. A conflict between the state and Buddhist activists led to its collapse.

This volume continues where *Building a Republican Nation* leaves off, covering the period after the fall of the First Republic in 1963. The coup that ended the First Republic brought in its wake an unstable period of military rule. North Vietnam accelerated the war and the United States responded with direct intervention. Despite such a hostile environment, the struggle for republican ideals continued, driving the generals in power to lift restrictions on opposition parties and the press in 1964. Owing in great part to popular demands, the military junta allowed the drafting of a democratic constitution that founded the Second Republic in 1967, which ushered in more meaningful popular participation than before.

Until the end of the Second Republic in 1975, war devastated South Vietnam. It not only destroyed countless lives and created millions of refugees, but also accelerated urbanization as American dollars, technology, and culture flooded the country. State leaders sought legitimacy through the popularly elected bicameral assembly. Yet the war threatened those institutions as US aid and the presence of Americans bred corruption and resentment, just as the state became more repressive toward civil society in order to cope with communist terrorism.[4] The interactions among the state, social groups, communist forces, and foreign powers created a situation in which the fight for republican ideals took place in myriad spheres and was motivated by a deep yearning for peace, a sense of civic responsibility, the pursuit of intellectual and artistic freedom, and an overall critical attitude toward the government.[5]

This volume uncovers just how war and outside intervention transformed the Second Republic. Whether about higher education, the printed press, the aid-dependent consumer economy, commercial music, or the civic culture of religious organizations, each chapter provides a different angle of that republic. The thematic diversity of this volume, as much as the cutting-edge research on Vietnamese republicanism, is what makes it novel. The volume does not stop with 1975; it covers the Vietnamese diaspora to explore how those republican ideals have endured after the war. Overall, the volume seeks to show Vietnamese, from political leaders to ordinary citizens, as agents of their history.

This introduction comprises three parts. In the first, we review recent trends in the study of post-1963 South Vietnam, one that gives greater agency to noncommunist South Vietnamese. The second section examines the relationship between warfare, the state, and society during the Second Republic.[6] The third explores what strains of republicanism have been kept alive in the Vietnamese diasporas and how.

RECENT TRENDS IN THE STUDY OF THE SECOND REPUBLIC

As the United States became increasingly involved in Vietnam in the 1960s, many scholars and researchers began to study the Second Republic more intensively. Most were government employees or contractors whose studies were meant to bolster American policy of defeating Hanoi-commanded communist forces. They had the advantage of conducting field work relatively free of constraints in areas under republican army control, especially if they were able to speak or read Vietnamese. This helped generate many informative works on RVN politics, economy, and society.[7]

Whether about village life, land reform, the economy, constitutional making, or elections, the picture that emerged was a mixed one that was constantly changing.[8] For example, in a major study of the South Vietnamese village economy, Robert Sansom argues that "considering the 1960–1967 period as a whole, the Viet Cong enjoyed the greatest support for their programs in the 1960–1964 period, before the war was escalated and Viet Cong taxes began to weigh heavily on the population. The [republican government's] benefits reached the population after 1965 and flowed generously through 1967."[9] If "the past was in the hands of the Viet Cong, the future favored the [government]." He concludes, "The tragedy of Vietnam was that the good and the bad were so evenly divided [between the government and the communist insurgency], thus the peasant had no clear choice. The bloodbath arose from the fact that the closest side [to the peasant] was always changing."[10]

Whether Sansom's conclusion is correct or not, the larger point is about a constantly shifting environment in the battle for hearts and minds. Between 1964 and 1967, republican ideals scored a major achievement in the establishment of a liberal constitution and elections for a bicameral assembly.[11] These institutions normalized the political process and expanded what Allan Goodman calls "the base of political community." He notes, "The attitude of political organizations during the period studied changed considerably. In 1967 political leaders interviewed tended to feel that their enemies were principally each other; in 1969, they had come to view their political opponent as the Viet Cong."[12] Charles Joiner also remarked in 1974 that "a considerable amount of political development transpired [after 1967], at least in terms of building political institutions.... Significant numbers of people were enmeshed in the legal political process."[13] Yet, as John Donnell shows, the situation after 1972 was precarious because of President Nguyễn Văn Thiệu's attempt to organize his own political party—the Democratic Party—as well as his effort to circumvent the democratic process.[14]

Since 2000, scholarly interest in the Second Republic has grown significantly, owing in part to a new generation of scholars with linguistic skills, and in part to the availability of fresh archival sources, especially from Vietnam, and the memoirs written by South Vietnamese refugees.[15] The new trend in scholarship seeks to restore agency to South Vietnamese as historical actors in their own right, despite the constraints that held them back. In the new scholarship, republican governments were no US puppets; nor did they lack domestic legitimacy. As Lien-Hang Nguyen argues, "often, American leaders were at the mercy of actors in ... Saigon."[16] South Vietnamese social and political elites drew deep inspiration from Vietnamese national traditions and modern ideas, from conservative to reformist to revolutionary.[17] Their anticommunism was shaped by their experience of the 1940s and 1950s, long before the United States became interested in Vietnam.[18] The large presence of American troops in South Vietnam after 1965, despite challenging the traditional conservatism of Vietnamese society and the sense of national identity, strengthened Vietnamese ethnic identification.[19]

Recent scholarship on elite politics has not contradicted earlier studies.[20] However, scholars have begun to examine broader aspects such as the republic's policies on education, economic development, and foreign relations.[21] New works have shed light on how Buddhists, Catholics, and students emerged as key players in Saigon politics.[22] Such civil society forces were diverse and fragmented, yet dynamic and influential. They helped democratize the RVN, first in the ousting of General Nguyễn Khánh, then in the decision of the ruling generals to promulgate a new constitution and organize elections in 1967. Their presence attested not to a lack of social cohesion, as some scholars have noted,[23] but to a measure of South Vietnam's democratic potential.

The Armed Forces of the RVN (RVNAF) is likewise undergoing scholarly reassessment. Even though new studies do not necessarily argue that Saigon could have won the war (and certainly not on its own while Hanoi continued to receive Soviet and Chinese support), they are challenging long-held myths about the RVNAF. Writing on the last two years of the RVN (1973–1975), George Veith argues, "By 1973, the South Vietnamese military, despite numerous internal and economic issues, had developed into a fighting force quite capable of defeating the North Vietnamese."[24] Andrew Wiest, who focuses on mid-level officers in the South Vietnamese army, comes to the same conclusion: "Although the upper echelon of the ARVN remained deeply flawed, the lower levels of the ARVN...fought with valor for years. And, while the strategic structure of the war rested on misguided assumptions, the U.S./ARVN alliance usually bested the vaunted [communist army] in battle and came tantalizingly close to military victory in the years after the Tết Offensive."[25]

With the new scholarship, it is now possible to understand the war from the South Vietnamese's perspective.

WAR, THE STATE, AND SOUTH VIETNAMESE SOCIETY

The Vietnam War, its length and scale, profoundly shaped the South Vietnamese state and society. The war's effects certainly varied by region. Much of the impact was due to the death and destruction. The RVNAF lost about 250,000 soldiers; three times as many were wounded. Perhaps no fewer than a million civilians perished. Among the most documented cases is Mỹ Lai, where about five hundred people were massacred by American troops in March 1968.[26] This happened a month after communist forces slaughtered about three thousand people and buried them in mass graves in Huế, an event that still awaits a serious study.[27] In 1968, 1972, and 1975, thousands of civilians died under communist artillery when fleeing the battlefields.[28] These events traumatized survivors for the rest of their lives, especially those who lost their friends and family members.

The war also disrupted the normal course of life. As thousands of young men were drafted into war, women were left to raise children and take care of the elderly. Many followed their husbands or fathers to wherever they were stationed, accepting temporary disruption rather than long-term separation. Millions became refugees or moved to the cities to avoid being caught in the crossfire.[29] Those who lived in slums eked out a living by taking on odd jobs. Towns were swollen with people and rice fields lay fallow. Given large numbers of American GIs and other foreign troops, a war economy emerged. Imported goods flooded the market and production shrank. The war upended the social status of many from traditional upper classes while raising that of anyone who could profit from the import economy.[30]

Southerners who did not directly experience the war found ways to build their lives, even devising opportunities for social mobility. Rapid urbanization and military expansion, for instance, created numerous nonagricultural employment opportunities.[31] Acquiring a modern education, even a graduate degree, became ever more feasible as thousands of new schools were built.[32] The government needed a strong workforce to man the new industries and services that sprang up.[33] Thanks in part to foreign aid, the living standards for employees in nonagricultural sectors improved as real wages doubled between 1958 and 1971 and continued to grow though at a slower and more volatile rate.[34]

As urbanization accelerated, foreign cultural products spread widely throughout the south, especially in cities and among youth. Former Minister Tôn Thất Thiện declared that "the American values—rejection of authority, the equation of success with wealth, the insistence of ruthless efficiency—combined with American political dominance have produced an explosive threat on Vietnamese society and culture."[35] Others, especially the young, welcomed the changed taste in food, clothing, language, music, art, literature, and lifestyle. From American jazz to French existentialism, intellectuals, writers, musicians, and artists tried their hands at what interested them, and in that way created an open, vibrant, and globalized culture in the heart of South Vietnam.[36]

The impact of war on religion was similarly complex. South Vietnam was religiously plural, Buddhism, Catholicism, Cao Đài, and Hoà Hảo being the largest groups. After the fall of the First Republic, the clergies of these churches took on prominent political roles, mobilizing their followers to vie for social and political influence. All three religions expanded during the 1960s and 1970s, opening their own universities and embarking on political activism.[37] As war tore society apart, bred social vices, and inflicted sufferings, it empowered religious leaders such as Thích Nhất Hạnh, whose philosophy of social engagement attracted a great following and spawned an active youth organization for social service, as Adrienne Minh-Châu Lê discusses in chapter 6 of this volume.

For the Catholic Church, as Tuan Hoang demonstrates in chapter 9, rising anticommunist sentiments and American intervention brought local churches into contact with foreign movements, helping them gain external support and attract new followers through new Catholic Action organizations such as the Blue Army or Cursillo.

The war posed the highest threat to the republican state and eventually destroyed it. As it escalated through the 1960s, it forced the Second Republic to depend more and more on US aid. As David Prentice and George Veith's chapters in this volume show, government officials, especially President Nguyễn Văn Thiệu, were deeply aware of the challenges facing their state, both internationally and domestically, both politically and economically. This awareness motivated them to propose peace initiatives, welcome Vietnamization with the promise of continuing US support, implement reforms to wean the economy off US aid, and support a democratic constitution in 1967 that gave birth to the Second Republic.[38] As Phạm Thị Hồng Hà shows in chapter 4, South Vietnam's dependence on US aid does not mean government officials and Vietnamese entrepreneurs did not have agency.

Similarly complicated was the relationship between the state and its citizens. War alienated many South Vietnamese, but it also helped the state cultivate anticommunist nationalism and forge a new relationship with many of its citizens. Facing privation, many southerners naturally reached out for help and relief from the government. As Heather Stur argues, "the notion of a give-and-take relationship between the RVN government and its citizens illustrates a sense of national identity and how the war facilitated the development of that national connection."[39] Another example of the rallying effect of war is the high number of young men who volunteered to fight for the republic and the broad support for the General Mobilization Law enacted in response to communist brutalities during the Tết Offensive.[40]

As southern citizens stood by the government and made great sacrifices for the war effort, government leaders were compelled to accept many of their demands, whether for emergency relief or for political representation. The move to promulgate a democratic constitution and to hold elections in 1966 and 1967 reflected a tacit bargain between the military government and various Buddhist groups in the "Struggle Movement," which led the revolt in central Vietnam in mid-1966.[41] Under the First Republic, republican institutions in the form of a constitution and an elected legislature had existed but were largely overshadowed by Ngô Đình Diệm's authoritarian government. Republican institutions in the

Second Republic would prove to be more robust. As Thanh Hoang and Tuong Vu argue in chapter 3 of this volume, the bargain also helped foster a vibrant print media. When the war intensified in 1972 and the state became more corrupt and repressive, it confronted a rebellious media that loudly demanded government accountability and fought courageously in defense of press freedom.[42]

The Vietnam War also shaped southern society in that it was a civil war overlaid by an ideological conflict. In the south, the war was deeply divisive. Many families had relatives fighting on both sides. Others were sympathetic to the communist cause or held allegiance to Hồ Chí Minh's government. Few were left untouched and most had to take sides. More than that, no clear border separated the two warring sides. The 17th parallel divided the North and the South, but much of the South became a battlefield. A village could be under government control during the day and by nightfall, the insurgents would take over. Communist bombings often killed more innocent bystanders than their primary targets for assassination.[43] As Gerald Hickey observes, "Without battle lines, without an identifiable enemy, the war was everywhere."[44] To strengthen their soldiers' loyalty and solidarity, communist propaganda portrayed the enemy as puppets, traitors to the nation, lackeys of foreign powers, and class enemies. Southern propaganda called their communist enemy bloodthirsty and evil. These dehumanizing terms not only justified the violence and hatred, but also permitted and even encouraged extraordinary cruelty.

Such intense enmity existed side by side with a liberal atmosphere and a vibrant civil society. These contradictory legacies of the Second Republic have endured in the highly partisan Vietnamese diaspora, which is striving to recreate the pluralism and cultural achievements of the late RVN.

THE VIETNAMESE DIASPORA IN POPULAR IMAGINATION AND HISTORIOGRAPHY

It is unknown just how many South Vietnamese fled when Saigon fell under communist rule. In different ways and at different times, they left, bound for any place that would accept them. Together, more than a million braved the high seas, the lucky ones finding themselves in Guam, Malaysia, Indonesia, Thailand, the Philippines, or Hong Kong.[45] To set off, they must have held fast to some hope of rescue, and most, if not all, turned to faith to steel their resolve.

More than 130,000 fled first, many airlifted out of the country as Saigon fell. Guam, first in a series of stopovers, would keep them in tent cities before they were taken to the United States. No sooner had they gotten on their feet than news of the crisis caught up to them. In 1977, fifteen thousand crossed the South China Sea—some leaving North Vietnam, their boats hugging the Chinese coast—to find asylum in neighboring countries. A year later, roughly sixty-two thousand Vietnamese crowded the camps there. With more than half a million refugees on their shores by 1979, Southeast Asian countries, overwhelmed and at a loss, would tow boats back to international waters.[46]

The 1979 Geneva agreement, the outcome of a spirited dialogue between sixty nations, set the terms for how to resettle them. The United Nations High Commissioner for Refugees (UNHCR) took the lead, setting up processing centers across Indonesia and the Philippines.[47] Until 1988, Vietnamese refugees would pass through these transit points on their way to Canada, Australia, France, the United States, and other countries as far away as Brazil and Israel. The measures put into place began to unravel, though, in 1989, when the number of Vietnamese taking flight again surged. Resettlement policies had tightened by then, so between 1989 and 1996, not all of the 120,000 Vietnamese screened found a home outside the camps. Some, long-stayers with nowhere else to go, remained in place for years.[48]

UNHCR and Vietnam's communist government had meanwhile reached an agreement in 1979 to allow people to leave the country safely. The Orderly Departure Program (ODP), an international effort to find legal migration channels, would reduce the number of Vietnamese crossing the sea. It would take years, however, before the plan came into being. ODP reached a high-water mark in 1991, at which point more than eighty-six thousand Vietnamese, especially Amerasians and political prisoners, had flown to thirty countries. By itself, ODP resettled about half a million Vietnamese, the United States taking the lion's share of reeducation camp detainees. This migration tapered off by the mid-1990s.[49]

On almost every continent, and against great odds, the Vietnamese are still making their mark. Tracing the routes they took is one way to understand how this diaspora came to be. The history of their flight—why they left, what troubles beset them, and how they fared at long last—could reshape the ways we see twentieth-century Vietnam. We may never know how many perished at sea, or died in the vast, still hardly understood network of prison camps. These stories would have implications for many years to come. Already, scholars, historians, artists, novelists, and many others are peering into this past, each finding some way to convey, above all, the triumph of the human spirit.

These are important steps, important because within Vietnam little is known or can be said about the refugees. Already in 1975, the revolutionary government had dismissed the exodus as fiction, as just another American ploy. Party newspapers called those who left slaves of the American empire. Communist parties in Germany and France, observing from afar, were happy to parrot that same conclusion.

In Vietnam, meanwhile, families were removed from their homes and sent to remote areas to break new land and settle there. More than two million would end up in gulags.[50] Bias against the South became more abstract. Believing that republican arts and letters stood in the way of the "new man," the government set about erasing traces of the ancien régime. To make a clean break, the authorities sent shock brigades to raid storefronts and private homes, burning what they could hunt down. All the while, the government, citing a right of property inheritance, called on Thailand, the Philippines, and other countries to return the vessels, the "hundreds of cargo planes and jet fighters," and "tons of gold" that the refugees had taken with them.[51]

By 1979, with war on its frontiers against China and Cambodia, communist Vietnam doubled down on its stance. The country seemed on the brink of collapse. Galloping inflation, famine, and "thievery and waste" big and small had exposed the shortcomings of collectivism. Subsidy—a system of rationing and price control set up during the war—could barely cover basic needs. Aid had slowed to a trickle.[52] In two publications—*Those Who Leave*, released in 1979, and *Vietnam: Which Human Rights?*, a year later—Hanoi laid the blame on China and the United States.[53]

It was the high noon of socialist ethics, and human rights had not long been a great truth. To party bureaucrats, the rights movement was little more than a "vast anti-Vietnamese campaign" to undermine its rule. Believing that socialist morality had outstripped every other ethical system, the regime in Hanoi claimed to have "given back to millions of Vietnamese their human dignity."[54] Still coy on the topic of reeducation, it asserted the right, as a sovereign country, to act freely on its own land. Vietnamese media at the time had only sharp words for the refugees. Work-shy, they were "too used to the life of the past regime ... easy life owing to external help ... so they flee."[55] At other times, the South Vietnamese were depicted gliding out to sea not so much to avoid work as to profit from an opportunity, spurred on by the prospect of an easier life in the West.[56] The common theme was that the refugees were good-for-nothings—prostitutes, drug addicts, criminals, and subversives.[57]

In the West, this story, pushed largely by those with ties to Hanoi, did not always fall on deaf ears. It was not uncommon for foreign correspondents who stayed after 1975 to be one-sided, so keen were they to stand up to American imperialism. Saigon came through, as often depicted during the war, as corrupt.[58] After American troops went home, a Belgian Marxist priest wrote, many Saigonese ran to other countries because they were "little inclined to accept a period of austerity."[59] Prison camps were "benign," "therapeutic," run with "due respect to persons."[60] New economic zones, another heavy-handed measure, became safe places where many with no jobs chose to go.[61] Never mind what the refugees had to say about what went on in their country; they had to "justify their departure."[62]

On new land, trying to earn their keep, the refugees bore their feelings alone. Had their Western colleagues read the hundreds of magazines and newspapers they founded in exile, their side of the story might have been known.[63] The associations they built to support refugees and prisoners of conscience seldom got a hearing in mainstream media. This long-standing bias against the South, the full impact of it, hit home in 1983. *Vietnam: A Television History* was playing on PBS. To the 9.7 million Americans who watched it, this landmark series tried to present a factual, even-handed account of the war. But in nearly all of it, the thirteen-part documentary omitted South Vietnamese voices. Between Americans, who struggled with a guilty conscience, and North Vietnamese, who came across as defenders of the home soil, the story unfolded. Perhaps it was too soon to call for a greater mix of perspectives because when the refugees tried to do so, the producers saw it as "anger and bitterness."[64]

In the smaller world of scholarly publishing, the same distrust festered. By the 1980s, Vietnam Studies had gone into decline and Vietnamese American studies (VAS), as a subfield, had yet to appear. Even so, a good many refugees in the West felt the need to research aspects of the war that even they had not understood. Few at the time were as well equipped. The exodus had brought to the United States many historians, scientists, economists, and sociologists who had the practical know-how and a native's grasp of the language and culture. Nguyễn Ngọc Bích and Huỳnh Sanh Thông, forerunners in this venture, had published books on Vietnamese poetry. Yet it is as true today as it was then that the refugees' desire and talent "have not been matched by the availability of research opportunities."[65] Old battle lines had also been firmly drawn.

Nevertheless, the refugees wrote and circulated works in their own language. More than the novel, more than historical studies, more, even, than poetry, memoir was the form many chose to set down their stories.

Reeducation camp memoirs became a genre all its own. Meanwhile, those at home with English spent their time translating. The hope was that, reading these works, the public would have a clearer picture of the war and its aftermath. Many others collected, restored, and preserved the trove of literary works from South Vietnam. Vernacular radio and television programs took off soon after, and these efforts have not slackened since.

By the time VAS came into its own, this Vietnamese-language archive laid wide open to scholars. It is by and large still untapped. As a branch of Asian American studies, VAS as we know it today may have had its start as critical refugee study (CRS), founded on the claim that traditional refugee studies had not gone far enough. The research conducted in the 1980s, it was said, tended to cast Vietnamese refugees either as victims who needed help or as model minorities.[66] The problem is not that the depictions are false, but that they shore up a myth of American rescue and care. CRS would reexamine the refugees' experiences to convey the full impact of American militarism around the world.[67] To do so, scholars follow the steps activists in the 1960s had taken. As Yen Le Espiritu wrote, "the stories of Vietnamese refugee flight must begin with this history of US military, economic, and political intervention in Southeast Asia."[68]

Although, thanks to CRS, we now have a clearer sense of how the first wave of Vietnamese refugees adopted this place and made it their own, the field has yet to engage area studies or Vietnamese-language scholarship. From Vietnamese studies, CRS might draw, for example, the scope of Soviet and Chinese military intervention during the war, and the three-way conflict involving communist Vietnam, Cambodia, and China from 1978 to 1989, which generated far more refugees than 1975. CRS has had little to say. Scholars of Vietnamese history are still grappling with the many strains of nationalism that caught on during the mid-twentieth century, but CRS has generally skirted the issue, presenting the conflict instead as an imperial war and ignoring the class warfare waged by the communist government against class enemies in the North after 1954 and in the South after 1975. Often, the Vietnamese come through as one people, driven by one cause, making the critique of American empire that much more potent.

The field is at its best when documenting how the refugees, having paid an extremely high price to do so, created their worlds abroad. Yet this scholarship still has to catch up to the rich discourse taking place in Vietnamese. The thousands of memoirs and poems about reeducation have yet to be touched. Mai Thảo, Doãn Quốc Sỹ, Đỗ Quý Toàn, and many others, each in his own way, have reflected on what war, death, and exile meant to them. Works on religion, philosophy, and literary criticism are no less copious. Today, Vietnamese-language discourse in the United States is moving at a much faster pace. Without reading a page or two of what the refugees have written, we may be no closer to understanding their flight than scholars of the 1980s.

Where CRS tends to cast the refugees as casualties of American imperialism, "restricted in their capacity to act as full subjects," other studies undertaken since 2000 place clearer focus on agency. Thien-Huong Ninh, Marguerite Nguyen, Quan Tue Tran, and Jana Lipman, among others, by bringing the minutiae of community life into relief, show how Vietnamese refugees leave their mark wherever they have settled. We see it play out in the earliest refugee camps, where Vietnamese men and women staged hunger strikes, sit-ins, and demonstrations to shape refugee resettlement policy.[69] In the American South, the Vietnamese, by tilling soil in the "manners and spirit of a people which preserve a republic," claim a space in the "American pastoral tableau."[70] Little Saigon's, now a "global brand" and a part of twentieth-century vernacular, exemplify the adaptive and self-sustaining communities the refugees create through "peaceful, yet diplomatically firm" engagement with others.[71] Standing together as a unified electorate, Vietnamese refugees in the United States have sent candidates to seats of government, where their voices on local and international issues can be heard. They organize commemorative rituals to remember their loss, all the while paying tribute to the places that became their refuge.[72] In this way and so many others, Vietnamese refugees are described as "frontier seekers" and "place builders."[73]

Nearly everywhere, the refugees' sense of community transcends national borders. A love of kin, or something similar, seems to resonate in the way they see the health of their community as connected to the well-being of their families in Vietnam. This could explain why affairs in the Asia Pacific, and the flow of people, goods, and ideas across the Pacific Rim, inform which way Vietnamese Americans vote. Through popular music, the refugees shape more than ever their former homeland's culture and their remittance has helped Vietnam's moribund economy recover.[74] This form of "transnational politics" has long set Asian Americans apart from other ethnic communities in the United States.[75]

This cultural and political landscape Vietnamese refugees have created owes a great deal of its richness to RVN republicanism. The chapters in this volume together provide something of a starting point for the post-1963 period. Each explores what republicanism may have meant in South Vietnam, showing how some stood up for the values they prized when they thought public interest demanded it.

In this light, the refugees' political and cultural life might mean something larger than it seems. Whether in France, Australia, Japan, or the United States, Vietnamese refugees carry forward the belief that "the good life" consists of active citizenship. Condemning human rights violations before the United Nations, denouncing Hồ Chí Minh's portrait in Little Saigon, then urging the Socialist Republic of Vietnam to claim sovereignty over China in an international court are not just expressions of anticommunism.[76] Were we to see them in the light of republican ideals, then the refugees are in each instance spurning arbitrary forms of power. As Thuy Vo Dang states, Vietnamese anticommunism means a great many things: "it may entail a rejection of Hồ Chí Minh-style communism born from colonial influences and nationalist revolutionary ideals or disdain for a series of communist endeavors to equalize classes through draconian methods of land reforms and purges."[77] Vietnamese refugees disavow totalitarianism at every turn because press freedom, civic virtues, and religious worship all have a place in their sense of liberty.

The diverse associational life they have forged through religion and the arts is yet another hallmark of RVN legacy. Temples, churches, and community centers, in a stricter sense, continue to be places where Vietnamese refugees cultivate a "love of home" and a love for one's own.[78] The Association of Former Military Police, the Institute for Historic Cao Dai Religion, and the Vietnamese Environmental Protection Society are among the hundreds of leagues founded in the spirit of democracy and cooperation. For members of such organizations, preserving their history and culture has been an underlying motive for them to remember a lost country and find new ways to raise its name.

THE CHAPTERS AHEAD

This volume gathers a diverse class of scholars and researchers from Australia, the United States, and Vietnam to examine the impacts of war on South Vietnamese society and the legacies of the RVN in the diaspora. Among them are historians, political scientists, literary scholars, and a librarian. The topics are just as diverse, covering different aspects of the war's complex and wide-ranging impact on South Vietnam and the diaspora.

In chapter 1, David Prentice analyzes President Nguyễn Văn Thiệu's

Vietnamization strategy. Rather than begrudgingly accepting Vietnamization, Thiệu was among its most ardent advocates as he sought the complete reassertion of the RVN's autonomy and self-sufficiency. Throughout the war, various South Vietnamese governments also made overtures of peace to its adversary as part of their strategy for survival. In chapter 2, George Veith discusses the origin and evolution of such peace initiatives from 1963 to 1973, showing the RVN leaders' complex calculations in response to pressure from outside and from their own constituencies.

Chapter 3, by Thanh Hoang and Tuong Vu, analyzes the printed press, showing how the relationship between the government and the press was more complex than commonly understood. Despite the government's sometimes repressive tendency, the press grew rapidly thanks in part to the war, which liberalized politics. The South Vietnamese press was able to play roles comparable to those in democratic political systems and was recognized as one of the freest and most vibrant in East Asia at the time.

In chapter 4, Phạm Thị Hồng Hà explores the Commercial Import Program, which the United States extended to the RVN as a way to finance the war. Although this program has been commonly understood as a political tool for the United States to dominate South Vietnam, Phạm demonstrates its economic benefits to US and South Vietnamese businesses alike. The Vietnamese governments harnessed the program to maximize revenues and stabilize the economy while maintaining a free market. In higher education, the topic of chapter 5, Trương Thuỳ Dung similarly argues that South Vietnamese educators collaborated extensively with their Western counterparts. Trương shows how a vibrant and diverse higher education system came into being in the early 1970s, with a dozen universities and several colleges all adhering to liberal values and offering rigorous academic programs to their students.

That vibrant intellectual environment formed the backdrop to the Buddhist revival movement. Chapter 6, by Adrienne Minh-Châu Lê, examines the activities of youth groups led by Thích Nhất Hạnh and his collaborators. As Nhất Hạnh traveled the world calling for peace, the youth groups went to South Vietnamese villages to help the victims of war. Because they refused to side either with the government or the communists, the youths' activities were suspicious to both. Some were murdered as a result. In chapter 7, Wynn Gadkar-Wilcox focuses on the monk Thích Minh Châu, an influential Buddhist scholar and rector of Vạn Hạnh University, who championed academic freedom. Through his work as a public intellectual, Thích Minh Châu sought to demonstrate that peace could only be achieved through the construction of a new system of education, one that would help rebuild faith in language and in a civil society.

Music, the topic of chapter 8, by Jason Gibbs, captured the sentiments of the average South Vietnamese. As Gibbs documents, the music industry in South Vietnam thrived as much on the profit motive as on the collective feelings and sympathies of the people. Composers, singers, and producers were paid handsomely and the music they produced shored up the public's support for RVN soldiers.

The last four chapters focus on how South Vietnamese republican values have survived in the diaspora. Chapter 9, by Tuan Hoang, traces the associational culture practiced by Vietnamese Catholics in the United States to South Vietnam. Hoang argues that mass mobilization during the war strengthened Marian devotionalism, which continues to thrive in the diaspora today. In chapter 10, Vinh Pham explores the diaspora's recreation, through music, of the lost republic. Rejecting the view that this music is merely a nostalgic expression, Pham makes the case that it is the cultural vehicle with which the diaspora sustains and rebuilds a republican national identity abroad.

The experience of exile is keenly explored in literature and philosophy as well. Chapter 11, by Phạm Vũ Lan Anh, examines Buddhist themes in the literary works of two Vietnamese-Australian writers. For these authors, Buddhism serves as a bridge to connect them with their homeland while giving readers a sense of the authors' complex diasporic identity. In chapter 12, Trinh M. Luu focuses on "Vietism," a doctrine developed by Vietnamese philosophers and writers living in exile. As a response to the Socialist Republic of Vietnam's human rights violations, the doctrine fuses folk beliefs, German romanticism, and Vietnamese nationalism to create a vision of the "new Vietnamese." This philosophy helped spawned a movement for cultural revival in the Vietnamese diaspora.

War determined the fate of the RVN from the beginning. Throughout the brutal and protracted war, South Vietnamese were not simply foreign collaborators, passive victims, or communist sympathizers. Many in South Vietnam, and later in the diaspora, were motivated by a vision of freedom and informed by nationalist sentiments, republican values, and the search for practical solutions to the problems of nation building. Together, the chapters in this volume will hopefully inspire future efforts to explore this neglected yet fascinating history.

NOTES

1. Miller, *Misalliance*, chapter 3; Chapman, *Cauldron of Resistance*.
2. Tran and Vu, eds. *Building a Republican Nation*.
3. For an extended discussion of republicanism and its neglect in Vietnamese studies, see Zinoman, "A Republican Moment."
4. On how Americans, Vietnamese, Koreans, and others profited from the black market, see Jamieson, *Understanding Vietnam*, 335-336. For a recent analysis of communist terrorism in Saigon and increased repression by the government in response, see Stur, *Saigon at War*, chapter 1.
5. For a perceptive analysis of these sentiments, see Jamieson's *Understanding Vietnam*, chapters 5 and 6.
6. The Republic's society refers to people living in the territory controlled or contested by the RVN government, practically Vietnamese territory south of the 17th parallel.
7. Goodman, *Politics in War*; Joiner, *Politics of Massacre*; Donnell and Joiner, eds. *Electoral Politics in South Vietnam*; Callison, *Land-to-the-tiller Program*.
8. A number of doctoral dissertations written during the period remain unpublished. A search on ProQuest Dissertation Abstract database yielded about half a dozen dissertations on the Second Republic, including Fredrick, "The South Vietnamese Constitution of April 1, 1967"; Lem, "Test of Survival"; Lee, "Role of the Military"; Sherry, "Evolution of the Legal System"; Moody, "Manufacturing Sector."
9. Sansom, *Economics of Insurgency*, 241, 237. Samuel Popkin echoes many similar points in his *Rational Peasant*.
10. Sansom, *Economics of Insurgency*, xv.
11. On the liberal character of the 1967 constitution compared with its 1956 predecessor, see Fredrick, "South Vietnamese Constitution."
12. Goodman, *Politics in War*, 254.
13. Joiner, "Elections and Building Political Institutions," in Donnell and Joiner, *Electoral Politics*, 9-10.
14. Donnell, "Prospects for Political Cohesion," in Donnell and Joiner, *Electoral Politics*, 151-172.
15. A recently published collection of testimonies is Vu and Fear, *Republic of Vietnam, 1955-1975*. See especially Tuan Hoang's review of important memoirs in "Political, Military, and Cultural Memoirs in Vietnamese," in Vu and Fear, *Republic of Vietnam*, 179-189.
16. Nguyen, *Hanoi's War*, 9.
17. Hoang, "Ideology in Urban South Vietnam"; Miller, *Misalliance*.
18. Hoang, "Ideology in Urban South Vietnam."
19. Tran, "South Vietnamese Identity."
20. Veith, *Drawn Swords*; Fear, "Ambiguous Legacy."
21. Dror, *Making Two Vietnams*; Toner, "Imagining Taiwan"; Fear, "Saigon Goes Global."
22. Topmiller, *Lotus Unleashed*; Miller, "Religious Revival"; Nguyen-Marshall, "Tools of Empire"; Nguyen-Marshall, "Student Activism"; Nguyen-Marshall, "Appeasing the Spirits"; and Dương, "Sóng Thần's Campaign," in Vu and Fear, *Republic of Vietnam*, 139-154; Stur, *Saigon at War*.
23. Woodside, *Community and Revolution*, 277-300.
24. Veith, *Black April*, 499.
25. Wiest, *Vietnam's Forgotten Army*, 302.

26. Jones, *My Lai*.

27. Dror, "Translator's Introduction"; Vennema, *Viet Cong Massacre*.

28. On the massacre by communist artillery in 1972, see Nguyen-Marshall, "Appeasing the Spirits"; Ngy Thanh, *Đại Lộ Kinh Hoàng*.

29. In 1970, the South Vietnamese government estimated that one-fifth of its population had at some point been a refugee. Cited in Nguyen-Marshall, "Associational Life."

30. Jamieson, *Understanding Vietnam*, 292–294.

31. The population of Saigon, the capital, quadrupled between 1955 and 1969, but the number of armed forces personnel increased by only 2.5 times between 1957 and 1967; and the number of government employees in Saigon also doubled in the same period. Cited in Nguyen-Marshall, "Associational Life." Apart from Saigon, other large southern cities include Cần Thơ, Đà Nẵng, Huế, Nha Trang, and others.

32. The number of students in South Vietnam quadrupled between 1955 and 1969. Cited in Nguyen-Marshall, "Associational Life." According to government data, the number of primary, secondary, and college students increased further by 25 percent, 40 percent, and 49 percent, respectively, between 1969 and 1974. Calculated from Phan Quang Dan, *Republic of Vietnam's Environment and People*, 178–180. Another source estimates that the total number of students increased by ten times between 1955 and 1973, college students by forty times, and vocational students by fourteen times. See Đặng Phong, *Lịch sử kinh tế*, v. 2, 947. On the expansion and internationalization of university education in South Vietnam, see chapter 5, by Trương Thuỳ Dung, this volume.

33. A source estimated that South Vietnam's industry grew by 2.5 times between 1962 and 1971 and declined 30 percent by 1974. See Đặng Phong, *Lịch sử kinh tế*, 858.

34. Đặng Phong, *Lịch sử kinh*, 957.

35. Cited in Joiner, *Politics of Massacre*, 276.

36. For testimonies of writers and artists in this period, see Nhã Ca, "Writers of the Republic" and Kiều Chinh, "Cinema Industry," in Vu and Fear, *Republic of Vietnam*. For intellectual and artistic culture, see Gadkar-Wilcox, "Existentialism and Intellectual Culture"; Schafer, "Death, Buddhism, and Existentialism." On how songwriters and performers benefited from the rising mass demand for their war-related music, see Jason Gibbs, chapter 8, in this volume.

37. Vo Kim Son, "Personal Reflections," 105–116. On issues related to Vạn Hạnh University, see Adrienne Minh-Châu Lê, chapter 6, and Wynn Gadkar-Wilcox, chapter 7, this volume.

38. Fredrick, "South Vietnamese Constitution."

39. Stur, *Saigon at War*, 154.

40. One source reported the number of volunteers under twenty at one recruitment center in Saigon more than doubled the planned intake of draftees three months after the offensive. See Nguyễn Công Luận, *Nationalist in the Vietnam Wars*, 330. According to historian Lê Mạnh Hùng (*Nhìn Lại Sử Việt*, 654), the General Mobilization Law to expand the RVNAF by two hundred thousand troops was quickly passed by the RVN's National Assembly on June 15, 1968, despite having been strongly opposed just five months earlier.

41. Goodman, *Politics in War*, 38–45; Fear, "Ambiguous Legacy," 13.

42. Goodman, *Politics in War*, chapter 10; Joiner, *Politics of Massacre*, 280–282; Joiner, "Elections and Building Political Institutions," in Donnell and Joiner, *Electoral Politics*, 1–12.

43. On communist commandos' terrorist activities and their assassinations of prominent politicians and officials such as Minister of Education Lê Minh Trí and Prime

Minister-to-be Nguyễn Văn Bông, see their post-1975 accounts in Hoàng Hà et al., *Trui Rèn Trong Lửa Đỏ*, esp. 110; Mã Thiện Đồng, *Biệt Động Sài Gòn*; Vũ Quang Hùng, "Tôi ám sát." For a careful analysis of the assassination of National Assembly Deputy Trần Văn Văn, see Lâm, "Assasination."

44. Hickey, *Village in Vietnam*, 279.
45. Robinson, *Terms of Refuge*; Sachs, *Life We Were Given*.
46. Van der Kroef, "Vietnamese Refugee Problem."
47. Espiritu, *Body Counts*, 58.
48. Robinson, "Comprehensive Plan of Action."
49. Kumin, "Orderly Departure from Vietnam?"
50. Vo, *Bamboo Gulag*; Huỳnh, *To Be Made Over*; Tran, *Lost Years*; McKelvey, *Gift of Barbed Wire*; Huy Đức, *Bên Thắng Cuộc Quyển I*.
51. "Foreign Ministry Claims Right to Property in South Vietnam, Abroad," Vietnam Center and Archive, 2223205006 01 May 1975, Box 32, Folder 05, Douglas Pike Collection: Unit 03—Refugees and Civilian Casualties, Vietnam Center and Archive, Texas Tech University [VCA].
52. Kim Ninh, "Renovating in Transition?"; Elliott, *Changing Worlds*; Tetsusaburo, *Vietnamese Economy, 1979–86*; Vu, *Vietnam's Communist Revolution*.
53. Vietnam Courier, *Those Who Leave*; Vietnam Courier, *Vietnam: Which Human Rights?*
54. Vietnam Courier, *Those Who Leave*, 33.
55. "The Vietnamese Ambassador in France," *Le Monde*, December 6, 1978.
56. Vietnam Courier, *Those Who Leave*, 22.
57. Vũ Hạnh, "Về vấn đề 'Tỵ nạn': Bổn cũ soạn lại," *Tuổi Trẻ*, July 20, 1979.
58. Earl Martin, "The New Vietnam: An Opposing View," *New York Review of Books*, May 12, 1977; Chandola, "Saigon Today."
59. Houtart, "Vietnam."
60. Houtart, "International Responsibility."
61. Chandola, "New Economic Zones."
62. Houtart, "International Responsibility," 279.
63. Nguyen Manh Hung, "Refugee Scholars."
64. Cited in Nguyen Manh Hung, "'Vietnam: A Television History,'" 79.
65. Nguyen Manh Hung, "Refugee Scholars," 94.
66. Espiritu, "Toward a Critical Refugee Study"; Nguyen, *Gift of Freedom*; Nguyen and Fung, "Refugee Cultures," 1–7; Bui, *Returns of War*.
67. Espiritu, "Toward a Critical Refugee Study," 423.
68. Espiritu, "Toward a Critical Refugee Study," 419.
69. Lipman, *In Camps*; Trần Đình Trụ, *Ship of Fate*.
70. Nguyen, "Vietnamese American New Orleans."
71. Collet and Furuya, "Enclave, Place, or Nation?," 1, 15.
72. Tran, "Remembering the Boat Exodus."
73. Mazumdar, "Creating a Sense of Place"; McLaughlin and Jesilow, "Conveying a Sense of Community."
74. Valverde, *Transnationalizing Viet Nam*; Small, "'Over There,'" 157. Vietnam began to open up its economy and legalize private enterprises in the late 1980s, but maintained many restrictions on economic exchanges with the external world, especially on remittances by overseas Vietnamese deemed by the communist government as subversive. The US embargo also made such exchanges difficult until 1995, when US-Vietnam

relations were normalized. Official data show that the amount of remittances by legal channels, not including unofficial transfers, in 1995 was equal to 1.4 percent of Vietnam's GDP, 14.3 percent of its foreign direct investment, and 34.1 percent of official development aid Vietnam received. From 1996 through 2000, its share rose to 3.3 percent, 50.4 percent, and 70.6 percent, respectively. During the next five years, from 2001 through 2005, its share rose further, to 5 percent, 80.5 percent, and 124.7 percent, respectively. In this period, remittance played nearly as big a role as foreign investment and a bigger role than foreign aid. See Chung, "Foreign capital inflows," 46.

75. Collet and Lien, *Transnational Politics*, 7.

76. "95% of Vietnamese People Want to Sue China in International Courts in a Referendum," *Star Gazette*, June 11, 2020, http://starsgazette.com/news/95-of-vietnamese-people-want-to-sue-china-in-international-courts-in-a-referendum/0227384 (accessed June 14, 2020).

77. Vo Dang, "Anticommunism as Cultural Praxis," 12.

78. Scruton, *How to Think Seriously*, 325.

CHAPTER 1

"Everything Depends on Us Alone"

President Nguyễn Văn Thiệu's Vietnamization Strategy

David L. Prentice

Unlike most of the contributors to this volume, I came to study the Republic belatedly. My initial focus was on Richard Nixon's first secretary of defense, Melvin Laird, and his strategy of American troop withdrawals—Vietnamization. From Laird's perspective, Vietnamization was a success: it brought virtually all US personnel home and reelected Nixon in a landslide. Even after South Vietnam's 1975 collapse, it provided a convenient and enduring scapegoat—Democrats in Congress. In my conversations with Laird, he was proud of Vietnamization and what it accomplished.

For the Republic of Vietnam (RVN), Vietnamization had no such happy ending. In memory, it became, as former vice president Nguyễn Cao Kỳ called it, a "gigantic con trick foisted on American public opinion" and the Republic.[1] Certainly, the strategy might have been a "minefield," as General Trần Văn Đôn remembered, though the Vietnamese were not "blindfolded," as he alleged.[2] Similarly, when President Nguyễn Văn Thiệu appears in the literature or postwar memoirs, he seems blind to American intentions, hopelessly indecisive, ever at the mercy of events, and an opponent of US troop reductions.[3]

Based on Vietnamese archival and other international sources, my research reveals that Thiệu was a complex figure who loomed large over events and American decision-making.[4] Rather than begrudgingly accepting Vietnamization, he was among its earliest and most ardent advocates.[5] Indeed, Thiệu developed a strategy of Vietnamization that he hoped would enable the Republic to survive America's exit from the Vietnamese ground war.[6]

Relating ends to means, intentions to capabilities, and objectives to resources, Thiệu grappled with a difficult domestic and international environment as he developed his Vietnamization strategy between 1967 and 1971. He understood, even before the Americans did, that the United States was on its way out of Vietnam.[7] He recognized that real peace was unlikely to come from the Paris talks. He knew a longer war lay ahead. He tried to prepare the Republic accordingly. His Vietnamization sought the complete reassertion of the RVN's autonomy and self-sufficiency—nothing less than the de-Americanization of the peace, the military, and the economy. That he failed diminishes neither his importance nor his agency.

"THE GREAT TACKER" AND HIS OPERATING ENVIRONMENT

In his ascent to becoming the Second Republic's first (and essentially only) president, Nguyễn Văn Thiệu had faced stiff challenges. Born along Vietnam's south central coast in 1923, he had modest origins. His father was a small farmer and part-time fisherman. Thiệu initially joined the Việt Minh and became a district chief of youth organization. He left their ranks in 1946 after he saw that communists dominated the group. In 1948, he joined the French-created Vietnamese National Army and fought against the Việt Minh. A committed anticommunist with political aspirations, he quietly and determinedly rose in the ranks of the newly formed Army of the Republic of Vietnam (ARVN).[8]

Ascending the Republic of Vietnam Armed Forces (RVNAF) hierarchy in the Ngô Đình Diệm and post-Diệm eras, Thiệu learned and then mastered the politics of survival. He had been a member of the patriotic, nationalist Đại Việt Party and remained a member despite that group's opposition to Diệm. He had also sided with Brigadier General Nguyễn Văn Hinh, who had fought a losing battle with Diệm over control of the Vietnamese National Army. Yet, as Diệm consolidated his power, Thiệu's loyalties shifted. He converted to Catholicism in 1957 and joined the Cần Lao Party in 1958. Thereafter, he went from commanding the Đà Lạt Military Academy to serving under General Dương Văn Minh and then heading the 5th ARVN division, which was stationed near Saigon. The US Central Intelligence Agency (CIA) judged in August 1963 that Thiệu was loyal to the Ngô family.[9]

Less than three months later, Thiệu would play a critical role in the coup against Diệm. General Dương Văn Minh impressed on Thiệu that the coup had American backing and that a new government could better fight the growing war. Thiệu reluctantly agreed to join the plotters. It was his forces that stormed the presidential palace. Yet he opposed the November 1963 murder of Diệm and his brother Nhu.[10] Seeing their corpses in the back of an armored personnel carrier sickened him. He would never forget how quickly and how deadly Vietnamese politics could become. Meanwhile, the coup failed to deliver the political stability or military progress its plotters and the US government had hoped for. Thiệu advanced anyway.[11]

From 1963 to 1967, Thiệu steadily outflanked competitors and gained the nickname "The Great Tacker" for his ability to deftly maneuver and advance even when the winds of fortune were against him. "Thiệu is intelligent and highly ambitious," observed one US officer after Diem's death. "He will remain a potential coup plotter until he is on top or dead." Despite the reservations of those who thought his loyalty too fickle, Thiệu became a full general. He then survived the coups and countercoups that defined the interregnum between the First and Second Republics. Part of a new generation of military men vying for national leadership—the Young Turks—he (then age forty-two) and Nguyễn Cao Kỳ (thirty-five) emerged on top of the ruling military junta in 1965 and 1966. Still, republican and Buddhist dissent, typified by the 1966 Buddhist uprising, challenged their policies and rule. Kỳ promised elections and a new constitution. Perhaps owing to his calm demeanor and southern background, Thiệu emerged on top of the military's ticket. Narrowly elected in 1967, the Great Tacker would face even greater headwinds as president.[12]

The war and the complexities of Vietnamese politics presented constant dangers. North Vietnamese regulars and their National Liberation Front (NLF) insurgents inflicted significant casualties on the RVNAF. Meanwhile, the NLF challenged the Republic for legitimacy and control, thus constituting an ever-present political, diplomatic, economic, and military threat.[13] Thiệu needed to secure the rural countryside and win peasant loyalty while countering communist propaganda abroad. Saigon politics was almost as challenging. Northern refugees, Catholics, anti-communist hard-liners, the generals, Buddhists, students, journalists, and a myriad of other groups created a continual maelstrom of political interests and conniving. Embracing republican constitutionalism gave Thiệu the domestic allies, philosophy, and legitimacy he needed to avert another coup and appeal for international aid. Allying with northern Catholics and hawkish parliamentarians, Thiệu would outmaneuver rivals and replace officials and generals whose loyalty was suspect. Politically secure and militarily confident by the end of 1968, Thiệu fixated on America's domestic situation.[14]

Having rescued South Vietnam from the brink of collapse from 1964 to 1966, the United States and its forces remained critical to the Republic's survival.[15] In 1968, the United States had more than half a million military personnel in South Vietnam, contributed more than $1 billion per year in aid, and provided significant logistical and airpower support. The US government could also play a large role in Vietnamese politics or pursue an independent settlement with North Vietnam and the NLF.

Although often portrayed as blind to American political realities, Thiệu followed US events, and American stamina loomed as his top strategic concern from 1967 to 1970.[16] His private secretary, Hoàng Đức Nhã, recalled that as antiwar protests and congressional dissent quickened in the United States in 1967, "Thiệu realized that the march to American disengagement was irreversible." That year, Thiệu predicted US troop withdrawals would be forthcoming and spoke of the need for the RVNAF to replace those forces.[17]

The 1968 Tết Offensive and its subsequent fallout in the United States, as reported by Ambassador Bùi Diễm, confirmed his instincts.[18] When on March 31, President Lyndon Johnson (LBJ) announced that he was implementing a partial bombing halt over North Vietnam, willing to pursue serious peace talks, and declining to run for reelection, Thiệu understood that the era of Americanization had ended. "There is now a serious danger that sooner or later the Americans will pull out," he explained to the British ambassador in Saigon. Or, as he told the National Assembly soon thereafter, "Everything depends on us alone."[19]

1968, DE-AMERICANIZING THE PEACE

Thiệu's de-Americanization (or Vietnamization) strategy followed two tracks in 1968: military preparations for the expected US troop withdrawals and diplomatic efforts to prevent the Republic's interests from being sold out by the United States in the Paris peace talks.

Militarily, he pursued the general mobilization of South Vietnamese manpower along with the modernization of ARVN forces to enable the Republic to replace American soldiers. Thiệu reasoned that by advocating US withdrawals he could ease American dissent and gain the goodwill, time, and aid necessary to survive. From April 1968 on, Thiệu was vocal on the need for the United States to reduce its forces in Vietnam.[20]

So much so, that US Secretary of Defense Clark Clifford would use Thiệu's confidence and mobilization to justify leveling off the American troop commitment.[21] Still, Thiệu's de-Americanization gained little traction in Washington because President Johnson rejected any drawdown.[22]

LBJ had his sights on terminating the war before his term expired in January 1969, and only a negotiated settlement could pull this off. He believed any unilateral US troop withdrawal would give Hanoi what it wanted and so reduce allied leverage in the talks. He was willing to halt the American bombing of North Vietnam to start negotiations. Even then, any halt was conditional on recognition of the Republic at the talks, respect for the demilitarized zone, an end to attacks on South Vietnamese cities, and a general understanding that North Vietnam would not "take advantage" of the halt. He also ordered US commanders to maintain maximum military pressure on the enemy in South Vietnam and increase the bombing of Laos. At the same time, his administration accelerated efforts to train, equip, and modernize ARVN forces.[23] Otherwise rebuffed on a Vietnamization of the ground war, Thiệu's strategic emphasis shifted to de-Americanizing the negotiations, especially as Johnson's haste to negotiate created genuine concern in Saigon.

Diplomatically, Thiệu feared a collapse of allied will similar to the French abandonment that followed the fall of Điện Biên Phủ in 1954: defeated in a major battle and weary of war, the French elected a government committed to extricating itself from Indochina with the subsequent Geneva accords dividing Vietnam in two. The Tết Offensive and the rise of prominent political doves—Eugene McCarthy and Robert Kennedy—signaled the same could happen in 1968.[24] As the Democratic nominee, Vice President Hubert Humphrey, tilted toward the party's left wing, Thiệu grew more apprehensive about the talks and the election. He and his officials wondered whether Johnson would compromise too much in Paris to improve his fellow Democrat's chances in the election or to achieve peace before he left office.[25] The Republic needed to affirm its diplomatic interests and bring its great power patron into line on negotiating procedures and the status of the NLF. Thiệu's position was precarious, though. As he once told his special assistant for foreign affairs Nguyễn Phú Đức, "I shall not place myself in front of an American rolling tank and get crushed, but shall remain next to the driver and try to influence him."[26]

Fixated on collusion between Richard Nixon's campaign, Anna Chennault, and South Vietnamese officials, the Johnson administration and historians thereafter misunderstood Thiệu's thinking and actions in

October and November 1968. Yet, he was remarkably clear, privately and publicly, on the Paris peace talks. He consistently opposed NLF participation as a distinct entity or delegation in the formal talks. America's chief negotiator in Paris, W. Averell Harriman, argued that a generic "our side/their side" formula would allow all "fantasies possible," but for Thiệu, appearances mattered.[27] An NLF presence would hurt his standing at home, give the Front legitimacy in Vietnam and worldwide, and raise the specter of a coalition government being imposed by an American settlement. Even if the United States refused to recognize the NLF in Paris, poorly negotiated procedures could effect the same end.[28]

Thiệu believed that if the North Vietnamese truly desired peace—predicated, of course, on the Republic's survival—then they would open direct talks with Saigon.[29] Regardless, South Vietnam should head the allied delegation and thus set a course for the "Vietnamization of the peace."[30] Thiệu communicated these concerns through televised addresses, private letters to President Johnson, discussions with US officials, and via Vietnamese diplomats in Washington and Paris. Believing his protests owed to Republican Party meddling, Johnson proceeded by announcing a total bombing halt of North Vietnam and his expectation of formal talks beginning after the American election.[31]

Having failed to thwart Johnson's breakthrough, Thiệu publicly broke with the United States on November 2. Addressing a joint session of the National Assembly, he declared that the Republic would boycott the Paris talks until Saigon, Washington, and Hanoi clarified procedural matters and the status of the NLF. His stand precipitated a groundswell of support in Saigon. His popularity and nationalist credentials had never been better. His break also sent a "warning" to the United States that the Republic would not blindly follow the American lead in Paris. That Johnson postponed opening the talks until Saigon was on board seemingly confirmed that it had a veto over North Vietnamese and American diplomacy. Thiệu understood that the war was far from over and that the Republic could not "kick America" at random. Still, his government felt they were on track to achieve "war and peace Vietnamization."[32]

Thiệu's efforts to Vietnamize the talks came at a great cost, though. He had made political gains in Saigon but had upset the American public and Congress. They would blame South Vietnam for sabotaging peace in 1968. Thiệu was right that Hanoi was uninterested in any peace that would have left the Republic intact—the only peace he or Lyndon Johnson would accept.[33] Ever the masters of diplomacy and propaganda, the North Vietnamese played up Saigon's refusal to end the war peacefully. They and their chosen NLF delegates took advantage of the delay to emphasize the latter's participation and de facto recognition. And though Saigon received some of the procedural concessions it demanded, the agreed-upon roundtable with no nameplates effectively granted the NLF the same status as the Republic: both could be portrayed as puppets or as legitimate governments. Indeed, when all sides convened for preliminary talks in January 1969, the communists took turns denouncing the Republic as an illegitimate puppet that they refused to recognize or negotiate with.[34] Thiệu and his advisers no doubt felt vindicated in their opposition to the talks, but in the propaganda war, the NLF would continue to score major victories in Paris.[35] Finally, Thiệu had failed to de-Americanize the peace talks. Learning from the diplomatic fandango, Nixon would pursue secret talks with even less regard for South Vietnam.

1969, DE-AMERICANIZING THE WAR

Even in announcing his diplomatic break from the United States, Thiệu was clear: "1969 would be a year for self-strengthening and self-reliance. We must strengthen ourselves and strive to achieve self-reliance to avoid being slaves."[36] Nixon's victory in the US election buoyed Saigon opinion and likely bought the Republic more time, but Thiệu maintained that American resolve was finite. He continued to express that "his greatest concern is American opinion about Viet-Nam."[37]

South Vietnamese officials appreciated that Nixon faced hard choices and that Congress and the news media would afford him a short political honeymoon. They recognized that North Vietnam and the NLF were far better at swaying US public opinion. They further understood that the 1970 midterms and 1972 presidential election were always on Nixon's mind. Saigon would have to accept responsibility and act quickly by embracing unilateral US troop reductions both to influence the new administration's direction and to secure American patience.[38]

Conversely, Thiệu believed the situation in South Vietnam had never looked better: the government was consolidating its control of the countryside and ARVN forces were growing in strength and numbers. He was confident that with enough equipment and economic assistance, his government could assume an increasing portion of the military burden while expanding GVN control of South Vietnam. "In 1965, we [were] like a patient afflicted with a serious disease. The patient's condition was serious," he argued. "And so South Vietnam called on the allies to come in and help treat our wounds. Now that we are on the road to recovery, we can gradually resume the duties they assumed during our illness, and permit them to go home."[39]

Thiệu's Vietnamization of the ground war rested on pacification and the replacement of American forces by a better trained, equipped, and expanded RVNAF.[40] As US and South Vietnamese forces beat back the enemies' 1968–1969 military offensives, they saw an unprecedented opportunity to expand the Republic's control. The prospect of substantive peace talks and a ceasefire dictated a "fast and strong" pacification campaign to establish an official presence throughout the country lest the communists claim much of the countryside.[41] Beyond diplomatic leverage and legitimacy, Thiệu badly needed rural manpower, resources, and taxes to make Vietnamization work. Throughout 1969, he and South Vietnamese officials developed and proposed political, economic, and land reforms to try and win rural loyalty. Perhaps owing to his experience of joining and then leaving the Vietminh, Thiệu invited NLF members to rejoin the Republic. He gave those cadre who rallied to the government relative immunity, proposed letting former communists participate in elections, and offered to negotiate directly with the NLF. Saigon could also cite these efforts when soliciting greater patience from the Americans.[42] Moreover, expanding government control gave Thiệu the confidence he needed to continue pushing for US troop reductions.[43]

As President Nixon struggled to choose his strategy in Vietnam, Thiệu maintained that the replacement of American soldiers by South Vietnamese forces should be the keystone of allied strategy. This "will decide the death or survival of the nation," he argued.[44] Relating objectives to resources, Thiệu believed US reductions, especially if the Republic proposed them first, would stave off American demands for a precipitate withdrawal and justify continued (and hopefully expanded) military and financial aid to South Vietnam. "We need weapons and money from the supporting Allies because we are a poor country," he explained. "But in bones and blood we are ready to replace the Allies here to fight to the last drop of blood despite losses."[45]

Overall, Thiệu's Vietnamization strategy made several assumptions about his domestic and international environments and about the future. He believed American troops could be exchanged for US patience, arms, and economic aid—at least as much as Hanoi received from its patrons. With these, he could expand the ARVN into a better equipped, mobile force that would be able to defeat the North Vietnamese Army (NVA).[46] At the same time, pacification and access to better arms would enable the Regional and Popular Forces to replace regular forces in secure areas.

Assuming sufficient foreign aid and security along with ongoing political and land reforms, Thiệu believed economic development and greater loyalty to the Republic would spread throughout the countryside. Vietnamization would begin to pay for itself. It would also help the Republic win more friends abroad as it showed itself a legitimate, popular government capable of self-defense. Unable to destabilize the Republic or match an improved, fully modern RVNAF with continued support from American airpower, North Vietnam would have little choice but to accept an uneasy peace. Theoretically, the strategy seemed sure to work.[47]

Thiệu pressed the US government to accept Vietnamization. America's top general in Vietnam, Creighton Abrams, also appreciated US political realities; he and Thiệu began drawing up Vietnamization timetables before Nixon's inauguration. In time, Nixon would accept US troop withdrawals, and the two presidents announced the first reduction on Midway Island, June 8, 1969. Nixon, though, privately doubted that Americans would back a long, Vietnamized war. He considered renewed and expanded bombing to compel an end to Hanoi's war against South Vietnam. Thiệu implored him to stick with Vietnamization.[48]

On July 30, 1969, Nixon visited Saigon to discuss with President Thiệu his plan to resume bombing North Vietnam. Thiệu sought to convince his counterpart that the "long-haul, low-cost" strategy of Vietnamization represented the best course possible. He explained that he was satisfied with the war's direction. Given time, his country would continue to expand pacification, build popular support, broaden the government, and eradicate the NLF without American help. As he understood it, Nixon could choose escalation "to speed up the war" or continue Vietnamization. "You help us so we can take over more and more," he reasoned. He understood that the upcoming 1970 congressional elections weighed heavily on the American president and although a devastating air campaign against Hanoi might shorten the conflict, it could destroy the US domestic support necessary for the long haul. Thiệu doubted the communists would ever give up their conquest of the South and believed that they had adopted a fight-talk-fight strategy so that they could endure a protracted war. Vietnamization would give the Republic of Vietnam the time and resources to do the same.[49]

Nixon would choose Vietnamization over a radical escalation of the war in 1969; thereafter, all parties understood American withdrawals were "irreversible."[50] Vietnamization proved politically popular, though. By the end of 1969, it seemed that Nixon had succeeded in squelching the antiwar movement and dissent in Congress. A "silent majority" of Americans opposed abandoning South Vietnam and indicated their willingness to endure the "long haul" of Vietnamization. Thiệu ended the year on a high note. He predicted that all US forces would leave South Vietnam in the next two years but that America would continue to provide logistical support and significant economic aid. "The President spoke with great self-confidence, zest and restrained optimism," one foreign diplomat observed. "He clearly believes that given time and continuing economic support he can make the policy of Vietnamisation work."[51]

1969–1971, VIETNAMIZING THE ECONOMY

Having chosen the long-haul, low-cost strategy of Vietnamization, Thiệu and his officials quickly confronted hard political and economic realities: the US Congress judged the costs too high, promised US aid and equipment were less than expected, Saigon politicians and rural peasants balked at higher taxes, and the South Vietnamese economy faced severe strains as American troops returned home. "Vietnamization requires a continued transfer of US resources to complement, and in many instances, to offset the local resources used in the war effort," the Ministry of the Economy noted. "Without such financial aid, it is impossible for Vietnam, a small and poor economy, to accommodate a major war."[52] Thiệu had expected "economic Vietnamization" to begin in Nixon's second term, but for his strategy to work, he had to implement economic reforms much sooner.[53]

Thiệu understood real Vietnamization required growing economic independence. "The economy is the key problem," he believed. "Though dealing with self-reliance and self-strengthening in our struggle, we do not have a self-sufficient economy." He exhorted top officials to do the impossible: reduce budget deficits, curb inflation, and promote economic growth while expanding the RVNAF. The Republic weighed devaluing the piaster, enforcing tax collection, raising taxes on luxury goods and some commodities, and striking nonessentials from the budget. Complicating matters, the Vietnamese context and US foreign aid Commercial Import Program encouraged the import of consumer goods even as these transactions gave the Republic the money it needed for government and military spending.[54] Import duties and austerity measures would likely reduce such imports, but the situation called for desperate measures. Addressing the people on the need for austerity taxes, Thiệu reminded them,

Allied troops are not inexhaustible nor is allied money. Our allies cannot aid us forever even if they want to. Should they want to aid us forever, they could not keep their aid at a high level forever. A dictum said: "One usually helps people in temporary need and never helps people in permanent poverty." Therefore, our allies will continue to provide aid, but only for those who are laborious and accept sacrifices and not for those who are lazy and dodge their responsibility.

Yet even discussing essential economic measures prompted dissent.[55]

In 1969, the Ministry of the Economy proposed austerity taxes on imported goods, luxuries, and gasoline to prevent inflation. When the National Assembly stalled, the Ministry cited a 1961 law to justify implementing the austerity taxes without legislative approval. Thiệu accepted the taxes but worried about the political backlash.[56]

The austerity taxes and import licensing restrictions ignited a flurry of protests in Saigon. The National Assembly balked at the move and the lower house staged an antitax walkout. Many solons called the move unconstitutional. The ensuing legislative revolt and protests made for a difficult situation. Needed reforms and sacrifices were opposed, weakened, or ignored. Tax revenue fell far short of government expectations. Speculation and hoarding rose. So did the cost of living.[57]

Hence the need for reform continued in the 1970s. Solons and government ministers well understood the gravity of the situation—the Republic they had worked so hard to build could founder on the shoals of spiraling inflation and budget deficits, all of which the removal of US soldiers and their money made worse. In 1970, the Assembly and Thiệu compromised on legislation that allowed the executive branch to set exchange, interest, and tax rates as it saw fit. Thiệu and his officials would get the flexibility they needed to make the tough decisions, though they would also receive the blame.[58]

The Republic quickly set to work. Tax reforms and modernization, including the implementation of a value-added-tax, steadily increased tax revenue and reduced inflation. The adoption of a floating exchange rate in July 1971 worked at further curbing inflation and the black-market currency exchange. With American backing, officials adopted liberal economic measures that emphasized free enterprise over government regulation and price controls. The economy improved, and South Vietnam attracted long-term foreign commercial investments and loans.[59] The Republic remained dependent on foreign aid, but Thiệu could reasonably argue that it was on the path toward self-sufficiency.[60]

Meanwhile, Thiệu hoped that control of the countryside along with land reform and efforts to improve tax collection there would enable villages to pay for their own administration and so free up additional money. Enacted in March 1970, the Land to the Tiller legislation aimed to end tenancy and so improve agricultural production and allegiance to the government. The program distributed 2.5 million acres of land and transformed almost a million families—making up more than one-third of the population—from renters to landowners. Thiệu wanted not just more farmers, but also better farmers. The Republic backed the use of miracle rice and encouraged rural banks to offer small farm loans to facilitate the spread of modern practices and seed stocks. These efforts to improve agricultural yields held out the promise of greater economic self-sufficiency. Ideally, civil servants would track these developments in the provinces and accordingly raise tax revenue.[61]

Yet in both villages and cities, corruption, hoarding, speculation, and other structural problems remained. Vietnamization continued to complicate matters, and the Republic remained heavily dependent upon foreign economic and military assistance. Still, Thiệu was hopeful America would deliver its promised aid. He reasoned that if America had helped postwar Germany, "Why not Vietnam?"[62]

1971–1975, STRATEGIC FAILURE

Thiệu's Vietnamization suffered a series of political, diplomatic, economic, and military setbacks after 1970, culminating in the Republic's fall in April 1975. Some of them owed to his mistakes and hubris; others to factors outside his control. Contingent though this process was, the assumptions underlying Vietnamization one by one proved unsound.

Politically, Thiệu's 1971 efforts to win reelection in a landslide backfired at home and abroad. To be clear, the National Assembly and Thiệu wanted to avoid a repeat of 1967, when too many tickets diluted the votes of both the anticommunist and liberal blocs. Yet the resulting legislation made it too hard for liberal and moderate candidates to get on the ballot. At the same time, prominent rivals like General Dương Văn Minh and Nguyễn Cao Kỳ realized they could not defeat Thiệu and so declined to get on the ballot. The resulting one-man election was a farce that harmed the Republic's legitimacy. Unlike the Democratic Republic of Vietnam, the Republic was in many ways accountable to its citizens, a relatively free press, and foreign observers.[63] Thiệu's mishandling of the election was part of a pattern: frustrated by factional politics and a critical news media, he would often take illiberal actions to do what he thought was necessary to stabilize the Republic. Yet these actions undermined the republican ideals he claimed to be protecting. Watching from afar, the US Congress would cite the election as proof of the Republic's undemocratic character, using it as a justification for aid restrictions and reductions. The American president's own relationship with Congress did not help.[64]

Diplomatically, Thiệu had a poor partner in Richard Nixon. Recalling Thiệu's attempts to de-Americanize the peace in 1968, Nixon and Henry Kissinger kept early talks with the North Vietnamese hidden from him. For his part, Thiệu deferred to the United States on the negotiations, believing that Hanoi would never settle and that he could veto a dangerous breakthrough or agreement. Instead, Nixon would coerce Thiệu to agree to the Paris Peace Accords by threatening to end US aid. Granted, the White House saw the agreement as critical to sustaining congressional appropriations for the Republic, but that necessity owed to Nixon's disdain for the legislature.[65]

Nixon's relations with Congress had been frayed from the beginning as liberal Republicans and Democrats increasingly turned on the war and defense appropriations generally.[66] As Secretary of Defense Melvin Laird understood from the onset, they were "money short" from the beginning.[67] Nixon's secrecy and bold moves made things worse. The 1970 joint incursion into Cambodia irrevocably damaged congressional relations. His use of airpower and resumption of the bombing of North Vietnam hurt as well. Escalation might have made sense militarily and diplomatically, given Nixon and Kissinger's efforts to coerce Hanoi into a settlement, but it undermined Vietnamization. The promised foreign aid and military assistance never materialized. Funds were short in 1969 and they were shorter still between 1973 and 1975. The Watergate revelations and hearings galvanized Congress to prohibit the use of US airpower in Laos and Cambodia, pass sweeping war powers legislation, and reduce aid to the Republic even further. These developments were out of Thiệu's hands, but he and Nixon had gambled they could act without Congress. They were wrong.[68]

Economically, the Republic made great strides toward self-sufficiency from 1971 to 1975, but these efforts proved insufficient and perhaps impossible. Without the necessary aid, the Republic could not maintain a fully mobilized and well-equipped RVNAF. The global economic context gravely complicated the situation. Nixon's decision to leave the gold standard meant, in real terms, that US aid decreased in value even if the absolute values remained the same. The 1973 oil shock and enemy attacks on South Vietnamese oil and gas depots meant that the Republic faced the highest oil prices in the world. Inflation swelled, unemployment increased, and the Republic faced an unsustainable budget deficit. Economic Vietnamization had advanced since 1967 but it could not finance a war against a stronger enemy.[69]

Thiệu's Vietnamization suffered its biggest defeats militarily. He had assumed US aid on par with what the Soviets and Chinese were giving North Vietnam.[70] Although true initially, American aid would fail to match Hanoi's patrons in quality or quantity. The communists gave North Vietnam the means to pursue economic development and a big war in the South. The 1971 ARVN invasion of Laos—Lam Son 719—demonstrated that the North Vietnamese were not preparing for an offensive like those the Republic suffered in 1968 and 1969 but something much, much larger. South Vietnamese forces unexpectedly met Soviet tanks, effective antiaircraft guns, and formidable North Vietnamese forces with modern firearms. From this engagement, Thiệu understood the Republic would need greater US aid and air support, but given the congressional context, such generosity was unlikely. The 1972 Easter Offensive further demonstrated that the Vietnamese battlefield had changed. The NVA, using tanks and heavy artillery, were able to retain a significant chunk of South Vietnamese territory. Thiệu's Vietnamized RVNAF, backed by American firepower, fought well but was unable to repulse the improved NVA. Dependent on US aid and airpower, the Republic would see these resources wither. Hanoi knew few such limits as the era of Vietnamization ended.[71]

From his inauguration as president, Thiệu understood America's internal difficulties demanded the Republic of Vietnam become self-sufficient diplomatically, militarily, and economically. He and his advisers understood America was giving the Republic one "last chance."[72] Everything would soon depend on them alone.

Conceptually, Vietnamization looked successful in 1970. Thiệu had stymied American unilateralism in Paris, expanded control of the countryside, strengthened the Republic's military forces, and begun economic reforms. On the surface, his Vietnamization portended of a "better war."

In reality, this progress masked lingering structural flaws. First, control was not the same as loyalty. Vietnamization failed both to control the countryside and to inspire devotion in cities and hamlets.[73] Second, military progress rested on joint efforts with American ground forces as well as Hanoi's decision to regroup and focus on military campaigns in Laos and Cambodia. Vietnamization did not enable the Republic to rout its enemies in 1972 or 1975.[74] Third, in the strategic theater Thiệu had judged most important, American patience and generosity continued its erosion, especially in Congress. Moreover, he failed to de-Americanize the peace or win more friends abroad.[75] Even with significant US aid, the Second Republic was far from being able to stand on its own.

Thiệu's efforts bought the Republic seven years and billions in aid.[76] But his Vietnamization strategy failed to account for what was likely an impossible situation: an inability to win hearts and minds, defeat the NVA, and plan for an end to American military and economic assistance. Like so many other prescriptions for crises in Indochina, what looked promising on paper proved elusive. As military historian James Willbanks concluded, "The idea was not in and of itself bad," though "Vietnamization, in the final analysis, failed and failed miserably."[77] A failure that would kill the republican state.

NOTES

1. Nguyễn Cao Kỳ, *Twenty Years and Twenty Days*, 125. On the debate over Vietnamization in the Vietnamese press in 1969, see Hoang and Vu, chapter 3, this volume.

2. Trần Văn Đôn, *Our Endless War*, 181, 183.

3. For instance, see Bùi Diễm, *Jaws of History*, 197–198, 276–277; Kimball, *Nixon's Vietnam War*, 149–150; Anderson, *Vietnamization*, 33.

4. This chapter draws on research from the Vietnam National Archives Center II (Hồ Chí Minh City, Vietnam), the National Archives of Australia, the Library and Archives of Canada (Ottawa, Canada), the Public Records Office (Kew, England), the Johnson and Nixon presidential libraries, as well as four other American archives.

5. President Thiệu often caused terminological crises over official and journalist use of the terms "withdrawal," "de-Americanization," and "Vietnamization."

6. John Lewis Gaddis defines strategy as "the process by which ends are related to means, intentions to capabilities, objectives to resources. Every maker of policy consciously or unconsciously goes through such a process." Gaddis, *Strategies of Containment*, viii.

7. Colonel Hoàng Ngọc Lung's essay on the Second Republic's "Strategy and Tactics" argues that Thiệu and the South Vietnamese did not understand that Vietnamization was more than modernization and expansion of the RVNAF; it was essentially a strategy that would require the Vietnamese to survive with greatly reduced American participation." As my research makes clear, Thiệu understood and publicly provided the latter definition of Vietnamization. Colonel Lung's essay appears in Sorley, *Vietnam War*.

8. Kevin Buckley, "No One Can Be Sure What Thiệu Is Thinking," *New York Times*, March 2, 1969; biography of Thiệu, US Embassy (Saigon), August 1, 1971, Folder "POL 15-1 VIET S 8/1/71," Box 2813, Record Group [RG] 59, National Archives II, College Park, Maryland [NA II]. I am grateful to Sean Fear for sharing the embassy biography.

9. Nguyen Tien Hung and Schecter, *Palace File*, 37–39; Moyar, *Triumph Forsaken*, 271; on Thiệu's biography, George Veith, email correspondence, December 8, 2019.

10. Veith, *Drawn Swords*, 62–63, 581–582.

11. Nguyen Tien Hung and Schecter, *The Palace File*, 74–79.
12. Biography of Thiệu, US Embassy (Saigon), NA II; Fear, "The Ambiguous Legacy of Ngô Đình Diệm," 8–12; Bùi Diễm, *Jaws of History*, 145–147, 158; and Buckley, "No One Can Be Sure." For more on the 1967 ticket, see Veith, *Drawn Swords*, 234–238.
13. See Clemis, *The Control War*.
14. On Saigon politics, see Fear, "Ambiguous Legacy," 27–30; Gawthorpe, *To Build as Well as Destroy*, 103–110. Kỳ remained a powerful figure throughout much of 1968 and spoke of favoring a coup to end the Second Republic so that a more decisive leader could replace Thiệu and the National Assembly. Embracing the Republic gave Thiệu a certain amount of "coup-insurance" in Saigon and Washington. On Kỳ, see Intelligence Information Special Report, CIA, March 6, 1968, #3a, "Kỳ-Thiệu," Box 2, National Security Files [NSF], William J. Jorden, Lyndon B. Johnson Presidential Library, Austin, Texas [LBJPL].
15. In 1965, Thiệu had favored Vietnamese mobilization to meet the military threat rather than what became the conflict's Americanization. See Moyar, *Triumph Forsaken*, 368.
16. For instance, Bùi Diễm's memoir argues that Thiệu ignored his reports and misjudged the political situation in America (*Jaws of History*, 248–249).
17. Buckley, "No One Can Be Sure"; Solberg, *Hubert Humphrey*, 311; Hoàng Đức Nhã, "Striving for a Lasting Peace," 59; FBIS Daily Report: Asia & Pacific, December 7, 1967, Folder 11, Box 2, Douglas Pike Collection: Other Manuscripts—FBIS-Asia, Vietnam Center and Archive at Texas Tech University [VCA].
18. For representative cables, see telegrams, Bùi Diễm (Washington) to the Foreign Affairs Ministry, February 5 and March 9, 1968, Hồ Sơ [HS] 851, Phủ Tổng thống Đệ nhị Cộng hòa, 1967–1975 [PTT], Vietnam National Archives Center II, Hồ Chí Minh City, Vietnam [VNAC 2].
19. Dispatch, Ambassador in Viet-Nam C. M. MacLehose (Saigon), "Call on President Thiệu, March 13," March 14, 1968, FCO 15/698, Public Records Office, Kew, England [PRO]; telegram, MacLehose to Foreign Office, "President Thiệu," April 2, 1968, DEFE 11/696, PRO; FBIS Daily Report: Asia & Pacific, April 11, 1968, Folder 11, Box 2, Douglas Pike Collection: Other Manuscripts—FBIS-Asia, VCA.
20. FBIS Daily Report: Asia & Pacific, April 3, 1968, Folder 11, Box 2, Douglas Pike Collection: Other Manuscripts—FBIS-Asia, VCA.
21. Memo, Rostow to LBJ, April 29, 1968, #1g, Folder "Meetings with the President, January-April, 1968 [1]," Box 1, NSF-Files of Walt Rostow, LBJPL.
22. Minutes of GVN meeting, July 12, 1968, HS 37, PTT, VNAC2; FBIS Daily Report: Asia & Pacific, July 19, 1968, Folder 5, Box 3, Douglas Pike Collection: Other Manuscripts—FBIS-Asia, VCA; "Interview with Vietnam President: US Pullback in Vietnam—When?," *U.S. News & World Report*, August 5, 1968, 42–46; dispatch, R. M. Tait (Canadian Delegation, ICSC, Saigon), "Vietnam: Honolulu Meeting July 20–21," August 7, 1968, File 20-22-VIETS-2-1 part 26, Volume 9401, RG 25, Library and Archives Canada [LAC].
23. Jeffrey Clarke, *Advice and Support*, 293–296, 301.
24. Dispatch, MacLehose, "Call on President Thiệu, March 13," March 14, 1968; cable to American Embassy Saigon, c.mid-April, 1968, #33b, Folder "Vietnam (18 Mar-29 April 68) [2]," Box 26, Clark Clifford Papers, LBJPL; "NVT Sees Gradual Pullout of Allied Troops Next Year," *Saigon Post*, April 26, 1968, 1.
25. For instance, see Nguyễn Phú Đức, *Viet-Nam Peace Negotiations*, 13, 20, 32–35.
26. Minutes of GVN meeting, July 12, 1968; handwritten memo, no author, "Dư án v/v theo dõi chính sách hóa đám của Hoa Kỳ," c. April 1968, HS 827, PTT, VNAC 2; Nguyễn Phú Đức, *Viet-Nam Peace Negotiations*, 102.

27. Telegram, Phạm Đăng Lâm (Paris) to the Foreign Affairs Ministry, October 21, 1968, HS 16374, Phủ Tổng Việt-Nam Cộng hòa, 1954–1975 [PTVNCH], VNAC 2.

28. President's Daily Brief, CIA, October 8, 1968, DOC_0005976397, Central Intelligence Agency-Electronic Reading Room; memo, CIA to Rostow and Rusk, "Reactions of the GVN and Vice President Kỳ Concerning the Proposed Bombing Halt," October 18, 1968, Folder "South Vietnam and U.S. Policies [X-File], Box 19, NSF-Rostow, LBJPL; minutes of GVN leaders' meeting October 19, 1968, 3:00 pm, HS 7431, PTT, VNAC 2.

29. On the evolution of Thiệu's various peace proposals, see chapter 2, this volume.

30. "Peace Should Be De-Americanised: Thien," *Vietnam Guardian*, October 28, 1968.

31. Cable, DIRNSA to White House, "Thiệu's Views on NLF Participation in Vietnamese Government," c. October 19, 1968, Folder "South Vietnam and U.S. Policies [X-File], Box 19, NSF-Rostow, LBJPL; telegram, GVN consulate (Paris) to Foreign Affairs Ministry, October 20, 1968, HS 16374, PTVNCH, VNAC2; "President Queried on Current Events," *The Vietnam Guardian*, October 21, 1968; memo, CIA to Rostow and Rusk, "President Thiệu's Views Regarding the Issues Involved in Agreeing to a Bombing Halt," October 26, 1968, Folder "South Vietnam and U.S. Policies [X-File], Box 19, NSF-Rostow, LBJPL; telegram, Thiệu to Bùi Diễm, October 23, 1968, HS 16374, PTVNCH, VNAC 2.

32. FBIS Daily Report: Asia & Pacific, November 4, 1968, folder 3, Box 4, Douglas Pike Collection: Other Manuscripts—FBIS-Asia, VCA; Keyes Beech, "LBJ—Most Hated Man in South Vietnam," November 4, 1968, 33, "VN 6I:11/68, Bombing Halt Reactions," Box 97, NSF-Country File Vietnam, LBJPL; dispatch, "Vietnam Peace Talks," November 6, 1968, File 20-22-VIETS-2-1 part 31, Volume 9401, RG 25, LAC; memo, Nguyễn Văn Hương, "Tóm Tắt Buổi Họp-Đồng Tổng-Trưởng Ngày 5/11/1968," November 11, 1968, HS 39, PTT, VNAC 2; memo, Tran-Van-Phuoc, "Khai Thác Thắng Lợi Chính Trị Của Việt-Nam Cộng-Hòa," November 15, 1968, HS 829, PTT, VNAC 2.

33. See Asselin, *Vietnam's American War*. Despite the Republic's doubts, Johnson had remained steadfast in his demand for the withdrawal of all North Vietnamese forces from South Vietnam and Laos and an end to North Vietnamese aid to the NLF. See memo, National Security Council [NSC], "Second Phase Instructions for Ambassadors Harriman and Vance," October 26, 1968, "Vietnam—Misc. Papers, Drafts, Memos Concerning Bombing Halt Decisions/Also Backchannel [1 of 2]," Box 136, NSF-Country File Vietnam, LBJPL.

34. Cable, Harriman (Paris) to State, "Detailed Summary of Procedural Meeting January 18," January 18, 1969, "Vietnam, Paris-Delto-Todel, Codeword, TDCS and Memos and Misc., etc.—'Bamboo' [1 of 2]," Box 260, NSF-Country File Vietnam, LBJPL.

35. Nguyễn Phú Đức, *Viet-Nam Peace Negotiations*, 161–162.

36. FBIS Daily Report: Asia & Pacific, November 4, 1968, Folder 3, Box 4, Douglas Pike Collection: Other Manuscripts—FBIS-Asia, VCA.

37. Memorandum of Conversation, Thiệu, Bunker, and Deputy Ambassador Samuel Berger, at Independence Palace, Saigon March 21, 1969, NSC 78:7, Richard Nixon Presidential Library and Museum, Yorba Linda, California [RNPLM]; memo, January 18, 1969, Folder "GVN Private Position 1969," Box 26, E-5408, RG 59, NA II; memo, Laird to RN, "Trip to Vietnam and CINCPAC, March 5–12, 1969," March 13, 1969, NSC 70:13, RNPLM.

38. Memo, Bùi Diễm (Washington) to Thiệu and GVN, "Một Vài Nhận Xét Và Đệ Nghị Đệ Trình Tổng Thống Và Chính Phủ Việt-Nam Cộng-Hòa," January 1969, HS 16671, PTVNCH, VNAC2; memo for the Prime Minister, "Tình hình chính-trị Hoa-Kỳ liên-quan tới Việt-Nam trong tháng 1–1969," February 7, 1969, HS 16671, PTVNCH, VNAC2; dispatch, Canadian Delegation to ICSC (Saigon) to External Affairs, "USA Troop Withdrawals—SVN Position," January 22, 1969, File 20-22-VIETS-2-1 part 33, Volume 9402, RG 25, LAC.

39. Memo, Trần-Văn-Phước, "Giải Thích Việc Quân Lực Việt-Nam Cộng-Hòa Sẽ Thay Thế Dần Quân Đội Hoa Kỳ," January 30, 1969, HS 17494, PTVNCH, VNAC2; memo, GVN H.Q.P., "Những Nhận Xét Sau 6 Tuần Lễ Tại Washington," March 10, 1969, HS 959, PTT, VNAC 2; memorandum of conversation, Thiệu, Bunker, and Deputy Ambassador Samuel Berger, at Independence Palace, Saigon March 21, 1969, NSC 78:7, RNPLM; "President Thiệu raps 'destructive' regimes," *Vietnam Guardian*, July 23, 1969.

40. Martin Clemis considers pacification and Vietnamization "two faces of a single strategic coin"; Andrew Gawthorpe calls Thiệu's village reforms "the civil side of Vietnamization." See Clemis, *Control War*, 192–197; Gawthorpe, *To Build as Well as Destroy*, 139.

41. Thiệu defined control as the ability of a civilian official to do their job during the day without being attacked. See Second ANZUS Security Consultations (Washington), October 23, 1969, Item 1727027 ANZUS-Official Consultations 1969, A1838, National Archives of Australia.

42. Thiệu thought his offers to negotiate with the NLF and allow their participation in supervised elections were "an assault weapon" he could use against the communists in the arena of international opinion. See "Peace Offer Anti-Red 'Assault Arm': Thiệu," *Saigon Post*, July 23, 1969, 1.

43. Memo, January 18, 1969, Folder "GVN Private Position 1969," NAII; memo, Nguyễn Văn Hương, "Tóm Tắt Buổi Họp-Đồng Tổng-Trưởng Ngày 5/11/1968"; "President Thiệu: Land Reform Sharpest Weapon to Fight Reds," *Saigon Post*, June 28, 1969, 1; Gawthorpe, *To Build as Well as Destroy*, 111–113; Kevin Boylan, "The Red Queen's Race, 1198–1201; Clemis, *Control War*, 219–220.

44. "Armed Forces Day Message: Nationalist Must Win Peace: Thiệu," *Saigon Post*, June 20, 1969, 1.

45. "President Underlines Readiness to Take on War Burden," *Vietnam Guardian*, April 18, 1969, 1, 6. Thereafter, South Vietnamese soldiers and officials derided Vietnamization as "the U.S. Dollar and Vietnam Blood Sharing Plan." See Hosmer, Kellen, and Jenkins, *Fall of South Vietnam*, 93.

46. Nguyễn Phú Đức recalled that America had been fighting a "rich man's war" that spent lavishly on airpower, soldiers' salaries, bases, food, and logistics. It seemed reasonable that the South Vietnamese could do far more with less. See Nguyễn Phú Đức, *Viet-Nam Peace Negotiations*, 232.

47. Thiệu outlined many of these assumptions in a July 1969 speech before civil servants and military officials. See FBIS Daily Report: Asia & Pacific, July 29, 1969, Folder 10, Box 5, Douglas Pike Collection: Other Manuscripts—FBIS-Asia, VCA.

48. Memo, Warnke to Clifford, January 25, 1969, #10, Folder "Vietnam, Documents 9-10," Box C31, Laird Papers, Gerald Ford Library, Ann Arbor, Michigan.

49. Nguyễn Phú Đức, *The Viet-Nam Peace Negotiations*, 225–229; letter, Bùi Diễm (Washington) to Thiệu, June 28, 1969, HS 1665, PTT, VNAC 2; Memorandum of Conversation, Nixon, Thiệu, et al., July 30, 1969, Folder "Personal Papers of William P. Rogers," Box 3, E-5439, RG 59, NA II; telegram, Tait, Saigon August 16, 1969, FCO 15/1009, PRO.

50. See Prentice, "Choosing 'the Long Road'."

51. Saving telegram, Mr. Moreton, Saigon December 29, 1969, FCO 15/1009, PRO.

52. Handwritten note from within GVN Ministry of Economy, c. mid-1970, HS 588, PTT, VNAC 2.

53. Nguyen Tien Hung and Schecter, *Palace File*, 34.

54. See chapter 4, this volume.

55. FBIS Daily Report: Asia & Pacific, July 29, 1969, Folder 10, Box 5, DPC: Other Manuscripts—FBIS-Asia, VCA; minutes, Nguyen Van Huong, "Tóm Tắt Phiên Họp Hội-Đồng Tổng-Trưởng Ngày 15,9,1969," c. September 15, 1969, HS 80, PTT, VNAC 2.

56. Nguyễn Đức Cường, "Building a Market Economy during Wartime," in Taylor, *Voices from the Second Republic*, 110; FBIS Daily Report: Asia & Pacific, November 3, 1969, Folder 7, Box 6, DPC: Other Manuscripts—FBIS-Asia, VCA.

57. Phạm Kim Ngọc, "Reform or Collapse," in Vu and Fear, *Republic of Vietnam*, 36–37; Simon Toner, "Imagining Taiwan," 785–786; "Austerity Taxes Spur Flurry of Protests," *Saigon Post*, October 27, 1969, 1; "House Stages Anti-Tax Walkout," *Vietnam Guardian*, October 28, 1969, 1, 6; Nguyen Duy Lieu, "More Austerity Measures Coming," *Saigon Post*, October 30, 1969, 1; Wendell Merick, "Behind Optimism about Vietnam," *U.S. News & World Report*, December 1, 1969.

58. Memo, GVN, "Chương-Trình Ổn-Định Kinh-Tế," n.d. (c. early 1970), HS 2185, PTT, VNAC 2; Nguyễn Đức Cường, "Coping with Changes and War," in Vu and Fear, *Republic of Vietnam*, 19.

59. On foreign investment in the period, see memo, Rogers to RN, December 8, 1969, Folder "NATO Ministerial Meeting, Brussels and Visits to Bonn and Paris 12/2–8/68," Box 13, E-5439, RG 59, NA II; memo, C. M. James (Saigon), "French Policy towards South Vietnam," September 14, 1970, FCO 15/1349, PRO; memo, C. M. James (Saigon), "France and Vietnam," November 19, 1970, FCO 15/1349, PRO.

60. Nguyễn Đức Cường, "Coping with Changes and War," 19–20; Phạm Kim Ngọc, "Reform or Collapse," 37–43; Toner, "Imagining Taiwan," 774–775, 784–788, 796–797.

61. Gawthorpe, *To Build as Well as Destroy*, 142–143, 182–184; Cao Văn Thân, "Land Reform and Agricultural Development," 47–55; Trần Quang Minh, "Decade of Public Service," 53–87.

62. Dispatch, Hart (Canadian Delegation to ICSC, Saigon) to External Affairs, "Views of President Thieu," May 28, 1971, File 20-VIETS-19 part 1, Volume 9377, RG 25, LAC.

63. Regarding its press, see chapter 3, this volume.

64. Fear, "Ambiguous Legacy," 49–54; Fear, "1971 Presidential Election."

65. Brigham, *Reckless*, 155, 158–159, 196–199, 208; Kadura, *War after the War*, 3–4, 57–60.

66. Johnson, *Congress and the Cold War*, 105, 153–154.

67. Laird quoted in telcons, Laird and Kissinger, 5:50 p.m., September 30, 1969, Henry A. Kissinger Telcons 2:7, RNPLM.

68. Julian Zelizer, "How Congress Got Us Out of Vietnam," *The American Prospect*, March 2007; Kadura, *War after the War*, 52–82. On Congress and the lack of sufficient aid after the accords, see, for instance, minutes of WSAG Meeting, October 2, 1973, and January 25, 1974 (US Department of State, *FRUS, 1969–1976*, vol. 10, 437–445, 507ff).

69. Kadura, *War after the War*, 91–99; Toner, "Imagining Taiwan," 792–796; Nguyễn Đức Cường, "Building a Market Economy," 103, 110–113.

70. Pursuing détente with the United States, the Soviets and Chinese reduced military aid to Hanoi in 1973. In 1974, the Soviets and North Vietnamese reached an agreement for renewed military aid. Military supplies and ammunition remained in short supply, but Hanoi had enough to escalate and then win its war in the South. See Asselin, *Vietnam's American War*, 219, 224, 226.

71. Nguyễn Phú Đức, *Viet-Nam Peace Negotiations*, 253–259, 279–281; Asselin, *Vietnam's American War*, 224–227.

72. Memo, Nha [Mỹ?] Châu, Liên Hiệp Quốc, "Một Vài Nhận-Định Về Chính-Sách

Của Hoa-Kỳ Đối Với Việt-Nam Trong Năm 1970," n.d. (early 1970), HS 20617, PTVNCH, VNAC 2.

73. Clemis, *Control War*, 281–307; Fear, "Ambiguous Legacy," 49–54; Gawthorpe, *To Build as Well as Destroy*, 187–189.

74. Willbanks, *Abandoning Vietnam*, 155–160, 278–287.

75. Fear, "Saigon Goes Global."

76. Thiệu proved overoptimistic on American aid but troop reductions largely followed his proposed timetables. As adopted, Nixon's rate of withdrawal followed and often mirrored Thiệu's proposals. And the Republic did receive a significant increase in American aid, going from nearly $1.9 billion in fiscal year 1968 to nearly $3.9 billion in fiscal year 1973. South Vietnam would receive about $1.6 billion in fiscal 1974. Conversely, Soviet military aid alone to North Vietnam was $1.7 billion in 1974. As long as communist assistance to North Vietnam remained so large, everything could not depend on the Republic alone. For aid figures, see Dacy, *Foreign Aid*, 200. For Soviet and Chinese aid, see Nguyễn Phú Đức, *Viet-Nam Peace Negotiations*, 417.

77. Willbanks, *Abandoning Vietnam*, 286.

CHAPTER 2

"All the Communists Must Leave"

The Origin, Evolution, and Failure of Saigon's Peace Demands, 1963–1973

George J. Veith

The Paris Peace Accords were a product of direct negotiations between the United States and the Democratic Republic of Vietnam (DRV). The ceasefire, exchange of prisoners, departure of American military forces and other modalities resulting from the accords primarily reflected the main principles of the United States and the DRV. The southern-based Republic of Vietnam (RVN) also had long-standing demands for peace, but both parties discounted the RVN's requirements. Although Washington labored to incorporate Saigon's requests into its overall negotiation strategy, it was unable to overcome the dichotomy between Saigon's desires and the Lyndon Johnson and Richard Nixon administration's domestic political needs. For Hanoi, acceding to Saigon's mandates would have defeated its primary aspiration—winning the war—and punctured its chief propaganda theme, that the RVN was a puppet of the United States.

Before the US military intervention in 1965, South Vietnam's government desired a military victory but occasionally sought to discuss peace with the National Liberation Front (NLF). After the 1968 Tết Offensive, the RVN realized that a political solution would be necessary to conclude the war. Consequently, beginning in 1969, Saigon repeatedly offered to hold elections that included the NLF, but the communists declined the proposals.

Saigon's conditions for peace evolved over the course of the war, a complex response to both its internal constituencies and external pressures. However, scholars have mostly concentrated on the diplomacy in 1972 and 1973 that concluded with the signing of the Paris accords. Historians such as Pierre Asselin, Jeffery Kimball, and Larry Berman have plumbed the archival records and produced an in-depth examination of the final round of talks.[1] Some of the main protagonists have also penned insider accounts.[2] Several other scholars have covered less well-known features of the intricate negotiations, such as the inclusion of either what was referred to as the Third Force or specific aspects of Saigon's foreign policy.[3] None, though, have discussed the origins of South Vietnam's peace policies or their evolution. This chapter attempts to address that gap and provide an overview of Saigon's demands for peace.

DEFINING SOUTH VIETNAMESE POLICY

President Ngô Đình Diệm never publicly articulated his position on achieving peace with the growing National Liberation Front. Instead, he focused on either population control through various pacification program such as the Strategic Hamlets or defeating the insurgency via advanced US weaponry and advisers. Only in the summer of 1963, under tremendous strain from both demonstrating Buddhist activists and the United States to reform his government, did Ngô Đình Diệm covertly reach out to Hanoi.[4] Rumors abounded in Saigon that he was contemplating everything from expanded economic ties with Hanoi to the neutralization of South Vietnam. Fear that Ngô Đình Diệm might convert the country to a neutral status was among the many reasons that General Dương Văn Minh and his co-conspirators overthrew him in November 1963.[5]

Postcoup, General Dương Văn Minh and his prime minister, Nguyễn Ngọc Thơ, believed that, in light of Ngô Đình Diệm's death, the noncommunist elements in the NLF could be convinced to join a political alliance with the anticommunists in South Vietnam's political framework.[6] They were preparing an outreach program to build a wider coalition in the South that included these supposedly disgruntled noncommunists. Rumors, however, again began circulating in Saigon that Dương Văn Minh and the ruling triumvirate were also secretly considering neutralization. General Nguyễn Khánh and several other generals used this same fear to spark another internal coup, and Dương Văn Minh was supplanted by Nguyễn Khánh on January 30, 1964.

In the spring of 1964, the NLF launched large-scale attacks, and the military situation in South Vietnam began to badly deteriorate. Frustrated by his declining military fortunes, in June 1964, Nguyễn Khánh made a covert effort to establish contact with the NLF to discuss peace. He enlisted one of his cabinet ministers, Lê Văn Hoạch, to convince the NLF to join in a coalition against the North.[7] Hoạch claimed he had reached an agreement with the NLF for a ceasefire, as did Nguyễn Khánh later in January 1965, but Nguyễn Khánh's erratic rule led to his ouster in February 1965 before any alleged accommodation was reached.

The military chose civilian politician Phan Huy Quát to replace Nguyễn Khánh as prime minister. Shortly after Phan Huy Quát's ascension, a senior Buddhist monk in Saigon named Thích Quảng Liên announced on February 28 the birth of a group dedicated to finding peace in Vietnam. Quảng Liên's program demanded the simultaneous withdrawal of both communist and American troops, followed by negotiations solely between the Vietnamese.[8] This was the first request by a nongovernment body for peace talks with the NLF, and Phan Huy Quát's initial cabinet meeting focused on responding to Quảng Liên's proposal. Phan Huy Quát's close aide (and future RVN ambassador to the United States) Bùi Diễm remarked that "Phan Huy Quát was against neutralism or a coalition. The consensus in the cabinet was that since Thích Quảng Liên appeared to favor the Communists, Phan Huy Quát needed to take a tough stance."[9]

Phan Huy Quát devoted his first news conference as prime minister to responding to Quảng Liên's proposal. He agreed with Quảng Liên that "the question of negotiation is entirely an internal Vietnamese matter" but "one the South Vietnamese government has never tackled." He then laid out his policies for negotiations. Phan Huy Quát said that though Saigon wanted peace, it would not settle for a "mere truce" that the communists would exploit. South Vietnam was defending itself against external aggression from the North, and if Hanoi truly desired peace, the communists must "end the war, infiltration, subversion, and sabotage," and should "guarantee the safety of South Vietnam." He then rejected any "international solution that has not received the agreement of the Government and people of Vietnam," a clear rebuke of recent French proposals for a resumption of the Geneva Accords.[10] Phan Huy Quát's peace conditions—defined by civilian politicians and not the military— were the first official post–Ngô Đình Diệm peace policy and became the basis for future RVN efforts.

Phan Huy Quát's forthright responses were completely overlooked when the US Marines landed near Đà Nẵng on March 8, 1965. Phan Huy Quát was loath to allow regular US combat forces into Vietnam, fearing that it would enable the Communist's potent propaganda machine to drive a "wedge...between the government and the people."[11] He was right. Trương Như Tảng, a covert NLF cadre living in Saigon, notes that the NLF had earlier decided to intensify the "political struggle" and "galvanize popular pressure in the cities for talks," thereby creating "a political crisis which the Americans would be powerless to affect. Our first step in this direction was to establish an open and legal movement...with no visible ties to the NLF."[12] Hoping that the Saigon government would collapse from internal strife, Trương Như Tảng helped form a group called the National Self-Determination Movement to advocate for peace talks. A second organization, the Committee for Peace, was also spawned by his effort.

Hours after the Marines waded ashore, the Committee for Peace held a press conference in Saigon. They demanded the removal of US troops and the start of negotiations between the RVN and the NLF but unlike Quảng Liên, they said nothing about communist forces withdrawing to North Vietnam. Fearing the Committee for Peace was a communist front, the military and anticommunist elements in South Vietnamese society such as the northern Catholics pressed Phan Huy Quát to forcefully respond. He quickly arrested the leaders of the two groups and had them deported. On March 12, Phan Huy Quát also publicly denounced Thích Quảng Liên's peace movement and proclaimed that his government was committed to a "total struggle" against the communists to win the war. Receiving no support from the Buddhist leadership, on March 17, Thích Quảng Liên resigned his church position and departed for a conference in Japan. Although Phan Huy Quát had successfully stymied an internal demand for peace talks, any group that appealed for direct talks with the NLF was now suspected of being a communist front.

Soon after Phan Huy Quát made his public statements about the RVN's peace stance, and with the Americans engaged in multiple covert peace initiatives, Deputy US Ambassador Alexis Johnson met with Foreign Minister Trần Văn Đỗ on May 1 to discuss the RVN's peace policy. Trần Văn Đỗ told Johnson that Saigon disagreed with a recent French proposal that convening another Geneva conference would achieve peace with Hanoi. For South Vietnam, the 1954 accords had proven futile. Trần Văn Đỗ pointed out that the International Control Commission had been useless in halting infiltration because without an "effective force which could be rapidly called to meet future aggression," the DRV had openly flouted both the 1954 and 1962 Laos accords.[13] Given Hanoi's track record, he remarked, why did anyone believe it would respect another pact? Much like Ngô Đình Diệm, Trần Văn Đỗ believed it was more important to achieve sway over the population given that "an agreement with the VC [Viet Cong] would be useless unless the RVN could control the villages." That required a ceasefire and a communist withdrawal. If the NLF did not withdraw its forces from South Vietnam, "all that would have been accomplished was the division of the country, and then the RVN would have to negotiate with the NLF. This is why the RVN had asked for the withdrawal of the VC.... [Dỗ] reiterated that a ceasefire without a withdrawal would be very dangerous and that neither the government nor the military could accept such an arrangement."[14]

Permitting communist troops to remain in South Vietnam was the chief issue over which President Nguyễn Văn Thiệu and the Richard Nixon administration would so vehemently disagree during the period before the signing of the Paris Peace Accords. They went to the heart of what constituted an independent South Vietnam. Although Nguyễn Văn Thiệu would only grudgingly agree to allow communist troops to remain in country in exchange for Nixon's promise of a continuation of aid and to resume bombing in response to a major violation of the ceasefire, he had not dreamed up these rationales for refusing to accept Kissinger's peace plan. The RVN had laid down these conditions long before the tumultuous events of October 1972 through January 1973.

The RVN asked for a meeting on May 26 between Phan Huy Quát and US Ambassador Maxwell Taylor to flesh out their respective positions. The Vietnamese claimed their objectives "stated in broad terms are restoration of peace with liberty and full sovereignty and independence of SVN." Regarding the NLF, the RVN's position was "absolutely firm." For Saigon, the NLF was a "creature of Hanoi," and Phan Huy Quát would not accept it as an "element in the RVN administration, either as a bloc or a political force or organization." Taylor agreed that even though the United States shared the South Vietnamese demand for a "securely guaranteed" independence, it favored the French offer to restart the Geneva Accords. Phan Huy Quát disagreed and stated the 1954 agreement was an "armistice between the French and the VC but not a political document governing the future of SVN," especially given that South Vietnam had not signed it.[15] However, if the two sides did return to a Geneva conference, the RVN wanted an American assurance that the United States would militarily respond if the communists violated any new treaty, another harbinger of the difficulties in resolving the future Paris accords.

Then the South Vietnamese revealed another anxiety: the challenging political climate inside the country to peace overtures. Because of the US proposals, the "Vietnamese press and opposition groups [are claiming] that basic decisions concerning South Vietnam are being made without RVN's being a party." For that reason, they said, the RVN had "made no attempt to initiate direct or indirect talks with the DRV" because of the "obvious political difficulties of appearing to deal with the enemy."[16] Phan Huy Quát could not offer negotiations without being accused that he was soft on communism. Saigon's sensitivities to its internal divisions would continue to shape the RVN's peace stance for years.

SAIGON REJECTS NEGOTIATIONS WITH THE COMMUNISTS

Shortly thereafter, the Phan Huy Quát government collapsed, and two military officers, Nguyễn Cao Kỳ and Nguyễn Văn Thiệu, assumed power. Nguyễn Cao Kỳ held the main leadership role but entered office woefully unprepared for the intricacies of foreign policy, something he initially considered of "little importance."[17] Nguyễn Cao Kỳ retained Trần Văn Đỗ as his foreign minister, but under pressure from the United States to announce Saigon's peace terms, on June 22, 1965, ordered Trần Văn Đỗ to publicly state the program discussed with the Americans on May 26. Trần Văn Đỗ announced the RVN's four major conditions for a settlement. First, an end to communist military and political subversion, the disbanding of the NLF, and the withdrawal of all infiltrators back to the DRV. Second, the right of South Vietnam to settle its own affairs. Third, the eventual withdrawal of friendly foreign troops. Fourth, effective guarantees of South Vietnam's independence and freedom. Ending with a strongly worded declaration, Trần Văn Đỗ proclaimed that if

> Hanoi sincerely wants peace, if it puts the interests of the nation above those of an ideology or a party, if it wants the Vietnamese people and the other peoples of Southeast Asia to live in peace instead of war, prosperity instead of poverty, freedom instead of slavery, it only has to put an end to aggression.[18]

Hanoi ignored Trần Văn Đỗ's eloquence. Moreover, Saigon's new leaders also disagreed that restarting the 1954 Geneva Accords was a logical beginning. In late July, Nguyễn Văn Thiệu made the

> spirited exposition to effect that their 'honor and political situation' did not permit them to recognize binding effect of document which French sought to impose upon them by signature of French General... Thiệu said they could accept the 'factual situation' created in 1954 by the Geneva

Accords [the division of Vietnam until reunification] but RVN could not change what had been consistent and basic position of all South Vietnamese since 1954. However, Nguyễn Cao Kỳ said that RVN could take position that, while RVN had not signed accords, they had always and would continue to respect their principles.[19]

Responding to the US request to continue to publicly articulate the RVN's peace policy, Nguyễn Văn Thiệu hammered on one theme; all the communists must leave. The path to reconciliation, he said, was for the communists to "withdraw their troops and cadres to the North. As far as we are concerned, the above preconditions have to be met if the VC want to talk about negotiations and peace." New US Ambassador Henry Cabot Lodge remarked that "Thiệu...seems determined to put his ideas on record to make certain that no negotiation or negotiating position is decided without RVN participation. There is no doubt he is reflecting opinions widely held within and outside RVN circles."[20] Lodge was painfully aware that Nguyễn Văn Thiệu's orations reflected the Nationalists' not-so-secret fear of "foreigners" making a peace deal that "sold them out" to the communists.

As US troops began to turn the military tide, Nguyễn Văn Thiệu and Nguyễn Cao Kỳ remained firmly against negotiations. In a discussion with Lodge in mid-October 1965, Nguyễn Văn Thiệu opined that the enemy would only agree to negotiate when "they were convinced they could not achieve a military victory with main-force units." Nguyễn Văn Thiệu believed that if the communists accepted peace negotiations, it was simply a tactic to wear down the United States. "The purpose of accepting an offer to negotiate would be to end or suspend the US military activities [so that] it would be difficult, if not impossible for us to continue operations."[21] For Nguyễn Văn Thiệu, true negotiations would only begin when Hanoi was convinced that it could not win the war. It was a position he would hold for years.

Despite repeated South Vietnamese statements rejecting negotiations with the communists until they halted their attacks and withdrew, President Johnson continued secret United States diplomatic activities. On January 14, 1966, Nguyễn Văn Thiệu gave the opening address to the Second Congress of the Armed Forces. Aware of the ongoing US efforts, he informed the assembled officers that the "war can be ended only by a complete victory, both military and political, and that peace for Vietnam can only be that of a country fully independent in terms of its territory and sovereignty."[22] Nguyễn Cao Kỳ also condemned the

American peace feelers. "No other nation," he stated, "is qualified and able to decide on our destiny...[and] we can never tolerate any interference harmful to our national sovereignty...There is no other alternative ...than to defeat the Communists and rout them from their strongholds."[23] Both men had now warned the United States not to make peace without considering RVN desires.

Having outlined its position, and convinced that Hanoi would not negotiate, for the remainder of 1966 and into 1967, the South Vietnamese leadership turned to more pressing internal issues. These included a renewed crisis with the Buddhists, followed by national elections in September 1966 for a Constituent Assembly that would draft a constitution. In April 1967, a new constitution was approved that called for a national vote to elect a president and a bicameral congress. Article 4, however, prohibited any "Communist or Neutralist" political activity. This article banning overt communist electoral efforts would serve as a shield for Nguyễn Văn Thiệu to defend his refusal to permit such action.

As candidates declared their intentions to run for the presidency, peace—and how to achieve it—became a major topic. At the onset of the presidential campaign in August 1967, pressure to outline his peace policy forced Nguyễn Văn Thiệu to modify long-standing RVN policy. He offered direct talks with North Vietnam.[24] By late August, he went a step further and dangled the possibility of a bombing halt—a tactic he had previously adamantly opposed—but only if Hanoi agreed to direct negotiations with Saigon. He even adapted his position regarding talks with the NLF by offering to speak with any individual from the Front, but only to discuss reconciliation. He would not speak with them as representatives of a rebel political entity. For Nguyễn Văn Thiệu, Hanoi's willingness to talk directly with Saigon was the litmus test of its sincerity. Doing so would concede the RVN's legitimacy and repudiate the Politburo's propaganda that the Nationalists were American puppets and that only the Front represented the South Vietnamese people. Regardless, Nguyễn Văn Thiệu did not believe Hanoi would respond to his offer of direct talks. He still judged that the DRV would only negotiate after it concluded that the North could not win militarily, or if the United States elections materially affected American policy. The only worse outcome in Nguyễn Văn Thiệu's mind would be if the Americans took over the negotiations and talked directly with Hanoi.

Most candidates agreed that negotiations should only occur between Hanoi and Saigon, and that RVN should not talk with the NLF. Only one contender, Trương Đình Dzu, ran on a platform of speaking directly to the NLF. Stunningly, he came in second behind Nguyễn Văn Thiệu and his running mate Nguyễn Cao Kỳ. Shortly after the election, Dzu was jailed for passing bad checks, but many believed he had been arrested for advocating peace talks with the NLF. However, Dzu's "mandate for peace" among the population was an illusion. Even though people were war weary, scholar Allan Goodman examined the September 1967 election and concluded that

> the magnitude of such a "mandate" was limited since eighty-two percent ...cast ballots for candidates who did not make peace more than a perfunctory campaign slogan and who expressed serious concern that a peace too hastily declared or one into which the Americans pressured the government would result in the take-over of the country by the Communists.[25]

NGUYỄN VĂN THIỆU TAKES OVER

In January 1968, Nguyễn Văn Thiệu gave his first foreign policy speech as president of the Second Republic. Nothing had changed. He warned Washington against succumbing to the "Communist stratagem of addressing themselves to the United States government only, while omitting the RVN." He pointedly reminded Washington that "this is our country." Saigon, he emphasized, should "have the central role in any developments relating to Vietnam....I regret to say that in the past our allies sometimes have not avoided...placing themselves at the center of peace efforts."[26] For a variety of reasons, including mistrust of Hanoi and the fear of a US deal with the DRV at Saigon's expense, Nguyễn Văn Thiệu continued to admonish the Americans not to negotiate directly with Hanoi.

At the end of January 1968, the communists launched the massive military assault known as the Tết Offensive. They attacked South Vietnam's cities, hoping for a popular uprising that would overthrow Nguyễn Văn Thiệu's government. Although the uprising failed to materialize, the offensive made President Lyndon Johnson consider appealing to Hanoi for direct peace talks between the two countries, the precise event the South Vietnamese were adamantly against.[27] In late March, US Ambassador Ellsworth Bunker warned Johnson that convincing Nguyễn Văn Thiệu to agree to US-led peace negotiations would be difficult. While Nguyễn Văn Thiệu "has shown himself to be very responsive to our wishes and needs he has made himself vulnerable to charges of being unduly influenced by the Americans, and... Thiệu could therefore find himself in a very delicate position if he should give his concurrence [for US-led peace efforts]."[28]

President Johnson disregarded Bunker's warning, and on March 31, 1968, offered a bombing halt over much of the DRV in exchange for direct negotiations. Several days later, Hanoi accepted. Accurately foreseeing the future, Bunker predicted that the "RVN will be very difficult to deal with in the matter of preparing for negotiations. Every move we make towards an accommodation with the Communists will raise lively and genuine fears of abandonment." Bunker then proposed his future tactics:

> focus on specific aspects of negotiations, discuss them in advance and in-depth with the top leadership...and try to bring them along as best we can without sapping their will to continue the struggle.... This will be a painful experience requiring patience and understanding, but it is vital to our objective of finding a political solution in Vietnam acceptable to the broadest range of Vietnamese Nationalist opinion.[29]

The peace talks formally opened in Paris in May 1968 but quickly stalled over procedural issues. Bunker met with Nguyễn Văn Thiệu and Nguyễn Cao Kỳ after each meeting to discuss the results and the US strategy, but the two provided little feedback. Nguyễn Văn Thiệu was furious that the United States was leading the talks—partly because the DRV refused to negotiate with Saigon—but was content to let the United States wrangle with the DRV negotiators, convinced that Hanoi was not serious about negotiations. Given the communists' intransigence, on October 7, Nguyễn Văn Thiệu addressed the National Assembly. He reiterated that he would not permit a coalition government, cede any territory, or allow the NLF to participate in any elections as a political entity. Buttressing his confidence was his belief that the military pendulum had swung his way. His army was growing, the communists had taken heavy losses in 1968, and new American weapons were improving the firepower of his troops.

Hanoi, however, had decided to change course. Shortly after Nguyễn Văn Thiệu's speech, chief DRV negotiator in Paris Lê Đức Thọ dangled a concession; if the United States halted bombing, then constructive talks could begin. Hoping a breakthrough had finally appeared, President Johnson promptly sent Bunker to gain Nguyễn Văn Thiệu's concurrence. The ambassador explained the new development and asked for Nguyễn Văn Thiệu's agreement on moving forward. Suddenly flexible, the South Vietnamese president promptly said yes. "After all," he replied, "the problem is not to stop the bombing, but to stop the war, and we must try this path to see if they are serious."[30] Nguyễn Văn Thiệu then asked about the NLF's status at the talks. Bunker said that the United States had informed Hanoi's delegates that it would not accept the NLF's presence at the table, but after Hanoi continued to demand the NLF's participation, Harriman had offered a your side–our side formula in which anyone could be seated with either party. The US plan was to sidestep Hanoi's demand while rejecting NLF flags, nameplates, or other insignia that would infer that the Front was a full participant in the talks.

On October 16, Bunker again visited Nguyễn Văn Thiệu and told him that US negotiators in Paris would soon meet with the DRV delegation. He wanted Nguyễn Văn Thiệu to sign a joint communique announcing the initiation of formal peace talks that included an RVN delegation. Nguyễn Văn Thiệu immediately convened his newly formed National Security Council (NSC) plus the leaders of the Lower House and Senate to discuss Bunker's request. After Nguyễn Văn Thiệu explained the situation, the NSC requested that he clarify the NLF's status at the talks before signing the joint communique or agreeing to send a delegation to Paris.

The next day, Nguyễn Văn Thiệu explained to Bunker the need to confirm the NLF's standing. "If I and the prime minister accepted," he said, "to go into a meeting without the NLF status clarified, there could be a violent reaction here." Nguyễn Văn Thiệu feared the hard-liners on his right would cause chaos. While he acknowledged that the world would blame him if Saigon declined to attend, he lamented that "I do not think I am strong enough to move; there are too many people here...who would use this as a pretext to make trouble."[31] Bunker advised Nguyễn Văn Thiệu to have greater confidence in his countrymen. Nguyễn Văn Thiệu, according to one aide, "did not share that line of thinking," and he "was willing to risk everything rather than accept the NLF as a separate delegation."[32] If the RVN agreed to speak to the NLF as an equal, Nguyễn Văn Thiệu believed it would destroy morale and undermine Saigon's contention that the war was aggression from North Vietnam.

With the United States unable to persuade Nguyễn Văn Thiệu that the Front's attendance did not constitute recognition, the two sides were at impasse. After President Johnson spoke on national television on October 31, 1968, to announce the formal start of negotiations between Hanoi and the United States, Nguyễn Văn Thiệu was faced with a stark choice: agree to attend or risk a rupture of US-RVN relations. In a speech on November 2 to the National Assembly, he rejected Saigon's attendance if the NLF was part of the Communist delegation. Talking with the Front was a line Nguyễn Văn Thiệu would not cross. The Assembly gave him a standing ovation, and most South Vietnamese supported Nguyễn Văn Thiệu's stance. Although many believed Nguyễn Văn Thiệu was the driving force in Saigon's resistance to negotiate with the NLF, in fact he was backed by many Nationalist constituencies, including the military and most National Assembly leaders and religious leaders. Granted, some South Vietnamese, including opposition deputies in the National Assembly and some Buddhist clergy centered on the Ấn Quang pagoda disagreed with his policy, but they held little political power.

Bunker, while upset at Nguyễn Văn Thiệu's refusal, nonetheless thought that Nguyễn Văn Thiệu's defiance of President Johnson had enabled him to "shed the image of an American-appointed chief executive and became a leader in his own right. By catering to ... nationalism, he has acquired the aura of a courageous patriot who is standing up to the foreigner."[33] Separately, Nguyễn Cao Kỳ agreed with Bunker, stating that "had Thiệu yielded [to the United States], the people would have called Thiệu's administration a US puppet and Thiệu might have been assassinated."[34] Despite allegations that the Nixon campaign had used Anna Chennault to pass messages to Nguyễn Văn Thiệu encouraging him not to attend, Nguyễn Văn Thiệu had refused for his own internal reasons, not because of Nixon's supposed entreaties.

By late November, Nguyễn Văn Thiệu had grudgingly agreed to send a delegation to Paris, but he remained adamant about not permitting NLF participation. Hanoi attempted to symbolically include the NLF by proposing a four-sided table, which Nguyễn Văn Thiệu immediately rejected. Outside observers blamed him for what seemed like an absurd impasse over the shape of the table, but he understood that procedural issues represented substantive ones, especially in Vietnamese culture.

On January 10, 1969, Bunker visited Nguyễn Văn Thiệu to convince him to halt further efforts to define the table. The ambassador explained that the new Nixon administration wanted to begin negotiations. As much as historians have discussed the tremendous influence that the Tet offensive had on President Johnson, few have realized that it also forced Nguyễn Văn Thiệu to confront the military reality. After listening to Bunker's plea, Nguyễn Văn Thiệu remarked that he was "no superhawk," and that he now understood that the war would not end with a military victory. "Eventually," Nguyễn Văn Thiệu said, "there would have to be political settlement involving competition with the Communists, a competition which would be decisive." Nguyễn Văn Thiệu, however, had left unspoken a key point; for years, RVN political and military leaders had demanded a military victory. Even mentioning a political solution was "defeatist" and risked arrest. Nguyễn Văn Thiệu now had to convince his people to accept something less, and

> that would take time.... The Vietnamese people now understand that there will be peace without victory, that they must expect a difficult contest with the Communists, and that the United States also wants and expects this. The question, therefore, has become how to make South Vietnam politically strong enough to win that looming contest.

Given this new reality, Nguyễn Văn Thiệu said, "the battle of propaganda is of the utmost importance. This is not only a matter of substance, it is equally, and sometimes even more, a matter of appearances, of face, of prestige.... Our common problem is how to win the political war and how to develop a propaganda position that will support that war." Nguyễn Văn Thiệu believed his dilemma was to simultaneously satisfy US opinion while maintaining "the morale of the Vietnamese people and armed forces to win in a political settlement."[35]

After an agreement was reached to use a round table with no flags, peace talks began. The formal opening of talks encouraged a few other South Vietnamese voices to clamor for peace. When prominent Ấn Quang bonze (Buddhist monk) Thích Thiện Minh called for direct negotiations with the communists, Nguyễn Văn Thiệu immediately rejected it, warning that South Vietnam was entering the most "dangerous period of its history" and that internal stability was "absolutely necessary" in this "period of political warfare."[36] Nguyễn Văn Thiệu ordered Thích Thiện Minh arrested, believing that national unity was crucial to winning the forthcoming political contest with the communists.

Despite his crackdown on those advocating talking to the NLF, Nguyễn Văn Thiệu himself was open to the concept. In January 1969, Vice President Nguyễn Cao Kỳ had mentioned to journalists that he was willing to meet in Paris privately with NLF representatives. On March 2, new US President Richard Nixon quietly encouraged this effort. Nixon told Nguyễn Cao Kỳ that it would be "very clever" if the RVN offered to speak with the NLF.[37] Nguyễn Văn Thiệu responded by telling Bunker in mid-March to inform Nixon that Saigon no longer sought "or speaks of complete military victory. We know the war cannot be won militarily." A peaceful solution required two things: "we need to be strong enough to win the political war with the Communists after peace is restored, and we must be assured that when we do make peace external aggression will cease... There can be no false solution as there was in 1954." To that end, the "North Vietnamese must withdraw and provide guarantees against renewed aggression, and the RVNAF [RVN Armed Forces] must be strengthened to enforce that guarantee."[38]

NGUYỄN VĂN THIỆU CHANGES COURSE

With Nixon's encouragement, on March 25, Nguyễn Văn Thiệu struck. In a dramatic announcement, he publicly offered to hold private talks with the NLF in Paris without any preconditions. To stymie any military backlash, he held a luncheon two days later with his senior commanders. After he had carefully explained his thoughts, the military leaders agreed that the proposal was useful and had stolen "the NLF thunder and put the RVN in a good public light abroad."[39]

Believing that he had the backing of South Vietnamese military and public opinion, on April 7, Nguyễn Văn Thiệu made another bold proposal for peace. In an address to the Assembly, he offered a six-point program for ending the war. In exchange for the withdrawal of North Vietnamese forces, a halt to violence, and their agreement to respect the constitution of the Republic of Vietnam, the RVN would extend full rights to anyone in the NLF. If they renounced violence and terrorism and did not call themselves communists, they could form their own political party and run candidates for elections. International monitors would guarantee their rights. Nguyễn Văn Thiệu also called for the dismantling of enemy bases in Laos and Cambodia, respect for the demilitarized zone, and the reunification of the two countries through a supervised election. Essentially, he had accepted the NLF as a political reality but not as a political entity. The communists once more declined to participate in elections.

On July 11, Nguyễn Văn Thiệu addressed the nation. He reviewed the history of the peace talks and pointed out that his compromise to permit the NLF to participate in elections as a separate entity demonstrated his good-faith pursuit of peace. He then made his boldest offer to date, again challenging the NLF to participate in internationally supervised elections, but only if it renounced violence and pledged to accept the results. Further, he offered to let the NLF help set up and monitor the elections, that there would be no reprisals after the elections and that the RVN would respect the election results no matter the outcome. He reiterated his earlier suggestions that he was willing to hold private talks with the NLF without preconditions to discuss the election logistics.

Hanoi immediately rejected Nguyễn Văn Thiệu's offer, calling it a "deceitful move" and an "election farce staged ... to maintain ... U.S. neocolonialism in South Vietnam."[40] His reaction was restrained. Privately he told Bunker that we "must make it clear we are not angry or shutting any doors."[41] Publicly, he responded by asking the communists to "think about" his plan while insisting that "I am a peaceful man who is trying to search for every conciliatory solution. I am not a war-like person, but neither will I surrender to the Communist."[42] He then declared that this was his last peace proposal. He had challenged the communists to an election contest but had reached his own limits and what was possible within Nationalist politics. It was now Hanoi's turn to respond.

After Nguyễn Văn Thiệu's offer was spurned by Hanoi, other Nationalists again sought to find peace by bridging the gap between the two sides. In late October 1969, RVN Senator Trần Văn Đôn officially announced a program that essentially offered neutralization and a coalition government between the NLF and the RVN. His declaration began discussions of a Third Force in South Vietnam that could offer a middle way between the foes. Although not quite "peace at any price," Đôn was simply the latest Saigon politician to seek a compromise with the communists. In 1965, the Peace Committee had first publicly broached the idea, followed in 1967 by Trương Đình Dzu, and then the Buddhist leader Thích Thiện Minh. As the previous efforts had done, Nguyễn Văn Thiệu also rejected those advocating the Third Force concept, but he could not arrest Đôn because the senator had parliamentary immunity. When the communists also dismissed Đôn's proposal, the talks remained stalled for another year.

On September 17, 1970, Nguyễn Thị Bình, the foreign minister of the newly proclaimed Provisional Revolutionary Government (PRG), which had replaced the NLF, publicized a revamped offer. She said that if the United States withdrew all forces by June 30, 1971, removed Nguyễn Văn Thiệu and Nguyễn Cao Kỳ from power, and formed a three-party coalition (PRG, Saigon, Third Force), then communist forces would not attack withdrawing US troops. Once a new coalition government was formed, voting would be held for a new Assembly that would write a new constitution. She rejected any elections if Nguyễn Văn Thiệu and Nguyễn Cao Kỳ remained in power. Saigon immediately vetoed her proposal. Instead, Nguyễn Văn Thiệu repeated his offer of the previous year to negotiate with the NLF and to hold elections under the supervision of an international committee to ensure fairness.

When Hanoi again scorned his overture, Nguyễn Văn Thiệu resumed his hard line. In a speech to the Assembly on October 31, he praised his government's military achievements and painted a picture of near victory. He resumed his denunciations of those "cowardly and defeatist people" who advocated a coalition or "peace in neutrality.... I will never betray our nation. I will never surrender to the Communists."[43] As much as he was proclaiming policy while attempting to convince Hanoi it could not achieve a military victory, Nguyễn Văn Thiệu was also playing to his base. A presidential election was scheduled for October 1971, and given these new peace offers, he needed to burnish his anticommunist credentials. To the South Vietnamese opposition, however, Nguyễn Văn Thiệu's rigidity remained anathema. Breaking a long silence, Dương Văn Minh rejected Nguyễn Văn Thiệu's stance. In a speech, Dương Văn Minh agreed that though the military situation had improved, solving Vietnam's problems "must be conceived by the Vietnamese in the interest of the Vietnamese people and nation."[44] Dương Văn Minh was rejecting US intervention in the peace process by discreetly proposing negotiations between the RVN and the PRG without risking arrest by overtly declaring his intention.

Much like in the 1967 election, how to achieve peace again become a huge issue in the new presidential race. Only two candidates would challenge Nguyễn Văn Thiệu in the 1971 election, Nguyễn Cao Kỳ and Dương Văn Minh. Much like Dương Văn Minh, Nguyễn Cao Kỳ began jockeying for votes by attempting to appeal for a political settlement to the war. Stealing a page from Trương Đình Dzu in 1967, Nguyễn Cao Kỳ said that Saigon "should try to...find ways to stop the fighting...[Thiệu] has talked about a political struggle, but how can this be done if the war still continues? Let's not talk about a military solution to the war."[45] Dương Văn Minh quickly agreed with Nguyễn Cao Kỳ, but by the summer of 1971, both candidates had withdrawn from the race over Nguyễn Văn Thiệu's repressive election tactics.

Nguyễn Văn Thiệu, however, continued his hard-line stance. He began articulating a policy that became known as the Four No's: no coalition government, no neutrality, no territorial concessions to the communists, and no communist political activity. He still believed that Hanoi would not negotiate "until there had been an all-out military confrontation with North Vietnamese forces." He predicted that the communists would wait until US ground forces had been withdrawn. Then they would then attack the "northern regions...to capture such cities as Quảng Trị and Huế." This would be the "final confrontation of the war." Nguyễn Văn Thiệu thought that Hanoi would then offer to negotiate, hoping to lock in any gains. Although Nguyễn Văn Thiệu remained adamantly against any communist political activity, he continued to propose elections to the PRG to end the war. He wanted to be remembered as the "president who brought peace to Vietnam."[46]

After he won the uncontested 1971 election, and with the negotiations in Paris still stalled, Nixon moved in January 1972 to jumpstart them. Nixon announced that his deputy, Henry Kissinger, had been secretly meeting with Lê Đức Thọ for several years, but without results. Consequently, Nixon now proposed that if the NLF would consent to elections, Nguyễn Văn Thiệu would resign one month before the vote, and the election would be run by an independent organization that the communists could join. Nguyễn Văn Thiệu, who privately was furious about the American tactic, took a measured tone in public, saying "I am always ready to sacrifice my own personal interests for the great interests of the country and people."[47] Despite having come close to meeting Bình's September 1970 proposal, Hanoi rejected Nixon's offer to for Nguyễn Văn Thiệu to resign and hold elections.

Nguyễn Văn Thiệu's prediction of a major enemy assault soon proved true. In late March 1972, Hanoi launched another massive offensive, this time backed by armor and heavy artillery. North Vietnam's forces initially made significant gains, but under heavy US aerial assault, the offensive bogged down. As the military tide began to reverse, by the summer of 1972, the Politburo decided to strike a deal. In early October 1972, Lê Đức Thọ offered a ceasefire and a prisoner swap in exchange for the removal of all US forces from South Vietnam. Most important, the Nguyễn Văn Thiệu administration could remain in power, a notable change from their earlier demands that Nguyễn Văn Thiệu had to be replaced. After the agreement, talks would be held between the RVN and the PRG to discuss a political solution, another major shift. North Vietnamese troops, though, would remain.

In late October, Kissinger flew to Saigon to gain Nguyễn Văn Thiệu's concurrence with the draft agreement. Nguyễn Văn Thiệu balked at many of the provisions, but his main sticking point was the failure to remove North Vietnamese forces from his country. This long-standing South Vietnamese demand was the key issue for both sides. Hanoi refused to withdraw, and Saigon was equally adamant that they leave. Given Nguyễn Văn Thiệu's rebuttal to this and numerous other articles, Kissinger was forced to return to the negotiating table to seek Hanoi's agreement on more than sixty changes demanded by Nguyễn Văn Thiệu. Lê Đức Thọ agreed to some, but under orders from Hanoi soon refused any further modifications. With the talks deadlocked, in late December, Nixon ordered a bombing campaign against Hanoi to force the Politburo to accept the changes. Eventually, both sides agreed to resume talks, and in early January 1973, they restarted. Under tremendous pressure from the United States, including the threat of a complete US aid cut-off, Nguyễn Văn Thiệu capitulated and allowed North Vietnamese troops to remain. On January 27, 1973, all four sides signed the Paris Peace Accords.

The accords called for the two South Vietnamese parties to discuss setting up a council to hold elections. In March 1973, the discussions began at La Celle-Saint-Cloud in Paris between the RVN and the PRG, which immediately stalemated over points both substantive and procedural. To break the impasse, Nguyễn Văn Thiệu offered his most comprehensive package yet on April 25. Saigon promised to remove the constitutional prohibition against communist political activity within thirty days and to "permit complete freedom for the Communists to wage their electoral campaigns."[48] After sixty days, both sides would convene a council to discuss the election and demobilize a portion of their troops. Within ninety days, the council would enact an election law, and a month later, a national election would be held that included all parties. The vote would be internationally supervised. Once more, the NLF and PRG declined this offer, and the fighting resumed.

Successive South Vietnamese governments had offered a path to secure peace in their war-torn land but were unable to achieve their goals. Initially, Saigon demanded that all communist forces depart the country or sought a military victory. Eventually, it challenged Hanoi for direct talks and adamantly requested that the United States not intercede diplomatically on South Vietnam's behalf. Successive RVN governments then attempted to repress South Vietnamese voices calling for peace, fearing they were either a Trojan Horse for the communists or would shatter efforts to convince Hanoi it could not win the war. After the Tết Offensive, Nguyễn Văn Thiệu changed course and offered to hold elections in which the NLF/PRG could participate if they renounced violence. The communists, however, continually rejected his offers. Although he realized a political compromise was the likeliest solution to achieve peace, Nguyễn Văn Thiệu believed that Hanoi would only negotiate in good faith once it accepted it could not win the war. After the 1973 Paris accords, he went a step further and provided a more far-reaching proposal that allowed the communists to freely engage in political campaigning. Hanoi's determination to win victory, however, precluded any acceptance of Saigon's overtures, which enshrined the status quo of two countries. Washington, while striving to include Nguyễn Văn Thiệu's conditions, ultimately decided to sign an agreement that allowed it to withdraw and recover its prisoners of war. Both countries had decided to serve their own interests rather than accept South Vietnamese proposals.

NOTES

1. For analysis of the Paris talks, see Asselin, *A Bitter Peace*; Kimball, *Vietnam War Files*; Berman, *No Peace, No Honor*.
2. Kissinger, *Ending the Vietnam War*. For the communist viewpoint, see Lưu Văn Lợi and Nguyễn Anh Vũ, *Le Duc Tho-Kissinger Negotiations*. The most detailed analysis of the Nationalist's perspective is Nguyễn Phú Đức, *Viet-Nam Peace Negotiations*.
3. For the Third Force, see Quinn-Judge, *Third Force*; Fear, "Saigon Goes Global."
4. For these maneuvers of Diệm, see "French Writer Describes 1963 Peace Bid," *Los Angeles Times*, December 15, 1968, quoting French writer George Chaffard. The piece accurately describes Nhu's efforts to contact Hanoi in various ways and provides other unconfirmed details.
5. For Vietnamese sources who mention these efforts, see Tôn Thất Đính, *20 Năm Binh Nghiệp*, 433; Đỗ Mậu, *Việt Nam*, 780.
6. Kahin, *Intervention*, 185.
7. Nguyễn Khánh, interview by Geoff Shaw, June 16, 1994, 45; Nguyễn Khánh, interview by Paul Van and Bui Duong Liem, June 14, 2009, YouTube, http://www.youtube.com/watch?v=xjTXJow2ZnI&feature=youtu.be.
8. "70 Meet in Pagoda on Antiwar Drive," *New York Times*, March 1, 1965, 6.
9. Bùi Diễm, interview, June 2, 2016, Rockville, MD.
10. "Saigon Rules Out Peace Until Reds Drop Their Role," *New York Times*, March 1, 1965, 6.
11. Bùi Diễm, *Jaws of History*, 130–131.
12. Truong Nhu Tang, *Viet Cong Memoir*, 92.
13. "Negotiations and a Settlement for Vietnam," Saigon Embassy Airgram A-828, May 7, 1965, Record Group [RG] 59, National Archives II, College Park, MD [NA II].
14. "Negotiations and a Settlement for Vietnam."
15. Memorandum of Conversation (Memcon), May 26, 1965, Personal Papers of Ambassador Bùi Diễm, Rockville, MD.
16. Memcon, May 26, 1965.
17. Nguyễn Cao Kỳ, *Buddha's Child*, 128–129.
18. Speech by Tran Van Do, June 22, 1965, Item #2120407033, Vietnam Center and Archive at Texas Tech University [VCA].
19. US Department of State, *FRUS, 1964–1968*, vol. 3, document 91.
20. AmEmbassy Saigon cable to Secretary of State [Saigon] #961, September 19, 1965, RG 59, NA II.
21. Saigon #1273, October 13, 1965, RG 59, NA II.
22. "Speech by Directorate Chairman Thiệu," Saigon Embassy Airgram A-443, January 27, 1966, RG 59, NA II.
23. "Ky Hints Against Foreign Meddling," *South China Morning Post*, January 15, 1966, 30.

24. "Thieu Says His Regime Would Talk with Hanoi," *Washington Post*, August 9, 1967, A11.
25. Goodman, *Politics in War*, 56; Joiner, "South Vietnam," 58–71.
26. "Thiệu Criticizes Attempts by U.S. to Open Talks," *Globe and Mail*, January 16, 1968, 8.
27. Berman, *Lyndon Johnson's War*, 176–180.
28. US Department of State, *FRUS, 1964–1968*, vol. 6, document 145.
29. Pike, *Bunker Papers*, vol. 2, 305–306.
30. Saigon #40220, October 14, 1968, RG 59, NA II.
31. Saigon #41345, October 20, 1968, RG 59, NA II.
32. Nguyễn Phú Đức, *Viet-Nam Peace Negotiations*, 107.
33. CAP 82720, from Rostow to Johnson, November 6, 1968, RG 59, NA II.
34. "Remarks of VP Kỳ on the Paris Talks Impasse," CIA Intelligence Information Cable, November 11, 1968, document 06923742, CIA Records Search Tool [CREST], https://www.cia.gov/readingroom/document/06923742.
35. US Department of State, *FRUS, 1964–1968*, vol. 7, document 277.
36. "Thieu Stresses Regime Safety," *New York Times*, February 9, 1969, 3.
37. US Department of State, *FRUS, 1969–1976*, vol. 6, document 28.
38. Memcon (Bunker), "President Thiệu's Overall View of the Situation We Face," March 21, 1969, Personal Papers of Ambassador Bùi Diễm, Rockville, MD.
39. Saigon #6858, April 3, 1969, RG 59, NA II.
40. Foreign Broadcast Information Service (FBIS), "Reaction to Thieu's Proposal for Elections," *Asia and Pacific*, July 14, 1969, L1.
41. Saigon #565, Bunker backchannel to Kissinger, July 14, 1969, RG 59, NA II.
42. "Pres. Thieu on Red Rejection of RVN Peace Proposal," *Vietnam Bulletin* 3, no. 43 (July 14–20, 1969), 5.
43. Thieu speech of October 31, 1970, to the National Assembly, Item #2321605001, VCA.
44. "Minh Hints at Race for the Presidency," *Washington Post*, November 2, 1970, A20.
45. "Ky calls for political settlement, viewed as bid to build candidacy," *Globe and Mail*, April 20, 1971, 10.
46. "Thieu Sees No Real Peace Till After Major '73 Battle," *New York Times*, September 17, 1971, 2.
47. "Thieu, on Radio, Endorses Election Plan," *New York Times*, January 26, 1972, 11.
48. Nguyễn Phú Đức, *Viet-Nam Peace Negotiations*, 411.

CHAPTER 3

War, Nation-Building, and the Role of the Press in the Second Republic

Thanh Hoang and Tuong Vu

Based on archival research of newspapers published in the Republic of Vietnam (RVN) between 1969 and 1973, this chapter sketches the development of the printed press and the roles it played in the Second Republic (1967–1975).[1] In the enormous literature on the Vietnam War, this important topic has not been studied. The press in any country is a crucial institution that reflects its level of development in terms of shared national identity, political freedom, civil society, and material culture. The press can be a tool of propaganda for a government, but it can also be a way for social forces to hold their government accountable.

The printed press is a useful window for a perspective into South Vietnam's social development and political system during wartime. In addition to news, entertainment, and advertisement, the printed press—whose producers and consumers made up most of the elites and numerous ordinary people—also published views about political issues. This press started out strong under the First Republic but was largely tamed by government repression in its last years. As war sharply escalated following the collapse of the First Republic, the press regained its freedom and grew in quantity and quality, thanks in part to the ruling junta's need for legitimacy, and in part to increasing demands for information, entertainment, and education in a rapidly urbanizing society. This South Vietnamese experience thus contradicts research that has found war to have adverse effects on press freedom, even in the United States, which has a strong tradition of free speech.[2] As this chapter shows, the case of Republican Vietnam suggests that not war alone but nation-building processes in tandem with war played an important role in the development of the press and press freedom.

The press's relationship with the government further challenges the common depiction in scholarship of the RVN as a repressive regime. Given such a depiction, one might expect a sycophant press in service of power, yet that was not the case. The authorities indeed from time to time sought to restrict press freedom by censoring news content, confiscating newspapers, and closing down opposition papers, especially as the war intensified after 1972. At the same time, the government not only created a legal framework for press freedom that was at times quite liberal, but also provided expensive subsidies for newspapers in the form of tax-exempt imported newsprint. Professional associations of journalists and publishers operated largely free from government intervention; sometimes they cooperated with and other times joined hands to protest against the authorities. As the press became increasingly powerful in the later years of the war, not only did newspaper pages come to reflect the multiple voices of many South Vietnamese, but the press also became a political force that fought against government censors to safeguard the South's civil society and democracy. In this sense, it is possible to argue that the South Vietnamese press played roles comparable to its counterpart in Western democracies.

In the first part of this chapter, we trace political developments in the RVN that over a decade slowly gave rise to a more inclusive national "political community" with shared interests despite significant tensions by the late 1960s. This story of South Vietnamese political evolution is crucial for understanding the evolving relationship between various Republican governments and the private printed press. The press became a more robust political force in the Second Republic just as a national political community emerged from under authoritarian rule. In the second part, we examine the contents of several newspapers and magazines published in 1969 and 1973. The analysis not only provides insights into the thoughts and feelings of many South Vietnamese in those critical years, but also demonstrates that the press in fact played roles similar to those of their counterparts in Western democracies. In conclusion, we reflect on the implications of our findings for understanding the relatively open political system of the RVN and the republican and democratic ideals embedded in it that offered opportunities for the press and civil society to grow amid a brutal war not of their choosing.

POLITICS OF NATION-BUILDING AND THE RISE OF
THE SOUTH VIETNAMESE PRESS

General knowledge of the RVN has been produced mostly by diplomatic historians, who tend to view South Vietnam as a hoped-for buffer for the United States in its containment strategy against communist expansion in Southeast Asia.[3] Most attribute the "artificial construction" of South Vietnam to the American pursuit of global hegemony and do not consider the regime worth studying on its own terms. Their work is generally aimed toward proving that, rather than fostering an independent South Vietnam with advice and aid programs, the Americans built "a castle on sand" that was doomed from the start.[4]

Relative to the communist North, Republican South Vietnam's population was much more diverse and included significant ethnic and religious minorities. Most of South Vietnam was inhabited by Vietnamese only since the seventeenth century, before that by the Chams, Khmers, and Chinese, among others. The diversity of the South Vietnamese society thus posed a significant challenge for the RVN as a young nation, which was in part why it took Ngô Đình Diệm more than a year after his appointment as premier to consolidate his regime. Nevertheless, the RVN was no artificial construction of the United States because its social and political elites had been active in the nationalist movement since the 1920s, when Vietnam was still a French colony. They were legitimate inheritors of that tradition as much as, if not more than, Hồ Chí Minh and his comrades were. Their disadvantage relative to the communist North, whose state had been founded in 1945, was the challenges of state-building in tandem with nation-building.

As the first president of the RVN, Ngô Đình Diệm was a modernizer with a deep vision for Vietnam's future and an active reformer.[5] Under his regime, South Vietnam nurtured its traditional culture while being open to influences from the West and from its Asian neighbors.[6] Ruling in an authoritarian style, President Diệm oversaw the creation of order out of chaos and of a centralized state out of fragments of colonial institutions. Despite his (unexpected) success in state-building, President Diệm failed in constructing an inclusive and vibrant nation. Not only were communists excluded but regional and religious tensions were also high under his administration.[7] Southerners, as opposed to those who were from North and Central Vietnam, and non-Catholics perceived or experienced marginalization even though they were the majority. By the early 1960s,

South Vietnam's fragile nation had unraveled. Hanoi had unleashed a communist insurgency in the South, gaining the support of many Southerners. Ngô Đình Diệm's family increasingly abused their power and alienated the political and military elites. As his regime confronted Buddhist monks and their followers who protested against the perceived favoritism toward Catholics in his regime, Ngô Đình Diệm refused to implement political reforms, against popular demands and American advice. With the Kennedy administration's tacit support, a group of generals launched the coup that ended the First Republic in 1963.

Following that coup, South Vietnam underwent political liberalization as well as a period of turmoil.[8] As military officers of various factions launched other coups to seize power, various political and religious movements took to the streets to promote their causes and demanded to be heard. Some coups and street protests were masterminded by the communists who also stepped up a military and terrorist campaign throughout the country, provoking US military intervention. The result was a series of short-lived governments, increasing division within the political and social elites, and frequent violent confrontations between the government and civil society. The chaos reached a climax when Buddhist groups in central Vietnam backed by a rebellious military faction brazenly defied the authority of the military government in Saigon headed by General Nguyễn Cao Kỳ.

The ruling generals confronted challenges from multiple fronts, including not just the war launched by Hanoi but also the clamor from various civil society groups for political representation, the pressure from the United States for improving stability, and the demands from elite groups and other military factions for sharing power. Even while Kỳ government suppressed the Buddhists, his government carried out an earlier promise by the generals to promulgate a new constitution and organize democratic elections, which inaugurated the Second Republic in 1967. It remains murky how Kỳ reached the decision to establish a constitutional and representative government. No direct US pressure to democratize was apparent.[9] Although pressure from civil society was strong, it was not enough to challenge the power of the military. The Kỳ government's motive likely came from a desire for political legitimacy and stability as well as for a more inclusive nation, which Ngô Đình Diệm had failed to build. Elections and representative government were a way to mediate contending elites (including those within the military) and popular interests (Buddhists, Catholics, the Cao Đài and Hoà Hảo, opposition parties, students, northern émigrés, Southerners, and others), making the nation more inclusive and potentially generating international legitimacy.

Regardless of the government's motive, under the generals' watch, a new republic with limited but unprecedented democratic freedom was born. A constitution modeled after the US constitution in which the freedoms of speech, press, and association were guaranteed was ratified.[10] In 1967, the first free presidential elections in which multiple political parties contested, General Nguyễn Văn Thiệu and General Kỳ were elected as president and vice president with a mere plurality of 34.8 percent.[11] Under the new regime, the generals still dominated politics but now had to contend, often in public and in constitutional and legal ways, with various societal interests.

The new institutions were robust enough to withstand the escalation of war during the communist Tết Offensive in 1968. Within a few years, evidence began to emerge of a political community with a shared interest in protecting the republic from both military dictatorship and communist subversion.[12] This community fought back at President Thiệu's alleged acts of electoral frauds in the presidential election of 1971 and at the government's attempt to muzzle the press and harass civil society leaders following the communist Easter Offensive in 1972.[13] Nevertheless, democratic institutions were under severe stress in the last two years of the war.

The more or less authoritarian style of Republican leaders from Ngô Đình Diệm to Nguyễn Cao Kỳ and Nguyễn Văn Thiệu is well known. The relationship between various Republican governments and the press in South Vietnam, however, was complex, shaped by larger political, social, and economic developments and an interplay of market forces, technology, social needs for information, and individual agency. As demonstrated by Jason Picard in his analysis of *Thời Luận* (Current Commentary), the most successful and outspoken newspaper in the First Republic, the massive migration of nearly a million Northerners to the South in 1954–1955 fueled the rise of *Thời Luận* whose owners, editors, main writers, and most readers were from the North.[14] The Ngô Đình Diệm government actually supported and encouraged the development of many newspapers that served Northern emigres in the first few years after Geneva. In early 1956, the government abolished the colonial system of censorship and replaced it with punishments if violations of press regulations were found later. Despite the hanging threats of punishment, this move allowed ambitious opposition politicians and courageous government critics to publish their uncensored writings. *Thời Luận* was not alone but it was most successful in this less politically restrictive yet commercially competitive environment. Thanks to *Thời Luận*'s publication of many incendiary criticisms of Ngô Đình Diệm's policies, it became extremely popular and sold tens of thousands of copies until the authorities finally closed it and arrested the owner and the main writer, prominent politicians Nghiêm Xuân Thiện and Phan Quang Đán, in early 1958, two years later.

The crackdown on *Thời Luận* marked the increasingly repressive trend of Ngô Đình Diệm's regime. During the last few years of its existence, the government imposed strict controls over the private press. Those controls, together with restrictions on political activism, were lifted after the 1963 coup that toppled the regime. As a result, the next few years witnessed a great boom in the number of newspapers. Given a growing urban population due to an intensified war in the countryside and the presence of American troops since 1965, a mass market for newspapers developed in many towns, catering to the public's rising need for news as well as entertainment. Newspapers became a lucrative business with low start-up costs but potentially high revenues if reaching a certain circulation.[15]

Yet rapid expansion led to cut-throat competition and a rapid turnover in the newspaper market. From twenty-five in late 1963, the number of private newspapers grew to ninety-one in 1964, forty-seven in 1965, and twenty in 1969.[16] The quest for profits led newspapers' owners to modernize production with new technologies, thus making newspapers cheaper and visually more appealing. But the same motive was also responsible for the flood of sensational news and media products deemed "culturally decadent" by many South Vietnamese. Many newspapers were mere mouthpieces of political parties—partisan propaganda tools in other words. In response to such developments, the military government ordered many confiscations and closures, which were viewed in press circles as arbitrary and repressive.[17]

Nevertheless, even during this period of naked military rule the relationship between the government and the press was not always confrontational. The new rulers, whether out of their sincere desire to abolish political restrictions under Ngô Đình Diệm or their practical need to cultivate popular support, oversaw the liberalization of the press and civil society by lifting censorship and allowing political parties to publish their own newspapers. Whether General Nguyễn Khánh was a demagogic dictator or empowered the South Vietnamese press during his rule in 1964 is debatable.[18]

It was under Khánh when the daily *Chính Luận* (Political Discussion) was founded. This newspaper, which would become the longest running and have the largest circulation in South Vietnam, was widely respected for its professionalism and balanced coverage. As American troops swamped South Vietnam and generated both admiration and contempt, readers raised many questions about what constituted Vietnamese national identity. In her analysis of the debates over this issue from opinion pages of *Chính Luận*, Nu-Anh Tran demonstrates that newspapers such as *Chính Luận* were effectively facilitating social and identity transformations among urban South Vietnamese in the middle of war.[19] The debates on *Chính Luận* suggested how the growing South Vietnamese press was shaping the emergence of an incipient South Vietnamese nation as they confronted a serious external challenge to their shared identity and culture.

Following the promulgation of a liberal constitution and establishment of a democratic system in 1967, the Nguyễn Văn Thiệu government issued Press Law 019/1969. This law continued the trend of press liberalization since 1963 but was also designed to rein in some of the excesses in the period since that event. It also affirmed press freedom as a fundamental right in the RVN mandated in the 1967 Constitution.[20] The law offered more specific guidelines for the government to regulate press freedom. For example, censorship was prohibited and newspaper suspension would require a judicial decision. Newspapers would not have to wait for the government to issue license to begin operation, and the government would have to provide the reasons if it rejected such licenses. Some professional restrictions were imposed on the press, such as the requirement that editor and publisher hold university degrees or have equivalent journalistic experience.

Although many of the problems with the press, such as the lack of professionalism, remained pervasive, the newspaper world appeared to continue to thrive after the law both in terms of quantity and quality. One American source estimated that in 1971 South Vietnam had about forty newspapers and 150 magazines, based mostly in Saigon. The largest newspapers had a circulation of between twenty-five and fifty thousand, total circulation nationwide being estimated at four hundred thousand.[21] As Nguyễn Ngọc Phách, who wrote the preface to the English translation of the new Press Law published in 1970, noted, newspapers that had once thrived on "yellow literature" and "blatantly saucy writing" such as *Trắng Đen* (Black & White) and *Điện Tín* (Telegraph) were no longer as popular, whereas *Chính Luận* had "matured" as a serious yet popular newspaper. Its owner had become wealthy and was "setting up one of the most modern newspaper printing plants in South-East Asia."[22]

The government and the press did not have smooth relations and were often in tension. When the government doubled the price of imported newsprint in 1970 as part of its austerity program to cope with budget shortfalls due to the reduction of US aid and the increased military burden of South Vietnam, newspaper owners, editors, and journalists formed a committee to protest that price change. Their protest couched in terms of press freedom eventually forced the government to back down and set aside a certain amount of newsprint for continued subsidy.[23] The government apparently treated the press carefully while seeking to manipulate its internal divisions. President Thiệu agreed to speak at the inaugural banquet of the Newspaper Editors Association in Saigon, founded in 1969, but did not appear at similar events of three other more established press associations, Syndicate of Publishers, the Federation of South Vietnamese Journalists, and Union of Journalists, whose membership, as Nguyễn Ngọc Phách disparagingly remarked, "reflects less concern for the improvement of the profession than petty interests as could be found in most Vietnamese professional leagues."[24]

As Hanoi unleashed a massive military campaign across South Vietnam in 1972, President Thiệu sought emergency powers granted by the constitution while attempting to limit press freedom. Decree 007-TT/SLU, issued in August 1972, required newspaper publishers to deposit 20 million đồng ($47,000) to operate, and impose other restrictions on publication and distribution. Ministerial personnel would go through the paper's contents four hours prior to distribution.[25] Newspapers had to show blank spaces or write the phrase "tự ý đục bỏ," "toà soạn đục bỏ," or "tự đục" (voluntarily deleted) if any perceived violations of the government's listed restrictions were found.[26] The new decree led to several closures and many journalists' losing their jobs.

Although the majority of newspapers survived, conflict intensified.[27] In late 1974, a few newspapers such as Sóng Thần (Tsunami) and Đại Dân Tộc (Great Nation) openly defied the government's order by publishing a public call for an investigation of President Thiệu for corruption.[28] Sóng Thần printed the call and then burned freshly printed issues in front of staff, distributors, and invited members of international news agencies when government agents arrived to confiscate the papers. When the government later issued a subpoena for the publisher of Sóng Thần, hundreds of lawyers and journalists with the support of press associations, opposition members of the National Assembly, and various religious and political groups, organized a march in downtown Saigon and boycotted government news. In the face of such a widespread movement, the prime minister dismissed the minister of information and canceled the trial a few days later.

Most of the history and politics of nation- and state-building in South Vietnam remains unexplored, but it is clear from recent scholarship that its leaders from Ngô Đình Diệm to the generals who succeeded him expended great efforts against overwhelming odds to construct a viable state and nation as an alternative to communist North Vietnam. The developments of the RVN through a personal autocrat (President Diệm) to military rule to a struggling electoral democracy did not stand out as abnormal given that Thailand, the Philippines, South Korea, and Indonesia had quite comparable experiences during the same period. It can be argued that the RVN's dependence on American support restrained the repressive tendencies of its leaders regarding press freedom. However, government repression of civil liberties in South Vietnam was arguably far less draconian than in other Asian countries that also depended on US support, including Thailand, South Korea, and Taiwan. It is a fact that the South Vietnamese government at times championed liberal ideas and presided over a vibrant civil society and a lively press. The printed press in turn contributed to the development of a national community while struggling to defend its own freedom. In the next section, we turn to examine the role of the press more closely by analyzing its contents in the two key years of 1969 and 1973.

ROLES OF THE SOUTH VIETNAMESE PRESS THROUGH CONTENT ANALYSIS

What roles did the South Vietnamese press play in politics? According to Clifford Christians and his coauthors, news journalists play four basic roles in a democratic process. The first is to provide surveillance of the social environment and relates to the basic element of news media embedded in monitoring the sociopolitical environment. The second is to form opinion pertaining to the meaningful agenda-setting of public discussions. Acting as messenger and public informant, news journalists encourage citizens to learn about the contemporary issues of the time. The third role is to play an active role in public life, engaging the government on behalf of the public and for the common good. The fourth is to take on the role of a watchdog, which generates mechanisms for holding officials to account and resisting outside efforts to subvert the independence of journalism.[29]

We argue that the press in South Vietnam performed all the above functions of its counterpart in a democracy even though the Second Republic had only an imperfect nascent democracy. This section analyzes press contents in the two critical years of 1969 and 1973 to demonstrate how those four key roles played by the press in South Vietnam at the time unfolded. Both years immediately followed one during which the war sharply escalated (1968 and 1972). The first, 1969, was when the democratic institutions established in 1967 went into full effect, whereas 1973 was a post–martial law year. In the debate on the Nixon administration's Vietnamization program that dominated the news in 1969, newspapers displayed their critical roles in monitoring and generating public discussions on that program that could have decided the fate of the Republic. In 1973, the press engaged the government to hold officials accountable to their alleged abuses of power and to defend its freedom.

Our materials include articles, opinion pages, and editorials of newspapers and magazines from a range of voices, including religious groups, leftist intellectuals, anticommunist citizens, students, and writers who were neither pro- nor anticommunist. Among those most critical of the government was the biweekly leftist journal, *Đối Diện* (Face-to-Face), which was published by two Catholic priests, Father Chân Tín and Father Nguyễn Ngọc Lan. *Đối Diện* provided frequent denunciations of the RVN government and US involvement in the war while supporting South Vietnamese youth activism and freedom of speech. In October 1972, the police raided its clandestine printing press and arrested thirty-five workers, "including ten deserters [from military mandatory service]." Father Chân Tín was sentenced to five years in solitary confinement by a military court but never arrested "thanks to the tacit protection of the Catholic Church."[30]

Other sources that were frequently critical of the government include *Tiếng Nói Dân Tộc* (National Voice), published and edited by Lý Quí Chung, and the first cooperative newspaper, *Sóng Thần* (Tsunami), co-founded by Trùng Dương (Nguyễn Thị Thái). Lý Quí Chung was a young activist at that time and an opposition member in the Lower House of the National Assembly from 1966 to 1975. Thanks to his legislative immunity, Lý Quí Chung could freely voice his criticisms of the Saigon government, US involvement, and the war in Vietnam.[31] Trùng Dương was a well-known female writer and *Sóng Thần* was one of three newspapers with the largest circulation in 1974.[32] With several offices from Huế to Cần

Table 3.1. Newspapers and Journals Consulted

	Publisher	Period of publication
Journals		
Đối Diện [Face-to-Face]	Father Chân Tín	July 1969–December 1973
Bách Khoa [Encyclopedia]	Lê Ngộ Châu	January 1969–December 1973
Trình Bầy [Presentation]	Thế Nguyên	August–November 1969
Vấn Đề [Issues]	Vũ Công Trực	January 1969–November 1970
Newspapers		
Chính Luận [Political Discussion]	Đặng Văn Sung	January–December 1969
		January–December 1973
Tiếng Nói Dân Tộc [National Voice]	Lý Quí Chung	April–November 1969
Sóng Thần [Tsunami]	Trùng Dương	January–December 1973

Source: General Social Sciences Library, Ho Chi Minh City.

Thơ, the paper was able to serve as a check on both local and central governments.[33]

Other newspapers and journals included in our sample are *Bách Khoa* (Encyclopedia), *Trình Bầy* (Presentation), *Vấn Đề* (Issues), whose editorial boards consisted of prominent journalists and scholars, as well as the daily *Chính Luận*, an anticommunist newspaper whose publisher was Đặng Văn Sung, a leader of the nationalist Đại Việt Party.[34]

THE VIETNAMIZATION PROGRAM, 1969

Vietnamization naturally brought deep anxieties for many Vietnamese about the future of their nation after three years of relying on US forces for the bulk of fighting. This concern is evidenced in President Thiệu's reported order that forbade newspapers to use the phrase, "the American withdrawal" (*Mỹ rút quân*) in their reports.[35] In his view, such a term might mislead the public into thinking that the Americans had agreed to the communist demand for unconditional American troop withdrawal.[36] On the first day of 1969, *Chính Luận*'s frontpage headline read "Friend Pushes in the Back, Foe Stabs in Front, and No Clue Where the Nation Is Going."[37] This headline fully captured South Vietnamese moods about the newly proposed strategy of Vietnamization (*Việt hóa* or *Việt Nam hóa*). Intense and prolonged debates over its nature, its goals, and its prospects cried out for readers' attention on the pages of Southern newspapers and journals for much of 1969.

How did Vietnamese writers and journalists see the nature and motives of Vietnamization? An editorial of *Chính Luận* described the new strategy as a reduction in American exposure to the war through a gradual withdrawal of troops while at the same time the United States would provide aid to train and equip the Army of the RVN (ARVN) for its defense and survival.[38] Based on various ambiguous statements by American leaders and with deep concerns, an editorial on *Chính Luận* speculated that Vietnamization suggested a decline in American commitment to defend South Vietnam—a reversion of Washington's earlier promises.[39]

The main reasons for that decline, according to Nguyễn Công Luận, a columnist of *Tiếng Nói Dân Tộc*, were the economic and political impacts of the war for the Americans.[40] In particular, the war had become unpopular abroad and American intervention in Vietnam had isolated the United States internationally. At home, the war had been a drag on the American economy, causing inflation and recession. Politically, the antiwar movement and the number of American casualties had created strong pressure on the US government to sue for peace. To carry out his campaign promises and to improve his chances for reelection in 1972, President Nixon had no choice but to move forward with Vietnamization.

Not all writers thought that the United States would soon abandon South Vietnam. Some *Chính Luận* columnists, such as Nguyễn Tấn Linh, Trần Văn Tuyên, Triệu Việt, and Việt Anh, firmly believed in the United States' commitment to defend South Vietnam.[41] They argued that despite domestic disagreements over the Vietnam War, the US government was committed to winning it. In the opinion of US policymakers, South Vietnam was an embodiment of the Free World fighting on the frontline against the communist expansion in Southeast Asia. It represented a permanent American interest whose protection was its responsibility. As a result, America would never betray or abandon the South Vietnamese.

American intentions aside, the reality was that South Vietnamese could no longer rely on Americans and other allies to fight for them. Burning questions thus emerged as to how and when the ARVN would be able to take the place of US troops. Would they be ready to adapt themselves to new challenges?[42] Some believed so, some disagreed, and others felt unsure. If in fact the goal of Vietnamization was to modernize the ARVN to defeat its communist enemy, *Chính Luận*'s writers hoped that the United States would continue to supply armaments while ceding full command of strategy and operations to the ARVN soon.[43] These authors argued that if the ARVN did not have complete and effective command, Vietnamization would create more difficulties for the RVN in the fight. More than other newspapers, *Chính Luận* displayed great confidence in the possibility to improve the ARVN's capability and performance under Vietnamization.

Even if the program achieved its desirable military outcomes, Vietnamization raised the questionable prospects of the South's long-term economic survival. Thuận Giao pointed out that, because South Vietnam's economy was underdeveloped and had depended on US aid and troops' spending, the American pullout would create a void in the services, trading, and banking sectors.[44] How could the RVN bear the burden of fighting the war alone, with an expected increase of up to 1.1 million troops? Beyond the enormous expenses needed to maintain such a large army, South Vietnam's government would need massive funds for war refugees and victims and for rebuilding infrastructure in villages and cities destroyed by war.

Expenses were to increase exponentially, but Tạ Văn Tài argued that raising taxes to cover them was not really an option because the government had exhausted the kinds of indirect taxes that could be levied, whereas direct taxes would require much greater state capacity than it had. Given the challenges of mobilizing resources that would demand great sacrifices from the South Vietnamese people, Tài believed that the RVN government had no choice but to consolidate democratic institutions so that various political factions and parties were willing to cooperate. The communists had been effective in organizing and mobilizing people, and the RVN must be able to perform as good a job if it were to prevail.[45]

Opinions and analyses about Vietnamization were not confined to the program itself but often extended to discuss bigger questions about the nature of the war and its prospects. Nguyễn Công Luận, a columnist of *Tiếng Nói Dân Tộc*, appreciated the sacrifices Americans had made and the reasons why the US government must pursue Vietnamization. He welcomed it as an opportunity for Vietnamese people to live their lives according to their traditional culture without control by a foreign power and free from the corrupting influences of foreign troops on their soil. For him, the problem was not Vietnamization itself but about what it would bring in the future: peace or war. If war continued, the provision of modern weapons from powerful allies on both sides would only bring annihilation to the Vietnamese race.[46] The view of South Vietnam as a victim of great powers' politics also came from journalists Trần Cam and Trần Thái Thủy of *Chính Luận*, who believed that Vietnam was merely a pawn in a geopolitical chess game.[47]

Similarly but far more critical of Vietnamese leaders in both the North and the South, Trần Thanh Việt of *Đối Diện* blamed the bloody civil war between the two regions on their leaders having lost their "national spirit" and allowed themselves to become proxies for foreign powers (the United States and China).[48] Applying Marxist terminologies, Việt considered class conflict to exist in Vietnam but not at the "oppositional" level (đối kháng). The war could only be resolved if foreign powers were no longer involved and the two Vietnamese regions could discuss and settle differences between themselves: for the sake of national unity, the North would institute democratic politics and the South would implement a socialist economy. Vietnamization was therefore a positive first step toward a settlement.

Casting US-Vietnamese relations in a similarly harmful light, Catholic priests Trần Văn Thọ and Chân Tín blamed American involvement for the escalation of the war in the first place. Even with generous aid from the United States, they said that the majority of South Vietnamese were fed up with the American presence. Vietnamese people could no longer accept such a domineering ally.[49] In the same vein, the "misalliance" between Saigon-Washington was compared by one writer with a fragile friendship between a rich man and a poor man, and by another writer with a marriage of a couple in which the husband is shorter than his wife (chồng thấp mà lấy vợ cao).[50] The marriage could still be salvaged but Saigon should be prepared to raising the chicks alone like the proverbial rooster.[51]

The wide-ranging and sophisticated discussion and debate on the pages of the Saigon press showed that South Vietnamese were not as easily misled as President Thiệu had worried. The press provided them with information and analyses that helped them understand the motives of the United States, the complexities of the domestic and global situation confronting American leaders, and the potentially positive and negative effects of Vietnamization. The press was not shy about criticizing the RVN leadership, its policies, and its dependence on the United States. Through newspapers, writers and analysts not only informed and educated the public but also raised many issues for the agenda to achieve successful Vietnamization and a lasting solution to the war. These are the first two roles of the press in a democracy, according to Christians and his coauthors. The other two roles are discussed in the next section with a close reading of press contents in 1973.

THE DEFENSE OF PRESS FREEDOM, 1972

Recall that decree 007-TT/SLU required a deposit of 20 million đồng ($47,000) for dailies (10 million for periodicals) and the submission of a few copies for review of each issue to the censors prior to distribution. According to a government spokesperson, the law was to make the press "more progressive and responsive to the needs of national security, while the fundamental principles of freedom of speech, press, and publication are completely respected."[52] Under the law, the number of dailies in Vietnamese language shrank from twenty-seven to seventeen.[53] One source claimed that 70 percent of journalists became unemployed when their papers closed for a lack of funds.[54]

Reactions from the press to the new law were immediate and livid.[55] *Bút Thần*, a newspaper owned by opposition Assembly member Lý Quí Chung, likened the law to a 130mm gunshot and announced its closure. *Chính Luận* and *Đuốc Nhà Nam* exposed the faulty logic of the government and questioned the constitutionality of the new law, which bypassed the Press Council and restricted press freedom.[56] Forty members of the Association of Newspapers Publishers (Hội Chủ Báo) met and rejected the new law, called on all newspapers not to publish for two days (August 22 and 23, 1972), and organized a campaign to lobby the Senate against it. *Đối Diện* ostracized the government for violating not just freedom of speech but also basic human rights. It argued that if the press accepted the situation, it would become a mere mouthpiece of the government and betray the purpose of journalism, which is to serve the public and the truth.[57]

Under the new law, the authorities appeared more aggressive in censoring newspaper contents, but great variations were found in the sample of newspapers and periodicals under study. Redactions on the front page to the inner pages of *Sóng Thần* were frequent, especially in articles discussing the RVN's social and economic measures or attacking corruption in the government. In contrast, redactions were found only intermittently in *Chính Luận*, which was known for its restrained style. We also found only two articles critical of high newsprint prices in September 1973 in *Chính Luận*. This was a great contrast to *Đối Diện*, which regularly published lengthy discussions of morality, freedom, and democracy in the South in 1973.

On the pages of the two most vocal publications, the anticommunist *Sóng Thần* and covertly communist *Đối Diện*, journalists and writers continued to voice their opposition to the press law and expose the government's failures and weaknesses. Among regular *tự ý đục bỏ* spaces on *Sóng Thần* was a semi-humorous column in the bottom right corner of the front page by the writer Chu Tử under the pen name of Ao Thả Vịt (A Duck Pond), or ATV, who satirized current events. When we retrieved

Sóng Thần issues for 1973, we found fifteen ATV commentaries on press freedom and democracy. *Sóng Thần*'s responses to state control, also written by Ao Thả Vịt, expressed deep frustrations toward the government. These articles often appeared with gaps created by government censors. In an article in May 1973 titled "An impassioned letter to President Nguyễn Văn Thiệu," Ao Thả Vịt linked his cabinet reshuffle with a question on possible reforms of press policies to meet new conditions in the South. The article argued that the nature of the regime affected journalistic performance, and that South Vietnamese hardship and depravation of the press would bring shame on the government. Despite the odds, Ao Thả Vịt asserted that the mission of a newspaper was to tell the truth. The president should understand this.[58]

Yet there were more than criticisms of the press decree such as those described here. Defining the role of the press as a watchdog, he wrote, "the government efforts to bring an end to corruption would be in vain but for the contribution of the press."[59] Indeed, *Sóng Thần*'s inner pages, the third and fifth ones, frequently carried articles on issues such as bribery and corruption complaints, reports on abuses by local leaders and police, and documents on investigations into residents' grievances over tax measures or economic and agricultural policies.[60]

Sóng Thần's ambition was to "strive for a new generation, a new ideal, a new human with a fresh mind and a new idea about life."[61] The paper saw itself as a vehicle for mobilizing a national social revolution, and its publisher and managing editors titled themselves the Democracy Group. The struggle *Sóng Thần* wished to embark on, he explained, was "a political struggle on a high level for humanistic values." Ao Thả Vịt identified himself not as an anticommunist writer, but a true admirer of "Liberty."[62]

With such a mandate, *Sóng Thần* launched attacks not only at the government but also at those posing as the opposition. On the launch of the newspaper *Dân Chủ* (Democracy), "the newspaper as the mouthpiece of the ruling party of President Thiệu fell short of expectations," ATV emphasized, "since *Dân Chủ* has nothing new to contribute to the South Vietnamese press."[63] ATV also criticized Senator Hồng Sơn Đông of *Điện Tín* (Telegraph), which began as a normal paper with few sales but later became popular thanks to billing itself as an opposition paper. In his view, by recasting *Điện Tín* as an opposition newspaper, Senator Hồng Sơn Đông merely competed for readership to make money.[64]

From the far Left, *Đối Diện* spared no words in its bitter and consistent denunciations of the oppressive atmosphere that enveloped press and other political activities. *Đối Diện* perceived itself as not only a forum for

Christians, but also a venue for all Vietnamese concerned about the country, regardless of religion and age. The magazine took a strong stance on freedom of thought, press, and democracy that the South Vietnamese government most likely failed to provide or protect. Father Nguyễn Ngọc Lan derisively called the Ministry of Information the Ministry of Confiscation, Censorship, and Deletion (Bộ Hốt Cắt Đục) to condemn its harsh censorship and frequent confiscations of *Đối Diện* and its sister newspaper *Tin Sáng* (Morning News).[65] In another article provocatively titled "The South Vietnamese Treadmill," written by Trương Bá Cần, the author argued that the South Vietnamese could not get off the treadmill (*cái vòng lẩn quẩn*) on which they had been living for nearly twenty years, lacking a clear reason for current regime's existence. South Vietnamese governments had all slid deeper into authoritarianism rather than defending a free and democratic society against communist invasion.[66]

Đối Diện went beyond the issue of press freedom to attack the United States and the RVN government's dependence on the United States. In a highly critical article, Trọng Phủ predicted that President Thiệu's regime would fall in just five minutes if the Americans cut off funding. For the author, relying on American aid, President Thiệu's regime was founded on military and police power.[67] In the same vein, Nguyễn Ngọc Lan chided the government for facilitating the domination of what he labeled "American cultural imperialism" over South Vietnamese society. "American cultural imperialism" dominated, he claimed, because the government restricted press freedom, raised the prices of imported newsprints (that is, cut subsidies for the Vietnamese press), and applied certain exchange rate schemes that made imported American publications cheaper in the local market than other foreign publications.[68] The solution for the South Vietnamese to escape US domination, the article proposed, was to "fight the Americans to save the country" (*chống Mỹ cứu nước*), which was perhaps not coincidentally the very slogan the communists deployed to justify their war in the South.

Đối Diện survived for a year after decree 007-TT/SLU. In its first issue, in October 1973, the magazine editorial team shared in the introduction how they had suffocated under the government's press oppression.[69] Proudly, the narrators wrote, "we were uncompromising in our rejection of the decree 007 that destroyed the free press and their livelihood. If our publications were suspended, this would not be the end of the South Vietnamese press. We believed that others would stand up so as to better serve the public's information needs." The last issue of *Đối Diện* in the archive was published in December 1973.

From what we have observed in this analysis of newspaper contents, press opposition was certainly tolerated despite the new law. There was still room for an independent press in the way the censorship bureau screened and approved articles. Those white spaces labeled "voluntarily deleted" did not limit understanding of the content as a whole. Strong criticisms of the government, the president, the ministers, and local leaders were still published. Many news publishers and journalists harshly and publicly condemned the authorities for stifling the free press, for its violations of the constitution, for its corruption, and for its dependence on a foreign power.

Nevertheless, for all the government's confiscations, financial requirements, and harassment of publishers and reporters, the recurring severe measures did not end South Vietnamese journalistic function as a government watchdog. In an article published in November 1974 and critical of the government's press policies, George McArthur, a *Los Angeles Times* reporter from Saigon, wrote,

> Despite censorship and seizures, the Saigon press is far freer and livelier (and more irresponsible) than the rest of the press in Southeast Asia—with the exception of Hong Kong and, nowadays, Bangkok. On any given day, the newspapers are full of criticism, innuendo, and scandal—often naming names and citing alleged details right up to the cabinet level.[70]

This chapter maps the politics of nation building at war alongside the rise of the South Vietnamese private press. The war was masterminded from Hanoi with the backing of China and the Soviet bloc. The United States intervened in the war ostensibly to help the RVN but ended up creating problems for it. As South Vietnamese elites tried to create a viable new nation out of a diverse population and in the midst of an escalating war not of their choosing, they not only fought against each other but also cooperated to create effective institutions to help them build a more inclusive national community and manage a rapidly changing society. In the process, a free press emerged and thrived, sometimes with the government's blessings.

Our textual analysis of the press has a number of possible implications for understanding the Second Republic's press and its role in politics. First, South Vietnamese publications such as newspapers and magazines are rich and diverse sources for research on the cultural, social, political, and even military aspects of South Vietnam. The lively public discussions and commentaries in the press collectively reflected the various attitudes and opinions of different groups in Saigon about the war and the government. It is clear from the newspaper pages that South Vietnamese editors and political journalists made great efforts to exercise freedom of expression by discovering, collecting, and selecting information of public interest; by processing information to generate news accounts and analyses; by providing background and commentary; and by publishing under conditions of war and turmoil. On the whole, they did translate those basic activities into a generalized role for the press in a democratic political system.

Second, the brave resistance of the press to state censorship suggests another aspect of democracy. The marches, demonstrations for freedom, or antiwar movements may have been built on individual leadership or spontaneous outbursts of contention, but also must have been part of a shared perception of possibilities for collective actions. The journalistic efficacy in the struggle for press freedom thus implies structural and political opportunities in a climate of generally open politics that greatly benefited diverse civil society groups. The liberalization of political parties under Nguyễn Khánh, the promulgation of the 1967 Constitution, the presidential and the National Assembly elections, and Press Law 019/69 manifested that climate. From that time onward, those institutions stimulated a broader process that involved the diffusion of republican and democratic ideas and the actions to defend press freedom. This analysis of press discourse demonstrates that, even under Press Decree 007/TT-SLU, government censors still condoned oppositional and critical thoughts. Thus we should not interpret social movement activists as mere victims of the South Vietnamese government without considering the incentives that the government had earlier created for them to act.

Last, the RVN tolerated dissident claims to the extent that publishers and writers bravely voiced their grievances, sometimes with personal impunity, as in the case of Father Chân Tín and Assembly member Lý Quí Chung. Despite the popular fear of government repression, the RVN state still offered a general space for many South Vietnamese to voice their concerns with a myriad of daily issues, including the future reunification of Vietnam, war and peace, US-Vietnamese relations, corruption, the economy, and freedom of expression. Given the tapestry of the relationship of the state, the press, and people in the RVN, this chapter provides a reasonable picture of the republican and democratic ideals embedded in the Second Republic.

NOTES

1. The authors thank Phạm Trần, Trùng Dương, Nu-Anh Tran, Jason Picard, Trung Nguyễn, Cường Nguyễn, and Joseph Bridge Du Barry for their helpful comments.

2. This is because wartime governments may be more sensitive to criticisms of their policies and may invoke seemingly legitimate excuses to circumscribe press freedom as well as other civil liberties. For a systematic study of the relationship between war and press freedom, see Vultee, "Second Casualty." On the United States, see Smith, *War and Press Freedom*.

3. Hopkins, "Historians and the Vietnam War"; McCormick, *America's Half-Century*; Young, *Vietnam Wars*.

4. Kahin, *Intervention*; Logevall, *Origins of the Vietnam War*, 35; Carter, *Inventing Vietnam*.

5. Miller, *Misalliance*; Stewart, *Vietnam's Lost Revolution*.

6. Nguyễn Tuấn Cường, "Promotion of Confucianism."

7. For the troubled relations between the Ngô Đình Diệm government and the religious groups such as Cao Đài and Hoà Hảo, see Chapman, *Cauldron of Resistance*.

8. Lâm Vĩnh-Thế, *History of South Vietnam*.

9. Goodman, *Politics in War*, 41; see also Penniman, *Elections in South Vietnam*, 7.

10. See Constitution of the Republic of Vietnam, http://spartanhistory.kora.matrix.msu.edu/files/6/32/6-20-101-116-UA17-95_000284.pdf.

11. Penniman, "Elections in South Vietnam," 69. This study offers a good overview of elections in South Vietnam, and detailed account of this and the 1971 elections as well as comments about them by foreign observers.

12. Goodman, *Politics in War*, 254; see also Joiner, *Politics of Massacre*, chap. 3.

13. For a discussion of those allegations, see Penniman, *Elections in South Vietnam*, 130. For Nguyễn Văn Thiệu's maneuvers to consolidate his grip on power, see Donnell and Joiner, *Electoral Politics*, chaps. 4 and 9.

14. Picard, "'Renegades'."

15. Joseph Treaster, "South Vietnamese Revising Outmoded Press Laws," *New York Times*, March 24, 1969, 3.

16. Nguyễn Việt Chước, *Lược Sử Báo Chí Việt Nam*, 120.

17. Treaster, "South Vietnamese Revising."

18. The latter view is expressed in Nguyễn Việt Chước, *Lược Sử Báo Chí Việt Nam*, 66. For an argument that Khánh was just a demagogue, see Trần Thúc Linh, "Góp ý kiến về báo chí Việt Nam," *Báo Chí Tập San* (Press Review) 1, no. 2 (Summer 1968): 174.

19. Nu-Anh Tran, "South Vietnamese Identity."

20. Bộ Thông Tin, *Quy Chế Báo Chí* (Saigon, c. 1973) includes Press Law 019/69 (1969) and Decree 007-TT/SLU (1972). For an official English translation of the 1969 law, see Republic of Vietnam, *New Press Law*.

21. George McArthur, "Saigon Press: Rumors, Astrology, but Little Truth," *Los Angeles Times*, October 4, 1971, E10.

22. Nguyễn Ngọc Phách, introduction to Republic of Vietnam, *New Press Law*, 3.

23. Trần Đại, "Nhân vụ tăng giá." After the government modified its policy to continue subsidizing newsprint, the protesters appeared fully complacent even though the prices for imported paper used for printing books remained high. For this, the author of this article criticized the press as not caring for anything other than their interests.

24. Nguyễn Ngọc Phách, introduction, 4–5.
25. For Decree 007-TT/SLU (1972), see Bộ Thông Tin, *Quy Chế Báo Chí*, 18–20. For a useful historical overview of censorship up to 1968 from a government official, see Nguyễn Văn Noãn, "Kiểm duyệt báo chí ở Việt nam."
26. Phạm Trần, "Life and Work of a Journalist"; Guimary, "Press of South Vietnam," 163-169. Against the government's wish, often the presence of "voluntarily deleted" contents helped sell newspapers.
27. James Markham, "Government Restraints Have Subdued Those Papers That Survive in Saigon," *New York Times*, August 21, 1973, 2D.
28. This paragraph draws on Trùng Dương, "*Sóng Thần*'s Campaign."
29. Christians et al., *Normative Theories*, 118–120.
30. Markham, "Government Restraints."
31. Lý Quí Chung, *Hồi Ký Không Tên*.
32. According to statistics conducted by the US Information Service in Saigon, *Sóng Thần* had a circulation of twelve thousand. Cited in Guimary, "Press of South Vietnam," 167.
33. Trùng Dương, "*Sóng Thần*'s Campaign for Press Freedom," 141–143.
34. For an interview of Đặng Văn Sung by Nguyễn Mạnh Hùng, see "Phỏng Vấn Đặng Văn Sung," March 16, 2022, https://usvietnam.uoregon.edu/phong-van-dang-van-sung/.
35. See David Prentice's contribution to this volume on Thiệu's strategy of Vietnamization.
36. "Mấu chốt" [The Key Point], *Chính Luận*, no. 1574, June 11, 1969, 1.
37. "Bạn đẩy sau lưng, thù đâm trước mặt, còn ở nước nhà không biết ra sao?," *Chính Luận*, no. 1461, January 1, 1969.
38. "Mấu chốt," 1.
39. Editorial, "Nửa đường," *Chính Luận*, no. 1557, May 23, 1969.
40. Nguyễn Công Luận, "Việt Nam hóa cuộc chiến hay là bước đi tới hố sâu diệt chủng," in *Tiếng Nói Dân Tộc*, no. 212, August 12, 1969.
41. Triệu Việt and Việt Anh, "Vài nét mới trong thời cuộc Việt Nam," *Chính Luận*, no. 1681/82, October 14, 1969. Trần Văn Tuyên was an important leader of the Vietnamese Nationalist Party, a former vice premier, and also a legislator.
42. Trần Thủy, "Những khó khăn của miền Nam trong những ngày sắp tới," *Chính Luận*, no. 1636-37, August 22, 1969.
43. See the following editorials: "Vấn đề Việt Nam hóa chiến tranh," in *Chính Luận*, no. 1528, March 29, 1969; "Khẩu hiệu mới: Việt Nam hóa cuộc chiến...nhưng không phải Việt Nam hóa bất cứ thế nào," in *Chính Luận*, no. 1593-1594, July 3, 1969.
44. Thuận Giao, "Việt Hóa Kinh Tế," *Trình Bầy*, no. 1, August 1970.
45. Tạ Văn Tài, "Phương diện kinh tế và chính trị của chương trình Việt hóa," *Vấn Đề*, no. 38, August-September 1969.
46. Nguyễn Công Luận, "Việt Nam hóa cuộc chiến hay là bước đi tới hố sâu diệt chủng," *Tiếng Nói Dân Tộc*, no. 212, August 12, 1969.
47. Editorial, "Con chốt đen con chốt đỏ trên bàn cờ Mỹ," *Tiếng Nói Dân Tộc*, no. 152, April 15, 1969); Trần Cam, "Giải pháp chính trị cho chiến cuộc Việt Nam," *Chính Luận*, no. 1554 (May 20, 1969; Trần Thái Thủy, "Những khó khăn của miền Nam trong những tuần sắp tới," *Chính Luận*, no. 1636, August 23, 1969.
48. Trần Thanh Việt, "Mâu thuẫn quốc gia và cộng sản," *Đối Diện*, August 1969.
49. "Đối Diện với phái đoàn liên tôn Mỹ" [Đối Diện and the American Interfaith Delegation], *Đối Diện*, July 7, 1969.

50. Tư Cầu Kho, *Tiếng Nói Dân Tộc*, no. 143, April 5, 1969; Editorial, "Nửa đường," *Chính Luận*, no. 1557, May 23, 1969. The term "misalliance" is used by Edward Miller.

51. The original, *gà sống nuôi con* (a rooster raises the chicks alone), is a Vietnamese proverb that refers to a challenging situation.

52. Quoted in Jacques Leslie, "Thieu Press Order Will Close Many Papers, Hurt Opposition," *Los Angeles Times*, August 6, 1972, 6.

53. The number of newspapers before the law is from Leslie, "Thieu Press Order," 9. The number after is official data cited in Nguyễn Việt Chước, *Lược Sử Báo Chí Việt Nam*, 79.

54. Phạm Trần, "Life and Work of a Journalist," 123.

55. See excerpts from major newspapers in "Dư luận báo chí trước vụ đạo luật báo chí" [The Press Opinion on the Press Decree], *Đối Diện*, no. 39, September 1972, 114–128. See also Leslie, "Thieu Press Order," 9.

56. Hội Đồng Báo Chí [Press Council] was an institution established under Article 39 of Press Law 019/1969, to be elected by a convention of all journalists and editors and to represent their professional interests. It met only once and did not have any influence.

57. Editorial, "Thái độ chúng tôi: Tạm biệt mà còn đó," *Đối Diện*, no. 39, September 1972, 129.

58. ATV, "Tâm thư gửi T.T Nguyễn Văn Thiệu," *Sóng Thần*, no. 544, May 5, 1973, 1.

59. ATV, "Sạch sẽ hóa," *Sóng Thần*, no. 439, March 13, 1973, 1.

60. Journalists Nguyễn Miên Thảo, Vũ Ngọc Long, Hùng Phong were in charge of the fifth page.

61. ATV, "Đi tìm con người mới," *Sóng Thần*, no. 496, March 16, 1973, 1

62. ATV, "Kiếp đọa đày," *Sóng Thần*, no. 483, March 3, 1973, 1.

63. ATV, "Nhật báo Dân Chủ," *Sóng Thần*, no. 609, July 13, 1973, 1

64. ATV, "Sơn Đông Mãi Võ," *Sóng Thần*, no. 514, April 3, 1973, 1.

65. Nguyễn Ngọc Lan, "Chế độ thông tin KKKK," *Đối Diện*, no. 35, May 1972, 37–42

66. Trương Bá Cần, "Cái vòng luẩn quẩn của miền Nam Việt Nam," *Đối Diện*, no. 37, July 1972, 118–122.

67. Trọng Phủ, "Miền Nam Việt Nam ba tháng sau ngày ngưng bắn," *Đối Diện*, no. 47, June 1973, 56–67.

68. Nguyễn Ngọc Lan, "Thưa ông thông tin đế quốc văn hóa Mỹ ghi ơn ông," *Đối Diện*, no. 32, February 1972, 10–18.

69. *Đối Diện*, "Số 50 thật đặc biệt," *Đối Diện*, no. 50, October 1973.

70. George McArthur, "Saigon Press Freedom: Whose Ox Is Being Gored?" *Los Angeles Times*, November 24, 1974, J3. Thailand experienced a brief period of freedom after General Thanom Kittikachorn, who had ruled since 1963, was forced to resign in October 1973.

CHAPTER 4

Reconceptualizing Foreign Aid

The United States' Commercial Import Program for the Republic of Vietnam, 1954–1975

Phạm Thị Hồng Hà

This chapter uses the case of the Commercial Import Program (CIP), an economic aid arrangement between the United States and the Republic of Vietnam (RVN) between 1954 and 1975, to shed further light on the impact and contours of US foreign aid projects.[1] Scholarly works on American commercial aid programs for the RVN in particular and its Third World allies in general have commonly considered these programs as a form of neocolonialism.[2] By providing economic and military aid to Third World countries, neocolonial powers seek to expand control over those countries and achieve global domination.[3] The view of aid as an exchange of economic assets for political gains was also expressed in many reports of US congressional hearings in the 1955–1975 period, which stated that the aid program for the RVN had led to an enormous economic cost on the part of the United States in return for political influence over its ally and the fulfillment of the US global anticommunist strategy.

Building on largely unexplored original sources from Vietnam National Archive No. 2, this chapter argues that the CIP as implemented in the RVN was not simply a matter of trading economic asset for political goals. As I show, the CIP came with many terms and conditions that helped American goods dominate South Vietnamese consumer markets and boost the growth of American manufacturers. More important, the process of aid provision of the CIP was also cleverly designed in ways that minimized the adverse effect on the US balance of payments. Instead of a simple give-and-receive arrangement between two governments, the

CIP was designed in complex ways, involving a wide range of actors, from American exporters to Vietnamese importers, and from the governments to the banking systems in both countries. Using this complex aid-giving mechanism, the United States actually spent most of the budget for the CIP domestically as payments in US dollars made directly to American manufacturers for their products. The United States then retrieved this sum, in Vietnamese piastres, from Vietnamese importers who paid for the imported products through a special mechanism called the Counterpart Fund administered by the US Agency for International Development (USAID), which was used largely to cover the military cost of the Vietnam War. This chapter thus argues that scholarly works on aid as a way of neocolonialism should focus not only on how global powers use aid to pursue political aims at considerable economic expenses, but also on the sophisticated strategies that aid providers use to maximize the cost-effectiveness of their aid.

I further argue that aid-giving was not a unidirectional process that depended solely on aid-providing countries, but a bidirectional process in which the volume and forms of aid were substantially determined by the government and businesses from aid-receiving nations. As I show, the Vietnamese government, banks, and importers actively devised creative strategies to harness various benefits from the CIP rather than being passive receivers of aid who were unable to craft an active course of action for themselves.

THE COMMERCIAL IMPORT PROGRAM AND ITS PROCEDURES

The CIP was a key component in the US anticommunist strategy in Asia during the Cold War. Launched in South Vietnam in 1954, the CIP was the most important form of economic assistance the United States provided to the RVN, accounting for 70 percent of total economic aid between 1954 and 1975.[4]

In the CIP, the United States did not provide money directly to the RVN government for fear that the latter would treat it as part of the national reserve and use the money at will. Instead, Washington granted Saigon an annual budget to help the latter import products for daily consumer needs. From 1954 to 1968 alone, the total value of CIP aid was around $2 billion.[5] As a consequence, the availability of imported consumer products in South Vietnam's markets, most of which were produced in the United States, increased dramatically, though a small portion came from Japan, France, Taiwan, Singapore, and South Korea.

Table 4.1. American Economic Aid to the RVN (in $ millions)

	1954–1962	1963	1964	1965	1966	1967	1968	Total
Nonproject aid								
- Cash transfers	0	6.3	3.0	0.3	0.6	0	0	9.9
- CIP	1,104.1	150.6	103.8	110.9	206.8	262.2	0	1,938.2
Counterinsurgency	0	10.7	18.8	43.8	38.4	62.9	67.2	240.8
Surplus Agriculture 402 Program	100.5	0	0	0	0	0	0	
PL-480 Program	120.2	36.6	139	65.5	78.8	172.9	90.96	1,328.2
Shipping Cost of PL-480	0	0	0	0	2.4	0.1	(2.1)	0.4
Project aid	139.2	41.5	35.1	30.5	33.3	72.4	72.1	424.1
Trust fund	0	7.6	1.1	1.3	1.5	2.2	1.1	14.8
Total	**1,464.0**	**253.0**	**219.8**	**252.3**	**361.8**	**572.5**	**229.5***	**3,352.9**

* Likely an error in the original report. The total amount for 1968 is 233.46
Source: "Tập đại cương của Nha Ngân sách ngoại viện về viện trợ Hoa Kỳ cho Việt Nam Cộng hòa từ năm 1954–1968" [Document of Bureau of Foreign Aid Budget About the US' Aid to the RVN, 1954–1968], Second Republic Presidential Office Fonds (1967–30/4/1975), File Number 2207, 10, National Archive II-Vietnam.

According to Vietnamese official documents, the CIP had two main functions. The first was to generate a budget in Vietnamese currency (the piastre) to finance defense operations and socioeconomic development projects. The second was to supply domestic markets with foreign imported goods without consuming the foreign currency reserve of the RVN government.[6] To achieve those two functions, the CIP was designed in a highly complex way and involved a wide range of actors.

At the beginning of each fiscal year, the US government would approve a fixed amount in US dollars to be used on the CIP. The RVN government would then notify Vietnamese importers and invite them to submit applications for authorization to procure products. The applications, however, were not submitted to the RVN government but instead to the USAID in Vietnam (USAID/VN) for consideration. Building on the applications submitted by importers, USAID/VN in collaboration with the RVN Ministry of Economy developed the Import Portfolio to spend the granted sum.

In the applications, the importers had to state the kinds of imported products, quantity, country of origin, shipping providers, place of sale, and expected time of sale. The USAID/VN retained the right to approve, reject, revise, and issue import licenses. Holders of import licenses would pay a sum, in Vietnamese piastres, equivalent to the value of the imported goods, to the Import Committee of Vietnam's National Bank. The money would be put into the Counterpart Fund, which was administered by USAID and released to the RVN government on a quarterly basis, to be used to cover the salary of South Vietnamese troops, a major component in the RVN's defense budget.

On receiving confirmation from the National Bank that the importer had completed payment, USAID in Washington (USAID/W), via banks, would pay US exporters (or in particular circumstances non-US international exporters) for their products. The payments were made in US dollars. The products would then be shipped to South Vietnam. Vietnamese importers would come to ports to claim their items under the supervision of the USAID/VN. If the amount of imported goods matched the amount stated in the import license, the importer would be allowed to receive the goods after paying import taxes.[7] Between 1955 and 1964, the total import volume under the CIP of the RVN was $1,486.6 million. The value increased to $2,534.2 million in the next decade.[8] From 1965 to 1969, the number of cars imported equaled that over the previous ten years.[9]

DOMINATING SOUTH VIETNAM'S CONSUMER MARKETS AND SUPPORTING AMERICAN MANUFACTURERS

A common view in reports of congressional hearings on commercial aid to the RVN was that the aid was an enormous waste of American taxpayer money. A report of the Committee for Government Operations in 1966 stated that USAID/VN did not monitor the CIP properly, allowing the program to be manipulated by Vietnamese officials for personal gain, thus nurturing corruption. A large quantity of items provided via the CIP had also been smuggled to areas under communist control.[10] Despite such criticisms from many members of the US Congress, the US government was determined to maintain the CIP for several reasons.

The first was to secure South Vietnam as a new and fertile market for American products and through which to support the US manufacturing sector. Securing new markets for US exports was indeed a major concern of American capitalism after World War II.[11] One of the major US foreign aid programs, the CIP for the RVN offered US manufacturers ample opportunities for exporting their products, mostly thanks to a series of conditions of aid that Washington imposed on the RVN and Vietnamese importers:

1. Vietnamese importers did not have the right to determine the place of origin of imported items. Almost all imported goods provided by the CIP originated from the United States or US-backed countries, although the average price of US goods was substantially higher than that of Japanese and European equivalents.[12] Since 1961, the United States added a new rule, preventing RVN from using US aid to procure goods from nineteen other capitalist countries, including France, Japan, the UK, and West Germany. This meant consumer needs in the RVN would be satisfied mostly by US manufacturers and businesses.
2. In principle, all goods in the CIP had to be shipped to South Vietnam on US-flag vessels although their shipping charges were among the highest in the world at the time. Before 1965, 50 percent of shipping cost was covered by the USAID/W and the remaining 50 percent by the RVN, which had the right to choose shipping carriers. After 1965, however, the RVN had to pay 100 percent of shipping cost and all goods had to be transported on US-flag vessels.[13]
3. Imported goods had to be transported out of Vietnamese ports within ninety days of the time of arrival. If importers failed to comply with this deadline, they would not be eligible for submitting new procurement applications. The aim of these rules was to speed up the importation of imported goods, thus generating more money paid to the Counterpart Fund.
4. To increase the competitiveness of American goods, the United States also pressured the Republican government to provide preferential treatments to Vietnamese companies that imported US products. They would be exempt from paying the fees for opening letters of credit. They were only required to pay a deposit worth 20 to 30 percent of the value of the goods they wanted to import if the goods were American made; the deposit for goods made in other countries was set at 100 percent. When applying for loans from commercial banks, if they planned to use the loan for purchasing American goods, the interest rate would be merely 8 or 9 percent, and that for loans to purchase goods produced from other countries was set at more than 12 percent. US goods were also subject to lighter taxes than goods made in other countries.[14]

With these terms and conditions, the CIP brought many benefits to American exporters and manufacturers, helping to transform South Vietnam into a fertile market for US tobacco, petrol, and pharmaceutical producers. In 1960, the total value of tobacco sold in South Vietnam reached $3.1 million, which increased to $4.5 million in 1961.[15] The share of US pharmaceutical products in South Vietnamese markets increased from 28 percent in 1960 to 47 percent in 1961; the share of French products decreased from 46 percent to 28 percent in the same period.[16] In 1967, the *Wall Street Journal* reported that sixty thousand pounds of antibiotics had been sold to South Vietnamese importers through the CIP, nine times the amount required to cover the need of the country's sixteen million people.[17] The United States was also the largest provider of petrol and oil to South Vietnam. In the 1972–1973 fiscal year, oil and petrol were the imported goods with the highest total value in the CIP: $67.5 million of $262.2 million of the entire import program, some 26 percent.[18]

Not only opening Vietnamese markets for the inflow of American goods, the CIP also helped American enterprises dominate markets in South Vietnam. In accordance with Article IV of the 1950 Pentalateral Agreement, the USG-GVN Economic Agreement, and specific USAID project agreements, the US government was entitled to duty-free treatment and exemption from taxation on the import of products, materials, or equipment furnished as part of its military and economic assistance programs. Much of this assistance was, of course, provided through the cooperation of firms under contract to the US government.[19]

Before 1961, products of US origin accounted for only 25 percent of all products on sale in the RVN. However, since January 1961, USAID declared that products from nineteen other developed countries, including France and Japan, were not qualified be to be goods that the United States used to provide to its allies as official aid.[20] By 1965, imported goods from the United States had increased to 45 percent, making the United States the largest source of Vietnam's imports.[21] Within the CIP alone, the share of American commodities in 1966 was 51 percent; those from Taiwan and other countries accounted for 22 and 22 percent, respectively. In 1970, the share of commodities of US origin increased to 81.3 percent; those from Taiwan and other countries further declined to 11.2 and 1.5 percent, respectively.[22]

Although the United States allowed countries receiving US aid to import goods from other nations, limits were strict as to the amount and kinds of goods that could be imported. A major rule was that the proportion of goods the RVN could import from other "Free World" countries such as Japan and Western European nations could not exceed 10 percent of the total goods imported through the CIP.[23] Furthermore, the RVN could only import goods from a third country when the goods in question could not be procured from American manufacturers.[24]

As table 4.2 shows, RVN import and export balance did not entirely depend on trade relations with the United States. In fact, commodities from various US allies still played an important part in South Vietnam's import portfolio. In 1965, although the United States had imposed the Buy American policy, which forbade the RVN from importing goods from Japan and other Western countries under the CIP program, Japan still emerged as the third largest supplier of goods to the RVN after the United States and Taiwan. In 1965, American commodities accounted for 45 percent of RVN import value, whereas those from Taiwan and Japan accounted for 13 and 9 percent, respectively.[25] In 1970, Japanese commodities accounted for 13 percent of the RVN's total import value, followed by French goods at 6.3 percent.[26]

In addition to manufacturers and service providers, American civil contractors also benefited substantially from the CIP. To assist the inflow of imported goods into South Vietnam, significant aid was spent on upgrading the country's seaports, particularly Saigon's, to accommodate the fast-growing volume of import and export. This meant ample opportunities for American contractors. In 1966 and 1967, the corporation RMK-BRJ won a contract worth $1.9 million to upgrade commercial docking stations of Saigon port. The road leading to the port was also upgraded with American money through an aid grant worth $688,000 to improve drainage, extend pavement in the Saigon port area, and improve lighting to permit more efficient round-the-clock operations, and fender the entire seawall to protect docks and ships from damage lighting.[27]

SOUTH VIETNAMESE AGENCY

The United States designed the CIP as a tool to maximize the cost-effectiveness of its aid and reduce the enormous overall costs of the war, but it did not have sole control over the process of aid-giving. The volume and kind of aid, as this section shows, were substantially decided by Vietnamese government, banks, and importers, who actively took advantage of the CIP for their own benefits rather than be passive recipients, merely complying with what the United States decided and not having the ability to craft an independent course of action for themselves.

The RVN Government

A major actor was the Saigon government, which used the CIP to achieve many of its economic goals, particularly containing inflation and increasing state revenues.[28] Since 1965, especially since the United States

Table 4.2. Republic of Vietnam's Export and Import Relations with Selected Countries, 1969–1970 (in $1,000) (calculated by the value of approved license)

Country of Origin	Export 1969 Value	Export 1969 % of total value of export	Export 1970 Value	Export 1970 % of total value of export	Import 1969 Value	Import 1969 % of total value of import	Import 1970 Value	Import 1970 % of total value of import
Austria	–	–	–	–	49	0.007%	43	0.006%
Switzerland	–	–	–	–	15,064	2.3%	9,978	1.5%
Netherlands	189	1.3%	360	3%	4,274	0.6%	9,518	1.4%
West Germany	901	6.2%	923	7.7%	19,223	2.9%	13,350	2.0%
Japan	2,265	15.4%	1,388	11.6%	166,525	25.0%	88,304	13.0%
United States	2,268	15.4%	1,311	10.9%	255,132	38.2%	331,117	48.9%
Total export and import value	14,693	100%	12,005	100%	667,000	100%	677,200	100%

Source: "Hồ sơ về tình hình khủng hoảng tiền tệ trên thế giới và sự ảnh hưởng của nó đối với Việt Nam năm 1971" [Documents about the Global Monetary Crisis and Its Impact on Vietnam in 1971], Vietnam National Bank Fonds (1955–1975), File no. 1030, 8, National Archives II-Vietnam.

deployed combat troops in South Vietnam, inflation had became a critical issue. Government officials thought the most effective solution was to reduce the shortage of consumer goods by increasing imports.[29] Fostering imports would also help contain inflation by reducing the total money supply as importers had to pay money to the National Bank to import products. Further, the larger the volume of imports, the more revenues the RVN government could raise from import taxes.[30]

A top classified report of the National Bank showed that between 1963 and 1965, South Vietnam's total import volume was around $300 million per year. In 1966, however, in the context of rising inflation and serious depreciation of the Vietnamese piastre in international and domestic markets, the National Bank recommended that the volume of import be raised to between $500 and $550 million and not be lower than $450 million.[31]

The RVN government also implemented a series of economic and financial policies in June 1966 under the name of Truth Operation or Sponge Cake Operation, which in effect permitted the unlimited import of all kinds of consumer goods to meet the fast-rising demand for consumer goods in South Vietnam.[32] The government held that "the crucial element for anti-inflationary action lies in the expansion of imports." Imports in 1966 increased by 60 percent over 1965.[33]

The RVN government also increased taxes to curb inflation, believing that new taxes would have an anti-inflationary impact of VND (đồng) 4 billion in 1966.[34] These measures were very much appreciated and welcomed by the International Monetary Fund: "There was no better measure for the problem of inflation in Vietnam than tax solutions,... which played a crucial role in maintaining political and social stability and gave the RVN a period of economic stability in nearly two years."[35]

Vietnamese economists affirmed the advantages of the measure to curb inflation in South Vietnam's economy, especially in the context of war. In an address at the formal opening of the First National City Bank's Saigon branch on September 15, 1972, Minister of Economy Phạm Kim Ngọc stated that "we have a fiscal policy designed to curb inflation as much as the war burden permits. This means that taxes are high, and they will be even higher in the future. The burden cannot be escaped: if it is not paid in taxes it will be paid in inflation."[36] As a consequence, in 1974, tax revenue from imports under the CIP brought VND 258 billion, equal to $469 million, accounting for 36 percent of the RVN's state budget.

Without this revenue, the budget deficit could have been more than 40 percent and inflation rate could have exceeded 100 percent.[37]

Tax was another way the government wanted to grant preferential treatment to the import of goods under the CIP program. Products imported into South Vietnam were subjected to two taxes, import tax (austerity tax) and perequation tax, the latter designed to give US goods an enormous advantage relative to goods from other countries. Vietnamese importers had to pay perequation taxes right at the moment the import license was issued. The tax rate was between 0 and 200 piastres per dollar of imported goods.[38] For US goods imported under the CIP program, the rate was between 5 and 10 piastres. For imports from other countries not included in the list of USAID-approved CIP goods, the rate could be as high as 210 piastres per dollar.[39]

Other than tax, a key measure of the RVN government to foster imports under the CIP was to maintain a high exchange rate between the Vietnamese piastre and the dollar. The exchange rates between the Vietnamese piastre and other currencies were determined by the Institute of Exchange Rate and the National Bank.[40] The exchange rate between the Vietnamese piastre and the US dollar, however, was a matter of negotiation between Washington and Saigon. In many instances, the United States pressured the RVN to devalue the Vietnamese piastre because the official exchange rate between the piastre and the dollar was set at a rate much higher than the actual value and much higher than the black markets rate. In the early years of the RVN, the official exchange rate was 35 piastres per US dollar. The exchange rate on black markets, however, was 90 per dollar. Even the RVN government acknowledged that this exchange rate set the value of the Vietnamese piastre "unreasonably high."[41] However, Saigon persistently tried to delay compliance with the United States' request and instead tried to keep the exchange rate at a high level, a measure intended to bring more profits to Vietnamese importers and increase the volume of the CIP.

In the early 1970s, under growing pressure to reduce the gap between the official exchange rate and that in the black market, the RVN government launched a "revolutionary" policy: to apply a floating exchange rate policy, effectively permitting a gradual devaluation of the piastre relative to the dollar.[42] However, in 1973, the RVN government promulgated Act 10/71, which established a system of "parallel exchange rates." The highest rate between the piastre and the dollar, 275 piastres, was applied on consumer goods imported under US aid programs, including the CIP and the PL.480 agricultural product aid program; a lower rate of

Table 4.3. Exchange Rates of the Vietnamese Piastre to US Dollar

Date of Effect	Official	Import using Foreign Reserve	CIP	Export
01.01.1955	35	35	35	35
15.11.1971	118	400	275	350
09.7.1972	425	425	290	500
03.01.1973	465	465	320	565
06.12.1973	550	550	455	575

Source: Lê Khoa, *Tình Hình Kinh Tế Miền Nam Việt Nam (1955–1975) Qua Các Số Liệu Thống Kê* [The Economic Situation of South Vietnam through Statistics] (Ho Chi Minh City: Vien Khoa Hoc Xa Hoi, 1979), 93.

400 piastres per dollar was applied on imported goods beyond those programs, that is, the import financed by the foreign reserve of the RVN government rather than by the United States. Thus, although the RVN government eventually devalued the Vietnamese piastre, it still intentionally applied a separate exchange rate between the piastre and the dollar for the CIP as a preferential treatment for Vietnamese importers and a way to contain inflation.

Vietnamese Commercial Banks

Another key actor that contributed substantially to the rapid growth of the CIP was Vietnamese commercial banks. In the RVN, commercial banks were colloquially referred to as foreign trade banks, because their operations focused predominantly on export-import activities.

In wartime context, Vietnamese banks were reluctant to provide credit, particularly long-term credit and credit for production activities in war zones. Credit for export and import activities, however, was an exception. Since the early years of the RVN, according to USAID, the largest need for credit in South Vietnam was credit for export and import, and about 80 to 90 percent of the credit provided by Vietnamese banks was used for import.[43] By July 1959, credit for import was VND 1,307 million, and that for export was merely VND 413 million. A confidential report by Governor of the National Bank Nguyễn Hữu Hanh to the Central Executive Committee on December 20, 1966, stated that credit provided by the banking system had played a crucial role in addressing importers' shortage of capital, thus facilitating the CIP and increasing at a stable rate the import of goods from the United States and US allies into South Vietnam.[44]

As the United States began deploying combat troops in South Vietnam and the volume of imported goods increased rapidly, the role of the Vietnamese banking system in financing imports became even more prominent. Statistics by the National Bank by December 31, 1972, showed that thirty-three banks and 178 branches in South Vietnam had provided a total credit of VND 51 billion for imports, accounting for 57.2 percent of the total credit, whereas the credit for exports was only VND 2 billion, accounting for merely 2.2 percent. Commercial banks even provided credit to importers to pay taxes, or sponsored their application for delayed payment of taxes in several months, a critical effect of which was that imported goods were transported out of ports as quickly as possible and the stockpiling of goods at ports was substantially reduced.[45]

The reason commercial banks prioritized credit for imports was because this was the most profitable type of lending operations, which could be completed within a short time, ensuring fast turnover of capital and minimized risks of wartime conditions relative to other kinds of financing operations. Normally a credit-for-export operation would be completed within between six months to a year. The likelihood of retrieving capital was also higher than that of financing operations in other fields, such as credit for production activities that were vulnerable to wartime destruction.[46]

Most important, banks could make a wide range of gains from financing import. Apart from interests, banks also gained profit from different fees, such as import license processing, communications, and commercial paper extension.[47] According to a press release by the National Bank in April 1974, the banking system in South Vietnam depended heavily on import operations to the extent that the governor of the National Bank even stated that "as long as import operations continue, the banking system will remain strong."[48]

Vietnamese Importers

Vietnamese importers were the third key actors contributing substantially to the proliferation of imported goods in South Vietnam under the CIP. They included small businessmen, large private corporations, and state import-export agencies. By 1968, USAID/VN estimated that nine hundred importers regularly imported products under the CIP.[49]

Importers had many motivations to participate in the CIP. First, as businessmen, given the highly unstable wartime conditions of South Vietnam, they saw it as risky to invest in manufacturing enterprises. At the same time, it was unwise to keep money in their pockets because wartime conditions meant that money would be devalued quickly. For example, the price of ordinary goods in South Vietnam often increased by 30 to 40 percent per year. Investing in purchasing and keeping imported goods therefore would be a much safer choice.[50]

Not only were imported goods less vulnerable to exchange rate fluctuations, but also, by participating in import activities, Vietnamese importers could gain legal access to foreign currencies, which were also less vulnerable to price fluctuations than Vietnamese currency. In South Vietnam at the time, it was illegal for nonstate individuals or entities to keep foreign currencies without declaring with the authorities.[51] An enterprise that imported products from the CIP could legally acquire US dollars whereas others had to get them from the black market. According to CIP protocols, when an importer received an import license, he could purchase foreign currencies, often in US dollars, from the National Bank in the amount stipulated in the license. He could also deposit foreign currencies in a foreign bank.[52] A *New York Times* report estimated that in the 1970s, about $200 million was deposited by Vietnamese importers in European banks, most of which were obtained through participation in the CIP.[53]

Another motivation for Vietnamese businesses to participate in the CIP was the official exchange rate, which favored import, as I describe. The unreasonably high official exchange rate brought importers a net profit of 20 to 30 percent of the value of imported goods at the time of importation (CIF). On average, an importer could get a striking profit of $102,000 to $153,000 per year.[54] Douglas Dacy reckons that in the context of massive inflation engendered by wartime conditions, importing foreign products was the safest and most lucrative business that could bring massive gains to importers, even when it took them months to sell their goods.[55]

Vietnamese importers not only took advantage of favorable conditions provided to them by the structural environment, that is, government policies, but also devised ways to create further advantages for their import businesses. Normally importers, as stipulated in the import license, were required to deposit 20 percent of the value of imported goods to a certified bank. Vietnamese importers often creatively transferred part of the burden of deposit to their customers, including wholesalers, retailers, and individual buyers. A farmer seeking to buy a US-made tractor was often required to pay an advanced payment to an importer so that the latter would place an order for the machine and guarantee that it would be delivered. The importer would then use the advanced payment to fulfill the duty of deposit to the bank. To facilitate the import of the tractor, the farmer might even provide an additional loan to the importer to help the latter make the required deposit to the bank as soon as possible.[56]

Vietnamese importers also resorted to illegal practices to gain from import activities. A common practice was to make secret arrangements with RVN officials. A report by the Ministry of Economy shows that import activities were dominated and even monopolized by a small number of rich businessmen with connections to provincial governors, generals, and even ministers.[57] These secret arrangements led to the emergence of dominant importers in South Vietnam, known as "king of rice," "king of flour," and "king of steel." Another report by the Ministry of Agriculture reveals that the market for imported fertilizers in South Vietnam was manipulated and controlled by five large corporations with connections to the Central Commission for Distribution and governors of many provinces, and it was those large corporations that made the rules and controlled the import of fertilizers into South Vietnam.[58]

Another example of how Vietnamese importers actively manipulated the CIP to their benefit was the common practice of reexport. As discussed, a major rule of the CIP was that imported goods could not be reexported to another country without USAID approval.[59] They had to be either consumed in Vietnam or further processed before they could be reexported. A USAID investigation report, however, revealed that a large quantity of CIP products had been reexported without further processing to Cambodia, Thailand, and even to territories under communist control. Investigations in January 1966 showed that eighty thousand tons of steel imported under the CIP had been reexported to Bangkok for a massive profit. This was made available by a complex network of large Vietnamese importers and their retailers. The retailers obtained CIP goods from the importers at a price much lower than that in the free market, then sold it on free and black markets at a much higher price. Some importers even arranged with retailers to stockpile goods that were in great demand to create artificial shortage so that they could sell those goods at a much higher price. Investigations discovered that forty thousand tons of fertilizers were being stored in cul-de-sacs and hard-to-spot warehouses across South Vietnam, and that some illegal warehouses had 1,500 tons of rice or 1,000 barrels of oil in stock.[60] Thanks to various advantages provided by the government and their own initiatives, Vietnamese businessmen gained an increasingly dominant role in the import sector. From the role of retailers for overseas Chinese importers, Vietnamese enterprises had become a new class of large-scale businesses that dominated import activities in South Vietnam.

ACTIVE OR PASSIVE? SOUTH VIETNAM AND SOUTH KOREA COMPARED

Despite the many examples demonstrating that the RVN government, banks, and importers played an active role in shaping the contour of the CIP, scholars commonly view the RVN as merely a passive recipient of American aid, unable to craft an independent course of action for itself. As evidence, they note that the RVN was forced by the United States to import largely consumer goods that would bring quick profit to American manufacturers, not production equipment and raw materials that would help South Vietnam develop an independent economy in ways some of America's Asian allies have done. Building on a comparison between the RVN and the Republic of Korea, I argue that any judgment of the former's responses to aid must be contextually situated. As I explain, the contexts in which South Korea and South Vietnam received and responded to US aid were quite different. Although the latter was unable to direct US aid toward developing the country's domestic manufacturing sector in ways the former did, it was not a passive and obedient follower of American orders. Instead, the RVN government's choice to prioritize the import of consumer goods was an active decision to harness as much benefit as possible from the very disadvantaged conditions externally imposed on them.

Like South Vietnam, South Korea was a major American ally in Asia and a major recipient of American aid. The initial aim of the US aid program for South Korea was also to meet short-term needs for consumer products rather than to provide production equipment and materials for longer-term development goals.[61] In the early years of the program for South Korea (1953 to 1960), three-fourths of imported goods were consumer items (food, beverages, manufactures oil, fertilizers), most of which were produced in the United States. Less than 10 percent of products imported were capital goods (raw materials, machinery and transport equipment).[62]

However, since the 1960s, the share of capital goods and intermediary goods in the CIP program for South Korea increased rapidly and gradually surpassed that of consumer goods.[63] This change was engendered by two factors. The first was the United States' new goal for its aid to South Korea. In the 1950s, in the context of the Korean War, Washington's top priority was to use the CIP to generate money to pay for military operations in South Korea. In the 1960s and 1970s, however, as the threat of war in the Korean peninsula receded and the political environment in South Korea began to stabilize, the United States began shifting the aim of its aid program from a focus on assisting war efforts to supporting South Korea in developing its economy, particularly its manufacturing sector.[64]

For the RVN, by contrast, the aim of the US aid program was always to support military operations and war efforts in South Vietnam. To achieve this aim, Washington's priority when implementing the CIP was to encourage the import of consumer goods at the expense of capital goods. As I explain, under wartime conditions, few Vietnamese businessmen wanted to invest in manufacturing enterprises and importers preferred importing consumer goods. It meant an aid program that prioritized capital goods would attract few importers and thus generate much less money for the Counterpart Fund, a major source of funding for the American war efforts in South Vietnam.

As a consequence, the United States consistently denied requests from the RVN government to prioritize capital goods and raw materials in the list of CIP products. On November 22, 1955, US Assistant Secretary of State Walter Robertson reported to Undersecretary Herbert Hoover that the RVN government wanted more capital goods and fewer consumer goods. This request was made again by President Ngô Đình Diệm in a discussion with Robertson and US Ambassador to Vietnam Elbridge Dubrow in a meeting in Washington on May 10, 1957, in which President Diệm stated that "It was necessary to strengthen the country from the inside by giving it means of production."[65] Washington consistently denied Saigon's requests, however, on the grounds that the key aim of the CIP was to generate as much money in local currency and as quickly as possible to cover military costs of the war.[66]

The main dynamic that led to a change in the US aid policy for South Korea, however, was the Vietnam War and the new bargaining power South Korea gained from deploying combat troops in South Vietnam. A key condition South Korea set out in exchange for the deployment of troops was that the United States would no longer impose the Buy American policy on its aid program for South Korea.[67] Although Seoul had sought to persuade Washington to abandon the policy since the late 1950s, not until South Korea started deploying troops in South Vietnam since the mid-1960s did Washington eventually accept the proposal.[68] South Korea promulgated a new policy of import liberalization in 1966. Unlike South Vietnam, South Korea was allowed to prioritize the import of raw materials, intermediate goods, and equipment inputs while erecting barriers to minimize the import of finished consumer goods that could compete with domestically manufactured equivalents.[69]

This chapter uses the case of the Commercial Import Program that the United States provided to the RVN between 1955 and 1975 to make three arguments about the impact and contour of US foreign aid projects. First, scholarly works on aid as a method of neocolonialism should focus not only on aid as an expensive tool for aid providers to pursue political aims, but also on the sophisticated strategies employed by global powers to minimize the costs to themselves. The CIP for the RVN came with many terms and conditions that helped American goods to dominate South Vietnamese consumer markets and boost the growth of American manufacturers. More important, the process of aid provision of the CIP was also cleverly designed in ways that allowed the United States to spend most of the budget for the CIP "at home" and at the same time made Vietnamese importers and consumers the actual payers for the imported products.

Second, I argue that aid-giving was not unidirectional but bidirectional, in which the volume and forms of aid were substantially determined by the government and businesses in aid-receiving nations. This chapter shows how the Vietnamese government, banks, and importers, rather than being passive aid recipients, devised active and creative strategies to harness a wide range of benefits from the CIP.

Finally, building a comparison between the CIP programs for South Vietnam and South Korea, this chapter highlights how local contexts shaped the aims and effects of foreign aid in very different ways. I argue that any judgment of the RVN's responses to aid must be contextually situated. Even though the RVN was unable to direct American aid toward developing the country's domestic manufacturing sector as South Korea had done, it was not a passive and obedient follower of American orders. Instead, the RVN government's choice to prioritize the import of consumer goods was an active decision to harness as much benefit as possible from the very disadvantaged conditions externally imposed on them.

NOTES

1. My sincere thanks to Phạm Kim Ngọc, former RVN minister of economy (1969–1973), and Nguyễn Đức Cường, former RVN minister of trade and industry (1973–1975), for their invaluable support during my research.

2. Phan Đắc Lực, *Vị Trí*; Nan, *Resolutely Struggle*; Trần Đình, "Vốn Lãi"; Athreya, "Perestroika"; Koshy, "Cold War to Trade War."

3. Nkrumah, *Neo-colonialism*; Sartre, *Colonialism and Neocolonialism*; Ruether, *Christianity and Social Systems*.

4. Hồ Thới Sang, *Kinh Tế Việt Nam*, 136; Đặng Phong, *Kinh Tế Miền Nam Việt Nam*, 157.

5. "Tập đại cương của Nha Ngân sách ngoại viện về viện trợ Hoa Kỳ cho Việt Nam Cộng hòa từ năm 1954–1968," File Number 2207, 10, Second Republic Presidential Office Fonds (1967–30/4/1975), Vietnam National Archives II, Hồ Chí Minh City, Vietnam [VNA II].

6. "Tập đại cương của Nha Ngân sách," File no. 2207, 12, VNA II.

7. "Phúc trình của Cơ quan phát triển quốc tế Hoa Kỳ ở Việt Nam (USAID/VN) cho Đại sứ Hoa Kỳ," File no. 27128, 45, Prime Minister Fonds (1954–1975), VNA II.

8. Dacy, *Foreign Aid*, 209.

9. "Tập tài liệu của Giáo sư Nguyễn Văn Hảo nhận định về tình hình kinh tế, tài chánh Việt Nam từ năm 1955–1970," File no. 2415, 32, Second Republic Presidential Office Fonds (1967–30/4/1975), VNA II. For a comparison, between roughly the same period from 1954 to 1975, the Democratic Republic of Vietnam (DRV) also received massive economic aid from their socialist allies, particularly the Soviet Union and People's Republic of China. There were, however, two important differences between the CIP program for the RVN and socialist countries' aid to the DRV. First, Soviet and Chinese aid to the DRV was provided through a relatively straightforward one-way give-and-receive arrangement between governments, without the participation of private entities such as importers and banks. Second, although the DRV indeed received a large amount of consumer goods from China and Soviet Union, the major share of economic aid from the socialist allies was in the form of raw materials and production equipment, which were used for the construction and operation of hundreds of new factories in northern Vietnam in the period of economic restoration after the end of the First Indochina War in 1954. See "Báo cáo tình hình quan hệ kinh tế của Việt Nam với các nước từ năm 1955 đến năm 1974 và phương hướng phát triển quan hệ hợp tác kinh tế với các nước trong những năm tới của Vụ hợp tác kinh tế—Uỷ ban Kế hoạch Nhà nước" [Report on Vietnam's economic relations with other countries between 1955 and 1974 and future plans of promoting economic cooperation in the years to come, Department of Economic Cooperation, State Planning Committee], State Committee for Planning Fonds, File no. 18025, Vietnam National Archives III [VNA III].

10. "Commercial (Commodity) Import Program for Vietnam (Follow up Investigation)," 2390112001, October 8, 1970, Box 01, Folder 12, 7, Douglas Pike Collection: Unit 11—Monographs, Vietnam Center and Sam Johnson Vietnam Archive at Texas Tech University [VCA].

11. Magdoff, *Age of Imperialism*, 12.

12. Võ Nhân Trí, "Sự Xâm Nhập Kinh Tế của Mỹ," 69.

13. Võ Đoàn Ba, *Ngoại Viện Hoa Kỳ*, 23.

14. Nguyễn Bằng, "Ngoại Thương Miền Nam," 43.

15. Szabo and Kuwabara, "Market for US Products," 8.

16. Szabo and Kuwabara, "Market for US Products," 9–11.

17. *Wall Street Journal*, "Agency's Charges of Drug-Firm Kickbacks to South Vietnam Importers Are Denied," August 3, 1967, 8. USAID in fact did not care whether the overimport of foreign products could impede the growth of domestic manufacturers in Vietnam. In 1966, a US Congress report showed that USAID/VN did not conduct any qualitative or quantitative survey on the actual needs for foreign goods in South Vietnam. Instead, it estimated the need through import license. For example, in 1967, a large stockpile of unused goods in South Vietnam threatened the survival of domestic textile and paper manufacturers. See "Commercial (Commodity) Import Program for Vietnam," 15, VCA.

18. "Bảng kê điện tín của Toà Đại sứ Mỹ tại Sài Gòn về giấy phép nhập cảng được Ngân hàng Quốc gia cấp năm 1973," File Number 779, USAID Fonds (1955–1975), VNA II.

19. "Annex, Logistics—re: The Pentalateral Agreement of 1950 [Best Quality]—Record of MACV Part 1," F015800240768, Box 0024, Folder 0768, Sam Johnson Vietnam Archive Collection, VCA. See also "Tập công văn của Nha Điều hành về công tác viện trợ năm 1960- 1973" [Official Documents of the Executive Department on Aid in 1960–1973], File no. 354, 4, USAID Office Fonds, VNA II.

20. Szabo and Kuwabara, "Market for US Products," 1.

21. "Tập tài liệu năm 1966 của Tổng bộ Kế hoạch và phát triển, Tổng bộ Kinh tế—Tài Chính, Các bộ Tài chính, Thương mại," File no. 186, General Department for Social-Cultural Development Fonds, VNA II.

22. "Report, Prepared by C/POB/CIP/ADCCA—The Aid Commercial Import Program for Viet-Nam," 0880126001, October 1970, Box 01, Folder 26, 3, Larry Flanagan Collection, VCA.

23. Commercial (Commodity) Import Program for Vietnam," 28, VCA.

24. "From the Director of the United States Agency for International Development Vietnam 1970," 8, A. S. Cook Library, Towson State University, Baltimore, MD.

25. "Tập tài liệu năm 1966," VNA II.

26. "Tập tài liệu của Ngân hàng QGVN, Quỹ Tiền tệ Quốc tế về cuộc khủng hoảng tiền tệ năm 1971–1973," File no. 1292, 221, Vietnam National Bank Fonds (1955–1975), VNA II. Japanese goods entered South Vietnam through various ways, not only under the CIP. First, in regard to Japanese goods entering the South Vietnamese market under the CIP, before 1961, when the United States had not applied the Buy American policy in Vietnam, Vietnamese importers could freely choose Japanese goods to import under the CIP. Because Japan had a good relationship with the United States, Japan enjoyed a relatively low tax rate in the South Vietnamese market. However, in exchange, Japan had to let the United States occupy Okinawa Islands. In addition, in exchange for US approval of the import of Japanese products to South Vietnam, Japan had to import more US goods. The United States would not pay dollars to Japan, but instead settle the payment by clearing debts or exporting US goods to Japan. After 1961, the Washington applied the Buy American policy, which prohibited Vietnamese importers from importing goods from nineteen countries, including Japan and Western Europe. However, the RVN government still imported Japanese goods using its own foreign currency reserve. Technically, the RVN government would provide its foreign currency only to public agencies or public-private enterprises to import goods, but in fact private importers were still granted foreign currency by the RVN government to import. Third, Japanese goods entered South Vietnam under Japan's war reparation program for Vietnam, which was worth $39 million paid in Japanese "goods and services."

27. "Improving and Expanding Transportation in Vietnam—Vietnam Feature Service (TCB-032)," 2321919001, no date, Box 19, Folder 19, 23, Douglas Pike Collection: Unit 06—Democratic Republic of Vietnam, VCA.

28. In the early days of the CIP for RVN, Saigon actually sought to persuade Washington to provide capital goods instead of consumer goods so as to help the RVN develop its domestic manufacturing sector. Saigon's requests, however, were consistently denied on the grounds that the key aim of the CIP was to generate as much money in local currency, and as quickly as possible to cover military costs of the Vietnam War. Thus the priority had to be given to consumer goods, which could be sold at a faster rate to raise money for the Counterpart Fund.

29. Nguyễn Văn Ngôn, *Kinh Tế Việt Nam Cộng hòa*, 116; see also "Tài liệu của Ngân hàng QGVN về tình hình kinh tế, tài chánh về tiền tệ của Việt Nam năm 1963–1967," File no. 71, 118, Vietnam National Bank Fonds (1948–30/4/1975), VNA II.

30. "Tài liệu nghiên cứu về chính sách tín dụng của Ngân hàng QGVN năm 1964–1974," File no. 1488, 2, Vietnam National Bank Fonds (1948–30/4/1975), VNA II.

31. "Tập tài liệu của Nha Tổng Kiểm soát Ngân hàng QGVN dùng để soạn thảo biện pháp ổn định kinh tế và tiền tệ năm 1965–1968," File no. 117, 192, Vietnam National Bank Fonds (1948–30/4/1975), VNA II. In practice the RVN government indeed followed the recommendation by the National Bank. In 1966, the total import value was $495.6 million. Import volume kept increasing over the years, reaching $802.7 million in 1971 and $725 million in 1972. See "Tài liệu của Ngân hàng QGVN về phúc trình thường niên năm 1970, 1971 liên quan tới dự trữ ngoại tệ, ảnh hưởng khủng hoảng tiền tệ thế giới và viễn cảnh chi phối sau năm 1971," File no. 186, Vietnam National Bank Fonds (1948–30/4/1975), VNA II.

32. Lê Tấn Tài, "Nhận Xét Về Một Số Biện Pháp," 12, VNA II.

33. "Tập tài liệu của Nha Tổng Kiểm soát Ngân hàng QGVN dùng để soạn thảo biện pháp ổn định kinh tế và tiền tệ năm 1965–1968," File no. 117, 256–257, Vietnam National Bank Fonds (1948–30/4/1975), VNA II.

34. "Tập tài liệu của Nha Tổng Kiểm," 257, VNA II.

35. "Hồ sơ v/v phân tích tình hình kinh tế, lạm phát tại Việt Nam Cộng Hoà theo quan điểm tiền tệ năm 1968" [Documents on RVN's Economic and Inflation Situation from Monetary Perspective in 1968], File no. 918, 92, Vietnam National Bank Fonds (1955–1975), VNA II.

36. "Tài liệu Khảo cứu về tình hình kinh tế Việt Nam năm 1972–1973," File no. 2493, 82, Vietnam National Bank Fonds (1955–1975), VNA II.

37. Nguyễn Đức Cường, "Building Market Economy," 97–100.

38. "Tài liệu Khảo," 93, VNA II.

39. Đặng Phong, "Kinh Tế Miền Nam Việt Nam," 163.

40. Phan Thiện Giới, "Chính Sách Quan Thuế," 223–224.

41. US Department of State, *FRUS, 1958–1960*, document 96.

42. According to SVN's policymakers (Minister of Economy Phạm Kim Ngọc and Minister of Trade and Industry Nguyễn Đức Cường), this measure was one of a series of structural reforms initiated in September 1970, so called "the new economic liberalism." Under these reforms, the RVN government let the exchange rate float, opened up the economy, and decontrolled domestic prices and economic activities—this was considered "revolutionary" at the time (Phạm Kim Ngọc, interviews, 2015; Nguyễn Đức Cường, email correspondence, 2015).

43. "Tập tài liệu về vai trò trung gian của Ngân hàng quốc gia trong giao dịch chứng khoán với vấn đề viện trợ thương mại Mỹ năm 1955–1957," File no. 1813, USAID Fonds (1955–1975), VNA II.

44. "Về phúc trình của Ngân hàng Quốc gia Việt Nam về áp lực lạm phát và chương trình ổn định kinh tế năm 1965–1967," File no. 23101, 48, Republic of Vietnam's Prime Minister Fonds (1954–1975), VNA II.

45. "Về phúc trình," 47, VNA II.

46. Thế Nhân, "Tương Quan Giữa Ngoại Thương," 12.

47. Thế Nhân, "Tương Quan Giữa Ngoại Thương," 13.

48. Vũ Tài Mạnh, "Nhìn Qua Tình Hình Ngân Hàng Thương Mại," 106.

49. Commercial (Commodity) Import Program for Vietnam," 9–11, VCA.

50. Dacy, "Foreign Aid," 153–155.

51. "Sắc lệnh, Nghị định, Công văn của Ủy ban Hành pháp Trung ương, Phủ Thủ tướng, Bộ Tài chánh, Ngân hàng Quốc gia Việt Nam về thể lệ hối đoái và ngân hàng năm 1965–1972," File no. 2029, Vietnam National Bank Fonds (1948–30/4/1975), VNA II.

52. Dacy, "Foreign Aid," 154.

53. Cited in Pho, "These Goodies," 25.

54. Võ Văn Sen, *Sự Phát Triển Chủ Nghĩa Tư Bản*, 180.

55. Dacy, "Foreign Aid," 158.

56. "Research Study, Simulmatics Corporation, contracted by Joint Economic Office of the U.S. Mission to Vietnam—A Study of Commercial Distribution of Agricultural Inputs in the Mekong Delta of Vietnam, 1968," 0880101001, 1968, Box 01, Folder 01, 53, Larry Flanagan Collection, VCA.

57. "Tập tài liệu của Nha Tổng Kiểm soát Ngân hàng QGVN," VNA II.

58. Laurence Stern, "(Another) Crusade Against Corruption Begins in South Vietnam," *Washington Post, Times Herald (1959-1973)*, October 1970, A14.

59. Stern, "(Another) Crusade."

60. "An Investigation of US Economic and Military Assistance Program in South Vietnam," 2184817011, November 9, 1966, Box 48, Folder 17, 17, 22, 26–37, Douglas Pike Collection: Unit 03–Legal and Legislative, VCA.

61. Kim, "Translating Foreign Aid Policy Locally," 419.

62. Krueger, *Development Role*, 71; see also Koo, *Korea and the United States*, 245.

63. In 1960, capital goods and intermediary goods accounted for 49.6 percent of the total goods provided by the CIP and consumer items for 24.6 percent. See Krueger, *Development Role*, 72.

64. Chung, *South Korea in the Fast Lane*, 310.

65. US Department of State, *FRUS, 1955–1957*, vol. 1, document 381.

66. US Department of State, *FRUS, 1955–1957*, vol. 1, document 277.

67. US Department of State, *FRUS, 1964–1968*, vol. 29, document 77.

68. In exchange for South Korea's deployment of troops in South Vietnam, Washington not only allowed South Korea to import raw materials and equipment inputs to develop its domestic manufacturing sector, but also opened the US market for Korean consumer products. During the Vietnam War, the volume of import from South Korea to the United States increased dramatically, from $35.6 million in 1964 to $760 million in 1972, a twenty-one-fold increase. See Park, *Military Authoritarian Regimes*, 33.

69. Kanesa-Thasan, "Stabilizing an Economy."

CHAPTER 5

Building Higher Education during War

South Vietnam's Public Universities in the Second Republic, 1967–1975

Trương Thùy Dung

This chapter examines the development of three major public universities of South Vietnam in Saigon, Huế, and Cần Thơ, focusing on the Second Republic period, when they had become firmly established but continued to grow. To assess these universities, I focus on their academic elements, ranging from admissions processes, curricula, and publications to examinations and accreditation. In examining the details of their operation as academic institutions, it is possible to gauge the degree by which administrators and faculty were able to rise to the challenges and serve the needs of their young nation at a time of war.

The Republic of Vietnam (RVN) was founded in 1955 after a nine-year war in which its French-trained military participated. That destructive war had been preceded by nearly a century of colonial rule. Although the French established a modern education system in Vietnam, its capacity was severely limited; its only institution of higher education was based in Hanoi and had a branch in Saigon. Given such conditions, the tasks facing the Republican elites were daunting given the massive need for a modern education system. By the early 1960s, war had begun to engulf South Vietnam, further burdening the resources of the Republic and making it more dependent on American assistance. Nevertheless, throughout two decades of its existence, the RVN was able to create a vibrant and diverse higher education system of a dozen universities and several colleges that adhered to liberal values and offered rigorous academic programs to its expanding population. Although still limited in many ways, South Vietnam's universities appeared on the path to approaching universal standards of university operations while serving national-level requirements.[1]

Until recently, Western scholarship on the Vietnam War generally ignored the RVN. Most scholars focus on the war as a military conflict, not as a social event. Scarcely any research has been done on the social and institutional history of South Vietnam during the war, including its education system.[2] Together with other chapters in this volume, this chapter offers a different perspective in which the South Vietnamese government and its people are assigned full agency as historical actors who sought solutions to practical problems as they coped with a war not of their choosing.

More specifically, existing research on education policy and intellectual culture in the RVN suggests that educators and researchers enjoyed significant freedom of thought while upholding and cultivating liberal values in their academic work and environment.[3] This was a remarkable feature given the RVN's anticommunist politics and life-and-death struggle for survival from the war. This chapter corroborates that insight but adds to it with a focus on the technical and professional aspects of higher education in the RVN. By focusing on the hardware of the system, so to speak, it is possible to observe that war not only generated destruction but also provided opportunities for the RVN to develop and modernize a national university system through its extensive collaboration with its American and Western allies. Although more research is needed, much more than Cold War politics seemed to be involved in the collaboration among educators from allied nations.

TRANSFORMATION OF SOUTH VIETNAM'S HIGHER EDUCATION IN THE 1950S AND 1960S

After 1954, the partition of Vietnam sowed various problems for education in general and higher education in particular. Too few schools were built, and curricula and teaching methods did not meet the developing requirements of South Vietnam. Technical education, which was almost nonexistent in Vietnam during the colonial regime, had to be established on all levels to deal with the pressing demands of reconstruction and development.[4] In addition, the general underdevelopment of Vietnam's higher education, including the lack of teaching staff, the scarcity of teaching and learning materials, the imbalance between student numbers and available seats in universities and colleges, required urgent solutions. Despite the difficulties, however, a number of factors encouraged the development of higher education in South Vietnam due to the circumstances of the 1950s and 1960s.

The first achievement in higher education's activities in the decade between 1955 and 1966 is evident in the construction of fundamental principles derived from realistic requirements of South Vietnam and adapted from cutting-edge models of higher education. These principles were proposed at the first National Education Convention in 1958 and reaffirmed in 1964 at the second convention. They provided a vision for the missions of the RVN's higher education, which emphasized three concrete segments:

1. Education must be a humanist education, respecting the sacred character of the human being, regarding man as an end in himself, and aiming at the full development of man.
2. Education must be a national education, respecting the national values, assuring the continuity of man with the natural environment (family, profession, and country), aiming at safeguarding the nation, its prosperity, and the collective promotion of its people.
3. Education must be an open education, respecting the scientific mind as a factor of progress, attempting to develop the social and democratic mind, and welcoming all the authentic cultural values of the world.[5]

Fulfilling educational principles and adapting to reality, higher education experienced rapid growth after the Geneva Agreement in 1954. Before 1954, the University in Saigon was only a branch of Indochinese University founded in Hanoi in 1906 by the French colonial government, and was the only institution of higher learning in South Vietnam.[6] In the first decade, not only did it become an independent entity, but many new public and private universities were also founded, among them the University of Huế (1957), Đà Lạt University (1958), Vạn Hạnh University (1964), and the University of Cần Thơ (1966). The increasing number of universities led to a surge of student numbers. In 1954, only three thousand students were enrolled at the university level; by 1967, the number steadily increased to approximately thirty-four thousand, multiplying eleven times in just over a decade.[7]

Together with independence from France was the establishment of Vietnamese control of universities in South Vietnam; for example, Nguyễn Quang Trình was the rector of the University of Saigon, Father

Cao Văn Luận the rector of the University of Huế, and Bishop Ngô Đình Thục the rector of Đà Lạt University. Government expenditures for education tripled: from VND 293,538,430 ($8,386,812) in the 1954–1955 school year to VND 900,000,000 ($24,459,688) in 1960, accounting for approximately 6 percent of the National Budget.[8] This portion was modest in comparison with the allocation for South Vietnam's national defense budget, yet it indicated the growing attention of the RVN's authorities for educational development.

To further opportunities for qualified students wanting to attend university, the tuition of national universities was nominal around VND 13 ($0.16) per year in 1968.[9] Even at private universities such as Đà Lạt University, the tuition fee was VND 500 ($6.25), which was higher than those in public universities but accounted for only an extremely small portion of the actual training cost for each student. In addition, to improve the opportunities to attend university, five thousand governmental scholarships were made available to children of disabled veterans, faculty members, or refugees.[10]

The scarcity of teachers, one of the most egregious problems of RVN higher education, was resolved gradually. After a call for the return of Vietnamese students from overseas, invitations to foreign professors, and more teacher training programs, the number of teachers grew steadily at almost all levels and in all types of training in universities and colleges. At the university level, 465 lecturers worked at three universities: the University of Saigon, the University of Huế, and Đà Lạt University in the 1960–1961 school year. The number rose slightly to 521 in the 1964–1965 school year for five universities, the three cited and two additional universities: Vạn Hạnh University and the University of Cần Thơ. Also in the 1964–1965 school year when it opened, the Agricultural College in Cần Thơ employed forty-nine instructors.[11] This figure was modest, yet significant for a brand-new agricultural education institution in South Vietnam. For unclear reasons, the number of lecturers in the technical colleges decreased from 172 to 129 between 1960 and 1965.[12] Nevertheless, the trend quickly reversed and showed a growing tendency in the years that followed.

DEVELOPMENT OF ACADEMIC ASPECTS IN MAJOR PUBLIC UNIVERSITIES (1967–1975)

Many fields were taught at public universities in the RVN. Each university had its own training strategy and focused on different strengths, although some duplication was unavoidable. For example, faculties of pedagogy operated in all three public universities in Saigon, Huế, and Cần Thơ, and faculties of medicine were run in both the University of Saigon and the University of Huế.

The University of Saigon, as known, had eight affiliated schools (faculties), comprised the faculties of law, science, letters, pedagogy, medicine, pharmacy, dentistry, and architecture. In the 1969–1970 school year, the Nha Trang Oceanography Institute was annexed to the University of Saigon for academic management. Yet the Nha Trang Oceanography Institute exclusively produced graduate programs for master and doctoral students.[13] In the initial stages, the University of Huế operated with four affiliated schools, comprised the faculties of science, letters, law, and pedagogy. The Faculty of Medicine and the Institute of Sinology were created and added later. The University of Cần Thơ had five affiliated schools and one center, namely, the faculties of science, agriculture, pedagogy, law and social sciences, letters, and the Foreign Language Center.

Admissions

In public universities, the requirements for student enrollment were significant: students generally were required to have earned the Bac II certificate (Baccalaureate Second Part Examination) in advance of being admitted for enrollment. As a report from that time states, the Bac II "is a very significant turning point in the lives of Vietnamese students. To be certified as a Bac II graduate is to be eligible for higher education.... Graduates of the twelfth grade who do not pass the Bac II are not considered high school graduates. They are subject to the military draft and opportunities for higher education are not open to them."[14]

Students usually had two opportunities, the last week of June and August, to take the Bac II examinations. The scoring and reporting procedures took about a month, so students who failed in their first attempt in June could reregister for the August exam. Depending on the time it took to get the results of the August test, universities postponed the opening of their fall term to the first week in October or even as late as mid-November.[15]

At the University of Saigon, admission requirements varied from faculty to faculty, with some similarities across its member schools. Among those eight schools, the faculties of law, science, and letters appeared to have relatively easier admissions. All students, with no limitation on age, who had earned the Bac II were qualified to enroll in these schools. Although creating more opportunities for students to enroll in Saigon, this policy resulted in the considerable problem of inadequate classroom capacity to accommodate all enrolled students. For example, thirteen thousand students were registered in the Faculty of Law in 1970.[16] This overwhelmed the school and, as a result, the faculties so affected raised their admissions criteria from the early 1970s. Certain exemptions that eased requirements were extended to students who were ethnic minorities, veterans, or the children of those killed in action.[17]

In contrast to the three faculties mentioned, the Faculty of Pedagogy had relatively higher admission prerequisites in regard to both age and qualifications. Candidates for admissions needed to be between eighteen and thirty years old. They were required to take entrance exams organized by the Faculty of Pedagogy, which included a written part and an interview. After passing both parts, students were required to undergo a general health check-up. Students who could not meet the health criteria for admission were rejected even if they had already passed all other qualifying exams.[18]

In the Faculty of Medicine, from the 1963–1964 through the 1969–1970 school years, applicants with the Bac II were qualified to attend the prep course (Année Prémédicale or APM) prior to becoming first-year students of medicine.[19] From the 1969–1970 school year, this prep course was abolished; instead students needed to acquire the PCB (physics, chemistry, and biology), SPCN (physics, chemistry, and natural sciences), or MPC (mathematics, physics, and chemistry) certificates in the Faculty of Science before being officially nominated as students of medicine. In the Faculty of Pharmacy prospective, students were subjected to a two-cycle examination, in the second cycle of which candidates took a multiple-choice exam testing their knowledge of physics, chemistry, and biology. They were also required to pass a foreign language qualification by translating written Vietnamese into either English or French.[20]

Given the important role of teacher training schools in the RVN's public universities, where the next generation of teachers for South Vietnam were trained, admissions were decided and given to candidates through austere evaluations. Students were required to pass a specialized entrance examination. At the Faculty of Pedagogy in Cần Thơ, applicants were required to be between nineteen and twenty-nine years old and to have Vietnamese citizenship. Depending on their interests and desired specialization, requirements were sometimes more stringent. Students who wanted to become teachers in history, geography, English, and French had to have taken those subjects in high school. Those wanting to be middle-school teachers (grade 6 to grade 9) had to complete several exams including essays and multiple-choice exams in English, French, history, geography, physics, chemistry, biology, and Hán-Vietnamese.[21] Maximum annual intake in this faculty was forty. As true for the Faculty of Pedagogy, those seeking entrance to the School of Agriculture at Cần Thơ needed to pass the usual entrance examinations and satisfy requirements of age, citizenship, and pre-college education in the same subjects. These included two-part exams in biology, chemistry, physics, and English in both multiple-choice and essay formats.[22]

Before 1973, those students who wished to study in the Faculty of Law and Social Sciences, the Faculty of Science, or the Faculty of Letters did not have to sit for entrance examinations. From 1973, to manage enrollment numbers and ensure the quality of admitted students, entrance examinations testing general knowledge and foreign language competence were required by the Faculty of Law and Social Sciences; with an additional essay and a foreign language test required by the Faculty of Letters; and a scientific knowledge test covering biology, physics, chemistry, and mathematics and a foreign language test required by the Faculty of Science.[23] Students at the University of Cần Thơ were required to learn a foreign language at its Foreign Language Center. Given the lack of teaching staff and course materials, most students studying at the University of Cần Thơ chose English or French for their foreign language subject.[24]

Despite doubling the number of university students from 1967 to 1975 (from 32,611 to 71,893), the ratio of university to high school students in South Vietnam remained unchanged during this period, at about 7 percent.[25] This figure was not a contradiction but demonstrated that the growth of high schools and university students was proportionate and that entrance examinations to enter universities in South Vietnam remained competitive. Although admissions criteria at public universities varied from institution to institution, all universities had more requirements for their prospective students than they had in previous years (in the 1950s and early 1960s), when students needed only the Bac II to be admitted. Diversification of examination designs, components of essay, interview and multiple-choice exam formats indicated the seriousness of educational administrators in evaluating their prospective students' competence. In the 1960s and 1970s, maintaining the quality of students increasingly preoccupied South Vietnamese authorities and educators. This was evidenced in particular requirements for specific curriculum tracks and the fact that not all classes at all universities reached their full capacity.

Teaching Methods and Curricula

By the 1960s and 1970s, a movement was launched in universities to reform the old methods of teaching that emphasized rote learning.[26] Breaking the traditional belief that teachers should shoulder all tasks in the teaching-learning process, South Vietnamese educators at the University of Saigon suggested that the role of teachers was primarily to instruct their students to rethink, research, and work independently. In this scenario, the teachers should be instructors, and the lectures (cours magistral) could be given to the students in advance. In doing so, teachers were better able to explain unclear points in the lessons to further students' understanding and encourage their participation in the discussions during lectures. This teaching method was legalized by Decree No.2661/GD/PC/NĐ, issued on November 28, 1967.[27] The decree instructed students to organize into groups of fifteen to thirty, which were considered to be ideal, in reviewing knowledge, in practicing what they had learned, in helping each other to overcome any inefficiencies of education facilities, and in enhancing their presenting skills.

South Vietnamese educators profoundly acknowleged the ineffectiveness of old teaching methods and aspired to change them. Since the late 1960s, South Vietnamese educators who had been trained abroad began to return home from the United States, England, Germany, Australia, New Zealand, and Japan. This paved the way for many innovations in the higher education system, including changes in teaching methods and a greater appreciation of academic freedom in South Vietnam's universities. Students of medicine and pharmacy faculties were excited to have access to up-to-date research from the United States. Those in the Faculty of Law were taught new subjects adopted from the American curriculum, such as statistics, methods of social sciences, politics, and international relations. At the Faculty of Letters, class discussions became regular activities under the guidance of professors both American-trained and French-trained. Students discussed and criticized philosophical theories, such as the existentialism of Kierkegaard, Heidegger, Sartre, and Merleau Ponty.[28] Rather than committing to memory, students acquired knowledge effectively by consulting auxiliary documents and references suggested by professors. This was not only useful to practice critical thinking but also decisive for them to build the skills crucial to a lifelong education.

A comparison of curricula of South Vietnamese universities in the 1950s with those in the 1960s and 1970s indicated some changes. Charles

Falk pointed out in his field study on higher education in the RVN around 1956 that

> The curricula are so distinct and specialized that there is no possibility of sharing professional staffs among various schools—for example, sharing of biology and chemistry professors (and laboratories) by the schools of Science and Medicine and the Higher of Pedagogy. Thus, where professional staffs are short-handed on all sides, there can be no coordination of activities to save laboratory costs and professional manpower.[29]

This situation gradually improved in the 1960s and 1970s. Several examples could be provided pertaining to cooperation and teaching task-sharing among faculties. An outstanding case was the faculties of science in the three universities: the University of Saigon, University of Huế, and University of Cần Thơ. These faculties took charge of teaching the natural sciences, such as physics, chemistry, and mathematics for students in pharmacy and medicine. The curricula of the same disciplines, more or less, were connected and agreed to among higher education institutions. The phenomenon of "suitcase professors" who traveled to teach in many universities across the country was popular in higher education. This, on the one hand, reflected the scarcity of teaching staff in public universities in South Vietnam, yet on the other hand, could promote collaboration in sharing teaching staff among institutions of higher learning.

Noticeably, as observed in curricula, Vietnamese professors rather than foreigners were teaching in almost all subjects of faculties, either general or specialized. This demonstrated a significant progress of Vietnamese higher education in the 1960s and 1970s relative to the early twentieth century. At that time, foreign professors were the majority in the Indochinese University. Until the late 1950s, the number of foreign teachers at the University of Saigon remained sizable; for example, foreign professors amounted to half the total teaching staff (twenty of forty-two) at the Faculty of Letters.[30] The growing number of South Vietnamese professors, more or less, illustrated the effectiveness of teacher training programs in pedagogy in the 1950s and 1960s. Another group who contributed in part to mitigate the domination of foreign professors at South Vietnamese universities were professors who had been trained abroad and returned in the 1960s and 1970s. Other contributing factors included the efforts of educators to use Vietnamese rather than French or English in teaching; and the rapid completion of Vietnamese terminologies in all disciplines that benefited Vietnamese professors in conveying and their students in acquiring knowledge.

From 1967 onward, in most faculties of public universities, duration for the bachelor's programs was four years (except the Faculty of Sciences at the University of Huế before the 1969–1970 school year). This curriculum design was similar to the undergraduate curricula at American colleges, suggesting an adaptation of South Vietnam's higher education from the American model in the late 1960s and early 1970s. General knowledge of all disciplines was taught in the first two years of these faculties and students who studied in different majors could study many similar subjects in the lower division. Specialized majors only started from the third year of bachelor's programs.

Moreover, a recommendation of American advisers "to combine the present Faculty of Letters, Science and some of the functions of the Faculty of Law into a common program combining humanities, social sciences, foreign languages, mathematics, and natural sciences" attracted the attention of RVN educators.[31] Combined courses commenced in the 1969–1970 academic year at some higher education institutions, such as in the applied science section at the University of Huế and the School of Mechanical Engineering at the National Technical Center in Saigon. Commenting on the effectiveness of applying combined courses at the School of Mechanical Engineering, Riley stated in his report that "these curriculum changes would not burden the teaching loads of the Engineering Faculty and will decrease the hours of contact the students have with the labs. They will also encourage the development and use of practical engineering level laboratories."[32]

In addition, academic programs began to take the interest and competence of individual students into account and added elective subjects. Under the newly designed curricula, students not only fulfilled general requirements of class hours (and later credit points) but also had opportunities to enhance their strength in their favorite subjects. The flexibility that allowed students to take courses in other faculties in common subjects, the implementation of combined courses, and the elective subjects, to a great extent, reflected the educational model of the Americans and its influence on higher education in the RVN.

Research and Publishing

Publishing was a new aspect for higher education in the RVN even in the second half of the twentieth century. Recognizing a modern trend in higher education, universities gave more attention to publishing activities from the late 1960s onward. This was meaningful in terms of not only solving the scarcity of educational materials but also supporting universities in fulfilling their duties comprehensively, including teaching and researching.

In general, South Vietnam experienced a conducive condition to publish in the 1960s and 1970s. According to a study of Lê Bá Kông, which was presented at the Conference of the Economic Aspect of Printing, Publishing, and Distributing Books in Manila in November 1974, there were approximately 180 publishing houses in South Vietnam. They were private entities operated on various scales and able to form without the need for governmental permission.[33] Some renowned publishers were Lá Bối, Lửa Thiêng, Khai Trí, Giao Điểm, Sống Mới, Nam Cường, and Hiện Đại. These publishers contributed significantly to facilitate the activities of academic communities by producing textbooks and reference works.

Most textbooks for all studying levels from primary school to university were printed at the Center of Educational Material (Trung tâm học liệu).[34] Aside from administrative offices, other offices, such as the Section of Drafting, Translating, and Printing and a publisher were also units of the center. In 1974, the center was made autonomous in its operations in order for it to cooperate flexibly with other publishers in the United States, England, and France. This cooperation allowed the center to print textbooks at lower cost and distribute them to all provinces in South Vietnam.[35] Given subsidies and assistance from foreign publishers, textbooks published by the center were much cheaper than those of private publishers. Nevertheless, the center did not monopolize publishing for several reasons. First, it alone could not meet the demands of South Vietnamese people. Moreover, other private publishers were able to compete with the center thanks to their personal relationships with educational institutes and the high quality of their publications. The center focused not only on publishing new books but also on republishing many valuable books during the 1960s and 1970s, such as the tenth edition of *Việt Nam Văn học sử yếu* (History of Vietnamese Literary Works) and the ninth edition of *Việt Nam thi văn hợp tuyển* (Selected Vietnamese Verses and Prose) written by Dương Quảng Hàm, and *Việt Nam Sử lược* (A Brief History of Vietnam) and *Nho giáo* (Confucianism) both written by Trần Trọng Kim.[36]

In the business of publishing university textbooks and reference works, Lửa Thiêng was a prominent name. It published approximately

130 books in the five years from 1969 to 1974.[37] Its publications covered all topics rather than focusing on a single field. Its publications included *Dân số học* (Demography), by Lâm Thanh Liêm, published in 1969; *Cơ cấu Việt ngữ* (The Structure of Vietnamese Language), by Trần Ngọc Ninh, published in 1973; *Văn chương Nam bộ và cuộc kháng Pháp 1945-1950* (Southern Vietnamese Literature and the Anti-French Resistance War in the Years 1945-1950), by Nguyễn Văn Sâm, published in 1972; *Lịch sử các học thuyết chính trị* (History of Political Theories), by Nguyễn Ngọc Huy in 1973; and *Triết học và Khoa học* (Philosophy and Science), by Đặng Phùng Quân in 1972.[38]

In addition, other publishing houses contributed to enriching references for students by publishing professors' lectures and research. Many textbooks published and republished during the late 1960s and early 1970s were written by South Vietnamese professors. For instance, *Nông học đại cương* (Introduction to Agronomy), by Tôn Thất Trình, published in 1967; *Phân cực* (Polarization), by Nguyễn Chung Tú, published in 1971; *Điện học* (Electrology), by Võ Đức Diễn, published in 1970; *Lịch sử Triết học Đông phương* (History of Oriental Philosophy), by Nguyễn Đăng Thục, published in 1968; and *Từ điển chữ Nôm* (Dictionary of Nôm Characters), by Nguyễn Quang Xỹ and Vũ Văn Kính, published in 1971.[39]

RVN professors overcame many difficult working conditions that consumed much of their time, such as traveling to teach in multiple locations, to enhance their research activities. Most professors had their own publications during the 1967 to 1975 period. Some of them published frequently, showing their diligence and devotion to research. Phạm Hoàng Hộ was one of the outstanding professors for fulfilling dual tasks, teaching and researching simultaneously. Within eight years (1967-1975), either in the capacity of rector of the University of Cần Thơ (1966-1970) or as faculty at the University of Saigon (1970-1975), he published seven books on biology, some of which are still valuable for students of Vietnamese botany.[40]

Examinations and Accreditation

Examinations were generally stringent if students were to pass their courses and earn credits. In the Faculty of Law at the University of Saigon, there were two examination periods for bachelor's degree students, one held in June and the other in September. Among the seven subjects that first-year students were required to complete were two writing and five oral exams. The writing exams took three hours each. If students passed these exams with a score of at least 10/20, they continued to the oral exams.[41] When students failed in the oral exams, they had the opportunity to retake them. However, if they failed both times, they needed to take all of the exams again, both writing and oral. Fourth-year students, who had to complete thirteen subjects, took two rounds of oral exams. The final score, which determined whether students passed or failed, was based on an average score of tests in the same oral round. Thus students whose scores of one or more than one subject were lower than 10/20 could still pass oral exams if their total score was 10/20 or higher. In oral exams of the second semester, students who failed in these exams were allowed to take them again in the first semester of the next academic year. However, they had only one opportunity to do so. If they did not succeed the second time, they were required to take exams for all subjects again, regardless how high their score in the first round of oral exams.[42]

Nguyễn Văn Cung and Nguyễn Văn Thắng, two former students at the Faculty of Law of the University of Saigon before 1975, stated that the exams organized by the Faculty of Law were strict. Statistics indicated how strict the examinations were. In 1970, thirteen thousand students enrolled in the bachelor's programs at this faculty. Four years later, in 1974, only 715 graduated.[43] On the one hand, the strictness of examinations contributed to training good students given the massive efforts required to pass each exam. On the other, it might be argued that examinations could not be a comprehensive tool to evaluate the competence of a student. Bad results in the exams were not definitive proof that the individuals would not be successful professionals.

In the Faculty of Agriculture at the University of Cần Thơ, students also had to take part in theoretical and practical sections as well as practical training at farms. If they were absent in 1/10 class hours per subject, they would not be allowed to take the final exams that year.[44] In the last year, students at this faculty presented their theses to a committee. This was a decisive element in their graduation. If the committees did not pass their theses, students had three months to prepare and represent. Without the agreement of the committee, students could not receive their certificates.[45] Among the faculties of the University of Cần Thơ, the Faculty of Agriculture was equipped sufficiently. The students of this faculty had better study conditions for their practice sections, including the use of laboratories and the facilities during their internships. Requirements for these students were therefore higher and stricter than for those in other faculties.

THE VIETNAM WAR SEEN FROM THE EDUCATION FIELD

In the twentieth century, Vietnamese people endured severe living conditions attributable to two protracted wars, the First Indochina War (1945–1954) and the Second Indochina War (1954–1975). War was catastrophic for generations of Vietnamese. At the same time, the way Vietnamese people tackled disastrous conditions revealed their resourcefulness and flexibility in approaching opportunities to develop.

Amid a seemingly endless war, Vietnamese continued to build their nation and their society. With the assistance of international parties, especially the United States and its Western allies, South Vietnamese yearned for and embarked on numerous ambitious civil projects that transcended the hostilities. The efforts of South Vietnamese educators and international experts, particularly from the United States, in expanding and modernizing higher education during the Second Republic period (1967–1975) tells another story about South Vietnam never told in scholarship preoccupied with the military struggle. In this context, military allies unintentionally became educational allies, and the RVN found assistance from external forces to share the burden of training its young generation. This is demonstrated in the cooperation funded by the US Agency for International Development (USAID) among American, South Vietnamese institutions, and American allies' organizations.

In the 1960s and 1970s, USAID focused on several critical fields of higher education in the RVN, including engineering, medical and dental education, and agriculture. The responsibility for assistance in each of these fields was assigned to a specific American institution. The University of Missouri–Rolla took the task of advancing engineering; the American Medical Association was responsible for developing the requirements of medical and dental education; and the University of Florida was entrusted with agricultural education. These institutions were aided in their tasks by educators from US allies and by the efforts of South Vietnamese educators to develop international connections abroad. This presented a multiparty engagement in the RVN's higher education system in the 1960s and 1970s, as Robert Russell LaFollette, the USAID Higher Education Adviser, explained the concept of "Many Flags" in advancing higher education in South Vietnam:

> New Zealand was helping to finance a new Science Building at Thu Duc and Canada was assisting in the expansion of the Faculty of Medicine at Hue, while West Germany was supplying the Hue Faculty of Medicine with

materials and two professors, and France was involved in the recruitment of faculty at both Saigon and Hue.[46]

The assembly of international institutions in the development of South Vietnam's higher education was even more meaningful, considering that this occurred in the distressed circumstances of war. The efforts of the RVN authorities in this area could be interpreted in many ways. It could be explained by the American pressure that pushed the RVN to reform and upgrade its education as a condition for continued American aid. Education could be seen as a political front in which the RVN could outperform the Democratic Republic of Vietnam in North Vietnam.

Nevertheless, the sincere aspirations of South Vietnamese, American, and other foreign experts in developing higher education in South Vietnam need to be taken into account. The tragedy of war could not defeat the will of South Vietnamese educators to build an advanced higher education system. This was demonstrated in the efforts of South Vietnamese professors in contacting many sources and asking for assistance from international institutions and organizations. One example is the Faculty of Medicine at the University of Huế: Rector Cao Văn Luận paid repeated visits to the offices of the USAID/Saigon, the French Embassy, and the German Embassy to seek assistance to establish the faculty. He did not receive any official assurances but did not give up until eventually the German Embassy through the University of Freiburg provided assistance.[47] Foreign support in this case was entirely due to the efforts of Rector Cao Văn Luận.

To be sure, from Washington's perspective, US educational assistance in South Vietnam served a political purpose. Nevertheless, numerous American organizations and agencies worked in South Vietnam during the war without considering the political element as a premise or the primary purpose for their operations. The Southeast Asian Development Advisory Group (SEADAG) is an example:

> SEADAG was created under the sponsorship of AID to bring together persons interested in Southeast Asia development from all professions without regard to their political views. Professional participants in SEADAG in no way implies a political commitment to any particular policy of the United States government. Such commitments are purely personal. SEADAG as an organization and the Asia Society as host of the meetings cannot be employed in any way directly or indirectly to demonstrate either approval or disapproval of United States policy in Vietnam.[48]

Politics is not the sole factor and occasionally not the decisive factor that drives and maintains relations among countries. For the American experts and other foreigners who worked in South Vietnam during the war, much more than politics was involved. An example is Lee Sherman Dreyfus, the former chancellor of the University of Wisconsin-Stevens Point, who was heavily involved in South Vietnam's educational development projects. In an interview with Thomas Reich in the early 2000s, when he was asked whether it was "realistic to expect a continued American influence in education once the military is removed," and whether he thought "the Vietnamese will have a reaction or resentment against us and throw us out without our military," Dreyfus did not hesitate to answer:

> I think it is a very real possibility, no question whether we ought to be doing anything on the basis of what many have projected later. I guess it is my own personal philosophy in education that as long as they are educators there, as long as they asked for certain help, which we are capable for providing them, and as long as we are in a position to provide, we ought to do it.[49]

Dreyfus expressed his opinion, but it was definitely not the only example of the sincere intention of international educators and experts in South Vietnam at the time. The considerable contributions of German professors at the University of Huế in particular and the humanitarian activities of West Germany during the Vietnam War were further evidence of a genuine desire of people to help others for the humanitarian purposes of education development. As mentioned, Western Germany sent several German professors to Huế in 1961 following the efforts by Rector Cao Văn Luận of the University of Huế. The names of those German professors—Horst Gunther Krainick, Erich Wulff, Kaufmann, Discher, Perings, and Holterscheidt among them—remain etched in the memory of former students who studied at the University of Huế.[50] Four professors—Krainick and his wife, Discher, and Alter Koster—were seized by communist forces during the Tết Offensive in 1968 and later found buried in a shallow pit.[51] The danger of the war, which they could have known or imagined before departing to South Vietnam, did not deter them. The presence of German professors in Huế at that time was strong evidence of their aspirations: to help in education and to help people in advancing their lives based on a good education. These aspirations were stronger than the fear of the danger they probably would face.

Further, after the end of the war, Professor Wulff returned to Vietnam to visit his Vietnamese friends in 1978.[52] If people had served in a country only from a sense of duty or other political reasons, after the war ended with the collapse of the RVN, they would have had no reason to go back there, a place that could remind them of sorrow images. Professor Wulff's visits to Vietnam in 1978 and later in 2008 underscored the humanitarian goals of international educators.[53]

This analysis of academic elements in the major three public universities in the RVN indicates how far they had progressed on the path of developing from scratch a modern higher education system when the events of 1975 befell them. Barely two decades from inextricable dependence on France from teaching staff to instructional language and curriculum, South Vietnamese universities were rapidly growing on their own in the late 1960s and early 1970s. In working to build a self-sufficient republic, they equipped their citizens with specific capabilities to take their country forward with modern concepts and technologies. Public universities promoted such a paradigm by being stricter in giving admissions to candidates in fields considered critical to the long-term development of the nation. The high dropout rates from year to year in South Vietnamese universities illustrated how much administrators and educators cared about the quality of their graduates and their seriousness in trying to approach universal standards in a higher education system.

Within a liberal intellectual culture, the passion of scholars and researchers for advancing higher education created a fertile environment for the remarkable growth of publishing activities associated with academic programs. Educational institutions matured in line with their publishing culture, an experience observed in more advanced countries such as Germany and the United States. Anyone doubting the progress of South Vietnam's universities and the competence of its educators should consider the huge number of valuable works written, translated, and published by Republican educators during their short tenure in the 1960s and 1970s.

To some extent, these features of the RVN's public universities reflected the larger aspirational nature of the Republic of Vietnam in its last years. Education was the key driver, tasked with forming "future" citizens and constructing the image and reality of the Republic of Vietnam as a modern developing nation. The open mind of Republican professors and administrators in emulating international models appropriate to their needs was critical to their achievements. The regime's collapse in 1975 should not be a basis for denying the RVN's many attempts and successes in the education field.

NOTES

1. As might be expected of any school system in a developing country, many intractable problems existed in South Vietnamese universities, such as their elitist character; the perennial inadequacy of instructors, programs, funding, and facilities; the culture of rote learning; and even occasional corruption scandals involving officials or instructors. With a vibrant civil society and with university autonomy (*tự trị đại học*) being granted in the 1967 constitution, student protests were also common for political as well as other causes. University campuses in fact became the battleground as both the government and underground communist agitators competed to rally students to their side. For personal accounts of communist activities in universities and their assassination of RVN Minister of Education Lê Minh Trí in 1969, see Hoàng Hà et al., *Trui Rèn Trong Lửa Đỏ*, esp. 110. For Saigonese youth's political activities, see Stur, *Saigon at War*, esp. chapter 3. These issues are beyond the scope of this chapter, which does not claim to provide a comprehensive study of higher education in the RVN.

2. Exceptions are Reich, "Higher Education in Vietnam"; Hoàng, "Giáo dục Đại học"; Trần, "Chương trình Giáo dục"; Dror, *Making Two Vietnams*; Vu and Fear, *Republic of Vietnam*.

3. Dror, *Making Two Vietnams*; Gadkar-Wilcox, "Existentialism and Intellectual Culture."

4. "Information on Education in Vietnam," December 4, 1959, File 1780839028, The Vietnam Center and Sam Johnson Archive, Texas Tech University [VCA].

5. "Information on Education in Vietnam," 6, VCA.

6. Đào Thị Diến, "Sự ra đời của Đại học Đông Dương qua tài liệu lưu trữ," https://vnu.edu.vn/btdhqghn/?C1654/N19219/Su-ra-doi-cua-dai-hoc-dong-Duong-qua-tai-lieu-luu-tru.htm (accessed April 5, 2017).

7. Data from "Decade of Expansion for Higher Education in Vietnam," File 2322018001, April 1971, VCA.

8. According to Vietnam's annual statistics, the exchange rate was roughly $1 to VND 35 in 1954, and VND 35,350 in 1960. See Bộ Kinh tế Quốc gia, *Việt Nam niên giám thống kê, quyển thứ năm, 1954–1955*, 219; Bộ Kinh tế Quốc gia, *Việt Nam niên giám thống kê, quyển thứ chín, 1960–1961*, 271. See also "Education in the Republic of Vietnam," 211.

9. In 1968, the exchange rate was $1 to VND 80. Nha Tổng giám đốc Kế hoạch, Phủ Thủ tướng, *Niên giám thống kê Việt Nam 1967–1968*, 206.

10. "Education in South Vietnam," September 1, 1968, File 0720510017, VCA.

11. "Education in the Republic of Vietnam," 214, VCA.

12. "Education in the Republic of Vietnam," 214, VCA.

13. Khánh Uyên, "Viện Đại học Sài Gòn và các trường trực thuộc," *Tạp chí Nghiên cứu và Phát triển*, no. 7–8 (2014): 110–123, 122.

14. O. W. Hascall, "The Baccalaureate Examination in the Republic of Vietnam," July 1972, File 2391104003, Part A, 4–5, VCA.

15. Hascall, "The Baccalaureate Examination," 11, 14, VCA.

16. Khánh Uyên, "Viện Đại học Sài Gòn," 112.

17. "Hồ sơ về tổ chức bộ máy và nhân sự của Bộ giáo dục năm 1968–1974," Hồ sơ số

7826, Phông Phủ Tổng thống Đệ nhị Cộng hoà (1967–1975), National Archives II, Hồ Chí Minh City, Vietnam [VNA II].

18. Khánh Uyên, "Viện Đại học Sài Gòn," 115.
19. Khánh Uyên, "Viện Đại học Sài Gòn," 117.
20. Khánh Uyên, "Viện Đại học Sài Gòn," 119.
21. Data from Phòng Tâm lý và hướng nghiệp Đắc Lộ's *Chỉ nam giáo dục*, cited in Phạm Thị Phương, *Lịch sử hình thành*, 87–88.
22. Cited in Phạm Thị Phương, *Lịch sử hình thành*, 101–102. Although this school was inaugurated at the same time with the University of Cần Thơ, it took two more years for it to build necessary equipment and infrastructure and the first entrance exams did not take place until 1968.
23. Cited in Phạm Thị Phương, *Lịch sử hình thành*, 91–97.
24. Lý Ngọc Lương, "Viện Đại học Cần Thơ," 27.
25. Data from the Ministry of Education's *The Postwar Development Group*, cited in Nguyen Anh Tuan, *South Vietnam Trial and Experience*, 373.
26. Lê Xuân Khoa, "Đại học miền Nam trước 1975, hồi tưởng và nhận định," in Ngô Bảo Châu et al., *Kỷ yếu Đại học Humboldt*, 545.
27. Lý Ngọc Lương, "Viện Đại học Cần Thơ," 17–18.
28. Lê Xuân Khoa, "Đại học miền Nam trước 1975," 545.
29. Charles Falk, *Higher Education in Vietnam*, cited in Nguyễn Văn Thuỳ, "Proposal for a Model Core Curriculum," 85.
30. "Ban Giảng Huấn," *Dòng Việt*, no. 6 (1999): 5–6.
31. "Public Universities of the Republic of Vietnam," April 1967, File 0720510011, 17, VCA.
32. Riley, "Report on the School of Mechanical Engineering," 27.
33. Quoted in Phạm Phú Minh, "Công việc xuất bản."
34. Trần, "Chương trình Giáo dục," 201.
35. Trần, "Chương trình Giáo dục," 202.
36. Trần, "Chương trình Giáo dục," 234.
37. Trần, "Chương trình Giáo dục," 238.
38. Trần, "Chương trình Giáo dục," 238–239.
39. Hoàng, "Giáo dục Đại học," 87.
40. Ngô Thế Vinh, "Những năm ảo vọng: Giáo sư Phạm Hoàng Hộ và bộ sách *Cây cỏ Việt Nam*"
41. Nguyễn Văn Cung and Nguyễn Văn Thắng, "Giới thiệu lịch sử."
42. Nguyễn Văn Cung and Nguyễn Văn Thắng, "Giới thiệu lịch sử."
43. Nguyễn Văn Cung and Nguyễn Văn Thắng, "Giới thiệu lịch sử."
44. Data from Phòng Tâm lý và hướng nghiệp Đắc Lộ's *Chỉ nam giáo dục*, cited in Phạm Thị Phương, *Lịch sử hình thành*, 105.
45. Phạm Thị Phương, *Lịch sử hình thành*, 105.
46. Reich, *Higher Education in Vietnam*, 178.
47. Cao, *Bên giòng lịch sử*, 292.
48. "Memo to SEADAG Members from Kenneth Young, Michael Moerman, Gayl D. Ness, Robert O. Tilman," April 7, 1967, File 0720619006, VCA.
49. "Memo to SEADAG Members," 444, VCA.
50. Hoàng Phủ Ngọc Phan, "Nhớ về các vị giáo sư người Đức ở Đại học Y Khoa Huế"

[Remembering the German professors at Huế Medical School], May 5, 2012, https://sachhiem.net/NDX/NDX024.php.

51. Karnow, *Vietnam*, 544. That the Germans were taken away from their residence by communist soldiers was a fact, but whether they were in fact executed is disputed. Alje Vennema, a Dutch medical professional who was in Huế during the Tết Offensive and who knew the Germans personally, claimed that they were "shot in the back of the neck and head at close range, their faces partly blown away." See Vennema, *Viet Cong Massacre at Hue*, 152. According to the same source, the German Embassy in Saigon announced in May 1968 that the Germans had been executed. Tôn Thất Sang, a medical student of the German doctors who claimed to have witnessed the excavation of their corpses from the grave also described that they had been executed. See Tôn Thất Sang, "Đi nhận xác thầy" [Identifying and receiving my professors' bodies], reposted on http://www.buctranhvancau.com/new-blog/2018/3/18/i-nhn-xc-thy-tn-tht-sang. Hoàng Phủ Ngọc Phan, another former medical student of University of Huế who had earlier joined the underground communist network claimed that a later investigation by the communist command showed that the doctors had been killed in the crossfire between their captors and gunfire from an American helicopter. See Hoàng Phủ Ngọc Phan, "Nhớ về các vị giáo sư."

52. Hoàng Phủ Ngọc Phan, "Nhớ về các vị giáo sư."

53. Hoàng Phủ Ngọc Phan, "Nhớ về các vị giáo sư."

CHAPTER 6

Buddhist Social Work in the Vietnam War

Thích Nhất Hạnh and the School of Youth for Social Service

Adrienne Minh-Châu Lê

On a warm evening in January 1964, a young Buddhist monk named Thích Nhất Hạnh sat with a group of students at Trúc Lâm Temple in Saigon. Having just returned to Vietnam after nearly three years overseas, he listened to their sad accounts of recent events. Despite mass demonstrations against the war, government and Buddhist leaders were not taking steps toward peace. "Vietnamese Buddhism, a thousand years old, was not offering a way out of the noose that had strangled our society for twenty years," the monk lamented. He sat with the students late into the night as they shared their hopes and fears, urging them to keep their faith alive. They discussed plans for their own social movement—one that would take a decisive stance against the war while addressing the immediate needs and suffering of the Vietnamese people. "Our numbers might be small," Nhất Hạnh told them, "but our hearts are strong."[1]

The Buddhist movement was the largest and most well-organized social movement in South Vietnam during the Republican era.[2] Monks, nuns, and students shook the foundation of the nascent Republic with persistent demands for civil liberties, representative government, and an end to the war.[3] Yet beyond the mass urban protests that captured global headlines, historians understand little about the underpinnings of this movement. Scholars have yet to explore the many beliefs and motivations of its leaders and participants, and how they sought to transform Vietnamese society in their everyday lives. Indeed, it would be an oversimplification to treat "the Buddhists" of South Vietnam as a whole. A full understanding of the Buddhist movement would require many studies on the diverse voices and personalities active during the war as well as early twentieth-century efforts to revive Vietnam's "national-cultural religion" in the face of colonialism and modernization.[4] Because only one book-length monograph and a handful of articles on the topic have been published, English-language scholars have only begun to sketch an outline of the Buddhist movement.[5]

Joining efforts to illuminate the history of South Vietnamese civil society and the Buddhist movement, this chapter examines the religious ideology and social work of Buddhist youth in the Republican era. It deals specifically with the philosophy and activities of the School of Youth for Social Service (SYSS), or Trường Thanh Niên Phụng Sự Xã Hội, the organization founded by Thích Nhất Hạnh and his disciples. Active from 1964 until 1975, the SYSS trained college-age students to lead rural development and emergency relief projects throughout central and southern Vietnam. Standing at the intersection of the twentieth-century Buddhist revival and the 1960s antiwar movement, SYSS organizers sought to build their nation through daily work toward education, economic development, peace, and reconciliation.

The SYSS was a facet of the Buddhist movement more concerned with rural aid and development than urban protest. It represents a previously unrecognized form of rural development in the Republic of Vietnam (RVN)—one that was neither state led nor directed by a foreign power. Further, the organization's refusal to pledge allegiance to either side— North or South, communist or anticommunist—challenges rigid, binary interpretations of the Vietnam War. The resolve of SYSS students to remain politically nonaligned shows how Buddhist youth rejected the uncompromising anticommunist ideology that government leaders tried to impose on them. Instead, they called for a ceasefire and negotiated settlement to Vietnam's civil conflict.

The first part of this discussion relies on Nhất Hạnh's writings from the 1950s and 1960s to outline the concept of socially engaged Buddhism, which was the ideological foundation of the SYSS. It also recounts some of Nhất Hạnh's struggles with conservative Buddhist leaders and the South Vietnamese and US governments. The second part explores the organizational practices of the SYSS and the violence endured by its students and staff, as pacifists who remained nonaligned in an ideological war. It is based on interviews with seven former SYSS students as well as written accounts from the time. Students witnessed the killing and kidnapping of dozens of their peers; one student ultimately self-immolated to shake the conscience of her fellow Vietnamese and inspire steps toward peace. These Buddhist youth not only fulfilled Nhất Hạnh's vision of socially engaged Buddhism—they also went beyond, devising their own ways to voice opposition to war and sow seeds for the future they envisioned.

ENGAGED BUDDHISM FOR THE MODERN ERA

Thích Nhất Hạnh emerged in the 1950s as one of the most outspoken advocates for a reformed Buddhism that could serve, materially and spiritually, a society being destroyed by war. His philosophy of engaged Buddhism, first introduced in a series of newspaper articles in 1954, was influenced by the Buddhist revival movement that began around the time of his birth.[6] Reformers of the 1930s believed Buddhism could help to preserve the integrity of Vietnamese society and culture in the face of colonialism and modernization; they advocated social action based on the idea of Buddhism for this world (*nhân gian Phật Giáo*).[7] The revival movement established and restored thousands of Buddhist schools, temples, publications, and lay associations across the country. Many societally engaged monastics arose from this era, including Nhất Hạnh and others who led the Buddhist antiwar movement.

Born as Nguyễn Xuân Bảo in 1926, Thích Nhất Hạnh became a novice monk at age sixteen at Từ Hiếu Temple in Huế.[8] His early training consisted of a mixture of Mahayana and Theravada traditions with a focus on mindfulness and *gathas*, or short verses recited silently as part of meditation. Unsatisfied with the curriculum in Huế, in 1949 Nhất Hạnh left for Saigon to pursue studies in science, literature, and foreign languages.[9] Throughout the 1950s, he traveled betwwen Saigon and Đà Lạt, teaching Buddhist history and Vietnamese literature to novice monks. He earned a bachelor's degree in French and Vietnamese literature from Saigon University—and became a prolific writer and editor-in-chief of *Phật Giáo Việt Nam* (Vietnamese Buddhism), the official journal of the Vietnamese General Buddhist Association.[10] In 1961, he left the country to study and teach at Princeton and Columbia Universities before returning to found Vạn Hạnh University (VHU), or Viện Đại Học Vạn Hạnh, and the School of Youth for Social Service.[11] In 1966, he left Vietnam again on an invitation to teach at Cornell University, taking that opportunity to conduct a peace tour in the United States and Europe, which led to his exile by the South Vietnamese government.[12] Expecting to be gone for only a few months, Nhất Hạnh would not return to his homeland for nearly forty years.

Nhất Hạnh's early writings reveal the mind of an ambitious, idealistic young monk who felt constrained by conservative institutions. In the 1950s, he wrote under at least eight pseudonyms, publishing short stories, folk poetry, literary commentary, and essays on Buddhist history and ethics. Most significantly, he advocated a turn to socially engaged Buddhism, "the kind of Buddhism that responds to what is happening in the here and the now."[13] To remain relevant, he believed, Buddhist leaders and institutions had to take the lead in improving the material conditions of people's lives. Nhất Hạnh repeatedly criticized the Buddhist hierarchy for focusing on traditional ceremonies while neglecting the urgent needs of their war-torn society. "A sermon in a suffering community means nothing," he declared. "The real sermon needed is action, the kind of action that can realistically stop the suffering being endured."[14] He also called for the "true and total unification of Vietnamese Buddhism," the creation of one national organization that could help bring together a divided country.[15] "The war has destroyed trust, hope, and all the constructive efforts of the past," he wrote. "Religion is the only institution left that can inspire unity and social responsibility. We must use the resources of our spiritual traditions to bring about change."[16] Nhất Hạnh's persistent and bold criticisms of the General Buddhist Association's leadership eventually led to his ousting as editor-in-chief of their journal in 1959. This event deeply affected the young monk because it proved that he could not rely on existing Buddhist institutions to do what he believed was necessary for peace and reconciliation in Vietnam.

Nhất Hạnh was certainly not the only Buddhist who saw the potential for religion to shape the future of his country. Several of his contemporaries also articulated and carried out their own ideas on how Buddhism should contribute to a modern Vietnamese nation. Thích Trí Quang became the most politicized—and most controversial—Buddhist figure as the leader of the urban protest movements of the 1963 to 1966 period.[17] The rector of Vạn Hạnh University, Thích Minh Châu, believed that Buddhist institutions ought to stay out of politics and pushed instead for education and intellectual debate as the main avenue for Buddhist influence on modern society.[18] Among his monastic peers, Thích Nhất Hạnh was the most focused on rural development in South Vietnam and antiwar activism on the global stage.

Believing that the United States was the main driving force behind the war, Nhất Hạnh left Vietnam to conduct a peace tour in 1966.

Arriving at the invitation of Cornell University and the Fellowship of Reconciliation, a US-based pacifist organization, Nhất Hạnh met with several US senators, seventeen congressmen, and Dr. Martin Luther King Jr., urging them to come out against the war in Vietnam.[19] He also had a thirty-three-minute meeting with US Secretary of Defense Robert McNamara, which he optimistically described as "a real dialogue."[20] On June 1, 1966, Nhất Hạnh published a statement from Washington, DC, that laid out five steps the United States should take to bring a diplomatic end to the Vietnam War, including "a clear statement by the US of its desire to help the Vietnamese people to have a government truly responsive to Vietnamese aspirations," "a cessation of the bombing, north and south," and the gradual withdrawal of US troops.[21] The following year, he published *Vietnam: Lotus in a Sea of Fire*—a book that detailed the experiences of Vietnamese people in the war and what he saw as the war's flawed moral logic. Nhất Hạnh's outspokenness against the war alarmed the US government, which was seeking Buddhist allies for its anticommunist agenda in Asia.

The month after Nhất Hạnh announced his peace proposal from Washington, a representative of a CIA proprietary called the Asia Foundation paid a visit to the School of Youth for Social Service.[22] The representative spoke with SYSS Director Thích Thanh Văn and offered a grant of $100,000 on one condition: he would have to sign and publish a statement declaring the school had no connection with its founder, Thích Nhất Hạnh.[23] A similar offer was made around this time to the leadership of Vạn Hạnh University. The timing of these offers, following on the heels of Nhất Hạnh's peace proposal, suggest that the US government sought to discredit his antiwar efforts by enticing other Vietnamese Buddhists to publicly renounce him.

The leadership of the SYSS, remaining loyal to their teacher and founder, never signed the document from the Asia Foundation.[24] Conversely, Vạn Hạnh University accepted the offer with strings attached. In the university's September 1967 newsletter, a statement by the rector, Thích Minh Châu, reads, "On page 58 of *Vietnam: Lotus in a Sea of Fire* by Thich Nhat Hanh, there is a reference to the 'School of Youth for Social Service of Van Hanh University.' I wish to point out that all connections between that school and Van Hanh University were severed in 1965, and that . . . Thich Nhat Hanh no longer serves this University as an adviser."[25] The very next issue of the newsletter features a front-page article about the inauguration of the new university library made possible by a donation of "over one million five hundred thousand" Vietnamese đồng from the Asia Foundation.[26] The foundation continued to support the university at least through November 1969, awarding large grants toward its printing press, faculty training program, salaries, library furnishings, auditorium, conference travel, and its new Center of Sciences and Technology.[27] Other Buddhist leaders also disassociated with Nhất Hạnh and the SYSS during and after his US peace tour. In June 1966, the press secretary for the Vietnamese Embassy in London wrote to *The Guardian* that

> the Secretary General of the Buddhist Institute for Secular Studies, the Venerable Thich Huyen Quang, issued a communique stating that any views expressed by the Venerable Thich Nhat Hanh were entirely his own and did not reflect the position of either the Institute in particular or of the Vietnamese Buddhists in general.[28]

It is reasonable to conclude that these public disavowals of Nhất Hạnh were a reaction to his antiwar activism. It was a matter of self-preservation to stay out of antiwar politics in South Vietnam given those who spoke out were being threatened, jailed, or otherwise silenced. Buddhist protestors clashed with the government several times between 1963 and 1966, resulting in dozens of deaths and arrests by the thousands in Huế, Đà Nẵng, and Saigon. By the end of 1963, the RVN held more than seventy-five thousand political prisoners, many of whom were jailed for taking part in the Buddhist movement.[29] Mass arrests of Buddhists continued at least through the summer of 1966. According to a document obtained by the Unified Buddhist Church, in 1968 Saigon's Chí Hòa Prison held a total of 1,870 prisoners—1,665 of whom were labeled as Buddhists and only fifty as communists.[30] Political activities led by Buddhists were fiercely suppressed through the end of the war.

Even without the support of fellow Buddhist leaders, and facing violent suppression from the government, Nhất Hạnh was determined to mobilize religious sentiments to serve the Vietnamese people. "Buddhism has much to contribute to this work, but we cannot wait for the religious hierarchy to act," he reflected in his journal. "They are reluctant to bring about change, and they've repeatedly rejected our efforts to create an engaged Buddhism. Our proposals lie in unopened folders on their desks, gathering dust."[31] Unable to spark social engagement and institutional reform among high-ranking monks, Nhất Hạnh turned to the community that had formed around him—and especially to Buddhist youth—as agents who would revive their religion for the modern age.

In 1965 and 1966, Nhất Hạnh published a series of seven articles titled "Speaking to Youth" (Nói Với Tuổi Hai Mươi), in which he discusses themes like love, loneliness, ideals, education, religion, and the state of their country. The series is poetic, full of reflections and lessons for life, and includes a call to action: "We have to patiently build a revolutionary foundation. We must start building from the ground up." The older generation was stuck in its ways; it was up to young people "to demand more, to create a new outlook and a new system for yourselves. You must stand up so the rest of us can follow your lead."[32] The next generation, discontent with the status quo, thirsty for new solutions, and full of youthful energy, would be the key to creating the future Nhất Hạnh imagined. That future began in the countryside.

"In recent years, I have put away some of my books on Buddhism, philosophy, and religion to read about community development, farm cooperatives, raising chickens and ducks," Nhất Hạnh wrote in early 1966. "I see that I need to contribute to the work of developing the countryside."[33] The bookish monk became concerned with farming and rural development, believing that only with a stable agricultural economy would Vietnam be able to stand on its own, independent from foreign powers. In his words, "Agricultural progress cannot be separated from issues of health care, education, and self-governance."[34] Given that nearly every village had a small temple with a resident monk, he felt that Buddhism could help bring about this development. "If every monk could be convinced to work with us to improve rural life, the movement would succeed in short time."[35] On returning from the United States in January 1964, Nhất Hạnh met with a core group of his students and began several experimental development projects they referred to as "self-help villages" (làng tự nguyện).[36]

In these villages, trained volunteers lived among the people, learned about their needs, and mobilized the community to improve its conditions. Volunteers first set up "demonstration projects" to spark the interest of the locals—such as planting straw mushrooms, raising chickens, or holding literacy classes for the children. Once the residents saw the value of these activities, they started their own initiatives to generate income for their families or improve community life.[37] Nhất Hạnh wrote in his journal about how this process unfolded in the first self-help village. The volunteers began by holding classes for the children under a big tree, teaching them to read and sing. After seeing how eager the children were to join, a man offered his house as a classroom. When the class grew too large for the man's house, residents pooled their resources—each family donating bamboo, wood, bricks, or labor—to construct a four-room community building to serve as the village school and medical clinic.[38] This self-powered uplift was core to Nhất Hạnh's vision for societal transformation. All that was needed was the existing local resources and a few dedicated organizers. By February 1964, Nhất Hạnh and his team had established four self-help villages—two in the south, in Cầu Kinh and Thảo Điền, and two in central Vietnam, in Khánh Hòa and Thừa Thiên.[39] With these models in place, they were ready to recruit more students and grow into an official organization, building on Nhất Hạnh's vision of channeling the energy and ideals of Buddhist youth.

BUDDHIST YOUTH AT THE HELM: THE SCHOOL OF YOUTH FOR SOCIAL SERVICE

The School of Youth for Social Service was established in the fall of 1964 under the auspices of Vạn Hạnh Buddhist University in Saigon. Its mission was to recruit and train college-age students to lead rural development projects in four key issue areas: childhood education, health, household economics, and community organization.[40] Nhất Hạnh explained that the goal was for SYSS students to be "equally knowledgeable about social concerns and religious teaching" and to "understand effective methods to combat poverty, disease, ignorance, and misunderstanding."[41] They would be pacifist agents in a war-torn society, helping people wherever they went without regard for political loyalties.

Nhất Hạnh traveled through Saigon and Huế in 1964, speaking at temples and advertising in newspapers to recruit students for the school.[42] The inaugural class of two hundred, made up of novice monks and nuns as well as laypeople, was selected from a pool of more than five hundred applicants.[43] The SYSS program consisted of two years of coursework with a one-month training period in between, followed by service assignments in villages throughout the south. As Nhất Hạnh had envisioned, they relied on Buddhist temples as local contacts. Teams of three or four students would stay and work for up to two years on each assignment before moving on.[44] The school prioritized recruitment of students from the countryside, believing they could better connect with rural residents and understand their needs.[45] In some cases, SYSS graduates returned to and served their home villages.[46]

Scholars might be eager to compare the development projects of the SYSS with those of the South Vietnamese government. Of course, the scale and reach of RVN agricultural programs dwarf those of the SYSS.

A few hundred volunteers could not possibly compete with multi-million-dollar programs backed by the South Vietnamese and US governments.[47] This chapter highlights not the numerical impact of SYSS programs—as measured in acres planted, livestock raised, or households uplifted—but instead the hopes and principles of Buddhist youth who resolved to risk death to improve the lives of their fellow countrymen, and who refused to take sides in the war. On a theoretical level, some similarities between Nhất Hạnh's self-help village model and the personalist model of direct democracy envisioned by the architects of the Strategic Hamlet Campaign are evident.[48] Both relied on local people as the basis of organization, trusting residents to make and carry out their own decisions. Both called for individual dedication and volunteerism for the common good. Both functioned on the belief that the central government was not necessary to democratic self-rule.

Yet the overwhelming fact remains that the government was first and foremost concerned with fighting and winning the war, and their approaches to rural development reflected this priority. Under Ngô Đình Diệm, the programs that were meant to "persuade rural residents that they should cast their lot with the government," were also counterinsurgency efforts that called for mandatory mass resettlement, the weeding out of suspected communists, and the construction of physical fortifications to guard against enemy infiltration.[49] Rural Development cadres went to their assignments armed and with military support.[50] According to the former director of cabinet for the Ministry of Land Reform and Agricultural Development, many personnel were trained to "defuse, deflect, derail, dismantle, demolish, defeat, and destroy communist tactics and strategies in the countryside."[51] SYSS students had no such political aims or training, and no armed protection. They relied solely on the trust of local people and Buddhist temples as they went about their small-scale, day-to-day work.

Following the self-help village model, SYSS students began by teaching young children how to read and sing folk songs while getting to know their families. Only if they gained the trust of the locals, when the villagers had accepted them as family, would they expand to other kinds of work—such as providing basic medical care, teaching handicraft and farming techniques, digging wells, organizing cultural events, and constructing schools, houses, and bridges. They often started their workdays at four o'clock in the morning.[52] Nhất Hạnh emphasized that their service was not charity; SYSS organizers shared responsibility with residents to improve their living standards.[53] Perhaps being mistaken for government workers, students were frequently asked how much they were paid and would answer that their motivations were not monetary but religious. As one student explained to a local resident, "We are doing volunteer work, for merit, Uncle. Our teacher says that doing good works to help our friends in the village builds merit, just like doing work in the temple."[54] Using connections with local temples and describing their work through the culturally embedded concept of merit made it easier for people to believe that SYSS efforts reflected genuine care rather than a desire for political or financial gain. Over time, many students came to be treated as sons and daughters, nieces and nephews, of the people with whom they lived and worked.

The work of the SYSS was carried out as the war raged on. Students and teachers organized relief missions, delivering truckloads of food, medicine, and clothing to areas devastated by floods and intense fighting. They helped console survivors and rebuilt some villages multiple times after repeated bombings.[55] The village of Trà Lộc in Quảng Trị province was bombed three times between 1966 and 1967 and each time SYSS volunteers helped comfort families and rebuild their school, homes, and medical center.[56] One former student recalls that when Trà Lộc was evacuated in 1972, she and her team fled with its residents to Đà Nẵng, where they organized aid for the displaced.[57] During the Tết Offensive in 1968, the SYSS campus itself sheltered thousands of refugees from the surrounding area. The school's director, Thích Thanh Văn, went out and spoke with military commanders on both sides to assure them that only unarmed civilians were being housed at the school and to ask them not to bomb the campus.[58]

Although the SYSS did not enjoy the support of the South Vietnamese government or other leaders of the Unified Buddhist Church, Nhất Hạnh was confident in their ability to carry on. "The staff is made up of able young people who are eager to get started," he wrote in his journal. "We have no money, but we have a plan, goodwill, and lots of energy."[59] This optimistic sentiment is echoed by those who enrolled in the school. Phạm Viết Nghiệm remembers feeling hopeless about his future before joining the SYSS: "In Vietnam we refer to each other as 'brother,' but in this war we were going out and killing each other. I didn't know which way to go." After reading a newspaper article about the opening of the SYSS, Nghiệm applied and was admitted into the inaugural class. "I liked the idea of the path of social service. I wanted that future for our society," Nghiệm said in a 2019 interview. "Doing volunteer work, I was happy."[60] Another former SYSS student, Thanh Hương, fondly recalls raising pigs and building a schoolhouse with refugees from the war-torn Quảng Trị province. Like many others, she recounts her experience with a mixture of pride and disbelief at her own youthful courage. "I can't believe I did all of that back then. I was young but so brave. I probably would be too scared to do it now."[61]

Pure intentions and good will did not shield SYSS students from the dangers and difficulties of a society at war, however. From the beginning, the school faced severe financial challenges, often unable even to provide adequate meals for its students. At times, they would eat nothing but rice with soy sauce and greens for months on end. They relied on donations from vendors of the Cầu Muối and Cầu Ông Lãnh markets—mainly greens that were too wilted to sell—and vegetables grown on school grounds.[62] In terms of infrastructure, for its first year the school depended on several temples that lent space for classrooms and dormitories—Từ Nghiêm Temple served as the main offices and lecture hall, and temporary dormitories were set up at Trúc Lâm and Huệ Lâm temples.[63] In its second year, the school was able to purchase several acres and built its headquarters next to Pháp Vân Temple, just outside the bustling city in Phú Thọ Hòa.[64] By then, a significant portion of the first class had dropped out, unable to withstand the stress of living so meagerly while studying from eight in the morning until ten in the evening every day.[65]

In addition to financial troubles, the polarized landscape of the war proved dangerous for SYSS students and staff. Being affiliated with neither the communist-led National Liberation Front (NLF) nor the South Vietnamese government, the school occupied a dangerous middle zone in which it could be mistaken as a tool of either side. As Nghiệm put it, "After starting down this path, I saw that it was even more dangerous than going down the other path [of joining the army]. By following our teacher, we got caught in the crossfire. Both sides wanted to kill us."[66] Between May 1966 and July 1967, the SYSS was attacked several times by unidentified assailants—resulting in the disappearance of eight students and the killing of thirteen. Dozens of others were injured or harassed.[67]

The first attack on the SYSS occurred at the end of the first year's training period, on the night of May 16, 1966.[68] According to a compiled account published a year after the incident, at around eight o'clock two strange men approached the school building. They were barefoot, wearing shorts and army helmets, and wielded grenades, daggers, ammunition belts, and a machine gun. An older SYSS student, Nguyễn Chí Tri, approached and informed the men that "we are students holding a training here with permission from the local government."[69] After a brief verbal altercation with Tri, the strangers turned around and threw a grenade into the meditation hall where students were gathered. The students ran to the back of the hall to take cover. The first explosion was followed by another two outside the hall, then a round of machine gun fire. When the dust had settled, the students were mortified to find their classmate Lê Văn Vinh lying on the ground in a pool of blood, his brains spilling out of his head.[70] Another student, Nguyễn Tôn, had also been injured by the first grenade. Some rushed to dress their friends' wounds while others went to alert the local police of the incident. When, after nearly an hour, the police had still not arrived, the students made their way to the hospital, eventually flagging down a car to drive them there.[71] Both Vinh and Tôn survived, though Vinh's brain damage resulted in his paralysis from the waist down.[72]

The following year, on the night of April 24, 1967, thirteen hand grenades were thrown into the SYSS women's dormitory, killing two and injuring thirty-one others.[73] Hồ Thị Minh Nguyện remembers hiding behind a small dresser in her room when she heard the commotion outside. Moments later, a grenade was thrown into the room. The explosion left her in shock; only when she looked down and saw her own blood did she realize she had been wounded.[74] The funeral for the two students killed that night was attended by members of the executive committee of the Unified Buddhist Church—who had not endorsed the founding of the school—along with hundreds of SYSS supporters.[75] Not knowing who was responsible for the attack, the students struggled to remain true to the principles of nonviolence and nondiscrimination that Nhất Hạnh had taught them. "We endured and tried to let go of the hatred and pain that arose from having two of our friends killed," wrote one student. "Their graves on the school grounds always reminded and guided us on the path. We had to keep going, to carry out the ideal that we all shared.... Because of this understanding, we did not hesitate to continue with our regular activities after that."[76] This resolve to carry on in the face of violence and death would be tested again and again.

On June 14, 1967, eight novice monk volunteers were taken from the villages where they were working, never to be seen again. The following night, twenty other students were awoken in the middle of the night and forced outside at gunpoint. After being tied and questioned, they were told that Bình Phước locals had reported them on suspicions that they were spying for the Americans. They were ordered to leave the village the next day "because the people do not want you here."[77] The final major violent incident against SYSS students occurred on July 5, 1967. Five student workers were taken in the middle of the night by a group of unidentified men to the bank of the Bình Phước River where they were questioned and then shot. Four died but one, Hà Văn Đính, survived after feigning death. According to him, when the students confirmed that they were affiliated with the School of Youth for Social Service, their captor had said, "I am sorry, but we have to kill you."[78] The funeral for the four students—Nguyễn Hy, Lê Thế Lành, Hồ Ngọc Tuấn, and Võ Văn Thơ—was held at the school's headquarters, their graves placed alongside those who had been killed just two months before.

Perhaps one of the most disturbing things about these incidents is that to this day it remains impossible to know who gave the orders to kill SYSS students—whether it was agents of the RVN or people affiliated with the National Liberation Front. Both sides were competing for control of the countryside at the time. The imperative to "pacify" NLF-dominated regions consumed South Vietnamese leaders and their US allies, and counterinsurgency proved to be dangerous work. The death and disappearance rates among RVN cadres is shocking—over seven months in 1966, a total of 1,015 Rural Development personnel were murdered or kidnapped.[79] It was not just attacks by NLF agents that set the programs back; whether due to a disastrous lack of coordination or the belief that a village had been taken by the communists, "all too often, Rural Development teams would make some progress, only to have it nullified when American aircraft bombed their villages."[80] With such chaos surrounding development efforts in the countryside, it was perhaps inevitable that the politically neutral SYSS got caught in the crossfire.

The resolve of SYSS students to stay true to the Buddhist principles of nonviolence and nondiscrimination is captured in the eulogies for their slain colleagues and friends. Their messages of peace were read aloud to the crowds that gathered in mourning. At the funeral for their two classmates killed in the dormitories, they announced, "We cannot hate you, you who have thrown grenades and killed our friends, because we know that men are not our enemies. Our only enemies are the misunderstanding, hatred, jealousy, and ignorance that lead to such acts of violence."[81] At the ceremony for the four executed at the riverbank, an SYSS representative addressed the shooters, thanking them for apologizing to their friends and saying that they were forced to kill them. "That proved that you did not want to kill us, but for your own safety, you had to do it. We hope that one day you will help us in our work for peace."[82]

Disregarding advice from neighbors and acquaintances, the SYSS never publicly denounced or tried to hold either of the warring parties accountable for the deaths of its students. It did not matter whether communists or anticommunists had killed their friends. Instead, students and staff held on to what they believed was a larger truth: the war had made all people desperate for survival; it had put regular people in a position where they had to kill or be killed. The individuals who attacked SYSS students were also victims. The only appropriate response was to refuse the logic of the war, to turn away from ideological hatred and to work for peace.

SYSS students struggled to make their message of nonviolence heard against the thunderous backdrop of the war. The written words and final act of one central organizer, Nhất Chi Mai, captures the painful reality experienced by those who called for peace and reconciliation. A soft-spoken primary school teacher, Nhất Chi Mai was like a big sister to other SYSS students. Few could have imagined that she would self-immolate as she did on May 16, 1967—setting herself on fire on the Buddha's birthday and sacrificing her life to inspire common people and government leaders to take steps toward peace in Vietnam.[83] Early that morning, Mai left home and went to Từ Nghiêm temple, a popular temple in Saigon and a sure destination for hundreds on Vesak. At the top of a staircase leading to the meditation hall she set up two small statues—one of the Virgin Mary, with arms outstretched, and another of Quan Thế Âm, the Bodhisattva of compassion. She also set up two placards on which she wrote her final words, a prayer to "use my body as a torch" to "light up the dark," to "awaken people's hearts" and "bring peace to Vietnam." She prayed to the Virgin Mary and Quan Âm, asking them to give her strength to remain composed and to recite the Buddha's name and her country's name while she was engulfed in flames. Then, thirty-three-year-old Mai doused herself with ten liters of gasoline and lit a match.[84]

Nhất Chi Mai left behind ten letters, addressed to her parents, friends, and various government and Buddhist leaders, along with a handful of poems. Together, these pieces capture the experience, ideals, and philosophical understanding of war that Mai shared with her teacher and fellow SYSS workers. They speak to the persecution endured by peace advocates, and the frustration that Buddhist youth felt toward government leaders who chose war at the expense of the people. Among Mai's final poems is one titled "With Palms Together I Kneel" (*Chắp Tay Tôi Quỳ Xuống*) that describes the silencing of those who called for peace and explains why she decided to self-immolate.[85] It follows here:

Sao người Mỹ tự thiêu?	*Why did an American self-immolate?*
Sao thế giới biểu tình?	*Why does the world protest?*
Sao Việt Nam im tiếng?	*Why is Vietnam silent*
Không dám nói Hòa Bình?	*Afraid to call for peace?*
Tôi thấy mình hèn yếu!	*I see that we are weak!*
Tôi nghe lòng đắng cay!	*I hear bitterness in our hearts!*
Sống mình không thể nói	*In life we cannot speak*
Chết mới được ra lời.	*Only in death can we be heard.*
Hòa bình là có tội!	*If you call for peace then you are guilty!*
Hòa bình là Cộng sản!	*If you call for peace, you're a Communist!*
Tôi vì lòng nhân bản,	*It is for the sake of humanity*
Mà muốn nói Hòa Bình.	*That I want to call for peace.*
Chấp tay tôi quỳ xuống	*With palms together I kneel*
Chịu đau đớn thân này	*And endure this physical pain*
Mong thoát lời thống thiết!	*Do not mourn over me!*
Dừng tay lại người ơi!	*Please put down your arms!*
Dừng tay lại người ơi!	*Please put down your arms!*
Hai chục năm hơn rồi,	*More than twenty years of war*
Nhiều máu xương đã đổ,	*With so much blood shed*
Đừng diệt chủng dân tôi!	*Do not kill our people!*
Đừng diệt chủng dân tôi!	*Do not kill our people!*
Chấp tay tôi quỳ xuống.	*With palms together I kneel.*

With her self-immolation, Mai aimed to cut through the ideological noise of the war and the silence of those who had become disillusioned and complacent with the state of their country. She wanted Buddhists and Catholics, communists and anticommunists, to work together for peace. Months before, Mai had written to Nhất Hạnh asking for his blessing to carry out a dramatic act that she hoped would move people to stand up and stop the war. Nhất Hạnh, who was in the United States at the time, wrote back forbidding her from carrying out such a sacrifice.[86] In the end, she followed her own volition. The profound courage and message of reconciliation captured in Mai's self-immolation moved thousands, including government officials and high-ranking Buddhist and Christian leaders. Despite censorship of articles covering Mai's act, news spread by word of mouth and her funeral procession flooded the streets.[87] Today, Nhất Chi Mai remains a powerful figure of the Buddhist antiwar movement. Altars are maintained in her honor across the south, including at Từ Nghiêm temple—where she self-immolated—and at Pháp Vân temple where, at the time of this chapter's publication, surviving SYSS students still gather twice a month.

Nhất Chi Mai was not the only young Buddhist willing to sacrifice herself to inspire peace and a better future for Vietnam. Among the eighty-eight recorded individuals who were killed or who self-immolated as part of the Buddhist movement, at least thirty-one were between the ages of twelve and thirty-five.[88] All the hundreds of SYSS students who dedicated themselves to rural development and aid projects knew they were putting their lives at risk every day. "Your life can be taken at any moment by a bomb or a sudden firefight," Nhất Hạnh wrote of their working conditions. "But our hearts compel us to go to the victims in these forbidden zones."[89] They believed it was worth the sacrifice to alleviate the suffering of communities afflicted by war and poverty.

Despite enormous financial difficulties and the unfathomable loss of students and friends, the SYSS continued to grow over the years. Four classes would graduate before the end of the war. Although many students—including one-third to one-half the inaugural class—were pulled out by their parents, drafted into the South Vietnamese army, or decided to leave on their own accord, those who stayed carried out the work wholeheartedly. They were driven by a profound aspiration that was difficult even for them to put into words. "Something compels us to plunge head on," one student wrote in 1967. "With so much division and violence flooding Vietnamese society...us young people deeply feel our responsibility. We believe in the future we are building."[90]

The School of Youth for Social Service brought Thích Nhất Hạnh's vision of engaged Buddhism to life. His investment in Buddhist youth bore fruit as its students demonstrated their will and ability to serve their fellow countrymen. "We are already, in our own way, bringing about a revolution in Buddhist teaching," Nhất Hạnh wrote. "Young people...are leading the way into new streams of Buddhist thought and action. They are giving birth to engaged Buddhism."[91]

With the fall of Saigon and the end of the war in 1975, Buddhist institutions ground to a halt along with the rest of South Vietnamese society. Vạn Hạnh University, which had nearly seven thousand students at the end of the war, was promptly shut down and designated a surrender point where RVN soldiers turned in weapons and uniforms.[92] The newly established communist government confiscated temples throughout the south, putting hundreds of monks and nuns under house arrest or in prison in the name of national security.[93] Local cadres closed down Buddhist-run schools, publishing houses, medical dispensaries, orphanages, and daycare centers.[94] The bank accounts and offices of the SYSS were likewise confiscated under the pretext that social services were to be the domain of the new government, not of religious organizations.[95]

The war had finally come to an end, but through military victory rather than negotiations as Nhất Hạnh, his students, and many other Buddhists had hoped. As the Communist Party raised its flag in Saigon, its leaders saw no reason to share political power. They continued to suppress the Buddhists who had caused so much trouble for previous governments with their calls for civil liberties and democratic representation. "We believe we can go along with a demanding program for social revolution," leaders of the Unified Buddhist Church insisted in their 1977 appeal to the communist government. "But we are not being allowed to do so. We want only to be Buddhist and socialist at the same time... to participate in the task of building life, not as machines but as humans with minds and hearts."[96] Nhất Hạnh would remain in exile while his fellow antiwar colleagues either escaped Vietnam or were imprisoned.

The history of the SYSS illuminates a significant yet little-known aspect of the Buddhist movement in South Vietnam. It also raises important questions about the legacy of Buddhism in postwar Vietnam. How different would the country be today had socially engaged Buddhists like Nhất Hạnh and his students been allowed to participate in unification and nation-building after the war? Survivors have been told by the current government that they should not talk about what happened to their school during the war, and annual commemorations for slain SYSS students are attended by plainclothes policemen to ensure that they do not include political content.[97] Former SYSS volunteers continue to distribute aid to rural communities today through an informal program called Love and Understanding (Hiểu và Thương), but the spirit of shared responsibility and communal work has been snuffed out. It became impossible to continue the training of Buddhist youth for social work or maintain projects like the self-help villages after 1975.

During his forty years in exile, Thích Nhất Hạnh established ten retreat centers across the United States, Europe, Asia, and Australia, published more than eighty-five books, and became known as the father of mindfulness and engaged Buddhism in the West. He was allowed to return to

Vietnam for the first time in 2005 after extended negotiations with the Vietnamese government.[98] Accompanied by a delegation of one hundred of his students from around the world, he conducted a teaching tour and published a dozen of his books in Vietnamese that are now displayed prominently in stores throughout the country.[99] In October 2018, Nhất Hạnh announced his final return to Vietnam and intent to remain in Huế until the end of his life.[100] Unable to speak or walk after suffering a stroke in 2014, Nhất Hạnh and his community continued to be monitored by the Vietnamese state until his passing at the age of ninety-five on January 22, 2022. On the question of whether their practice of engaged Buddhism will have a chance to flourish in Vietnam, Sister Chân Không, an SYSS cofounder and now the eldest nun in the community, says, "That is up to us... If the deep energy of ancestors wants this to be a peaceful place, if we practice well and try to love those who oppose us, then every day will be better."[101]

NOTES

1. Thích Nhất Hạnh, journal entry, February 5, 1964, *Nẻo Về Của Ý*, 210–211.

2. For historiography on the Buddhist protest movement, see Miller, "Religious Revival"; McAllister, "Only Religions Count in Vietnam"; Topmiller, *Lotus Unleashed*. Some including Mark Moyar have argued, with too little evidence, that the South Vietnamese Buddhist movement was linked to the communist war effort and that some Buddhist leaders were agents of the Communist Party (see Moyar, "Political Monks"). Moyar relies on unconfirmed suspicions and accusations in US State Department memos, CIA reports, and American news articles to argue that Tri Quang was most likely a communist. This chapter joins other scholarly works in debunking his view.

3. Given an estimated 70 to 80 percent of the population identifying as Buddhist and a network of five thousand temples throughout South Vietnam, Buddhist leaders could mobilize masses with relative ease. Roughly one million, or one in ten South Vietnamese Buddhists, actively participated in demonstrations. "The Buddhists in South Vietnam," US Central Intelligence Agency, Office of Current Intelligence, Special Report, SC No. 00598/63A (June 28, 1963), Central Intelligence Agency-Electronic Reading Room; ; Topmiller, *Lotus Unleashed*, xi.

4. Thích Thiện-Hòa, *50 Năm*, 126.

5. For scholarly articles and chapters on the Buddhist movement, see DeVido, "Buddhism for this World"; King, "Thich Nhat Hanh," 329–334. The sole book-length monograph on the topic is Topmiller, *Lotus Unleashed*.

6. Thích Nhất Hạnh, "History of Engaged Buddhism," 30. For more on the twentieth-century Buddhist revival, see DeVido, "Buddhism for this World"; Nguyễn Lang, *Việt Nam Phật Giáo Sử Luận*.

7. DeVido, "Buddhism for this World," 252.

8. Tăng Thân Làng Mai, *Đi Gặp Mùa Xuân*, 15.

9. Tăng Thân Làng Mai, *Đi Gặp Mùa Xuân*, 35 and 40.

10. Tăng Thân Làng Mai, *Đi Gặp Mùa Xuân*, 51–53.
11. Document from Ministry of Interior, Republic of Vietnam, 5 September 1963, folder 4218, Phủ Tổng Thống Đệ Nhị Cộng Hoà, Vietnam National Archives II, Ho Chi Minh City.
12. Michael Parks, "Saigon Moves Against Monk Taking Peace Plea to the World," *Baltimore Sun*, May 7, 1971.
13. Nhất Hạnh, "History of Engaged Buddhism," 30.
14. Nhất Hạnh, "Struggle for Peace in Vietnam," 130.
15. Dã Thảo (Thích Nhất Hạnh), "Thống Nhất Toàn Vẹn," *Phật Giáo Việt Nam* 9–10 (April-May 1957), 11–13.
16. Nhất Hạnh, journal entry, February 5, 1964, *Nẻo Về Của Ý*, 226.
17. For more on these protests and Trí Quang's motivations, see McAllister, "Only Religions Count"; Topmiller, *Lotus Unleashed*.
18. Thích Minh Châu's political stance is articulated in Vạn Hạnh University publications *Tư Tưởng* [Thought] and *Vạn Hạnh Bulletin*. See Wynn Gadkar-Wilcox, chapter 7, this volume.
19. Bryce Nelson, "Buddhist Monk Pleads Here for End to War," *Washington Post*, June 4, 1966; Max Zahn, "Talking Buddha, Talking Christ," *Tricycle: The Buddhist Review*, September 30, 2015.
20. Nelson, "Buddhist Monk Pleads Here." It was around this time that McNamara began to change his mind on the Vietnam War. As George Herring put it, "As early as summer of 1966, McNamara . . . was troubled by the destructiveness of the war, particularly the civilian casualties, and by the growing domestic opposition." Herring, *America's Longest War*, 176, citing McNamara to Johnson, May 18, 1967, in Sheehan, *Pentagon Papers*, 580.
21. "Statement of the Venerable Thích Nhất Hạnh, June 1, 1966, Washington, DC," in Thích Nhất Hạnh, *Vietnam*.
22. Ford, *Cold War Monks*, 2.
23. Chân Không, *Learning True Love*, 91.
24. Chân Không, *Learning True Love*, 91.
25. Thích Minh Châu, "Notice," *Van Hanh University: A Newsletter for Friends and Neighbours*, September 1967.
26. "Inauguration of Van Hanh University's Library," *Van Hanh Newsletter*, October 1967.
27. In November 1969, the president of the Asia Foundation, Haydn Williams, was honored with a university ceremony. Details of donations from the Asia Foundation can be found in Van Hanh newsletters, 1967–1969. "News on Van Hanh University," *Van Hanh Bulletin* 1, no. 3 (November 1969): 36.
28. Phan Trong Quy, "LTE: Phan Trong Quy Press Secretary, Embassy of Vietnam," *The Guardian*, June 28, 1966.
29. King, "Thich Nhat Hanh," 329.
30. Military forces under Nguyễn Cao Kỳ detained an estimated seven thousand Buddhists in major cities in 1966. Kahin, *Intervention*, 430; Hassler, *Saigon, USA*, 42; Forest, *Unified Buddhist Church*, 34.
31. Nhất Hạnh, February 5, 1964, *Nẻo Về Của Ý*, 226.
32. Nhất Hạnh, "Nói Với Tuổi Hai Mươi," *Giữ Thơm Quê Mẹ* 7–8 (January 1966): 43–54.
33. Nhất Hạnh, "Nói Với Tuổi Hai Mươi."
34. Nhất Hạnh, journal entry, February 5, 1964, *Nẻo Về Của Ý*, 219.
35. Nhất Hạnh, journal entry, February 11, 1965, *Nẻo Về Của Ý*, 272.
36. Nhất Hạnh, journal entry, February 5, 1964, *Nẻo Về Của Ý*, 207.
37. Nhất Hạnh, journal entry, February 5, 1964, *Nẻo Về Của Ý*, 207.

38. Nhất Hạnh, journal entry, February 11, 1965, *Nẻo Về Của Ý*, 273–275.
39. Nhất Hạnh, journal entry, February 5, 1964, *Nẻo Về Của Ý*, 208, 225.
40. Kenneth W. Morgan, "Buddhists in Saigon," *The Christian Century*, January 26, 1966.
41. Nhất Hạnh, journal entry, February 5, 1964, *Nẻo Về Của Ý*, 226.
42. Phạm Viết Nghiệm, interview, Ho Chi Minh City, January 3, 2019; Võ Thị Dương Mai, interview, Ho Chi Minh City, July 17, 2019; Lê Văn Đính, interview, Huế, July 28, 2019; Hồ Thị Minh Nguyện, interview, Huế, July 28, 2019.
43. Vương Pen Liêm, *Những Vụ Án Tối Tâm*, 11; Lê Văn Đính, interview; Hồ Thị Minh Nguyện, interview.
44. Vương Pen Liêm, *Những Vụ Án Tối Tâm*, 89–90; Võ Thị Dương Mai, interview.
45. Nhất Hạnh, journal entry, February 11, 1965, *Nẻo Về Của Ý*, 272–273.
46. Võ Thị Dương Mai, interview.
47. For more on these RVN programs including the Accelerated Protein Production Program, the Land to the Tiller Program, and the Accelerated Miracle Rice Production Program, see Trần Quang Minh, "Decade of Public Service."
48. The philosophy of the Strategic Hamlet Campaign is discussed by Duy Lap Nguyen in Tran and Vu, *Building a Republican Nation*, chap. 6.
49. Miller, *Misalliance*, 197. For more on Diệm's development and counterinsurgency programs, see Miller, "Development, Space, and Counterinsurgency"; Miller, *Misalliance*, 162–234.
50. Trần Quang Minh, "Decade of Public Service," 58–61.
51. Trần Quang Minh, "Decade of Public Service," 50, 59.
52. Lê Văn Đính, interview.
53. Nhất Hạnh, "History of Engaged Buddhism," 35.
54. Nhất Hạnh, journal entry, July 12, 1965, *Nẻo Về Của Ý*, 284.
55. Nhất Hạnh, journal entry, December 12, 1964, *Nẻo Về Của Ý*, 242.
56. Chân Không, *Learning True Love*, 85; Berrigan and Thích Nhất Hạnh, *The Raft Is Not the Shore*, 132–133.
57. Võ Thị Dương Mai, interview.
58. Chân Không, *Con Đường Mở Rộng*, 316–319; Lâm Uyên, interview, Ho Chi Minh City, January 3, 2019.
59. Nhất Hạnh, journal entry, February 5, 1964, *Nẻo Về Của Ý*, 227.
60. Phạm Viết Nghiệm, interview.
61. Thanh Hương, interview, Ho Chi Minh City, June 16, 2019.
62. Vương Pen Liêm, *Những Vụ Án Tối Tâm*, 13; Chân Không, *Con Đường Mở Rộng*, 254.
63. Vương Pen Liêm, *Những Vụ Án Tối Tâm*, 11; Hồ Thị Minh Nguyện, interview.
64. Vương Pen Liêm, *Những Vụ Án Tối Tâm*, 12; Chân Không, *Con Đường Mở Rộng*, 220–222.
65. Vương Pen Liêm, *Những Vụ Án Tối Tâm*, 13; Võ Thị Dương Mai, interview.
66. Phạm Viết Nghiệm, interview.
67. For more, see Chân Không, *Learning True Love*, 10, 89, 105–106; Chân Không, *Con Đường Mở Rộng*, 261–267; R. W. Apple Jr. "Young Buddhist Says War Perils Her Country's Human Values," *New York Times*, May 17, 1967.
68. Chân Không, *Con Đường Mở Rộng*, 261.
69. Vương Pen Liêm, *Những Vụ Án Tối Tâm*, 32–33.
70. Hồ Thị Minh Nguyện, interview.
71. Vương Pen Liêm, *Những Vụ Án Tối Tâm*, 35–36.
72. Chân Không, *Con Đường Mở Rộng*, 261–262; Chân Không, *Learning True Love*, 89.

73. Apple, "Young Buddhist"; Chân Không, *Con Đường Mở Rộng*, 264.
74. Hồ Thị Minh Nguyện, interview.
75. Vương Pen Liêm, *Những Vụ Án Tối Tâm*, 56–61.
76. Vương Pen Liêm, *Những Vụ Án Tối Tâm*, 65.
77. Vương Pen Liêm, *Những Vụ Án Tối Tâm*, 103.
78. Vương Pen Liêm, *Những Vụ Án Tối Tâm*, 109–130; Chân Không, *Con Đường Mở Rộng*, 267; Chân Không, *Learning True Love*, 106.
79. Herring, *America's Longest War*, 158–159; and Blaufarb, *Counterinsurgency Era*, 205–242.
80. Herring, *America's Longest War*, 159.
81. Chân Không, *Learning True Love*, 89.
82. Chân Không, *Learning True Love*, 106.
83. Thích Thiện-Hòa, *50 Năm*, 188–189; Chân Không, *Con Đường Mở Rộng*, 242; Hồ Thị Minh Nguyện, interview.
84. Nhất Chi Mai, final letter written before self-immolation, May 15, 1967, in Thích Thiện-Hòa, *50 Năm*, 199.
85. Nhất Chi Mai, "Chấp Tay Tôi Quỳ Xuống," in Thích Thiện-Hòa, *50 Năm*, 192. Translation by the author.
86. Chân Không, *Con Đường Mở Rộng*, 251.
87. Chân Không, *Con Đường Mở Rộng*, 291–292.
88. Fifteen of these young Buddhists were associated with the SYSS. For a list of the eighty-eight individuals who died taking part in the Buddhist movement, see Thích Thiện-Hòa, *50 Năm*, 104–122.
89. Nhất Hạnh, journal entry, December 12, 1964, *Nẻo Về Của Ý*, 243.
90. Vương Pen Liêm, *Những Vụ Án Tối Tâm*, 48–49.
91. Nhất Hạnh, journal entry, July 12, 1965, *Nẻo Về Của Ý*, 286.
92. "News on Van Hanh University," *Van Hanh Bulletin* 2, no. 1, 2 (February 1970); "News in Brief," *Van Hanh Bulletin* 6, no. 3 (September 1974): 54; Quinn-Judge, *Third Force*, 180.
93. Central Executive Council of the Unified Buddhist Church of Vietnam, "An Appeal Made by the Unified Buddhist Church of Vietnam for the Protection of Human Rights in the Socialist Republic of Vietnam" (translated by the Vietnamese Buddhist Peace Delegation in Paris), June 9, 1977. In Forest, *Unified Buddhist Church*.
94. Thich Huyen Quang, "Letter to the Prime Minister re: violations of the policy for freedom of worship in South Vietnam," March 17, 1977. In Forest, *Unified Buddhist Church*.
95. Sister Chân Không, interview, Huế, December 28, 2018.
96. Central Executive Council, "An Appeal," 3, 5.
97. Võ Thị Dương Mai, interview.
98. For more on this 2005 teaching tour, see Chapman, "The 2005 Pilgrimage," 297–341.
99. Nhất Hạnh returned to Vietnam again in 2007, 2017, and 2018. "Plum Village Practice in Vietnam," Plum Village, January 3, 2014, https://plumvillage.org/blog/monastic/plum-village-vietnam-background/; "Thay Arrives in Vietnam," Plum Village, August 29, 2017, https://plumvillage.org/news/thich-nhat-hanh-arrives-in-vietnam/.
100. Nhất Hạnh, "English Translation of Thay's letter to Root Temple Descendants, October 2018," October 26, 2018, https://plumvillage.org/letters-from-thay/tnh-letter-to-root-temple-descendants/.
101. Chân Không, interview.

CHAPTER 7

Political Philology and Academic Freedom

A Defense of Thích Minh Châu

Wynn Gadkar-Wilcox

Thích Minh Châu (1918–2012) was a founder of Buddhist institutions in the Republic of Vietnam. He was also an institution in his own right. Hailing from a family of intellectuals in Quảng Nam province, he received ordination in Huế in 1946 and proceeded to spend almost two decades in Sri Lanka and India studying Pali manuscripts and the Pali language. In 1961, he received his PhD from the Nava Nalanda Mahivara (then part of the University of Bihar), under the directorship of the noted philosopher, Sanskritist, and Indologist Satkari Mookerjee.[1] Shortly after returning to Vietnam in 1964, he became vice-president of the Institute for Higher Buddhist Studies, also known in English as the Saigon Buddhist Studies College, an institution developed by Thích Nhất Hạnh (1926–2022) and others that was in the process of expanding into Vạn Hạnh University.[2] Thích Minh Châu grew this institution into a full-fledged university with the aim of producing a modern version of the ancient Buddhist Nalanda University in Vietnam.

In his position as rector, he also oversaw the creation of, ran the finances of, and for several years edited two journals. The first, *Tư Tưởng* (Thought), ran irregularly but roughly bimonthly from its inception in 1967 to just before the fall of Saigon in the spring of 1975. It featured contributions in the humanities and on comparative philosophy from members of the Vạn Hạnh faculty and from prominent intellectuals across the Republic of Vietnam (RVN) and occasionally from Europe or the United States. The second was launched in 1967 as *Van Hanh*

Newsletter and continued from 1969 to 1974 as *Van Hanh Bulletin*. It began as an English-language magazine to "make new friends," to inform potential supporters of the activities and academic philosophy of Vạn Hạnh University, and to ask for donations in the form of books for a library, glass for the windows, small scholarships for students, and a working heating and air conditioning system.[3] As sources of funding—most notably from the San Francisco–based, CIA-founded Asia Foundation—began to increase, *Van Hanh Bulletin* supplanted *Van Hanh Newsletter*. It operated primarily as a redacted version of *Tư Tưởng*, focusing less on requests for donations and descriptions of basic activities and more on the philosophical and academic foundations of Vạn Hạnh University.

As the chairman of the editorial board of both *Tư Tưởng* and *Vạn Hạnh Newsletter* and as rector of Vạn Hạnh University, Thích Minh Châu held a large and powerful microphone. His articles were frequently at the front of these journals and set the tone for the others. Moreover, his substantial contacts with international scholars and public officials made him a significant public intellectual in his own right.

This chapter articulates Thích Minh Châu's political and academic philosophy in order to defend his most controversial action: his decision to cut ties with Vạn Hạnh University's cofounder Thích Nhất Hạnh, most likely to secure the support of the Asia Foundation, which was about to give Vạn Hạnh University a substantial grant.[4] I argue that this action was consistent with Thích Minh Châu's vision, which held that peace could only be achieved through a long-term process of rebuilding faith in language and integrity in civil society, and that those processes required the construction of a new system of education appropriate for the development of Vietnamese youth.

This presentation contrasts Thích Minh Châu's thought with the positions taken by Thích Nhất Hạnh and the School of Youth for Social Service (SYSS), which Adrienne Lê describes in chapter 6. The different approaches to the war these two monks took demonstrate the pluralistic nature of the RVN, in which many views—about the war, about the nature of engaged Buddhism, about European and Indian philosophy—were allowed to compete. As the introduction to this volume notes, pluralism is a hallmark of the republican experience in the RVN. However, this freedom of thought did not come without some constraints, which profoundly affected Thích Minh Châu's decision-making as a university administrator in that he required the backing of American nonprofit organizations for his university to thrive.

AS TRAITOR AND SELLOUT

To the extent that recent English-language scholarship has considered Thích Minh Châu, it has focused on his role as a political figure in the Buddhist movement of the mid-1960s. Viewed from this perspective, Thích Minh Châu appears as a traitor who sold out the more radical leaders of the Buddhist movement in order to ensure American funding for the enlargement of Vạn Hạnh University.[5]

The argument for this claim focuses on events in the spring of 1966, at the height of the so-called second Buddhist crisis, which arose when Buddhist leaders became concerned with not only the protracted and deadly nature of the Second Indochina War but also the slow pace and general uncertainty about the restoration of democracy in South Vietnam. Thích Minh Châu shared those concerns and participated in the March 13 press conference of the Viện Hóa Đạo, usually translated as the Institute of Secular Affairs. This was the political advocacy wing of the United Buddhist Church (UBC), which called for the immediate restoration of democracy and the return of all exiled generals.[6]

Shortly after, well-known UBC leader Thích Nhất Hạnh decided to return to the United States, where he had found employment as a lecturer in comparative religion at Columbia and Princeton Universities from 1961 to 1963. This time, Cornell University Political Science Professor George T. Kahin (1918–2000) invited him, ostensibly to present a talk titled "The Revival of Vietnamese Buddhism," but also to join a forum on US policy on Vietnam and to give a lecture tour sponsored by the Nyack, New York-based antiwar interfaith group Fellowship of Reconciliation, which had formed the International Committee of Conscience on Vietnam.[7]

In the course of this tour, which continued into the summer of 1966, Thích Nhất Hạnh met a number of influential religious, political, and cultural leaders, such as Rabbi Abraham Heschel, Martin Luther King Jr., Pope Paul VI, Robert McNamara, and Arthur Miller.[8] He also gave a series of provocative speeches suggesting that "the Saigon government is corrupt and a puppet of Washington," that the influx of new American troops would only "convert more people to the Viet Cong," and that pacification programs were "of no use" because pacification workers were "U.S. agents."[9] Finally, he held up his work with SYSS, which was the one part (of three) of Vạn Hạnh University that he directed, as an alternative to US pacification efforts. On June 1, 1966, Thích Nhất Hạnh announced in Washington, DC, a five-point peace proposal calling for a better government in South Vietnam, an immediate halt to bombing, an abandonment of offensive military operations, a specific US declaration of intent to withdraw from Vietnam within months, and a US commitment to repair the damage it had done.[10] Meanwhile, the SYSS's student union, whose president was Thích Nhất Hạnh's disciple Sister Chân Không, issued a similar call for peace.[11]

Thích Minh Châu was well known for believing that a university education should not be mixed with overt political work. He therefore acted. In the summer of 1966, he dissolved the student union and ended Vạn Hạnh University's affiliation with the SYSS. He also forwarded his statement dissolving the union to the police and reportedly accused Sister Chân Không of being a communist—a less-than-trivial statement in Saigon in 1966. He also implied that Thích Nhất Hạnh could not be exonerated from the same charge.[12] The following year, he issued a clarification in *Van Hanh Newsletter* in response to the 1967 publication of Thích Nhất Hạnh's book *Vietnam: Lotus in the Sea of Fire* that not only was the SYSS not affiliated with Vạn Hạnh University but also Nhất Hạnh was no longer an adviser to the school.[13]

Thích Minh Châu's initial decision to dissolve the association between the SYSS and Vạn Hạnh University may have been the result of his personal convictions. His decision to publish a notice publicly repudiating any association between the university and Thích Nhất Hạnh, however, was the result of foreign influence. In October 1967, the *Van Hanh Newsletter* announced that due to an Asia Foundation grant of VND 1,500,000 (at that time, roughly $10,500), Vạn Hạnh University would be able to open a spacious and well-stocked library.[14] In 1966, by the CIA's own admission to the 303 Committee, an internal oversight body, the Asia Foundation was "almost totally dependent on covert funding support from this agency."[15]

One might be tempted to argue that this unflattering portrait of Thích Minh Châu is the result of the writing of a partisan observer. Most secondary accounts of these events rely on the memoir of Sister Chân Không, who not only was removed from her position of president of the student union but also played an integral role in attempting to keep SYSS afloat after Thích Minh Châu banished the program from Vạn Hạnh University. Despite her apparent reason to depict these events in an unfavorable light, however, Thích Minh Châu appears to have at least implicitly confirmed some link between the Asia Foundation's support and his actions as rector by emphasizing their "major financial support" in an interview with Buddhist scholar and historian Robert Topmiller years later.[16]

IN DEFENSE: AN INTERPRETATION

If these facts are not to be disputed, and I am not in a position to dispute them, then defending Thích Minh Châu's ideas and actions seems a difficult task. However, he left a very extensive body of writing, and reading those articles and books reveals a remarkably coherent, consistent, unified, and defensible philosophy. It is, furthermore, one single philosophy, despite drawing from disparate sources, including Buddhist texts and examples (the Dhammapada, Nagarjuna, Emperor Aśoka, commentaries on right speech), Kant (*Perpetual Peace, Critique of Practical Reason*), phenomenology and existential philosophy (Karl Jaspers, Gabriel Marcel), and humanistic psychology (especially Erich Fromm). Thích Minh Châu's view of politics cannot be substantially distinguished from his view of how a university should be administered and how scholars should behave. In turn, his view of the role of the university was indistinguishable from that of Buddhist institutions.

Thích Minh Châu believed that protracted war in Vietnam rendered members of Vietnamese society at least temporarily incapable of meaningful political and social change. The politics and rhetoric of propaganda and sloganeering—not only from communists, but also from any number of noncommunist groups—had clouded the meaning and intent of ideas such as "peace" and "religion." Political leaders used these terms in bad faith for ends that corrupted the meaning of the ideas, so that no community or society of believers existed that could meaningfully or quickly build coalitions around them.

What was needed was a reconstruction of civil society so that peace and democracy could be built on a foundation of agreement about the structure of society. A reconstruction of civil society required a reconstruction of agreement about the basic meaning of words and ideas, and could only be achieved through a university centered on the humanities. Vạn Hạnh University was particularly well suited to fit the role of preparing young people to foster future democratization and pacification in Vietnam because it combined the best features of a Western university with the principles of the original Nalanda Mahavihara of a millennium earlier. The first he understood as a reliance on reason, academic freedom, and freedom of inquiry more broadly. The second entailed a focus on intense scholarly debate within the Buddhist principles of compassion and right speech.

AS A POLITICAL PHILOLOGIST

Thích Minh Châu first and foremost was a philologist. He was someone who carefully read, translated, and attended to the language and meaning of texts. His training in the Pali language and in hermeneutics profoundly inflected his view of the world. This attention to the language and meaning of texts, and to education, was a family trait. His father, Đinh Văn Chấp (1893–1953), was the top doctoral graduate of the 1913 Palace Examination, spent a career as the education officer (Đốc học) for Quảng Nam province, and was known as a translator. In addition to providing critical early translations of Lý and Trần Dynasty poems from Chinese into *quốc ngữ*, Đinh Văn Chấp also translated a Buddhist text on the cessation of suffering written by the well-known monk Thích Đôn Hậu (1905–1992).[17]

Thích Minh Châu followed in his father's footsteps. Through his life, his scholarly writing rarely strayed from philology; it focused on translating texts between languages and offering critical commentary about the meaning of texts by focusing on the interpretation of single sentences or even single words. In his doctoral dissertation, he closely compared the *Madhyama Agama/Zhōng Ahánjīng* (中阿含經) (Middle-length discourses), which only survives in literary Chinese form, and the *Majjhima Nikāya*, a corresponding text in Pali. His aim was not only to demonstrate that the *Madhyama Agama* was a part of the Sarvastivadan canon, which clarified the route of transmission of Chinese ideas, but also to show through close linguistic analysis the striking similarities between the two texts. These suggested the close lingages and doctrinal similarities between the Theravadin monasteries and the schools that in the nineteenth and twentieth centuries have come to be known as Mahayana.[18] In the introduction to the work, Satkari Mookerjee reflected on the painstaking scholarly detail of the study, noting that despite Thích Minh Châu's background as an ordained monk, "his work is that of a scholar, critical, cautious, and faithful to the truth."[19]

A similar attention to the meaning of individual words and ideas was reflected in his other early academic studies. While at Nalanda, Thích Minh Châu also carried out a similar comparative study of the Pali and literary Chinese versions of the *Questions of Milinda*, a text purporting to record the queries of the Indo-Greek King Menander I (165–130 BCE) to the Sarvastivadan Buddhist sage Nagasena (fl. 150 BCE) regarding, among other things, the status of karma during the transition of a soul from one existence to another. He said he prepared this study with the aim of preparing a new Pali–Literary Chinese dictionary.[20] The concern with language is also evident in his 1963 biography of the famed Buddhist pilgrim Xuanzang, which Thích Minh Châu completed while serving as a lecturer in Pali at the Nava Nalanda Mahavihara after finishing his PhD. Thích Minh Châu evidently admired Xuanzang, whose journey to Nalanda in some ways mirrored his own many centuries later. Revealingly, his biography includes a substantial section emphasizing Xuanzang's importance as a translator.[21]

This emphasis on clarifying the meaning of words and ideas persisted in his writings on the Second Indochina War and the political and cultural situation in the RVN. Discussing the utility of religion as a path for liberation in Vietnam and the world at a gathering at the Saigon Baha'i headquarters on World Religions Day in 1967, he first emphasized that the wartime situation that had been ongoing in Vietnam for more than twenty-five years had provoked "a crisis in spirituality and values." To speak of Vietnam was to speak of war, political polarization, and a decline in cultural and human values. Therefore, any religious tradition attempting to bring peace to Vietnam needed first to address the root cause of polarization, economic desparities, and declines in cultural values: "the collapse of language."[22]

Thích Minh Châu suggested that rather than a series of symbols designed to represent reality, to be used in consideration of others, words such as "peace," "public service," and "religion" were being manipulated by ideologues to "produce propaganda," "protect individual interests," and "inflate people's egos." The result of this corruption of language was that these key words for reforming society had become empty signifiers— "empty nouns" (*danh-từ trống rỗng*)—that anyone could use in any way they saw fit. This process denied the moral import of these words or their power in decision-making. "Our sacred language is becoming a means of acquiring cheap goods in the marketplace," Thích Minh Châu lamented, "which anyone is capable of buying and adorning with the decoration of superficial actions in the current deadlocked atmosphere today."[23] He seems to be suggesting that rather than exercising right and compassionate speech as an end in itself, modern society encouraged people to manipulate words to inflate their importance or achieve their career or political aims. As a means to an end, words had become a commodity; their meaning was determined by whatever would have the most value in getting the speaker to his desired political end. If declaring that an act of war was an act of peace fooled people into believing an act was just, a modern politician would resort to such a twisting of what "peace" could mean.

In an extended essay on how to use the best of Western and Eastern thought, he quoted the American linguist Benjamin Lee Whorf, who said that "whenever agreement or assent is arrived at in human affairs...the agreement is reached by linguistic processes, or else it is not reached."[24] For Thích Minh Châu, this meant that a common understanding of language was a prerequisite for dialogue and deliberation, which were themselves prerequisites for peace and functioning democracy. The solution to this problem was to "disinfect our language," to restore meaning to these words. This aim could be achieved if people who wanted to use these words for their truth value and not for political manipulation could educate others on their proper meanings.[25] The point was not that any particular language, such as Vietnamese, was uniquely suspect to such corruption. It was rather that by the late twentieth century, popular discourse in politics and in the media was so subject to ideological manipulation that the very terms of what would constitute peace, or liberation, or religion were called into question.[26]

Speaking at his annual talk to Vạn Hạnh students during Vesak celebrations in 1969, Thích Minh Châu warned that the malaise caused by a lack of spiritual strength was making Vietnamese shirk their personal responsibility to produce peace in Vietnam. Vietnamese people could not rely on political parties or ideologies to which they were committed to bring to a close the war that had "resulted in the massacre of countless thousands over these decades" and "turned our country into a place in which the whole population needs to be buried."[27] The constant barrage of bad news from the war, combined with propaganda on all sides, had numbed the Vietnamese population and caused many ordinary Vietnamese citizens to attempt to continue their lives as if the war were not ongoing. "The power of propaganda and the constant sloganeering," he explained, "have lulled the people of today to sleep with the rhythm of crisis."

To resolve this problem, the Vietnamese people needed to awaken their spirits and avoid the temptation of endorsing a politically motivated "false movement toward peace," which was how he characterized the Paris peace talks, since they were, in his mind, only aimed at an armistice, not at the actual prevention of future war. These politically oriented talks were self-interested and duplicitous, and therefore were in violation of the requirement of "right speech" in the eightfold path:

We have seen that in the Noble Eight-Fold Path, the Buddha taught right speech. "Right speech" means: do not lie, do not slander, do not say hateful, discordant, or aggressive things. "Right speech" also means not saying things that are poisonous, malevolent, coarse, gossipy, or vain. We can observe that the aspect that is missing today, with everyone speaking of peace, is "right speech."[28]

The solution to this problem was for the Vietnamese people to be dedicated to learning, developing knowledge of, and disseminating a truthful and good-faith interpretation of the meaning of such words as peace. In that case, a pacification "that lies within the spirit and the meaning of the Noble Eight-fold Path and the Middle Way, characterized by the return to peace, wisdom, enlightenment, and Nirvana" was possible.[29]

During the 1971 Vesak celebrations at Vạn Hạnh, Thích Minh Châu further clarified that this path forward should be to follow the teaching of the Buddha. Right speech would involve striving for personal improvement through a faithfulness to truth and human values. "No foreign country and no foreign people can help us," he opined, because for peace and prosperity to return to Vietnam, the "bankrupt society" would first have to be reformed. And that involved a long-term process in which all Vietnamese people tried to "improve ourselves; then our families, our schools, and our society will improve."[30] Such a process would start with language.

That, he added in a final paragraph of his speech addressed directly to the students of Vạn Hạnh, was the task and the teaching he was trying to pass on to them. A revival of human values through a careful study of words and their meaning was fundamentally a long-term academic process involving the teaching of youth, and it was necessary for peace, which required not only political action but also a fundamental social, psychological, and spiritual change in each person.[31]

Thích Minh Châu was not opposed to political action. His goal was for the Vạn Hạnh University students to be the "future leaders of the nation."[32] Certain outcomes for which he advocated, such as "economic development" based on "happiness" rather than on "enslavement of people to materialism," a conquering of "fanaticism," and an end to war, required some political action for their achievement. What was necessary, however, was to "start our new political life based on the Dhamma," and that meant that one should only engage in political activities that cultivated respect for "truth, life, and human values."[33] To create a politics consistent with the Dhamma would take a reorientation of the entire society, however, and that would take time and require a fundamental change that could only be brought about through education. Because education was the way to a fundamentally different conception of politics, such a transformation was possible only if educational institutions were safe havens, away from the political chaos of the broader society. In other words, such a politics was possible only after a collective shift away from a materialist conception of politics and toward a spiritual one.

AS A BUDDHIST EXISTENTIALIST

Though Thích Minh Châu's philosophy focused on a reform of language, he also engaged with historical ideas about how this reform could be put into practice. These ideas came chiefly from two sources: classic Buddhist texts from ancient times and continental philosophy from the nineteenth and twentieth century, particularly phenomenology and existentialism.[34]

The first significant Buddhist text for Thích Minh Châu was the *Dhammapada*. One of the most widely read scriptures of the Pali canon, the *Dhammapada* consists of a series of short sayings from the Buddha regarding particular situations. Because of its somewhat aphoristic nature, it is easily quotable and recognizable to a Vietnamese Buddhist audience. Thích Minh Châu used this to his advantage. In an essay introducing the issue of Buddhism in the modern world, he began with the epitaph of verse 303 from the *Dhammapada*: "Sitting by himself, resting by himself, going by himself without being tired, only the person who can do this will be happy in the forest."[35] He uses this quotation as an illustration of having a method and possessing both self-control and a sense of personal responsibility for the transformation of society as something essential in the modern world. In a collection of his writings, he cites verse 146—"Why is there laughter? Why is there joy although [the world] is always burning? Shrouded in darkness, why not see the light?"—in the context of suggesting that the ceaselessness of war in Vietnam both offered a danger of despair and an opportunity to realize enlightenment based on the very seriousness of the situation.[36] Later, in stressing that the cessation of war requires first the attention of each person in reducing craving and anger in themselves, he cites the Buddha as saying in verse 103 of the *Dhammapada*:

> If you win over a thousand enemies in battle
> Such a victory cannot be equated with

A victory over oneself
Self-victory is the highest victory.[37]

The second Buddhist source of Thích Minh Châu's political thought comes from history: the example provided by the conversion story of the Emperor Aśoka (304–232 BCE). He famously conquered the state of Kalinga in a massive and bloody battle and then felt a wave of remorse after seeing the consequences of his actions: the bloody bodies of soldiers stacked on the battlefield the day after the battle, which reportedly resulted in more than one hundred thousand deaths. According to the famous Aśokan pillars, this remorse caused Aśoka to convert to Buddhism and commit to nonviolence.[38] For Thích Minh Châu, Aśoka's actions are proof that a true Buddhist-oriented transformation of politics is indeed possible if the desire for peace is not "dictated by a particular ideology" but instead motivated by a self-realization of the need for moral purpose. In emphasizing that peace is a primary meaning of nirvana, Thích Minh Châu argues that Aśoka's actions are an example of this teaching, "because this Indian King, in the midst of the greatest victory in the greatest battle, felt regret for his actions in conquest, and underwent a self-transformation to follow the teachings of Buddhism."[39]

A third major influence on Thích Minh Châu's Buddhist thought is the nondualist Buddhist philosopher Nagarjuna (ca. 150–ca. 250 CE). Thích Minh Châu applies Nagarjuna's ideas when making his oft-repeated point that achieving peace in Vietnam or in the world is impossible without Vietnamese people achieving peace within themselves first, not least because inner peace and outer peace are not fundamentally distinguishable. To make this point, he cites Nagarjuna's argument that "there is nothing whatsoever of *samsara* distinguishing [it] from nirvana; there is nothing whatsoever of nirvana distinguishing it from *samsara*."[40] When trying to stress the importance of nonduality as a transition point between Buddhist philosophy and Western philosophy, Thích Minh Châu cites Nagarjuna's argument that "when emptiness is possible, everything is possible/were emptiness impossible, nothing would be possible."[41]

Thích Minh Châu relies on Nagarjuna because Nagarjuna's writing confirms that easy declarations of stable ideological truths were illusory. This also explains his interest in contemporary continental philosophy, particularly phenomenology and existentialism. In linking Buddhism and existentialism, Thích Minh Châu taps into an existing popular intellectual discourse in the Republic of Vietnam that interpreted both theories as rejecting overarching ideologies in favor of self-cultivation.[42]

However, Thích Minh Châu begins his emphasis in continental philosophy with Kant. He uses the *Critique of Practical Reason* to show that faith is an essential element of even secular belief, if we are to believe in moral laws.[43] Additionally, in an extensive discussion of the insufficiency of the Paris peace negotiations to achieve lasting peace, he draws extensively on the *Essay on Perpetual Peace*. In that discussion, Thích Minh Châu draws a parallel between Buddhist notions of peace and Kant's first appendix, "On the Opposition between Morality and Politics with Respect to Peace." Thích Minh Châu summarizes Kant's critique of three basic political rules as follows:

1. *Fac et excusa* (do and apologize): Do what you want, then find a way to justify the incident after the fact;
2. *Si fecisti, nega* (if you did it, deny it): Whatever you have done, do not acknowledge that you are at fault, but blame others or blame humanity;
3. *Divide et impera* (divide and conquer): Sow division between you and your partners and your enemies. Pretend to help the weak, and you will conquer them all.[44]

In interpreting this passage, Thích Minh Châu makes several points. First, he notes that these political criteria "absolutely contradict those of the eight-fold path." Second, he notices, in regard to the Paris negotiations, that "the political strategies of the West and of the Communists are both loyal to these slogans, as much as any one has been since the year 1795."[45] Kant's alternative to this political order, which consisted of advocating for a series of conditions or rules for the foundation of a moral and political order in which peace was possible, was broadly consistent with Thích Minh Châu's suggestion, in the context of his citation of Kant, that "self-rectification, which often means the cleansing of the spirit, makes the spirit strong, calm, and peaceful, [in order] to live a spiritual and moral life according to the noble eight-fold path."[46]

Thích Minh Châu cites twentieth-century exponents of phenomenology and existentialism even more frequently than Kant. He views these traditions as fundamentally affirming his perspective that to seek either peace or truth, political ideologies and values needed to be set aside and put into brackets in favor of an inner search—a view he also finds reflected in his interpretation of Nagarjuna. Thus he cites Heidegger's insight that "every valuing, even where it values positively, is a subjectivizing," by which he means that placing culture or art or science on a human pedestal reduced those ideas to mere instruments of human appreciation or consumption, rather than things in themselves.[47]

Thích Minh Châu's appreciation for existentialism came mainly from his reading of Gabriel Marcel (1889–1973) and Karl Jaspers (1883–1969). He borrows from Marcel the idea that peace was internal and spiritual, and that purely external and political appeals to peace were most likely the work of ideologues. "An ideologue is a spirit that lets itself be caught up in the mirage of pure abstractions," Marcel says. Thích Minh Châu uses this quotation to show that "true peace is not the same as the peace dictated by a particular ideology. The ideologies are only self-delusional and cheat us with illusory abstractions."[48] Marcel contends that "peace is an eschatological concept" belonging to a "suprasensible dimension" rather than referring only to terrestrial events; Thích Minh Châu, revising Marcel's conception, argues against any permanent distinction between sensible and suprasensible dimensions, and between action in the world and action within the self, so that both needed to be pursued.[49]

Thích Minh Châu also relies on the ideas of Karl Jaspers, primarily to support his interpretation of Kant's perpetual peace. Jaspers stresses the importance of actors avoiding bad faith in negotiations to end war. Jaspers claims that "he who wants peace must not deceive. The lie is a principle of war, and of all politics geared to potential war." Jaspers argues, in explaining Kant's view, that "to represent an armistice as peace is a fraud." Thích Minh Châu uses this to explain his own view that negotiations between the United States and the Democratic Republic of Vietnam (North Vietnam) were being done in bad faith and in political self-interest, and therefore could not result in true peace.[50]

A final influence on Thích Minh Châu was the humanistic psychologist Erich Fromm (1900–1980). Fromm's 1964 book *May Man Prevail* suggests that if the world wanted to avoid global thermonuclear war, the United States would have to accept a neutralist third world, withdraw from global conflicts, and have "a renaissance of the spirit of humanism, of individualism, and of America's anti-colonialist tradition."[51] Thích Minh Châu uses Fromm's ideas to show that war could only be abated through truthful dialogue, cooperation, and mutual understanding, not by trying to win over the world's population with propaganda or slogans. He approvingly quotes Fromm's statement that "the present struggle is a struggle for men's minds. One cannot win this struggle with empty slogans or propaganda tricks, which nobody except their own authors believe."[52]

The antecedents to Thích Minh Châu's political beliefs came both from the classic texts of Buddhism and from nineteenth- and twentieth-century Western philosophy. He argues that these texts had the same aim, and that this aim connects to his philosophical and linguistic views: that the world is awash with propagandistic ideology, that the only way toward peace in the world is through truth, and that truth can only be arrived at if each person sets aside what they think they know based on ideological preferences and attempts to seek peace and truth internally. To do so, however, requires educational and social institutions that can help young people cultivate those skills.

AS A PROPONENT OF A BUDDHIST ACADEMIC FREEDOM

Although Thích Minh Châu was a translator, an academic, and an occasional political commentator, his fundamental identity during the zenith of his writing in the late 1960s and early 1970s was as a university administrator. In developing a vision for the continued success of Vạn Hạnh University, Thích Minh Châu consistently emphasized that this goal was directly related to Vietnam's wartime situation, and that the education his students were receiving would put them in a position to lead the country in a direction of future peace and democratization.

Thích Minh Châu's vision for accomplishing this goal was to create a Buddhist university based on the inculcation and development of Buddhist notions of wisdom and compassion, while incorporating the best of a Western-style humanities education's "investigation, analysis, and comparison." He would do so through coursework focusing on comparing Buddhist logic and philosophy with the traditions of continental and Anglo-American philosophy, and comparing techniques of Buddhist meditation and mindfulness with "modern psychotherapy."[53]

At a long speech given at Vạn Hạnh's first graduation ceremony on May 26, 1969, Thích Minh Châu elaborated on Vạn Hạnh's aims in a very specific way. First, he argued that the contemporary world offered only one university system, that originating in the Western universities that began to be established in England and Italy in the twelfth century. These had grown out of theological study, yet universities were profoundly changed by the Enlightenment, which brought "the humanist spirit" and "the scientific spirit." These developments reached their pinnacle in the nineteenth century with the German universities in Halle, Göttingen, and Berlin, where respect for authority and hierarchy were replaced with "university freedom and university autonomy." Summarizing, Thích Minh Châu argued that Western universities were founded on the spirit of God—"the Christian spirit of the middle ages and the reformation," the spirit of Man—"the humanist spirit of the renaissance," and the spirit of Science—"the scientific spirit" of the eighteenth to twentieth centuries.[54]

However, Thích Minh Châu asserted, the Western university was in spiritual crisis, because all three of its values—God, Man, and Science— had been fundamentally challenged. God, of course, had been challenged by Nietzsche, but also perhaps more damagingly by Christian existentialists who denied the centrality of organized theology, such as Paul Tillich (1886–1965). The relevance and importance of "Man" in the sense of renaissance humanism was fundamentally challenged by the empiricist tendencies of scientific inquiry. But even the faith in science, after Werner Heisenberg's (1901–1976) uncertainty principle showed that the more precisely the position of a particle can be determined, the less precisely its momentum can be known, and after Kurt Gödel (1906–1978) showed that any consistent computable system must be incomplete and that axioms could not be shown to be consistent within their own system, the reliability—and the knowability—of empirical, scientific knowledge about the world was called into question as well.[55] This accounted for the crisis in universities around the world in the 1960s.

He believed that it would therefore be "absurd" for Vạn Hạnh University to "follow the steps of the West while it is undergoing a crisis."[56] The solution was for it to follow instead "the tradition of Eastern university education of Nalanda," an education based on five fundamental divisions—grammar and linguistics, medicine, logic, letters and aesthetics, and philosophy—yet also follow the model of the *Quốc Tử Giám* (National University) in Vietnamese tradition. Although Thích Minh Châu was not very clear on how to use the *Quốc Tử Giám* as a model, he did stress that the examination system in Vietnam was first established under the Lý dynasty, whose existence owed a great deal to the Buddhist master Vạn Hạnh for whom the university was named. Presumably, because the *Quốc Tử Giám* under the Lý dynasty combined Buddhist and Confucian values to form an indigenous system of education, Vạn Hạnh University could take that as an inspiration to do the same.[57] Together, these would constitute an Asian model for a humanities education, to engender a "radical spirit" or "new values" that would overturn values that are not working. The radicalism of this proposal lay in its attempt to create a modern university while seemingly rejecting the enlightenment values on which most modern universities were based.

The primary values that Vạn Hạnh University inculcated in its students were truth, freedom, and humanity, which were "values of every human culture," but also values not present in the wartime circumstances of Vietnam: "Van Hanh University starts its activities in circumstances which negate all the values to which the university has been trying its best to give effect in following the course that it has charted."[58] The problem was that the meaning of these words had become unclear. Truth, freedom, and humanity also "have no unchanging meanings," which allow them to be exploited by political parties. The task of the students at Vạn Hạnh was to discuss and debate their meaning in a university context, where the spirit was neither one of a political organization nor even of a religion, but instead an "open spirit of dynamic collectivity" so that, out of these debates, a collective consciousness about how to pursue these ideals would arise untainted by the political pressures of a hopelessly divided and increasingly economically bifurcated Vietnam in the middle of a war.[59]

To complete a vision of this kind of humanistic university, Thích Minh Châu relies also on several Western sources. He begins by discussing Plato's notion of *paideia*, which he links to Plato's allegory of the cave, suggesting that education was about developing techniques to perceive light in an atmosphere of darkness.[60] In another context, he describes *paideia* as "the realisation of the potentialities of man in all the intellectual and spiritual aspects of life," and therefore "an embodiment of human nature, leading it to its ultimate fruition." In this context, *paideia* is the essence of a humanities education in "truth, freedom, and humanity," which together means "the awakening of the creative spirit of man on the road to the enlightenment of mankind."[61]

In a 1970 article emphasizing education as an antidote for perpetual war, Thích Minh Châu cites a number of nineteenth- and twentieth-century sources on the philosophy of education to argue that true education would open the mind of students for action in the world. He had first and foremost been inspired by the educational writings of Ralph Waldo Emerson (1803–1882), who argued that American education had become sterile and rote both in its teaching style and its content. School had become a place in which "day creeps after day, each full of facts, dull, strange, despised things, that we cannot enough despise—call heavy, prosaic, and desert."[62] Education had become "cold" and "hopeless," and "a treatise on education, a convention for education, a lecture, a system, affects us with a slight paralysis and a certain yawning of the jaws."[63] The antidote to this problem was to create an education system based on the principle of giving "hope," rather than "despair" to students, and that was to give a moral education to inflame the spirit of students through engaging with them and earning their perpetual respect.[64]

The result of this kind of education is that it would produce a student body that was cognizant of truth and able to work for peace. Thích Minh Châu insisted that "it is precisely because of the war that we must build a university." "War is destructive" and "war means pessimism," but the university was "constructive and optimistic," because it provided "a focus for the hopes of the people." Whereas war was destroying the moral fabric of Vietnam, Vạn Hạnh University reinforced that moral fabric.[65] The professors of Vạn Hạnh could not be in the "ivory tower"; they had to be awakening the "sacred consciousness" of truth, freedom, and humanity, "in the hearts of the students," and by taking seriously their "responsibility before history." "Arousing Freedom, Truth, and Humanity in the hearts of men, and rejecting all political tendencies, all religious divisions, enslavement by dogmas, biases born of traditions, and above all, narrow factional spirit," the students and faculty at Vạn Hạnh could determine "whether mankind will rise or fall," not only for "Vietnam, but in regard to the whole of mankind in this earth."[66] The spirit of Vạn Hạnh, and only that spirit, could end the war.

In his prolific writings in the 1960s and 1970s, Thích Minh Châu produced a coherent political philosophy that justified his actions in leading the university as the most constructive way to respond to the realities of war. This chapter presents a defense of his views. Thích Minh Châu contended that the factionalism evident in the political arena, both locally and globally, rendered the words such as "peace" and "truth" and "public service" so fungible as to be virtually meaningless. He argued that politically, culturally, and socially, the RVN was hopelessly divided, and that these tendencies were making Vietnamese youth feel disillusioned and disinclined to engage to end the war and improve their society. He maintained that to ameliorate this situation, a fundamental transformation of values had to occur and a new kind of civil society had to be built. Moreover, that kind of society could only be constructed if students had the opportunity to debate and discuss what their new culture should look like, outside the overwhelming pressure of the Cold War and of everyday politics in the RVN. The only way to produce a real peace was to restore meaning to language and to restore dialogue to the youth; the only way to do those things was to build a university not beholden to existing interests.

Returning to our initial question, we can now consider anew whether building Vạn Hạnh University justified the distasteful nature of what could be considered the institution's inaugural act: Thích Minh Châu's decision to dissolve the student union, cut ties with the School of Social Service, and announce the university's total separation from its founder, Thích Nhất Hạnh, forswearing his version of "engaged Buddhism" in the process, all to receive donations that almost certainly originated with the CIA.

Reasonable arguments can be made against being an apologist for this act. One might say that the ends of achieving peace through education cannot possibly justify the means of taking money from the CIA insofar as the ends were not achieved: Vạn Hạnh University students did not end the war. After the fall of Saigon in 1975, institutions associated with the United Buddhist Church were repressed and Vạn Hạnh University was closed.[67] A small temple and research center, renamed as the Vạn Hạnh Institute, was allowed to continue. Thích Minh Châu stayed there, working on translations from Pali into Vietnamese, for the rest of his life. It can also be argued that this founding act contradicted many of the principles that Thích Minh Châu was trying to inculcate: one cannot, in a sense, found a university that was supposed to be removed from the politics of the Cold War if that university is ultimately only made possible by funding, offered with explicit strings attached, from a Cold War source. Moreover, for all of Thích Minh Châu statements of approval of free debate and references to the tradition of university and faculty autonomy dating back to the nineteenth-century German universities, his actions in separating Vạn Hạnh from the SYSS, dissolving the SYSS, and removing Thích Nhất Hạnh contradict the open debate he was seeking to endorse.

Yet, on the other hand, these actions were probably necessary for the survival and success of the university. When the first issue of *Van Hanh Newsletter* was published in June 1967, the university was still seeking small donations so that glass could be put in the windows and chairs provided for classrooms. The university had no generator; rooms did not have consistent power; and students studied by flashlight. Conditions were dire.[68] Moreover, after the Asia Foundation grant, Thích Minh Châu and other Vạn Hạnh administrators were able to make connections that led to more grants and monetary aid that surely contributed to the expansion and success of the university. The Asia Foundation gave Thích Minh Châu a travel grant to visit the East-West Center in Honolulu; as a result, Kokua Van Hanh, a charitable organization of Hawaiian Buddhists, was founded to give monetary assistance to the university.[69] Later, Vạn

Hạnh was the recipient of a large grant from OXFAM to provide relief to the victims of war and natural disasters.[70] In the final days of Vạn Hạnh University in 1975, the faculty were awarded a Ford Foundation grant for teaching and performing Vietnamese traditional music.[71] It is doubtful whether funding these grants would have been possible without the initial Asia Foundation grant, or whether the university would have even survived long enough to receive them.

Moreover, the argument that Thích Minh Châu was unsuccessful because Vạn Hạnh students did not have the opportunity to build a new society or end the war misses the point, because it presumes that any action available to a person such as he could have ameliorated the conditions in Vietnam at the time any better. Justification for Thích Minh Châu's argument that a lasting peace and a permanent, more democratic society in Vietnam required fundamental social, cultural, and educational change is considerable; we might even say that the persistent lack of achievement of Thích Minh Châu's latter goal even today in Vietnam is evidence of how fundamental a change is required.

Even today, many of us make compromises necessary to carry out the work of teaching our students so that they may contribute to making a better world. Many of us may choose to teach or study at universities where educational or disciplinary decisions can be altered by powerful donors, or where university educational goals are farmed out to consulting firms.[72] Many of us have friends or know colleagues who work at universities with Confucius Institutes, despite overwhelming evidence that these institutes, which are funded through the Chinese Ministry of Education, restrict the topics that can be discussed in its programs and discriminate against instructors based on their political and religious views.[73]

To say this is not to criticize these decisions; it is instead to say that they are justified, because working at a university is the only way we can educate our students in a way that will allow them, in the future, to not live in a society that is beholden to such outside political and economic forces.

That is what Thích Minh Châu knew, and he was right.

NOTES

1. "Thích Minh Châu (1918–2012)," in Buswell and Lopez, *Princeton Dictionary of Buddhism*, 905; "Thích Minh Châu," in Luân Hoán, *Tác giả Việt Nam*, 601; Bhiksu Thich Minh Chau, *Chinese Madhyama Āgama*, 1–2; *Nava Nalanda Mahvihara: History Past and Present*, http://navnalanda.com/nava%20nalanda%20mahavihara.html (accessed August 28, 2019).

2. Chapman, "Return to Vietnam," in Taylor, *Modernity and Re-enchantment*, 301; Soucy, "Thích Nhất Hạnh," in Payne and Halkias, *Oxford Research Encyclopedia*.

3. *Van Hanh University: A Newsletter for Friends and Neighbours* [*Van Hanh Newsletter*] 1 (June 1967), 1–2.

4. The purpose of this defense is not to cast moral judgment on either Thích Minh Châu or his detractors, but to provide an analytical justification for his actions. Thích Minh Châu elected to remove any reference to Thích Nhất Hạnh's affiliation with Vạn Hạnh because he believed that doing so was necessary to attract funding from US sources; that without that funding, Vạn Hạnh University would not survive; that the survival of independent universities was critical for the long-term peace and success of the Vietnamese people; and, finally, that these first three ends justified the means of excluding Nhất Hạnh. This chapter uses historical contextualization to show that Minh Châu had ample justification for these beliefs—in other words, that it is more likely than not that but for his actions, these eventualities would have come to pass. Of these, only the fourth, which speaks to whether such utilitarian calculi are appropriate, can be considered a moral argument. Even in that case, however, the focus is not on whether Minh Châu was a good person or a bad person, or a good Buddhist or a bad one, but on whether the historical circumstances in which he found himself provided an analytical justification for the beliefs he held.

5. The Western-language sources that exclusively focus on Thích Minh Châu's role in distancing Vạn Hạnh University from Thích Nhất Hạnh, dissolving the student union, and severing Vạn Hạnh University's ties to the SYSS include Chapman, "Return to Vietnam," 301–303; Quinn-Judge, *Third Force*, 99–100; Topmiller, *Lotus Unleashed*, 49

6. Topmiller, *Lotus Unleashed*, 49. On the organization and typical English translation of Viện Hóa Đạo, see McLellan, *Many Petals of the Lotus*, 103.

7. See International Committee of Conscience on Vietnam, "Vietnam and the American Conscience: A Tribute to Thich Nhat Hanh, Leading Buddhist Monk from Vietnam," Flyer, Douglas Pike Collection, Vietnam Center and Archive at Texas Tech University, Virtual Vietnam Archive, Lubbock, TX [VCA].

8. International Committee, "Vietnam and the American Conscience," VCA.

9. Los Angeles Fellowship of Reconciliation, "Statement of the Venerable Nhat Hanh, May 16, 1966," Douglas Pike Collection, VCA.

10. Chapman, "Return to Vietnam," 303; Chan Khong, *Learning True Love*, 83–84.

11. Chapman, "Return to Vietnam," 302.

12. Chan Khong, *Learning True Love*, 86.

13. *Van Hanh Newsletter* 3 (September 1967): 8; Chan Khong, *Learning True Love*, 91–92.

14. "Inauguration of Van Hanh University's Library," *Van Hanh Newsletter* 5 (October 1967): 1. See also Quinn-Judge, *Third Force*, 99–100. For monetary conversion rates, see "Saigon Black Market Exchange Rates 1955–1975 in Dong Per US Dollar," *Coins and Banknotes in Vietnam and French Indochina*, https://art-hanoi.com/library/rates/ (accessed August 28, 2019).

15. Price, *Cold War Anthropology*, 182.

16. Topmiller, *Lotus Unleashed*, 165. The full text reads, "The inclusion of Thich Minh Chau in this group [calling for the restoration of democracy] is particularly noteworthy, as he consistently opposed Buddhist political activity and emphasized that Buddhists should focus on education and cultural projects. He is still the rector of the Van Hanh Institute in Ho Chi Minh City, an educational facility dedicated to training monks and

nuns. During our interview, he told the author that the institute received financial support from the Asia Foundation before 1975. The author suspects the Asia Foundation was used to channel CIA money to friendly groups. When the author mentioned this to [George] Kahin, he also thought it could be true."

17. Đinh Văn Chấp, "Dịch thơ đời Lý và Trần"; Thích Đôn Hậu, *Muốn hết khổ*.
18. Bhiksu Thich Minh Chau, *Chinese Madhyama Āgama*, 13–18.
19. Mookerjee, foreword to Bhiksu Thich Minh Chau, *Chinese Madhyama Āgama*, 2.
20. Bhikkhu Thich Minh Chau, *Milindapanha and Nagasenabhiksusūtra*.
21. Bhiksu Minh Chau, *Xuanzang*, xvii–xxii.
22. Thích Minh Châu, "Tôn giáo phải là con đường giải thoát cho Việt-Nam và Thế Giới" [Religion is the path of liberation for Vietnam and the World], *Tư Tưởng* 1 (August 1967): 363–364.
23. Thích Minh Châu, "Tôn giáo phải."
24. Thích Minh Châu, "Làm thế nào chúng ta có thể phụng sự cho sự hòa điệu giữa những nền văn hóa đông phương và tây phương để cung hiến nền hòa bình thực thụ cho nhân loại?" [How can we work for the harmony of the cultures of East and West, in order to provide for real peace?] *Tư Tưởng* 4-5 (1967): 16–17; Whorf, *Language, Thought, and Reality*, 212.
25. Thích Minh Châu, "Tôn giáo phải," 364–365.
26. Thích Minh Châu, "Tôn giáo phải," 365.
27. Thích Minh Châu, "Khả tính của Phật Giáo đối với vấn đề hòa bình" [The Capabilities of Buddhism in Relation to the Issue of Peace], *Tư Tưởng* (New series) 2 (July 1969): 3–4.
28. Thích Minh Châu, "Khả tính của Phật Giáo," 9.
29. Thích Minh Châu, "Khả tính của Phật Giáo," 4.
30. Thích Minh Châu, "Đức Phật và vấn đề cải tiến xã hội" [The Buddha and the Issue of Social Reform], *Tư Tưởng* 4, no. 3 (May 1971): 14; see also Thich Minh Chau, "Buddha and the Problems of Social Reform," *Van Hanh Bulletin* 3, no. 4–6 (April-June 1971): 23.
31. Thích Minh Châu, "Đức Phật và vấn đề cải tiến xã hội," 14.
32. Thích Minh Châu, "An Aspect of University Guidance," *Viet Nam Bulletin* 2 (August-September 1969): 4.
33. Thich Minh Chau, "Buddha and the Problems," 22–23.
34. Mohandas Gandhi is the one intellectual and political influence of Thích Minh Châu's who does not fit into this schema. Thích Minh Châu spoke approvingly of Gandhi's political philosophy, in particular of the idea of *satyagraha* or "truth struggle" as a process of forcing the true meaning of words and ideas to be made manifest to political power. Thích Minh Châu, "Bất Bạo Động của Đông Phương: Sức Mạnh của Kẻ Mạnh Nhất" [Nonviolence of the East: The Power of the Strongest], *Tư Tưởng* 3, no. 2 (June 1, 1970): 23–27.
35. Thích Minh Châu, "Lời tòa soạn: Phật giáo đối mặt với thế giới hiện đại" [Introductory remarks: Buddhism in the face of the modern world], *Tư Tưởng* 3, no. 3 (July 1, 1970): 2.
36. Thích Minh Châu, *Trước sự nô lệ của con người*, 234. In the same discussion, in discussing the difficulty of attaining peace through conventional political discourse, he quotes Herbert Marcuse as observing, "Does not the threat of an atomic catastrophe which could wipe out the human race also serve to protect the very forces which perpetuate this danger?" (239).
37. Thich Minh Chau, "Speech Delivered by Venerable Thich Minh Chau, Rector of

Van Hanh University, on the Occasion of the Buddha Jayanti Celebration 517, on 17 May 1973 at Van Hanh University," *Van Hanh Bulletin* 6, no. 2 (June 1973): 10; see also Thích Minh Châu, "Đức Phật và Con Người Hiện Đại" [The Buddha and Modern People], *Tư Tưởng* 6, no. 5–6 (July-August 1973): 11.

38. Gethin, *Foundations of Buddhism*, 100.
39. Thích Minh Châu, "Khả tính của Phật Giáo," 5–6.
40. Thích Minh Châu, "Khả tính của Phật Giáo," 7. See also Batchelor, *Verses from the Center*, 129. Batchelor translates the passage as follows: "Life is no different from nirvana/nirvana no different than life/Life's horizons are nirvana's/the two are exactly the same."
41. Batchelor, *Verses from the Center*, 124; Thích Minh Châu, "Làm thế nào chúng ta," 24–25. Thích Minh Châu's English translation of this passage is "All is harmony indeed for him who in śunyatā conforms/All is not harmonious for him who conforms not to śunyatā."
42. Gadkar-Wilcox, "Existentialism and Intellectual Culture."
43. Thích Minh Châu, *Trước sự nô lệ của con người*, 81; see also Kant, *Kant's Critique*, 223.
44. Thích Minh Châu, "Khả tính của Phật Giáo"; see also Kant, "Appendix," in *Principles of Politics*, 127–128.
45. Thích Minh Châu, "Khả tính của Phật Giáo," 8.
46. Thích Minh Châu, "Khả tính của Phật Giáo," 8.
47. Thích Minh Châu, "Làm thế nào chúng ta," 22; Heidegger, "Letter on Humanism," 265. Thích Minh Châu sees a fundamental connection between Heideggerian notions of being and Buddhism, in particular what he sees as its emphasis on being present in the world. Thích Minh Châu, *Trước sự nô lệ của con người*, 36–37.
48. Marcel, *Paix sur la terre*, 44; Thích Minh Châu, "Khả tính của Phật Giáo," 6.
49. Marcel, *Paix sur la terre*, 57–58; Thích Minh Châu, "Khả tính của Phật Giáo," 7.
50. Jaspers, "Kant's 'Perpetual Peace.'"
51. Fromm, *May Man Prevail?*, 250.
52. Fromm, *May Man Prevail?*, 251.
53. *Van Hanh Newsletter* 1 (June 1967): 1.
54. Thich Minh Chau, "Searching for a Cultural Philosophy," *Van Hanh Bulletin* 1, no. 1 (July 1969): 8–9.
55. Thich Minh Chau, "Searching," 10.
56. Thich Minh Chau, "Searching," 12.
57. Thich Minh Chau, "Searching," 13–14.
58. Thích Minh Châu, "Chân lý, tự do, và nhân tính" [Truth, Freedom, and Humanity], *Tư Tưởng* 2–3 (1968): 25; Thich Minh Chau, "The Role of the University," *Van Hanh Newsletter* 10 (June–July 1968): 1.
59. Thích Minh Châu, "Chân lý, tự do," 26–27; Thich Minh Chau, "Role of the University," 2.
60. Thích Minh Châu, *Trước sự nô lệ của con người*, 286–287.
61. Thích Minh Châu, "Chân lý, tự do," 29; Thich Minh Chau, "Role of the University," 2.
62. Emerson, "Education," 108.
63. Emerson, "Education," 109; Thích Minh Châu, "Phê bình giáo dục thực dụng Tây Phương và xác định đường hướng giáo dục Phật Giáo" [Critique of Pragmatic Western Education and Determination of the Direction of Buddhist Education], *Tư Tưởng* 3, no. 4 (August 1, 1970): 21–22.

64. Thích Minh Châu, "Phê bình giáo," 22; Emerson, "Education," 111–112.
65. *Van Hanh Newsletter* 1 (June 1967): 1.
66. Thích Minh Châu, "Chân lý, tự do," 30–31; Thich Minh Chau, "Role of the University," 8.
67. Thich Quang Minh, "Vietnamese Buddhism in America," 104.
68. *Van Hanh Newsletter* 1 (June 1967): 2.
69. "Kokua Van Hanh," *Van Hanh Newsletter* 2 (July 1967): 4–5.
70. Thích Minh Châu, "Diễn văn của thượng tọa Viện Trưởng" [Speech of the Abbot], *Tư Tưởng* 8, no. 2 (July 20, 1974): 11.
71. Many thanks to Mark Sidel for sharing with me the documentation of this grant.
72. Colin McEnroe, "Architect of Titanic Higher Ed Fiasco will Steer Ship," *Hartford Courant*, September 11, 2015, https://www.courant.com/opinion/op-ed/hc-op-mcenroe-ojakian-wrong-man-for-higher-ed-job-0913-20150910-column.html (accessed August 30, 2019); Gabriella Debenedictis, "Government Less Transparent than Before," *Hartford Courant*, July 7, 2019, https://ctmirror.org/2019/07/07/government-less-transparent-than-before/ (accessed August 30, 2019); Hunt, *University of Nike*, 211–229.
73. Sahlins, *Confucius Institutes*.

CHAPTER 8

Songs of Sympathy in Time of War

Commercial Music in the Republic of Vietnam

Jason Gibbs

Perhaps the most enduring and appreciated vestige of the Republic of Vietnam (RVN) in Vietnam today is its music. Within a pell-mell marketplace of creators and audiences searching for the novel and sensational, a core of music was created that was in harmony with collective values of a sizable portion of the nation's people. The songs that have endured from that time emphasized humanity, sentimental attachments, and deeply felt emotions. Following commercial and musical practices long familiar in the West, this marketplace was nevertheless built locally. The songwriters themselves did much to guide the conditions for this lively scene where creative musicians had extensive opportunities to profit from their works and to achieve and maintain a high standard of living.

The musicians and audiences of that time participated in a vibrant and meaningful musical marketplace, shaping the sound of the Republic. I look at the songs and songwriters, the ways musicians earned a living, and the role of broadcasting and live performance in disseminating the music. I look at sheet music, its production, and cultural significance. Last, I look at the recording industry, taking into consideration how technological innovation changed musical practice.

SONGS AND SONGWRITERS DURING THE FIRST REPUBLIC

The first Vietnamese popular songs written in Western styles date from the late 1930s. The earliest works were often love songs or patriotic songs drawing on heroes and events of Vietnam's past.[1] At the outbreak of the

First Indochina War, a large number of songwriters evacuated to rural Vietnam to join the Việt Minh, where they were active creating and performing music and skits. Songs written in the early years of that war hand an independent, romantic tone, but because the communist party took on a totalizing role in the creation and dissemination of culture such songs were at first discouraged and later prohibited. This music, along with earlier love songs became the basis of a genre known as *nhạc tiền chiến* (antebellum music), which was enjoyed and esteemed by musicians and audiences throughout the Republican era. Because they were suppressed in the communist Democratic Republic of Vietnam (DRV), these works exemplified the freedoms of the RVN. On partition, many Northern musicians who created this music moved to Saigon. The earliest distinct musical trend of the RVN were songs written about the collective sadness and longing of the nearly million Northerners who emigrated south in 1954 and 1955.[2]

Prior to this mass migration, a genre of musical theater called *cải lương* had been the dominant entertainment in the south. *Tân nhạc* (new music), the term used in the South for Western-influenced songs, made slower inroads. The audience for modern popular song had originally been the urban educated upper classes. Ballroom dance was popular with this group and many *tân nhạc* songs were composed to dance rhythms. In the mid- to late 1950s, up-tempo Latin dance rhythms like rumba and chachacha came into vogue. A new style of lively music employing folk-like pentatonic melodies became familiarly known as *dân ca* mambo (mambo folksongs). The lyrics to these songs were a celebration of and a yearning for an idealized village life for new immigrants to the cities many of whom were displaced because of unrest or economic factors.[3] Conservative musicians shocked by these "fiery rhythms" disparaged such music.[4] The audience for these Westernized songs widened owing to the appeal of song lyrics that were more direct than *nhạc tiền chiến* songs, which had been full of metaphor and literary allusion.

The Ngô Đình Diệm government employed cultural propaganda to promote its political and civic agenda, especially through the radio airwaves. Songs that did not mention RVN soldiers often could not be broadcast.[5] One songwriter reported that in those days he wrote about four propaganda songs every month strictly for the remuneration.[6] Such music made few inroads in the marketplace and was largely broadcast and forgotten. Musicians later repudiated this work as being forced on them and unworthy of their talent.[7] Although radio broadcasts devoted a large part of their music programming to songs about Republican soldiers, only the more romantic ones were recorded or published.[8] Members of the military, their families and loved ones were a significant market, but they were not moved by bellicose songs. This subject matter needed to be approached in a sympathetic way. One songwriter realized that his audience was the young people coming of age in a country at war and thus he had to "put himself into their place to learn their concerns and their hopes."[9]

Idyllic songs of true love forced apart became a constant source of inspiration, often expressed metaphorically. A vagabond or wanderer stopping at a small roadside stand described a soldier's life far from home. Young women were sometimes represented as waiting flowers rooted to a place. Some songs described chance encounters between a soldier and a local woman. Others expressed the emotions of soldiers stationed in faraway jungles and highlands. Songs were also written from the perspective of the girlfriend or wife on the home front who longed for a soldier at the front.

Many of the songs created at this time were composed to a bolero rhythm, a slowing down of the *dân ca* mambo tempo. This rhythm became a dominant idiom throughout the RVN beginning in the late 1950s until the end of the Republic. The slow, steady rhythmic engine of the bolero provided a framework for melodies ornamented with the vocal inflections of southern folk music.[10] This also led to a new genre of song and sound recording called *tân cổ giao duyên* (songs new and old of predestined affinity) also known as *tân cổ*, where *tân nhạc* was interpolated with the *vọng cổ* (longing for the past) aria of *cải lương* (reformed musical theater). This transformed existing songs into mini dramas. The intersection of Westernized song with traditional melody found a large audience among working-class Southerners.

SECURITY FORCES AND PSYCHOLOGICAL WARFARE

Nearly every man creating commercial music (they were almost entirely men) had to join some branch of the security forces of the RVN. Musicians were rarely combatants, but instead members of artistic troupes or involved with musical programming, logistics, or psychological warfare. They played an ever-present role in the musical marketplace of the Republic. During the First Republic, psychological warfare campaigns focused on forming mobile squads equipped with loudspeakers that engaged with the rural population performing skits and songs.[11] Their aim was to "entertain the populace and propagate the Vietnamese government's policies and line."[12] Music for the Open Arms (Chiêu Hồi) programs were often like siren songs calling enemy combatants back to their wives or girlfriends.[13]

The fall of the Ngô Đình Diệm regime resulted in a reorganization of the psychological warfare program. The Psychological Warfare Bureau (Cục Tâm Lý Chiến) became part of the larger Political Warfare Office (Tổng cục Chiến Tranh Chính Trị). The resulting Performing Arts Department (Phòng Văn Nghệ) demonstrated a new emphasis on supporting creative workers like poets, playwrights, and songwriters in the creation of works to support the government and armed forces. Many of those who worked for the Performing Arts Department of the Psychological Warfare Bureau were familiar with the cultural program of the communists and opposed such a doctrinaire approach realizing that it would not reflect the values of their nation or succeed in a republic that promoted liberty and viewed itself as the alternative to the totalitarian North.[14] One aim was to create works to "expose the lies and cruelty of the enemy" while not disparaging them. They praised their own side, but did not overamplify their successes. The songs portrayed Republican soldiers facing hardship but faithful to their loved ones and to their country.[15]

SONGS AND SONGWRITERS AFTER 1963

After the fall of the First Republic, censorship relaxed considerably. Songs that been previously banned made it into publication and onto the airwaves.[16] This easing of restrictions also resulted in greater commercial competition in the music marketplace. Music had become more lucrative than ever; songs that stood out owing to their novelty or through effective publicity had greater opportunities. Despite a desire among cultural leaders to promote an optimistic culture that supported the Republic and its cause, they had to acknowledge that a free country could not ban sad songs as the communist North did. There were attempts to keep them off of the airwaves, but this proved difficult because many songwriters, music publishers and record labels resorted to bribery to get their songs broadcast.[17]

Newspaper critics lamented the growing popularity of inexperienced songwriters who pandered to the public. Although the music broadcast during Ngô Đình Diệm's time may have been too bellicose, songs were now too individualistic and sentimental and did not do their part for the war.[18] Others complained that the songs merely expressed trite sentiments or were an extended lament about fate.[19] One commentator protested that songwriters and singers had created such an attractive product that they impaired the judgment of the gullible majority of the listening audience.[20] Another criticism was that melodies sounded like *cải lương,* meaning they had the sad affect of the *vọng cổ* aria.[21]

To combat this problem some songs were not permitted to be broadcast. A March 1967 newspaper article announced that twenty-three "maudlin" (*ủy mị*), so-called anti-war songs had been banned from the Voice of the Armed Forces radio and on Armed Forces television.[22] Some of the offending music was created by psywar songwriters.[23] Those were only a small number of the songs that expressed the soldier's ambivalence about his lot. Some describe his longing for city life and the love he left behind there. In others, soldiers lamented their uncertain futures with the regret that war interrupted what should have been the prime of their lives. Some expressed the close bonds among Republican soldiers. RVN composers also wrote many songs for Tết, the spring New Year's holiday when families gather and celebrate. Many of the songs were specifically written for RVN soldiers, both giving loved ones at home a reminder of soldier's life at the front and expressing a hope for peace.

Psywar songs effectively depicted the destruction inflicted by the enemy on the civilian population of the South in songs. The strongest manifestation of collective sentiment came after the attacks of the 1968 Tết Offensive. A number of songs were written about the death and devastation in the beloved imperial capital Huế. These songs reinforced a growing popular sentiment toward the republican government and armed forces.[24] The Tết Offensive was a shock to the people of the RVN. Songs of the following years reflect the circumstances of soldiers were unable to return home to their families for the holiday—a soldier's duty kept him from performing a son's duty. As the Paris Peace Accords were being negotiated and after they were signed, many songs reflected a collective hope for peace and a return to normal life.

An alternative to the prevailing slow, melancholy songs emerged in the late 1950s and early 1960s with a style of music known as *kích động nhạc* (action music). This rock music with electric guitars and drum sets began to thrive after the fall of the Diệm regime. At first there were only covers of Western pop and rock music, but soon songwriting professionals began to write their own rock songs.[25] The stars of this genre were Hùng Cường and Mai Lệ Huyền, the former portrayed a swashbuckling RVN soldier and the latter his fun-loving girlfriend who thinks soldiers are the best and tries not to blame them for being gone so much while defending the nation in glory.

Two developments in the 1970s I think would have shaped future Vietnamese popular music had the RVN continued after April 1975. The first was this growing influence of rock music. The phenomenon of students forming cover bands to play Western rock music became known as *nhạc trẻ* (youth music). The young musicians, most notably the Phượng Hoàng Band, moved from covering songs to creating their own. Their songs expressed both a disillusionment with lives shadowed by constant war and an appreciation of the love and beauty they sought within these circumstances.[26] They attracted an audience of students already drawn toward Western pop and rock music.

The second trend was the tendency of songwriters to create songs with simpler melodies and lyrics for the lower rungs of society. These songs thrived during the period of relative peace after 1972 with subject matter that frequently reflected the realities of lives of the poor and directly addressed the limitations that poverty placed on their choices in life, especially their hopes for love and marriage. Songs of this type, I believe, would have come to dominate the music marketplace after 1975.

THE MUSICIAN IN THE MARKETPLACE

The majority of musicians in the RVN were at least part-time soldiers. In addition to their military service, they could be involved in a variety of ventures, such as performing, teaching, recording, sales, and publishing.[27] Their work within the armed forces often only occupied them during working hours, leaving evenings and weekends for their music activities.[28] Typically these musical side jobs provided their principal source of income. Musicians have told of a nightly transition from a military uniform during the day to a formal jacket at night when they played music at restaurants and dancehalls.[29] Performing music in Western popular styles for GIs and other foreigners helped many musicians earn a substantial living. One soldier-musician described paying off sentries at his post so he could sneak off to make money playing music at American clubs at night.[30]

Nhạc trẻ musicians, often still teenagers, made great efforts to learn a repertoire of music to entertain foreign soldiers and civilians stationed in Vietnam. They taught themselves the necessary styles and repertoire by working with more experienced musicians and by listening to imported long-playing records. These rock groups had many lucrative opportunities to entertain foreign soldiers at bases all over the country. They were transported by military planes to posts near and far, sometimes directly to the front. The Vietnamese performers were treated with respect on the bases because this entertainment was so important to the troops. American soldiers even carried their equipment onto the stage.[31]

To earn extra money many musicians also offered private lessons or taught classes. Others trained singers or worked as vocal coaches. Singers were the main face of the new music. A 1967 newspaper article reported that there were around six hundred singers who regularly performed for radio and television programs, and of those only thirty were top-tier professionals. The very top performers could earn as high as 100,000 đồng for an appearance. Those on the lower tier earned around 40,000 đồng a month.[32] Most of the broadcast vocalists were students or had other jobs and might appear on air once or twice a month, more vocalists were female than male, and around 60 percent of the performers were under twenty-five. A television producer acknowledged that television singers must have three qualities—be photogenic, be able to sing well, and gesture as they sing.[33] The personal lives of young women performers became fodder for tabloid-like treatment.[34] Singers were also conscious of their role in supporting the military and frequently performed at benefits and traveled to bases to entertain the Republic's troops. One popular female singer wrote an open letter to a newspaper expressing her concern and admiration for RVN soldiers and her appreciation of the fan mail she received from them.[35]

Ballroom dance had been a popular leisure activity since the colonial era. When the government shut down the dance halls between 1959 and 1963, the response of musicians and people who enjoyed nightlife was to move live entertainment to tea rooms (phòng trà). Each tearoom had a house band. A succession of singers traveled from venue to venue sometimes singing at as many as eight venues, a practice known as chạy sô (running shows).[36]

In 1964 the dancehalls reopened. Some of these establishments, especially those in Chợ Lớn (the Chinese nightlife district in Saigon), catered to an affluent clientele and paid high wages for the best musicians. These musicians were often Chinese or Philippine, but a growing number of Vietnamese met these high standards. Chợ Lớn clubs also brought in well-known vocalists from Hong Kong and Taiwan; taxi dancers were also a very important feature of these night spots.[37] Some locations like Văn Cảnh, Grande Monde, and Maxim's also had elaborate floor shows. For the sake of variety musicians moved from nightclub to nightclub every three to six months. Some also got jobs in more remote locations like Đà Lạt and Đà Nẵng. Because there was a midnight curfew, dancehalls only opened their doors from 8 until 11 p.m. During the summer offensive of 1972, known as the Mùa hè đỏ lửa (Summer of red flames), the government closed the dancehalls and the musicians returned to the tea rooms.[38]

From the early days of the RVN, musicians organized troupes to perform music and skits, sometimes at the direction of the government other times for profit. Such troupes also performed in theaters in Saigon and toured the provinces.[39] These musician-entrepreneurs set up musical extravaganzas known as đại nhạc hội (music festivals).[40] The programs at some of Saigon's larger theaters lasting two to three hours drew audiences of between one and two thousand.[41] On some weekends there were competing festivals each trumpeting its own cast of stars. This form of entertainment aimed to appeal to audiences of all ages and backgrounds. The programs were like vaudeville performances with singers, comedians, skits, and dancing demonstrations. A major appeal of these shows was the possibility of seeing the celebrities of the stage, radio, television, and recordings in person.

After the change of government in 1963, organizers of these shows tried ever more outrageous ways to pull an audience away from their competitors. Shows sometimes included martial arts demonstrations, beauty pageants, and sexy dance routines. Some were also organized around cải lương, presenting excerpts from plays, shorter dramas along with other variety show elements. Performances of cải lương plays themselves became more like variety shows, incorporating rock music, Vietnamese and foreign songs, and sometimes risqué dance routines.[42]

In 1965, Trường Kỳ organized the Đại Hội Nhạc Trẻ Taberd (Taberd Youth Music Festival) at his Catholic High School run by Lasallian brothers that featured young people playing rock and roll cover songs. He also regularly organized the "Hippies à go go" rock music programs at nightclubs. The Political War Office also hired him to put together nhạc trẻ programs as a benefit for the wounded veterans and war widows. His crowning achievement was an International Outdoor Youth Music Festival held at Hoa Lư Stadium on May 29, 1971. Sponsored by the Political War Office, this concert featuring nineteen rock bands from five countries attracted an audience of seven thousand as well as international press coverage, a propaganda victory for the RVN.[43]

BROADCASTING

Radio-France-Asie (known in Vietnamese as Đài Pháp Á) had been run by the State of Vietnam as a subsidiary of the Radiodiffusion-Télévision

Française (French Radio and Television Broadcasting). It was handed over to the government of the RVN in February 1956 and was renamed Đài Vô Tuyến Việt Nam (Vietnam Radio, or VTVN).[44] Over time, its signal was made more widely available through a system of regional substations.[45] The other major broadcasting station aimed at listeners in the Republic was the Đài Phát Thanh Quân Đội (Armed Forces Radio), a branch of the Psychological Warfare Bureau. Later stations included the Tiếng Nói Tự Do (Voice of Freedom) created in 1964 under the tutelage of the Voice of America to broadcast for audiences in the North. Mẹ Việt Nam (Mother Vietnam), Gươm Thiêng Ái Quốc (Sacred Patriotic Sword), and Giải Phóng Nam Bộ (Southern Liberation) were all stations set up for American psywar purposes.[46]

VTVN and Armed Forces Radio were both commercial-free, government-funded stations. In the early 1960s, VTVN offered around four and a half hours of cultural programming on weekdays, broken into thirty- to fifty-minute blocks. These were live broadcasts that included poetry, Western classical music, folk music, traditional musical theater, as well as *tân nhạc*.[47] The most popular programs were broadcast on weekends and included live *cải lương* performances. Sundays featured audience participation shows like talent search programs for singers and an all-request song program.[48]

Although VTVN did not have commercial aims, it did provide modestly paid, stable government jobs to its editorial staff, program directors, and musicians. The various live music shows employed bandleaders as subcontractors who hired instrumentalists and vocalists and were positioned as gatekeepers into the musical marketplace. A newspaper writer complained that these bandleaders just rented the airwaves during their time slot to whoever paid to promote their songs.[49] The radio stations often promulgated rules limiting the number of songs that could be broadcast by a single songwriter; rules evaded through the use of pseudonyms.

Radio reached its widest audience with the proliferation of cheap transistor radios in the early to mid-1960s.[50] In November 1965, VTVN moved to a twenty-four-hour broadcasting schedule. These additional programming hours were made possible because of newly introduced technologies such as transcription discs and magnetic reel-to-reel tapes for prerecording or rebroadcasting programs.[51] Radio programs also increasingly relied on commercially released recordings to fill out their programs.

The media landscape would change significantly in February 1966 when the RVN introduced its first television station. The government had insisted that the American authorities construct these broadcast facilities as a concession for their setting up an English-language channel for their own armed forces in Vietnam.⁵² At the outset the viewing audience was small because there were so few television sets, but after a time television cut deeply into radio's audience. RVN television programming also had limited hours. In the beginning the broadcast day began at 7:30 p.m. and ended at around 10 p.m. The content was locally produced with news and public affairs programs, plus short plays, *cải lương*, and a few *tân nhạc* programs.⁵³ Television being less staid than radio also included programs of *nhạc trẻ* that appealed to younger audiences. The English-language American television stations in Saigon and Đà Nẵng occasionally featured Vietnamese rock groups.⁵⁴ Musicians also worked in film. Composers with classical training who wrote soundtracks and popular vocalists sometimes also appeared on screen.

SHEET MUSIC

Sheet music was a popular music commodity through the history of the RVN. Printed sheet music only notated the words and melody of a song without written piano accompaniment or chord symbols to assist a guitar player. A song's cover page was illustrated with an offset print of one or multiple colors, or with a photograph often of a singer or celebrity. Because the songs were displayed in shops and kiosks, the cover art played an important role in enhancing the music's appeal. The music itself was printed on the two interior pages. The final page was usually an advertisement for the publisher, for a music class, or for a songwriter's other works.

 Although sheet music was attractive because of its packaging and sentiment expressed by the songs, it was also popular because it was inexpensive. It was an easily affordable treat or gift that carried a sentimental meaning. Used sheet music from that time often shows handwritten inscriptions that are either messages to the recipient of a song or tell of the feelings or circumstances of the buyer. Sometimes a song sheet became a memento of a meaningful event or relationship. The sheet music also had other social meanings. Some bought it just to learn song lyrics, to sing the song to themselves in a moment of solitude, or to sing together and share with friends. During the Tết Offensive families confined to their homes sang from sheet music to entertain each other.⁵⁵ Groups of young men also gathered in the alleys of Saigon singing from sheet music accompanied by a guitar to send off a friend who was about to join the armed forces.

A number of major publishers had already been established in the State of Vietnam before 1954. The Tinh Hoa publishing house, founded in Huế in the 1940s, moved south to Saigon in 1956 becoming Tinh Hoa Miền Hoa, an imprint that appeared on several hundred songs. An Phú publishing house, founded in 1951, also published hundreds of titles, over time becoming more active as a distributor than as a publisher. It was not a storefront but more of a counter or stall.[56] An Phú also had smaller retail branches in provincial cities. The Diên Hồng publishing house was established in 1955, and was also an important sheet music distributor. A number of small publishers opened and closed during the 1950s such as Lúa Mới, Lam Sơn, and Mỹ Tín. Principally a musical instrument workshop and store, the latter also published a half dozen *dân ca* mambo songs.

Minh Phát emerged in 1963 as one of the RVN's most successful publishers and distributors releasing well over a hundred songs, but its success lay primarily in its distribution network. The imprint was run by Nguyễn Đăng Minh, who set up shop on the countertop of a cart he stored on the sidewalk in Saigon's central business district. He pulled his wares from within these carts and packed them up at the end of the day. Although not a musician, he was adept at identifying a song's commercial potential. His approval allowed composers who self-published their works to get them distributed far and wide. For tax purposes, he sometimes preferred to issue his own imprints as if they were published by the songwriters themselves.[57]

Some songwriters started their own publishing house to release their own songs and those of others. Hoàng Thi Thơ published under the Ly Tao imprint. A 1964 newspaper column noted that the hottest songs were being published by 1,001 Bài Ca Hay, directed by Duy Khánh, a psywar officer and popular singer-songwriter.[58] Nhạc Hay Của Bạn was the publishing house of songwriter Trần Thiện Thanh, another psywar officer who was also a singer and recording artist using the name Nhật Trường. Thùy Dương Nhạc Tuyển was the imprint for Châu Kỳ, a musician who had been a pioneering vocalist during the late 1940s and early 1950s. Song Ngọc's Tình Ca 20 company also opened a two-story shop of the same name in Phú Nhuận that sold sheet music and sound recordings. Tiếng K Thời Đại was started by Nguyễn Khuyến, Saigon's best-known magician, who wrote songs using the penname Bảo Thu. In 1965, Nguyễn Văn Đông, who was also a military officer, started the successful Trăm Hoa Miền Nam (One hundred flowers of the south) music publishing company named after the short-lived Chinese free expression movement.

The Sóng Nhạc music imprint was directed by Lê Minh Bằng, pseudonym for a group of songwriters—Lê Dinh, Minh Kỳ, and Anh Bằng. They published over two hundred songs that were often concurrently recorded on the Sóng Nhạc record label. The Việt Nam record label also started a sheet music imprint called Việt Nam Nhạc Tuyển. At the outset, they focused on *kích động nhạc* but subsequently printed many best-selling songs in other styles.[59]

The period between 1965 through 1972 was the peak of printed music publication and corresponds to the years when the American economic presence was strongest in the RVN. In the later years, songwriters increasingly opted to self-publish and rely on existing distribution networks. Two new companies in the publishing and distribution business also came into being. The Mỹ Hạnh company entered in 1966 and specialized in reprinting earlier classic songs. Nhạc Mới, started by Ngọc Chánh in 1972, introduced many foreign songs with Vietnamese lyrics and *nhạc trẻ*.

Although no official documentation attests to sheet music sales, writing songs could be a very lucrative profession. Reports are numerous of the most popular songs selling five hundred thousand or more copies.[60] Revenues from the sheet music sales of a single blockbuster song could pay a songwriter enough royalties to buy a new car. Another songwriter told me that a successful song could support him for five or six months.[61]

SOUND RECORDING

The commercial recording of Vietnamese music began in the earliest years of the twentieth century and was for many years controlled by multinational record labels from Europe and America. Asia Records, founded by Ngô Văn Tri and Ngô Văn Mạnh (Năm Mạnh) in 1936, was the first Vietnamese-owned record label. They quickly dominated the local market because of their understanding of the Vietnamese audience and because they manufactured their records cheaply and locally undercutting the price of their competitors.[62] Possessing the only disc manufacturing equipment in French Indochina, Asia was the only label to issue new recordings during World War II. They continued to make new recordings with the label well into the early years of the RVN.

Although the vast majority of Asia's recordings were of *cải lương* and its *vọng cổ* aria, they also released a small number of *tân nhạc* recordings.

In 1954, Asia took a foray into the *dân ca* mambo market with the subsidiary Việt Thanh label operated by Ngô Thị Kha (Ngô Văn Mạnh's sister). She also played a role in the company's move to seven-inch 45 rpm records with the affiliated Asia Sóng Nhạc label. Her husband Nguyễn Tất Oanh (Tám Oanh) became the company director.[63] The label owed much of its success to the artistic direction of the Lê Minh Bằng songwriting trio. Sóng Nhạc began releasing seven-inch *tân nhạc* records in 1961. These and most other Vietnamese seven-inch discs were extended play recordings with two songs per side. Over a decade, Sóng Nhạc released more than two hundred recordings in this format.

Hãng Dĩa Việt Nam (Vietnam Records) also had roots in colonial French Indochina. Lê Văn Tài, the original owner, had been the primary agent for Victor Records in Cochinchina. He began releasing recordings in the late 1940s. After he passed away, the label was run by his daughter Lê Ngọc Liên (cô Sáu Liên). The company sold sound recordings continuously through 1978, when the new government seized its property.[64] The Việt Nam label released several dozen *tân nhạc* discs on 78 rpm discs in the 1950s. Beginning in 1958, it released hundreds of seven-inch recordings of *tân nhạc* and *tân cổ giao duyên*. They also released *cải lương* performances in sets of up to twelve seven-inch records or in sets of up to four 33 rpm ten-inch, long-playing discs.

The Hoành Sơn label was an early competitor that manufactured its 78 rpm records on modern equipment in Europe to try to gain an edge in quality over their competitors.[65] Lam Sơn was another important record label of the early days of the RVN. During the 1950s, it issued more than 150 78 rpm releases, some in sets of as many as ten discs of mostly *cải lương*. In the early 1950s, it became affiliated with the Hồng Hoa label devoted to *cải lương, vọng cổ,* and *tân cổ giao duyên*. The Tân Thanh (New Sound) label recorded both *tân nhạc* and *tân cổ* on 78 and 45 rpm discs. The Việt Hải label also started out producing 78 rpm recordings and later released around a hundred mostly *vọng cổ* performances on seven-inch records.

During the 1960s, several additional labels devoted to *tân nhạc* released seven-inch records. These labels included Capitol (no relationship to the American company), which made more than fifty releases of *tân nhạc* and *tân cổ giao duyên,* and Dư Âm, which released more than thirty discs. The Nhạc Ngày Xanh, Thiên Thai, Tình Ca Quê Hương, and Nhạc Tuyển Vô Tuyến companies were all doubled as music publishers and record labels.

Nguyễn Văn Đông was artistic director of Continental Records. Closely connected with his Trăm Hoa Miền Nam publishing house, the label released more than 150 seven-inch records through 1972. Continental also released at least twenty sets of *cải lương* plays presented on up to four 33 rpm ten-inch discs. He later started the Sơn Ca record label in 1967 entirely devoted to *tân nhạc*. He noted that *cải lương* recordings largely underwrote the recording of *tân nhạc* songs. The initial release of a *cải lương* was an issue of ten thousand discs, but only five thousand discs of a *tân nhạc* recording would be manufactured. A typical *cải lương* program sold seventy thousand copies whereas a *tân nhạc* recording usually only sold five thousand. The former had an audience throughout all of rural Vietnam while the latter's audience was largely concentrated in the cities. Nguyễn Văn Đông attributed the success of the Continental label to his constant attention to the tastes and preferences of his audience. He stayed in close contact with thirty-six sales representatives all over the republic to get a sense of what kinds of subject matter was welcomed by listeners.[66]

The years 1966 and 1967 marked a turning point in the music market of the RVN, when sound recordings began to overtake sheet music in promoting songs.[67] Records and record players had always been a relative luxury. So were reel-to-reel tape recorders, which became more common at this time. Labels began to create album length programs for this medium that could play back more than an hour of music. Cassette tape technology soon followed. It was welcomed in the developing world in the late 1960s and soon became ubiquitous given the production of inexpensive, battery-powered portable cassette players. This new format put sound recordings into the hands of more people than ever. It also resulted in an increase in music piracy. Because cassette technology allowed for both playback and recording, it opened up the production of music to a wider range of musical entrepreneurs.[68]

The earliest cassette tape releases in the RVN date from around 1969 and paralleled existing reel-to-reel tape programs. With seven-inch records, listeners could enjoy only two to four songs. Tracks were limited to three or four minutes in length, thus songs had to be performed at brisk tempos. The technology for duplicating cassettes was simpler and less expensive than that for records. Furthermore, a cassette tape could easily hold eighteen tracks, nine on each side of the tape. Existing record labels soon focused their attention on the cassette business. Continental started off by pulling together tracks from earlier disc recordings to assemble cassettes programs organized by recording artist or theme. Soon they began to release new recordings only on reel-to-reel and cassette tape. Familiar songs were frequently reinterpreted with more up-to-date instrumentation (usually more electric guitar centered) and with slower tempos because tape allowed for longer tracks.

This easily accessible technology allowed for new kinds of commercial recordings. In January 1970, songwriter Phạm Mạnh Cương released a monthly series in twenty-six installments of recordings made in Saigon's tea rooms that capture the atmosphere of that musical culture.[69] The audio cassette was a boon for *nhạc trẻ* performers, who began to be featured on tapes that documented many of the singers and bands that played in American clubs. These were presented on cassette labels such as Nhạc Trẻ, Tình Ca Nhạc Trẻ, Nhạc Hồng, and Thế Giới Nhạc Trẻ. New labels benefiting from the cassette explosion of the final years of the RVN included Diễm Ca, Hoạ Mi, Kim Đằng, Mây Hồng, Nghệ Thuật, Nhạc Vàng, Nhã Ca, Phượng Hồng, Shotguns, Tơ Vàng, and Thương Ca. Best-selling singers produced reel-to-reel and cassette albums in their own names.

Entrepreneurs opened stalls at the Thương Xá Crystal Palace, a modern, four-story shopping mall in Saigon's commercial center. The advent of cassette tapes made these businesses even more profitable. In October of 1969, the Trung Tâm Băng Nhạc Jo Marcel opened a large air-conditioned store where music lovers could sample and choose the programs they liked. They advertised heavily and at times struggled to keep up with the high demand. To further profit from this phenomenon, they opened a recording studio and released over thirty-seven original albums recording more than five hundred tracks.[70]

Others saw opportunity in creating bootleg recordings. A young entrepreneur named Trịnh Quan set up a number of kiosks around Saigon that created custom reel-to-reel, cassette, or eight track tape programs on demand, drawing from a large supply of source tapes.[71] Attention to the needs of the customer was a good way to do business but the beginning of the crippling problem of intellectual property theft that has harmed Vietnamese musicians ever since.

The music life of the RVN provided a stark contrast with that of the DRV. The DRV government maintained total control over all cultural institutions; there were no independent cultural or business outlets. Government companies held a monopoly on sheet music and sound recordings. All musicians and musical ensembles were directly employed by the government. The state held a monopoly on all media. Musicians could not form their own ensembles or companies.

The music of the RVN arose from within a larger Vietnamese nation in conflict with itself with two competing visions for Vietnamese society. Its government was not in a position to command its artists and people to strictly adhere to its policies. By promoting intellectual and creative freedom the state distinguished itself from ideology and governance of the DRV. Musicians created works that were welcomed and rewarded by audiences and consumers of recordings and sheet music. Psychological warfare played a significant role in guiding songwriters' creative output and certainly shaped the creative works that entered the musical marketplace. Government programmed radio and television broadcasts also helped form popular taste. But the government's influence was limited as commercialized music came to dominate the airwaves. The government's public broadcasters were unable to do anything about programmers who succumbed to bribery from musicians or companies that wanted exposure for their music.[72]

The war and the presence of foreign armed forces and civilians pumped a great deal of money into the Republic's economy and the wallets of independent musicians. Nightclub performers and the bands who performed on American bases made a very handsome living. With possibilities like this it is not surprising that songwriters or publishers would resort to whatever they could to gain an audience for their work. Vocalists also had myriad opportunities to earn money performing songs and became highly paid celebrities.

The cultural and governmental authorities of the RVN, by allowing for a proliferation of songs of sentiment and affection instead of aggressive martial music, created a people more unified behind the country. Songwriters felt as if it was part of their duty to write music that was in sympathy with the people's feelings.[73] Much like Olga Dror has described in her study of textbooks in the RVN, popular song frequently expressed both hopes for future peace and sorrow for the destruction brought by war. Some of the songs expressed anger about the acts of the enemy, but none denounced the enemy soldier, perhaps because of an underlying understanding that they were all one nation and they hoped their foe could be brought to the right cause. This contrasted with the attitude of the Hanoi government, which had a clear and unforgiving view of its enemy as stooges of the Americans.[74]

The DRV and the Socialist Republic of Vietnam (SRV) that came into existence in 1976 banned the music of the RVN to its fullest abilities. They derided this music as *nhạc vàng*, a word that in Vietnamese could mean either golden or yellow music. This term derived from the Maoist concept of *hoangse yinyue* (黄色音乐) where the color is unambiguously yellow, and by implication, sickly.[75] Nhạc vàng was especially noxious because of its relationship to "colonialist imperialism" and the global exploitation of capitalist market forces. Aspersions to these songs being a psychological warfare scheme of propaganda were not unreasonable.

In 1976, a DRV musicologist and songwriter wrote a cautionary analysis of *nhạc vàng* highlighting the dangerous attraction of the music's sad desperate lyrics, relaxed flowing melodies, and overly emotional singing. This music was a greater danger than any politically reactionary music because it "horns its way into the soul like a night shadow and lulls one's vigilance because of its sweet and gentle appearance."[76] As this article was being published, music of the RVN had already become pervasive in the postwar North after having been brought back by soldiers as spoils of war. In fact, this *nhạc vàng* had already been a troubling specter during the war showing up at the movie theaters, weddings, and schools of the North.[77] The DRV government had arrested and sentenced some Hanoians to prison for furtively listening to RVN radio and singing the songs.[78]

The communist government worried that this soft music would sap the will of young people to take up arms to fight and deplete their energy to build a socialist state. Government officials and intellectuals of the RVN had had much the same fear. Looked at generously some of them complained that the music of the marketplace was full of too many meaningless love songs written following the whims of fashion.[79] Of particular concern was the disheartening effect this "debauched" music would have on young people and that it would "kill off the nation's will to live."[80]

The music was as dangerous as the communist government believed because it provided such an appealing antidote to the outlook and way of living the government promoted. After 1975 the SRV remained on a permanent war footing with enemies within and without. The entire musical corpus of the RVN remained banned until 1989. Since that time, more and more songs from the Republic have gradually entered legal circulation.[81] Although prohibited, these songs had never been absent from Vietnam. Audio, videocassette, and compact disc duplication spread this music everywhere, inside and outside Vietnam. Today, nearly the entire RVN song repertory is easily accessed online.

Naturally, the musical legacy of the RVN has played a crucial role in the lives of diasporic Vietnamese. Songs that reflected the emotional and personal sacrifice made by soldiers and their loved ones during the war could come to represent the sacrifices families made when leaving their homeland to live on foreign soil. Working within the communities living in refugee camps and newly settled in the United States, ethnomusicologist Adelaida Reyes describes how immigrants presented this music as an important part of Vietnamese identity.[82] One interviewee said that when she was growing up in Vietnam she had been indifferent to these songs and only grew to love and appreciate them after she left the country behind her.[83]

The musical era that gave birth to these songs ended almost half a century ago. The generation that created and popularized this music is approaching the end of their lives, yet the music of the RVN has continued to touch and resonate with listeners in successive generations. The songs were created during the most difficult period of recent Vietnamese history and arose from events that took place long ago, yet these songs deliver messages that resonate with Vietnamese audiences everywhere. Songs that appeal to people's sympathies with each other and with their nation continue to endure and to heal.

NOTES

1. Lê Thương, "Thời tiền chiến trong tân nhạc (1938–1946)," in *Nhạc tiền chiến*, ed. Đỗ Kim Bảng, 62–70.

2. Gibbs, *Rock Hà Nội*, 99–101. These songs carried a message that corresponded with the North-South Compassion Campaign mentioned in Jason Picard's "They Eat the Flesh of Children."

3. Trương Hoàng Xuân, interview, Hồ Chí Minh City, June 10, 2012.

4. Nguiễn Ngu Í, "Bách Khoa phỏng vấn giới nhạc sĩ: Thẩm Oánh," *Bách Khoa* no. 156 (July 1, 1963): 95–96.

5. Thanh Sơn, interview, Hồ Chí Minh City, November 15, 1998.

6. Trương Hoàng Xuân, interview.

7. Phạm Duy, *Hồi ký thời phân*, 93.

8. Thanh Sơn, interview.

9. Nguiễn Ngu Í, "Bách-Khoa phỏng vấn giới nhạc sĩ: Minh Kỳ," *Bách Khoa* no. 158 (November 1, 1963): 107–108.

10. Gibbs, "Songs of Night's Intimacy."

11. Roberts, *Psychological War*, 105–106. For a description of the activities of one of these troupes, see Diệu Tân, "Thi sĩ, kịch sĩ Anh Bằng," in *Kỷ niệm về nhạc sĩ Anh Bằng*, 138–147.

12. Nguyễn Long, *Ký ức của một người Việt*, 94.

13. Lê Dinh, "Anh Bằng và tôi," in *Kỷ niệm về nhạc sĩ Anh Bằng*, 31.

14. Nguyễn Công Luận, *Nationalist*, 190.

15. Đỗ Kim Bảng, Facebook message, June 22, 2019. Some examples of psywar campaigns included the tiller gets a field, calls to enlist, communist denunciation, and the open arms program. Lê Dinh, "Anh Bằng và tôi," 31.

16. Mặc Thế Nhân, interview, Lái Thiêu, Việt Nam, November 12, 1998.

17. Ngô Liên, "Nhạc kể lể con cà con kê," *Chính Luận*, May 23–24, 1965, 4; Nguyễn Ánh 9, interview, Hồ Chí Minh City, August 3, 2015.

18. HH Lan Hà, "Thực trạng của nền tân nhạc VN hiện tại," *Bình Minh*, April 21, 1967, 2.

19. "Lành mạnh hóa âm nhạc Việt-Nam là một nhiệm vụ cấp thiết," *Chính Luận*, September 4, 1965, 5.

20. Tinh Tú, "Sự phổ biến ca nhạc bừa bãi cũng do sự thiệu phê bình chỉ trích của dư luận," *Bình Minh*, December 10, 1967, 2.

21. "Một khía cạnh của thúi nát xã hội: Văn nghệ sa đoạ," *Tiếng gọi miền Tây*, June 25, 1966, 6–7.

22. "23 bài hát ủy mị ngưng phổ biến," *Bình Minh*, March 31, 1966, 2.

23. Representatives of the Đại Hội Văn Hóa Dân Tộc [National Culture Congress] charged that psywar songwriters were trying to out-do their competitors on the outside by writing lyrical, romantic songs. "Tân nhạc rũ rượi—du dương của các đài phát thanh bị lên án," *Chính Luận*, August 19, 1966, 4.

24. Taylor, *History of the Vietnamese*, 604.

25. Nguyễn Công Luận, *Nationalist*, 234, 238.

26. Gibbs, "Phượng Hoàng," 17–32.

27. Đỗ Kim Bảng, Facebook message, June 26, 2019.

28. Nguyễn Văn Đông, interview, June 18, 2009.

29. Trương Xuân Hồng, interview; Nguyễn Ánh 9, interview.

30. Trần Đăng Chí, interview, Garden Grove, CA, June 11, 2016.

31. These groups consisted of four or five band members plus a female vocalist, two go-go dancers and a stripper. Quốc Vượng, interview, Hồ Chí Minh City, June 13, 2012.

32. The value of the đồng frequently fluctuated at this time. In 1967 the official rate was 118 đồng to the dollar. Thus 100,000 đồng equaled approximately $847 and 40,000 đồng equaled $339. This was at a time when the annual per capita gross domestic product in the RVN was $148. United Nations, *Statistical Yearbook*, 600.

33. Xuân Huy, "Hoạt động của giới nhạc trẻ đang lên tại Saigon," *Bình Minh*, September 14, 1967, 3; September 15, 1967, 3.

34. Throughout the latter half of 1967 a long series of reportage concerned the personal lives of young female vocalists in the *Bình Minh* newspaper.

35. Lê Hiếu, "Nữ danh ca Minh Hiếu một trong những người em gái hậu phương gửi bức tâm thư đến các chiến sĩ," *Hậu Phương*, July 4, 1965, 3.

36. Nguyễn Long, *Ký ức*, 155. The newspaper *Báo mới* of October 13, 1962, featured advertisements for seven tea rooms in Saigon and Chợ Lớn.

37. Tám Lang, interview, Hồ Chí Minh City, June 13, 2012; Trần Đăng Chí, interview.

38. Huỳnh Hữu Thạnh, interview, Hồ Chí Minh City, June 9, 2012.

39. Nguyễn Long, *Ký ức*, 99–102, 107–110.

40. Trần Quang Hải, "Trần Văn Trạch (1923–1994), nhạc sĩ hài hước của làng tân nhạc Việt Nam," *Thế giới nghệ sĩ* 114 (April 14, 2017): 8–9, 11.

41. Lam Phương, interview, Garden Grove, CA, September 23, 2003.

42. Ethnomusicologist Terry E. Miller, stationed as a GI in 1970, attended *cải lương* performances in Saigon and compared them to a "crazy sideshow." Miller, "Music and Theater."

43. Trường Kỳ, *Một thời nhạc trẻ*, 121–123, 226, 265–266, 281. Trường Kỳ helped change the name of rock music from *kích động nhạc* to *nhạc trẻ*. For him, *kích động* implied

something shocking and *nhạc trẻ* represented a sound that was "youthful, new and unusual." See Gibbs, "How Does Hanoi Rock?," 14.

44. The station was also known as the Đài Phát Thanh Quốc Gia [National Radio] or Đài Phát Thanh Saigon. "La radio à Saïgon," *Saigon / Vietnam*, http://saigon-vietnam.fr/radio-saigon_fr.php (accessed August 29, 2019).

45. Smith et al., *Area Handbook*, 290–292.

46. Nguyễn Huy, "Cựu nhân viên đài Tiếng Nói Tự Do, Mẹ Việt Nam hội ngộ," *Người Việt* March 19, 2017, https://www.nguoi-viet.com/little-saigon/cuu-nhan-vien-dai-tieng-noi-tu-do/.

47. A schedule for 1961 is found on the back cover of the sheet music to Lê Bình, "Sầu gieo cung oán." Nguyễn Đình Toàn, interview, June 15, 2019.

48. "Tin vắn âm nhạc," *Bình minh*, April 7, 1967, 2.

49. Trung Phong, "Đài phát thanh Saigon có nên duy trì chủ trương 'Chỉ huy tân nhạc,'" *Bình minh*, September 19, 1967, 3.

50. Xuân Huy, "Hoạt động của giới nhạc trẻ." The number of radios increased tenfold in the Republic of Vietnam from 125,000 in 1960 to 1,300,000 in 1969. United Nations, *Statistical Yearbook*, 804.

51. Nguyễn Đình Toàn, interview. This schedule was printed in *Chính Luận*, November 6, 1965, 4.

52. Roberts, *Psychological War*, 140–141.

53. Mai Lệ Huyền, interview, Newport Beach, CA, March 29, 2011.

54. Tùng Giang, *Hồi ký nhạc sĩ Tùng Giang*.

55. Phạm Công Luận. *Sài Gòn*, 156. Lưu Na, interview, Westminster, CA, June 15, 2019.

56. Phượng Vũ, interview, Anaheim, CA, June 15, 2019.

57. Phượng Vũ, interview. Hoàng Trọng, interview, Mountain View, CA, April 3, 1997.

58. "Trong làng tân nhạc có gì lạ," *Bình Minh*, July 12, 1964, 10.

59. "Cô Sáu, Lê Văn Tài thấm mệt vì 'V. N. Nhạc Tuyển,'" *Chính luận*, August 27–28, 1966, 3.

60. Lam Phương, interview; Phượng Vũ, interview; Nguyễn Long, *Ký ức*, 297–298.

61. Nguyễn Đình Toàn, interview; Phạm Thế Mỹ, interview, Hồ Chí Minh City, April 8, 2001.

62. See Gibbs, "A Missing Legacy."

63. Trần Tử Trung, Facebook message, April 24, 2019.

64. The family lost the business for a time during a government movement to strike down capitalists (*đánh tư sản*). Phạm Công Luận. "Hãng đĩa Lê Văn Tài: Dư âm còn vọng," *Người Đô Thị*, May 24, 2017, https://nguoidothi.net.vn/hang-dia-le-van-tai-du-am-con-vong-8234.html (accessed February 13, 2023).

65. Ngành Mai, "Hãng đĩa hát Asia chèn ép đĩa Hoàng Sơn," *Người Việt*, September 14, 2012, https://www.nguoi-viet.com/giai-tri/Hang-dia-hat-Asia-chen-ep-dia-Hoanh-Son-3922/.

66. Nguyễn Văn Đông, interview.

67. Trung Phong, "Khi ba hãng đĩa lớn."

68. Manuel, *Cassette Culture*, 28–31.

69. Nguyễn Ánh 9, interview.

70. Nguyễn Long, *Ký ức*, 294–296.

71. Sài Gòn Xưa, "Có ai còn nhớ những dãy kios này không," Facebook, September 2, 2018, https://www.facebook.com/oldsaigon75/posts/1859345700781024.

72. Trung Phong, "Đài phát thanh Saigon"; Văn Lương, "Các đài phát thanh cần rút kinh nghiệm sau 1 năm phục vụ thính giả. Cần thanh lọc nội bộ cần duyệt lại chủ trương, cần nghe ngóng dư luận thính giả," *Bình Minh*, December 10, 1967, 2.

73. Song Ngọc, interview, Houston, TX, April 7, 2009.

74. Dror, *Making Two Vietnams*.

75. Gibbs, *Rock Hà Nội*, 113–126.

76. Tô Vũ, "Nhạc vàng là gì," *Văn hóa Nghệ thuật*, May 1976, 43–46.

77. Đỗ Nhuận, "Nhạc vàng," in *Âm thanh cuộc đời*, 354.

78. Gibbs, "Capitalist Music Brings Jail."

79. HH Lan Là, "Vào thế giới ca nhạc," *Bình Minh*, May 25, 1967, 2–3.

80. "Một khía cạnh của thúi nát xã hội," 6–7.

81. Until recently, the Cục Biểu Diễn Nghệ Thuật (Performing Arts Office) maintained a list of songs that were permitted. Recently also, the Ministry of Culture decided to do away with that and to deal with the recording and performance of offending songs on an individual basis. Việt Tuấn, "Chính phủ chấp thuận chủ trương bỏ cấp phép ca khúc trước 1975," *VNExpress*, February 11, 2019, https://vnexpress.net/giai-tri/chinh-phu-chap-thuan-chu-truong-bo-cap-phep-ca-khuc-truoc-1975-3879722.html (accessed February 13, 2023).

82. Reyes, *Songs of the Caged*.

83. Lưu Na, interview. Elsewhere in this volume, Vinh Phu Pham examines the legacy of this music in the Vietnamese diaspora (see chapter 10).

CHAPTER 9

Pray the Rosary and Do Apostolic Work

The Modern Vietnamese Catholic Associational Culture

Tuan Hoang

The scene occurred forty-three years after the demise of the Republic of Vietnam (RVN) in Little Saigon, Orange County, southern California. The site was the Mile Square Regional Park, a convenient location for large gatherings of Vietnamese Americans in Orange County thanks to its size and proximity. The date was July 15, 2018, which saw hundreds of local members of the National Cursillo Movement USA and their families together for the annual Grand Ultreya Picnic. The gathering began with a Vietnamese-language Sunday mass and continued with a picnic lunch of Vietnamese and American food. The chaplain of Vietnamese Cursillo in the Diocese of Orange and a visiting priest from Vietnam presided over the mass and a choir led singing over loudspeakers. Cursillo themes were evoked during the homily and the prayer of the faithful, but the ceremony was notable for many references to a current situation in Vietnam, whose government has alledgedly considered leasing three "economic zones" to Chinese investors for ninety-nine years. At the beginning of the mass, the chaplain asked cursillistas to pray especially for their Vietnamese country under "the threat of loss." This theme of national loss was repeated during homily and the prayer of the faithful. Before the final blessing, the lay president of Vietnamese Cursillo in the diocese spoke to the gathering and made a strong denunciation of the Vietnamese government. He also invited participants to purchase tickets for a special raffle, whose profit would be sent to funds supporting Vietnamese political dissidents, including dissident clergy.[1]

The chaplain's words provide an example of the nationalist and anticommunist orientation that Vietnamese American Catholics share with non-Catholic members of their ethnic cohort. Moreover, the gathering exemplifies the larger associational culture among Vietnamese American Catholics, whose membership is made up of former refugees, immigrants (including 1.5-generation immigrants), even second-generation Vietnamese Americans. Only a small number of Vietnamese American Catholics have taken a weekend retreat with the organization and an even smaller number have continued to participate in its monthly meetings. Yet their participation has been important enough to make up a major division within Cursillo USA and to merit the inclusion of the Vietnamese language on the organization's website (along with English and Spanish). More significantly, Cursillo is just one among many organizations in which Vietnamese American Catholics have participated at the parish, diocesan, national, and international levels. There are also the Association of Catholic Mothers (Hội Các Bà Mẹ Công Giáo), Marriage Family Enrichment (Thăng Tiến Hôn Nhân), the Legion of Mary (Đạo Binh Đức Mẹ), the League of the Sacred Heart (Liên Minh Thánh Tâm), Lay Fraternities of St. Dominic (Liên Đoàn Giáo Dân Đa Minh), the Eucharistic Youth (Thiếu Nhi Thánh Thể), the Boy Scouts (Hướng Đạo), the Society of the Little Flower (Đạo Binh Hồn Nhỏ), and Charismatic Renewal (Canh Tân Đặc Sủng), among others. Many members of these organizations have been active also in liturgical groups such as Eucharistic ministers, lectors, and altar servers. They participated regularly in ethnic activities at the parish or diocesan levels such as teaching catechism and the Vietnamese language to children on weekends.

What is the background of this associational culture? How was it formed? Answers to these questions necessarily lead us to Catholicism as practiced in Vietnam before 1975.

DEVOTIONALISM AND CATHOLIC ACTION BEFORE 1954

The associational culture of Vietnamese Catholics in the United States grew out of a devotional culture rooted in indigenous and global interactions in Vietnam. During the eighteenth and nineteenth centuries, anti-Catholic persecution led to the devotion to Our Lady of La Vang in central Vietnam and devotion to the Vietnamese martyrs across the country. The growth of indigenous devotionalism further benefited from the spread of ultramontanism from Europe. The ultramontane movement began as a reaction to the aftermath of the French Revolution and, more generally, the secularization of European society. It advocated for papal authority in politics and culture as well as in matters of faith. It also created a revival of religious institutions, especially religious orders, and promoted pilgrimages and other devotional practices, especially on the Virgin Mary, the Sacred Heart, the Eucharist, and the sacrament of penance.[2]

The combination of ultramontane and indigenous practices set the foundation for a modern devotional culture emerging in the nineteenth century. Marian devotionalism provided an example of this culture. In the 1850s, for example, the missionary bishop of Huế began the Association of Our Lady (Hội Đức Bà). By the end of the century, his successor declared "Our Lady Protector of Christians" as patron of a new church in La Vang. The influential Trần Lục, the best-known non-martyr Vietnamese priest from the nineteenth century, built churches after the Immaculate Heart of Mary and wrote poetry attributing a hybrid of Christian-Confucian feminine virtues to the Virgin Mary. In 1895, the LaSallians who ran the Taberd Lycée in Saigon organized the first Indochinese chapter of the Sodality of Our Lady (Hiệp Hội Thánh Mẫu), a global and popular organization of lay spirituality founded by a Belgian Jesuit in the sixteenth century. Originally geared toward youths and students, this sodality eventually drew older members and still exists in Vietnam today. In 1932, the missionary Sisters of Vincent de Paul established the first Vietnamese chapter of the ultramontane-inspired Children of Mary (Hội Con Đức Bà) in suburban Saigon. Growing in popularity, these and other devotional organizations tended toward the local rather the national at the time.[3]

Four interrelated developments led to national organization of the devotional culture. First, Vietnamese Catholics began to view Marian devotionalism in a global context. Ultramontane priests and religious certainly helped popularize non-Marian forms such as the devotion to the Sacred Heart and St. Thérèse of Lisieux the "Little Flower." But Marianism remained most prominent. In particular, missionaries and Vietnamese clergy widely circulated stories about Our Lady of Lourdes. Among Vietnamese Catholics, her miraculous healing of ordinary people such as carpenters, soldiers, and disabled children made Lourdes the best-known foreign Marian site until the popularity of Fatima in South Vietnam during the 1960s. After World War I, some of the workers and soldiers that went to Europe to support France made pilgrimages to

Lourdes itself. Such ultramontane devotions coexisted with the more indigenous ones, especially devotion to the Vietnamese martyrs, especially ninety-two that were beatified at three occasions during the 1900s. Those events brought much pride to the Catholics and enhanced their allegiance to the papacy. In sum, ultramontane influence helped bring about a major shift in Vietnamese Marian devotionalism, which became global and modern in outlook and vision.[4]

The second development was the creation of Catholic Action, which began in nineteenth-century Europe as a response to anti-clericalism but shifted by the next century to new issues such as industrialization and labor unions. Although much of the leadership of Catholic Action came from the clergy, it aimed at the laity and depended heavily on lay participation. Catholic Action received ringing endorsement from several popes, especially Pius XI, as a way to transform and re-Christianize society during the 1930s and 1940s. They included Young Catholic Workers (Thanh Niên Lao Động Công Giáo), Rural Catholic Youth (Thanh Niên Thôn Quê Công Giáo), the Valiant Hearts and Souls (Hùng Tâm Dũng Chí), the Eucharistic Crusade (Nghĩa Binh Thánh Thể), and Catholic Boy Scouts. Most of these organizations aimed at recruiting young men but also teenagers and even boys and girls. Young Vietnamese and a new wave of missionaries from Europe and Canada were instrumental in introducing Catholic Action to Vietnamese. The growth and appeal of these organizations reflect, among other things, the first modern era of mass participation in Vietnam.[5]

Third, the momentum toward a modern associational culture came partly from the desire and advocacy for the establishment of a national church. For reasons of centralization, the Vatican wanted to create a primarily indigenous hierarchy and change the administrative status from missions to ordinary dioceses. For their own reasons, Vietnamese Catholics desired greater autonomy from missionaries. As a result, the first Vietnamese bishop was consecrated in 1933, followed by two others in the next three years. These developments culminated in the establishment of the national church with a large majority of Vietnamese bishops in 1960. Even though the 1960 event was significant in itself, more crucial was the activism among the indigenous clergy since the 1930s. The Vietnamese clergy fueled greater Vietnamese control of Catholic lay organizations, including Marian ones. The first Vietnamese bishop, for example, formed a new chapter of the Sodality of Our Lady in his diocese not long after he became bishop. The second bishop organized another chapter at the seminary in his diocese. In 1945, the priest Phạm Ngọc Chi, later an ardent anticommunist bishop in South Vietnam, announced the creation of a chapter aimed at children and youths in his diocese. European missionaries had been instrumental in promoting ultramontane devotionalism while the Vietnamese clergy and lay leaders eagerly spread it among the growingly nationalist Catholic population.[6]

Still, a fourth factor was the rise of global and then local communism, which threatened the institutional influence of the Church as well as Catholic modernity embodied by Catholic Action. Vietnamese Catholics followed the lead of the Vatican and European bishops in reaction to the Russian Revolution, and their small but vocal press propagated against the threat of communism even before there was a communist party in Vietnam. By the early 1930s, however, they began to react against revolutionary violence within Indochina when a communist-led rebellion in north-central Vietnam burned down a church and killed a priest and several lay Catholics. Vietnamese Catholics might not have supported colonial policies, but they rivaled the colonial authorities in denouncing the theoretical and practical ills of revolutionary communism. This development would carry significant consequence in South Vietnam later.[7]

In some respects, anticommunism and Catholic Action came together during the decolonization of Indochina to form the foundation for a nationalist and anticommunist variety of Marian devotionalism in South Vietnam. In particular, the August Revolution in 1945 created a violent intra-Vietnamese conflict of mutual extermination between the communists and a multitude of nationalist and religious groups. Among the Catholics, some initially supported the communist-led Việt Minh during the First Indochina War as others stayed neutral and waited out the war. Others, especially in the Catholic regions of Bùi Chu and Phát Diệm, armed their Catholic communities against Việt Minh infiltration. After 1950, anticommunist themes were increasingly prominent among devotional and Catholic Action organizations. In particular, Our Lady of Fatima, already an anticommunist symbol in Europe and the Americas, began to take a special hold among the faithful thanks to efforts by a small number of missionaries, native clergy, and Vietnamese musicians, who composed popular hymns in her honor.[8]

The associational culture was limited during the first phase of the First Indochina War because many Catholics moved among different zones controlled by the Việt Minh or the French. The situation became better during the early 1950s, when a number of Catholics, including lay leaders, returned to their communities from Việt Minh zones. Equally important was the arrival of international organizations. Most spectacular was the growth of the Irish-founded Legion of Mary, whose first Vietnamese chapter (called "presidium") was established in Hanoi in 1947. By 1952, five praesidia were in Hanoi and six were in Huế; two years later, the number grew to thirteen in Hanoi and spread to nearly all mission dioceses in Vietnam. The rapid growth proved auspicious for the future of the Legion of Mary in South Vietnam later. In 1966, the count was 862 senior praesidia and 202 junior praesidia with 12,420 full members and 1,791 young members, plus 6,112 "sponsoring" members, and 58,322 supporters in Saigon alone.[9]

Initiatives for Marian devotionalism and the associational culture also came directly from the Vietnamese. A prominent example is Trần Đình Thủ, a diocesan priest from the heavily Catholic and anticommunist area of Bùi Chu. In the early 1940s, Thủ began organizing a number of seminarians and lay people who dedicated themselves to the Immaculate Heart of Mary. In 1948, Thủ received permission from the local bishop to turn one of these groups into a men's religious institute. In 1953, the Vatican permitted him to form this group as the Congregation of the Mother Co-Redemptrix (CMC). The following year, the CMC moved entirely to the south and suburban Saigon. The humble beginning would turn the CMC into the leading promoter of the devotion to Our Lady of Fátima in South Vietnam and the official leader of the Movement for the Reparation to the Immaculate Heart of Mary (Phong Trào Đền Tạ Trái Tim Vô Nhiệm Đức Mẹ).[10]

Still, it took until 1953 and pressure from the Vatican for the bishops to centralize Catholic Action by appointing Gerárd Gagnon to be national director. A Canadian Redemptorist priest, Gagnon had introduced Vietnamese to the ultramontane and Quebec-founded sodality League of the Sacred Heart (Liên Minh Thánh Tâm), which later grew to be a major men's organization in South Vietnam and the diaspora. During a turbulent period, Gagnon purchased a center in Đà Lạt that would be used for retreats and training of thousands of Catholic Action members and associates. He also assisted many Northern members when they moved south in 1954 and 1955. Between this migration and communist repression of the Church in the North, Catholic Action concentrated virtually completely in the South over the next twenty years.[11]

THE ASSOCIATIONAL CULTURE IN THE REPUBLICAN SOUTH

The pre-1954 context of Catholicism in South Vietnam was therefore multifaceted. Its culture was an outcome of modern religious movements, disruptive warfare and burgeoning anticommunism, and the consolidation and centralization of a national Church. Out of this combination arose a new associational culture that was both devotional (that is, prayer- and ritual-oriented) and apostolic (action-oriented). Although they were created for different age groups and sometimes with different foci, these associations shared the goal of empowering the laity. Leaders organized meetings, retreats, and volunteer "apostolic" work such as visiting the sick, communal cleaning of public areas, and raising funds for leprosy.

This development contributed handsomely to the vibrancy of Marian devotionalism specifically and the associational culture generally in South Vietnam. Not surprisingly, the division of Vietnam from 1954 to 1975 had a direct and dramatic impact on the associational culture. The Southern Church benefited partially from the losses in the North, which saw more than six hundred Catholics, including large numbers of priests and nuns, moving to the South after the Geneva Conference. The Northern church also suffered severe restrictions and sometimes prohibitions imposed by the government on the ordination of new priests, seminary training, participation in civil associations, communication with the global church, and a host of other issues. Like the rest of Northern society, the Church necessarily endured warfare, including American bombing. The momentum toward growth stopped and survival became its primary goal.[12]

Even though the Southern Church was also affected by national partition and warfare, it saw a flourishing of associational life and exchange of ideas for several reasons, including frequent interactions with the Vatican and the global church, support from the RVN and non-Catholic foreign organizations, Catholic administration of many educational and medical institutions, and a vibrant Catholic press. After a short delay at the beginning of the partition, the national office of Catholic Action became a highly active leader in organizing retreats and gatherings for many lay organizations. In November 1960, the Vatican formally recognized the Vietnamese national Church and raised the status of mission vicariates to dioceses. By the early 1960s, all dioceses in South Vietnam had a local director of Catholic Action to coordinate diocesan activities. In 1966, the following Marian organizations, most of whom were members of Catholic Action, counted some three hundred thousand Catholics in metropolitan Saigon alone: the Legion of Mary, the Movement for Reparation to the Immaculate Heart of Mary, the Blue Army of Our Lady of Fatima (Đội Binh Xanh), the Associated Sodality of Our Lady (Hiệp Hội Thánh Mẫu), the Rosary Society (Hội Môi Khôi), the Society of

Children of Our Lady (Hội Con Đức Mẹ), and the Union of the Immaculate Heart of Our Lady (Đoàn Tận Hiến Đức Mẹ Vô Nhiễm). For a different example, the 1970 annual pilgrimage festival to the Shrine of Our Lady of Perpetual Help in Saigon drew thirty thousand attendants over four days of festivities, including members of Marian sodalities and other devotional organizations.[13]

Marian devotees, of course, were not required to belong to a sodality or organization. Nonetheless, Marianism affected the devotional life of most Catholic Action organizations and at times served as a venue for and expression of anticommunism. The Saigon government certainly encouraged the anticommunist nationalism among Catholics, especially but not exclusively Northern émigrés. For example, Ngô Đình Thục, the archbishop of Huế and older brother of President Ngô Đình Diệm, organized and headlined the 1961 festival of Our Lady of La Vang. The largest of several triennial festivals at the site of La Vang, this event saw the active participation of many Catholic Action organizations during masses, devotional gatherings, and group meetings. In addition, one of the six days of the festival was designated specifically for Catholic Action. In important aspects, the festival functioned as religious mass rally of hundreds of thousands of Catholics to mourn national division, condemn the communist threat, and hope for peace and national unification through constant prayer and apostolic work. In a similar fashion, the leading Catholic Action periodical in South Vietnam opened an article about Our Lady of Fatima by asking, "What must Catholics do to bring about peace for the country?" The answer is found in the "Fatima messages: Repent and do reparation" because it is "the magical weapon against communist from Our Lady of Fatima [and] the key to peace for the country."[14]

Vietnamese orientation toward Our Lady of Fatima served as anticommunist devotionalism as well as an illustration of at least one new organization in the Catholic Action landscape, the Blue Army of Our Lady of Fatima mentioned earlier. It was in fact Vietnamese initiative that led to the establishment of the Blue Army in South Vietnam. In early 1964, a military officer from South Vietnam visited the Catholic Information Center in Washington, DC, during a break from studies at Fort Bragg in California. He learned about the Blue Army and contacted its founder, the American priest Harold Colgan. Interested in starting the movement in South Vietnam, he also wrote the archbishop of Saigon for permission to begin a chapter in the country. It led to the creation of the Blue Army in Saigon in September 1964 then an opening mass that saw "over 1000 members."[15] Almost a year later, the chaplain of the Belgian chapter of the Blue Army formally introduced the idea for a tour of the Pilgrim Virgin in South Vietnam. Nonetheless, it is difficult to imagine this tour without a formal presence of the organization in South Vietnam. The inspiration for the tour itself was global, stemming from a tour of the Pilgrim Virgin to South Korea in December 1952, an event that devotees believed to have caused the signing of the armistice eight months later. In the Vietnamese case, Colgan and Haffert readily supported the tour but there was also complication due to delayed mailing. Not to frustrate the desire among Vietnamese Catholics for a tour, the president of The Blue Army's Australian chapter helpfully intervened and managed to bring the original statue to South Vietnam.[16]

A different kind of Catholic Action organization was Cursillo, which came to South Vietnam not through Europe or North America but the Philippines. After US direct intervention in March 1965, a number of Filipino engineers and workers were contracted for construction projects in the country. Despite the lack of any clear evidence, it appears that they introduced this organization to the Vietnamese Catholics. In any event, the first retreat took place during the last weekend of January 1967 in Saigon. Participants included twenty-seven Vietnamese and twenty-three Filipinos, including priests, religious, and a laity among the Vietnamese. The import of this event also lay in the fact that a Filipino bishop came to help directing the retreat and the Vietnamese bishops of Saigon, Huế, and Đà Nẵng stopped by the retreat for short visits. Although the number of cursillistas in South Vietnam by 1975 is still unknown, "dozens" of such retreats were held in Saigon, Xuân Lộc, Nha Trang, and other localities. In any event, the gathering described at the beginning of this article could be traced eventually to the retreat in January 1967.[17]

The Second Vatican Council (1963–1965) further gave momentum to the involvement of the laity and clergy in Catholic Action. The Catholic press in South Vietnam distributed many articles about the Council's teachings on renewal and involvement of the laity. It frequently discussed the challenges of abrupt change, such as the laicization of many clergy and men and women religious in Europe and the United States, that occurred in the immediate aftermath of the Council. In particular, the subject of missionizing and evangelizing the faith to non-Catholics received an emphasis in the discourse among priests, religious, and leading laymen and laywomen. "Urgent Evangelization" screams the title of a lecture given at the Missionary Center in Vĩnh Long in 1971.

While praising the works of the Council, the lecturer warned against the "extreme progressive" elements within the Church that opposed traditional affirmation on birth control, priestly celibacy, and other teachings. He also emphasized the messages of Our Lady of Fatima as the main reason for caution against the contemporary threat of atheism. Last but not least, he called for Vietnamese effort to evangelize to non-Christian peoples throughout Southeast Asia, even other parts of Asia. In the same year, indeed, the South Vietnamese bishops reorganized the top leadership of Catholic Action. Instead of having one bishop in charge of Catholic Action, they established three committees on education, development, and, especially, evangelization to non-Catholics in the country. The postconciliar action and clarion calls for missionary work was a new development in the history of Vietnamese Catholicism.[18]

ASSOCIATIONAL CULTURE AMONG THE REFUGEES IN THE UNITED STATES

The momentum of evangelization generally and Catholic Action especially came to a screeching halt when the RVN ceased to exist in April 1975. Along with much else in the civil society of South Vietnam, Catholic activities were heavily curtailed and Catholic Action largely ceased to exist as a viable entity. It took years, even decades, before the associational culture returned to life, albeit in altered forms.

In the meantime, Catholic refugees in the United States found themselves away from danger but had to face many challenges in the first few years following the fall of Saigon. Most urgent was the issue of survival in a wealthy yet culturally different society; learning English and finding employment were their foremost priorities. Yet whenever and wherever they could, they also resorted quickly to the faith practices from their homeland. Most immediately, it meant mass, confession, and communal devotion in their language. Next was the search for local stability, especially in terms of having a more permanent location. During the first ten years in the United States, it was rare that a Catholic refugee community received permission from the local bishop to establish an ethnic parish. More often, a community was assigned to an existing parish and given a limited amount of time each week for masses and other activities. During its first year in existence, for example, the community in Portland, Oregon, rented an apartment to have masses and carry out activities such as choir practice.[19]

The organization of human resources was primarily liturgical at first, with choirs and altar boys among the most important service for masses on Sunday and holy days of obligation. On special occasions, a community might organize flower girls to perform a May Crowning. Yet it did not take too long for the associational culture to begin resembling itself, if in a much diminished capacity. Again, it began with devotional and liturgical practices. Praying the rosary at church or individual residences was common, and even the smaller communities organized Marian and Eucharistic processions. Many a community, alone or with other communities, organized annual or occasional pilgrimages to Marian shrines within driving distance.

Although most pilgrimages took place at shrines already established in the United States, the most important was the annual one to Carthage, Missouri, under the organization of the CMC, then and now the largest Vietnamese American religious order of men. A number of regional pilgrimages had been organized, but the gathering at the CMC headquarters in Carthage during the first weekend of 1978 marked the first major national pilgrimage among the Catholic refugees. Organized as a "Day of Reparation for the Immaculate Heart of Mary," it drew participants from at least thirty-three refugee communities from as far as Salem, Oregon. Appropriate for an event about Marian reparation, the most prominent sodality at the pilgrimage was the chapter of the Movement for the Reparation from Wichita Falls, Texas, which had been constituted informally. At the end of the pilgrimage, however, the CMC announced that the diocese's bishop had given permission to establish the movement in the United States.[20]

It did not take long for this Fatima- and anticommunist-inspired organization and affiliates to be formed and reformed among the Catholic refugees. Indeed, the late 1970s and early 1980s marked a serious effort at reconstituting the associational culture. Between 1979 and 1986, for example, the community in Fort Worth, established its chapters of the League of the Sacred Heart and the Sodality of Families for the Reparation to the Immaculate Heart (Hội Gia Đình Đền Tạ). This chapter of the league drew "many members" from the beginning and about twenty families joined the sodality. Over time, however, the sodality became inactive due to a new rotation format for communal praying of the rosary but also because of the establishment of new sodalities such as Association of Catholic Mothers (Hội Các Bà Mẹ Công Giáo) and the Eucharistic Youth (Thiếu Nhi Thánh Thể). For another example, the community in Portland, Oregon, established in 1981 its chapters of the League of the Sacred Heart and the Association of Catholic Mothers with approximately thirty and fifty members, respectively. Although their numbers were smaller than those of the League or the Association, about fifty former members of Cursillo, mostly in California and Louisiana, began a national effort to reestablish a Vietnamese presence in the United States in 1979. This effort led to the first retreat of Vietnamese cursillistas, which was held in the Diocese of Lafayette, Louisiana, in September 1981.[21]

There were probably many motives and goals behind the reestablishment of Catholic Action organizations among the refugees. Among the most significant, however, were the grief among the refugees over national loss and their fear of losing their Vietnamese Catholic identity to the more materialistic American society. Ecclesiastical and other developments during late colonialism and the Republican era had attuned them to a more active participation in the life of both church and society, and it was most difficult to leave aside that identity while facing the uncertain future in the United States as well as that of their loved ones in Vietnam. Moreover, their grief and fear made them ever determined to hold on to their faith practices while adapting to the ways of the new society. It was within this context that we can fruitfully approach the regeneration of the associational culture in America.[22]

Many other developments during the 1970s and beyond helped account for the current associational culture among Vietnamese Americans. Moreover, the associational culture in the south of the country was severely curtailed after 1975 but also began to return by the 1990s. The same occurred in the north, if more slowly. By the 2000s, many devotional sodalities and associational organizations have been reestablished or created for the first time in most parishes throughout Vietnam.

This chapter modestly presents a historical perspective on connections among the colonial, republican, and refugee experiences. These experiences were distinct due to disruptions caused by warfare, national division, and regime changes. Yet the disruptions only slowed the making of the modern associational culture. The First Indochina War, for instance, slowed the momentum of Catholic Action during the late 1940s and early 1950s, but it could not extinguish the interests among many of the laity and clergy. Or, the disruption caused by the fall of Saigon only led to the recreation of Cursillo and other organizations as a mode for association in the diaspora. Most notable was the period of South Vietnam, whose culture allowed for the late-colonial momentum toward Catholic Action and modern devotionalism to flourish. An examination of the Vietnamese Church since 1975 is beyond the scope of this chapter. Nonetheless, it behooves us to recognize that the revival of the postwar Catholic associational culture since the 1990s could not have happened without a model provided by institutional flourishing between 1954 and 1975.

NOTES

1. This description comes from observations and notes kept by the author at the gathering. As of September 2018, the national service administrator for all of Cursillo USA is a Vietnamese.
2. See Hoang, "Ultramontanism, Nationalism," 13-14.
3. Hoang, "'Our Lady's Immaculate Heart.'"
4. Keith, *Catholic Vietnam*, 150.
5. Keith, *Catholic Vietnam*, 155-162; Trần, "*Thanh-Lao-Công*." For a different example of organized religion and mass participation, see Hoang Duc Ngo, "Building a New House."
6. Keith, *Catholic Vietnam*, 89-117; Phan Phát Huồn, *Việt Nam Giáo Sử*, 508.
7. Hoang, "From Reeducation Camps," 50-52.
8. See Đoàn Độc Thư and Xuân Huy, *Giám Mục Lê Hữu Từ*; Van Chi, *Catholic Choral Musi*, 72-73.
9. *Trái Tim Đức Mẹ* [Immaculate Heart of Mary] (August 1968), 14-19, 35-36; *Trái Tim Đức Mẹ* (December 1966), 157.
10. Congregation of The Mother Coredemptrix, *Biểu Chứng Đức Tin*, 60-71.
11. Phan Phát Huồn, *Việt Nam Giáo Sử*, 486.
12. As indicated by *kỷ yếu* (yearbook or commemorative publication) of northern dioceses published since 2000, many parishes and missions lost the majority of their members to the migration of 1954-1955. Infrastructure also suffered after the migration, often severely, since there was little money and scarce materials and manpower for maintenance and repair of churches and other physical structures. Before 1954, for example, the parish An Vỹ in the Diocese of Thái Bình was divided into seventeen missions in addition to the main church. After the majority of parishioners moved south, only four missions were left and the government used the main church building for storage. See *Kỷ Yếu Giáo Phận Thái Bình*, 430.
13. *Trái Tim Đức Mẹ* (November 1966), 105, 129; *Liên Lạc* [Communication] (March 1970), 62-63.
14. The entire issue of *Đức Mẹ Lavang* [Our Lady of La Vang] (September 1961) is devoted to reports about the festival. *Tông Đồ Giáo Dân* [Lay Apostolic] (March-April 1968), 1-3. For more analysis of Marian anticommunism, see Hoang, "Our Lady's Immaculate Heart."
15. *Sacerdos: Linh Mục Nguyệt San* [Sacerdos: Priestly Journal] (January-February 1968), 50-53; *Trái Tim Đức Mẹ* (November 1965), 96.
16. *Trái Tim Đức Mẹ* (October 1965), 91; *Trái Tim Đức Mẹ* (November 1965), 96-98.
17. *Sacerdos Linh Mục Nguyệt San* 61-62 (January-February 1967), 78-80; *Sacerdos Linh Mục Nguyệt San* 63 (March 1967), 147-148; *Dân Chúa* [People of God] (April 1979), 39.
18. *Tông Đồ Giáo Dân* (May-June, 1971), 41-44; *Tông Đồ Giáo Dân* (March-May, 1971), 3-6.
19. *Kỷ Yếu Giáo Phận*, 11-12.
20. *Trái Tim Đức Mẹ* (January-February 1978), 20-22.

21. "Sơ Lược Tiểu Sử Giáo Xứ Chúa Kitô Vua, Fort Worth, Texas" [A Summary History of the Christ the King Parish in Fort Worth, Texas], https://www.chuakitovua.org/tieusugiaoxu; *Kỷ Yếu Giáo,* 48–52; *Dân Chúa* (April 1979), 39; *Liên Đoàn* [Federation] (November 20, 1981), 6.

22. For a longer development among Catholic refugees in the diaspora, see Hoang, "Ultramontanism, Nationalism."

CHAPTER 10

Rhizomatic Transnationalism

Nhạc Vàng and the Legacy of Republicanism in Overseas Vietnamese Communities

Vinh Phu Pham

They say that every Vietnamese household has at least one bottle of fish sauce, a set of *phở* bowls, and a karaoke set with accompanying copies of either *Paris by Night* or *Asia*. Although from the outside, the first two items seem more necessary than the latter, I can be almost certain that a sizable number of overseas Vietnamese, most likely sitting shirtless in a car garage with a Heineken in hand, would argue the opposite. Taking their side, I too have witnessed how crucial and integral these videos and live shows have been to the Vietnamese community in the United States and elsewhere—this is not only because, until much more recently, they are in effect one of the few media outlets for overseas Vietnamese artists and performers to celebrate their culture, but also, and more important, one of the main arteries keeping Vietnamese republicanism alive.[1] In other words, this cultural space in which South Vietnamese political sentiments—namely anticommunist, democratic, and sympathetic to the United States—was made to prosper. This is evident both in the general aesthetics and content of the shows, which often feature songs and skits about the Republic of Vietnam (RVN), as well as its main audience, who were mostly diasporic Vietnamese. In fact, one of the main hosts of *Paris by Night*, Nguyễn Ngọc Ngạn, is a Canadian writer himself and one of the many boat people who left Vietnam after 1975, and the other, Nguyễn Cao Kỳ Duyên, is the daughter of then RVN prime minister Nguyễn Cao Kỳ.

Indeed, one need not look hard to find all the traces of the former republic in these live shows, since many of the songs that they perform are *nhạc vàng* (yellow music) and the song writers they choose to host and celebrate, such as Lam Phương, Phạm Duy, Anh Bằng, or Trịnh Công Sơn, are polemic figures, even before the fall of Saigon.[2] Nonetheless, many of the songs sung during these shows were still banned in Vietnam and therefore their performances were "opportunities to listen to music suppressed by the state."[3] It is undeniable that the genre of *nhạc vàng* and war time music as a whole was crucial in the production of nationalist sentiments in the RVN. Still, far too little critical attention is paid to how its production and propagation abroad has affected the Vietnamese overseas communities. Aside from Adelaida Reyes's convincing *Songs of the Caged, Songs of the Free*, Kieu-Linh Caroline Valverde's *Transnationalizing Viet Nam*, or Deborah Wong's more general *Speak It Louder*, most critiques of these forms of music production tend to rely on the figures of nostalgia and melancholy as their main point of departure.[4] Although these commentaries are certainly valid and necessary, I find that they can also seem passive and politically ineffective, not active cultural agents that continue to fuel nationalist sentiments.[5]

In this chapter, I focus on Lam Phương's "Chiều Tây Đô" and some of its interpreted performances as primary examples of cultural agents that fuel nationalist sentiments for the RVN from abroad. Because of this, I posit that qualitative terms such as "melancholic" and "nostalgic" are incomplete descriptors of *nhạc vàng* and that their continual use is a way to brush over the sentiments of loss from those who maintain a nationalist identity with the RVN. However, rather than looking at this nationalism as a concrete, monolithic ideology attached singularly to the physical homeland, here, I take it as a performance that locates the space of the nation within the diasporic imaginary of the impossible return—a form of rhizomatic transnationalism linked together by differentiated networks of belonging, which has no real center.[6] Like Alexander Cannon, I think that Vietnamese music production (and its criticisms) ought not to be centered on any of the diasporic capitals but instead that it is a performance, one that seeks to build a transnational space rather than recover a lost territory.[7] As with the example of the karaoke sets and the copies of *Paris by Night*, what makes the cohesion of this transnationalism possible is the wide distribution and repetition of songs with common ideals such as "Chiều Tây Đô," which, from my perspective, despite its name, refers more so to a shared identity based on departure and return than to an actual territory or locality.

THE PROBLEM WITH NOSTALGIA AND MELANCHOLIA

In the *Asia* rendition of "Chiều Tây Đô" with Hoàng Oanh, the video starts off with a wide shot of the stage made to look as if it could be any milieu in the Mekong Delta.[8] Dressed in the traditional *áo dài*, Hoàng Oanh's silhouette stands on a dock against the sunset backdrop where she begins to sing a segment in *cải lương*. Around her are several small boats and palms fronds populating the screen. As the segment about returning to the homeland comes to a close, she approaches the foreground and begins the main song. These shots, interspersed with scenes of rivers and women in small boats not only establish a sense of place but also perpetuate an idyllic image of Vietnam as a rural, agrarian society.[9] At a first glance, the juxtaposition of the visuals with the lyrics that Hoàng Oanh sings seem to merely provoke a sense of nostalgia and melancholy about a lost country. Yet a more critical gaze would reveal that such terms do not fully nor adequately capture the imagery that is at hand, nor do they account for the political stakes such imagery implies. The decision to have Hoàng Oanh—a singer who has been around for decades and who built her fame and career during the height of the war—perform a song about exile and the former republic should not go unnoticed.

Hoàng Oanh, whose birth name is Huỳnh Kim Chi, was already a recognizable public figure and an established performer by the time she and her family left Saigon in 1975.[10] Born on June 11, 1946, in Mỹ Tho, she had already won her first singing competition at the age of five with *Radio France Asie*.[11] From there onward, she would continue her trajectory as a singer, appearing regularly on stage and television, which would later lead her to many collaborations with some of the most talented musicians of the time such as Châu Kỳ, Duy Khánh, Phó Quốc Lân, Mạnh Cương, Lam Phương, and others. Indeed, by the time she performed "Chiều Tây Đô" with *Asia*, Hoàng Oanh was already well established among the Vietnamese communities as one of the most emblematic voices of exile.[12] Take, for example, her performance of Lam Phương's "Chuyến Đò Vĩ Tuyến" for *Asia 12*, in which the prelude includes archival footage of the mass migration of people from the North to the South with the numerals 900,000 in a white arrow to indicate the number of people moving south of the 17th parallel.[13] Just as the video transitions from the prelude to the main song, viewers are presented with an animated map of wartime Vietnam in which the northern part begins to fill in with red and a horizontal line labeled "17 degrees" cuts across the center.[14] Given her prior work in the RVN and videos such as these, by the time Hoàng Oanh appeared in "Chiều Tây Đô," fans and overseas Vietnamese listeners in general had been primed in that her image was already associated with not just one but two types of exile, one internal, the other external.

As for the composer of "Chiều Tây Đô," Lam Phương (real name Lâm Đình Phùng) was already one of the foremost lyricists and prolific musicians associated with *tân nhạc* (new music) and *nhạc vàng* prior to 1975. Born in 1937 to a poor family in Rạch Giá, Kiên Giang, Lam Phương was fortunate enough to go to Saigon at the age of ten to continue his studies while staying with family.[15] At age fifteen, he wrote his first song, "Chiều thu ấy," but it would not be until a few years later that he would gain recognition. The poverty that he was born into would later prove to be an asset when he wrote "Kiếp nghèo" and "Chuyến đò vỹ tuyến," songs that launched his career in the Saigon music scene.[16] In 1958, Lam Phương joined the South Vietnamese Army (Quân lực Việt Nam Cộng hòa) and in 1970 he wrote his other well-known ballad "Thành phố buồn." Like many others, in 1975 he fled the country with his family. A more extensive discography can of course be found elsewhere, but what I want to highlight here is that Lam Phương, like Hoàng Oanh, was already well associated with a certain trend of music in the RVN prior to his departure. Thus, when he wrote "Chiều Tây Đô" in Paris, the song became not only a hymn for the diaspora, but also a reminder of a country that is no more. What I emphasize here is that even though composers such as Lam Phương carried on with the same musical traditions, these songs were written in exile—quite like other composers, such as Phạm Duy, Anh Bằng, Trầm Tử Thiêng, Nhật Ngân, Hoàng Thi Thơ, which all constitute a particular strand of *nhạc vàng* that have similar lyrical narratives.

Indeed, for much of the listening public in and outside Vietnam, songs like those written by Lam Phương are often seen as purely nostalgic for the pre-1975 era, not only because of the war thematic, but also in the aesthetics of the performances, which draw on traditional motifs such as the *áo dài* or the backdrops with scenes from the countryside. Resting with this surface perspective, however, one would grossly miss out on their political critique, their influence, and, ultimately, the rationale for why some of these songs were banned in Vietnam. As Phillip Taylor points out, if one were to go to most cafes or bars in southern Vietnam in the 1990s, the music would most likely have been pre-1975 music recorded in Orange County and smuggled back into the country by *việt kiều* (overseas Vietnamese).[17] Seen as a tool of neocolonialism, this music represented a huge risk for the communist party's tight grip on cultural and ideological hegemony. The issue with *nhạc vàng* is that it was living proof of the vestiges of the old republic, and that it could be smuggled in and maintained a listening public, which undermined the party's appearance of absolute control within the country. Yet even when critics agree that such music had profound political implications, the language used to describe it still relied on such terms as melancholy or nostalgia as primary descriptors.[18] Certainly, this rhetoric did not come from nowhere given that, aside from the emotive imagery that the songs themselves illicit, it was also the main charge that the communist party used to criticize the consumerist and "weak" culture of the RVN.[19] The underlying dual implication, then, is that although the music is too *lãng mạn* (romantic) and *yếu ớt* (weak), it was also, for some, *đầu độc* (poisonous) and *phản động* (reactionary).[20] For this reason, *nhạc vàng*'s strong potential for corroding the social cohesion and public "morality" cannot be ignored. As a result, this strange contradiction of cultural objects being both weak but also dangerous, imbues terms such as "melancholia" and "nostalgia" with a symbolic dimension that merits more critical attention.

In his essay "Mourning and Melancholia," Sigmund Freud characterizes both the states of mourning and melancholia as being related to the loss of the loved object.[21] Yet what distinguishes the two is that with melancholia, "one cannot see clearly what it is that has been lost" and therefore "it is all the more reasonable to suppose that the patient cannot consciously perceive what he has lost either."[22] This distinction is significant in the sense that if melancholia is a pathological form of reaction to the lost loved object that is unconscious to the patient, then it would be even more difficult to pinpoint what it is that has been lost and, consequently, how to treat the symptoms. Foreseeing possible objections to my claims, I take the opportunity here to clarify why psychoanalysis might be an appropriate analytical approach to looking at *nhạc vàng* in this context. First, it is that psychic effects and their diagnoses are at the core subject dependent. What I mean is that development of any form of prognosis, whether for an individual or a collective body, necessarily involves subjects and a process of addressing whatever issue is at hand. Second, psychic states, as they emerge within cultural mediums, do not readily lend themselves either to a singular reading or to a legible dialectic. This implies that the purpose of any analytical tool, whether psychoanalysis or any other system, is to offer possible insight and not guaranteed causal contributions. In other words, if one is to seriously take up *nhạc vàng* as a genuine medium through which RVN sentiments are being transmitted, that is, culturally specific objects that carry affective potential, such as certain nationalist sentiments, it cannot be said that a more "objective" system might be better suited—for what current analytical system would offer a quantifiable and accurate account of nationalism or the feeling of loss within these songs? Or, should all readings of *nhạc vàng* from this historical period be treated merely as examples of cultural ethnographies? Of course not.

The point to remember is that something about these cultural objects exceeds their historical specificity and apparent message. In the same way that nationalism and loss cannot be determined by their approximate degree, as empirical measurements fall short, so too should psychoanalysis be understood as an attempt to address the excess of artistic production, which also has no predetermined parameters for its proximity to some underlying truth. Like nationalism, the modus operandi of psychoanalysis is one of complexity, where the claim is less a hidden structure than a nonrecognized relationality, which guarantees an ultimate truth. Put differently, the application of Freud's theory is not a claim for the veracity of whatever is kept underneath or behind a cultural object; it is instead an entryway to understanding the object as being more multifaceted than it would otherwise appear. I should also add that in using some of the clinical terms, I am not suggesting that listeners of *nhạc vàng* should be understood as patients, in the strict sense of the term, but that if the leverage against the *nhạc vàng* has been deployed in a manner that denotes a deviation from the expected psychic norm by terms such as *yếu ớt* or *lãng mạn*, then what psychoanalysis offers is a questioning of the terms of those norms. These songs are, after all, cultural objects that produce and engender psychic affects, to see them as neutral or worse, as simply nostalgic or melancholic for the lost object, would be to deny the strong political undertone that has maintained their social relevance.

In the case of the RVN, although one cannot doubt the immense psychological processes that accompany the idea of a lost object in all its forms, I argue that at least within the literary and musical representation, this loss has been cathected to the very real loss of the southern republic. Even in popular speech, those who identify with the RVN refer to April 30, 1975, as *Ngày mất Nước* (the day the country was lost), rather than the communist commemoration of *Ngày Giải phóng miền Nam* (the liberation of the South). In other words, rather than accepting the lost loved object as something inarticulable of the unconscious, this loss has been encapsulated and explicitly named within the object of the country. This is to say that whatever this absence might imply, here, loss must take the form of both the unimaginable, and also that of a nameable thing. To further this point, we can take Việt Khang's "Việt Nam Tôi Đâu" (where is my Vietnam?) or Lam Phương's "Mất" (loss/lost) as two cultural objects that directly reference this loss as something that must be identified.

In the example of the song "Mất," this loss is described in the second stanza with the lines:

> Anh có biết ngày ba mươi mất nước
> Ngày chia ly, ngày của tù đầy
> Em phiêu lưu vào khung trời mây xám
> và tứ bề là biển rộng mênh mông.[23]
> Did you know that April 30th the country was lost
> The day of separation, the day of full prisons
> I venture out into the gray skies
> And where all around me is the vast sea.

This first line, which is more of a question, serves as an inquiry into whether the lover, who has been exiled, knows that the republic has been lost; the following lines detail the exile. In "Chiều Tây Đô," the same sentiment is replicated in the lines "Ghé hỏi cỏ cây, cỏ cây khóc, gió than van—Kể từ khi mất quê hương gió ra khơi đưa người vượt biển" (I stopped to ask the grass and the trees, the grass and the trees cried, the wind told me that ever since losing the homeland, the wind has come to take people across the seas), where the loss of the country is once more immediately followed by exile.[24] For our interest, it is the singing voice's conscious knowing and articulation of this loss in both examples that makes mourning, at least from the Freudian perspective, a more suited term for describing the reactions and subsequent sentiments.[25] Indeed, the sense of loss was so evident in "Chiều Tây Đô," as a loss to the ego that, the nature, represented by the wind and the trees, are also implicated in this act of mourning. To draw further attention to the differences between these two states, later on in his essay, Freud explains that

> melancholia contains something more than normal mourning. In melancholia the relation to the object is no simple one; it is complicated by the conflict due to ambivalence ... For this reason the exciting causes of melancholia have a much wider range than those of mourning, which is for the most part occasioned only by a real loss of the object, by its death. In melancholia, accordingly, countless separate struggles are carried on over

the object, in which hate and love contend with each other; the one seeks to detach the libido from the object, the other to maintain this position of the libido against the assault.[26]

In other words, we might say that because melancholia is the product of competing processes within the patient, which does not allow for a clean detachment between the libido and the object, it would therefore complicate the patient's capacity to determine the loss object and achieve a resolution. More important, however, it makes it difficult for the patient to make direct claims about his distress. Of course, my obsession with this differentiation is not without reason because the lack of resolution and proper sense of cause not only produces confusion for the individual, but also implies a sense of hopeless passivity. Conversely, because mourning is a symptom of a conscious loss of the object, it can be perceived as a more active process of working through the loss. Following through with these definitions, in my reading, the critiques offered in the songs are in no way passive or undetermined. Take this example:

> Mẹ chờ thư về ngồi thèm thuồng miếng trầu cay
> Trẻ thơ lang thang vì cơn đói suốt bao ngày
> Vợ chờ tin chồng ngày về quá xa xăm
> Bao năm giải phóng như thế này phải không anh?[27]
> Mothers sitting, waiting for letters while chewing betel nuts
> Young children roaming around out of hunger every day
> Wives waiting for news of their husbands, their returns so far off
> So this is what all those years of "liberation" is like?

In the same way, the phrase *bà con* (everyone/folks), which gives the image of women and children to represent large groups of people, so the three images are offered here as a heuristic for Vietnamese society. Starting with the Vietnamese mother waiting for her son who has gone into exile, followed by the children roaming the streets and then wives missing their husbands, the draw of the stanza is the misery caused by disassembly of the familial unit leaving the most vulnerable members behind. Here the cause of the singer's lament is embodied within the people the revolution should have taken care of. The last line can be read as the culmination of the critiques, which actively challenges what the party really stood for, given that the result is the suffering and dismantling of Vietnamese society.

Looking at the Vietnamese community since 1975, anticommunist sentiments were never necessarily hidden, those who stayed were often jailed for either having been a part of the former republic or risking their lives to escape. From abroad, small Vietnamese refugee communities around the globe were actively establishing anticommunist newspapers and magazines, as well as participating in rallies and protests.[28] Even in more recent decades, this opposition to the communist party did not soften as protests were held among the diaspora in the United States against having normalized ties with Vietnam. Some notable examples are the protests in Irvine when in 2014 a city council member wanted to establish a twin city relationship between Irvine and Nha Trang, and in Little Saigon, Orange County, in 2019 when protesters marched to demand human rights in Vietnam.[29] The list could go on, but the main point is that even at the heart of one of the *nhạc vàng* producing capitals, lamenting the past was never really passive nor simply apolitical.

My conviction, then, is that the communist party's insistence on terms such as melancholia to describe *nhạc vàng*, which many critics adopted, functioned to detach the idea of this loss to something concrete. In other words, to ensure the cohesion of the party's narrative, it has to also deny the lost loved object as a real object and therefore to delegitimize it as a form of mourning. Similarly, even seemingly descriptive terms such as nostalgic are not neutral in their deployment, because to be nostalgic implies a certain acceptance of the past as past and, in a certain way, an acceptance of the present. However, given the examples of the politically active overseas Vietnamese communities, and the way *nhạc vàng* has been used to bolster their nationalism, neither the people in these communities nor the rhetorical question in "Chiều Tây Đô" is in any way a sign of acceptance of this past. Instead, the line is an active contestation to the party's politics. In this way, the continual usage of these terms as critical terms ignore the purpose of what songs like these actually do, which is to actively engage as a form of catharsis as well as provide the space for dissent and mourning.

RHIZOMATIC TRANSNATIONALISM

In Louis-Jacques Dorais's study on Vietnamese people in North America, he tries to trace the dimensions of the separate Vietnamese communities by showing how different groups have varying attachments and relationships to diaspora. Crucial to defining what makes this "diasporicity" relatable to each group is the distinction between those groups that see their transnational values as either more collective or more individual, the former being diasporic and the latter nondiasporic.[30] Although my main interests are not necessarily limited to this distinction, I do find Dorais's work to suggest something important—that is, regardless of where the communities are scattered, their identification with a more collective identity is hinged on their relationship with transnationalism.[31] Put differently, this diasporic, collective identity is not limited only by spatial categories proximity or distance, given that transnationalism already implies some form of separation from the localized nation, but also by whether they maintain a channel with the politics of their wider community.

In this view, I argue that companies like *Paris by Night* and *Asia*, which have reached countless Vietnamese people around the globe by playing nhạc vàng, represent a constitutive force in this shared identity. What needs to be emphasized, however, is that this shared identity is based less on a monolithic definition of nationalism, or even republicanism, which are singularly attached to the physical homeland, than it does with idea of the impossible return, represented in songs like "Chiều Tây Đô." So, although the lost object in nhạc vàng might be attributed to the very real territorial loss of the RVN, the type of transnational self-identification that those songs promote are not. In other words, what sustains the connection with this type of transnationalism are the networks that spring about as a condition of exile. This is a pertinent clarification because it frames nationalist sentiments differently than the center-periphery model, wherein collective association is hierarchized by proximity and attachment to the physical homeland. Here, such a model cannot function given precisely for the reason that the homeland no longer exists. There is no longer a South Vietnam. Instead, from my perspective, the desire and longing in these songs are directed overwhelmingly toward the voyage of return, which has no fixed locality because there is nothing to return to and therefore is concentrated on the process of movement toward that imagined nationalist space rather than any real, fixed destination. Put differently, the shared lost object of the diasporic community cannot be said to be cathected only to these songs or the RVN itself, but also to that notion of an impossible return.

In Gilles Deleuze and Félix Guattari's *A Thousand Plateaus*, going against Noam Chomsky's linguistical model, they describe rhizomes as something that can not only "assume diverse forms," but also be linked to one another, like assemblages, without having any fixed points or hierarchy.[32] Unlike trees, which have roots and thus a sense of order to them, rhizomes might be better understood as freely associating themselves with the larger whole. In other words, they are less individual units in a sense than they are forms of multiplicities. Earlier, I suggested that discourses on overseas Vietnamese music and cultural production, more broadly speaking, should not be focused on the diasporic capitals such as Orange Country, Paris, and San José because their purpose was to produce a transnational identity detached from center or centers. This is because, like rhizomes, diasporic nationalism cannot be determined individually or quantifiably arranged and ordered in a particular hierarchy—for who is to determine which of them exceeds another? Even though many diasporic capitals exist as cultural capitals for the community, in my view, they function less as fixed points where nationalistic thinking is concentrated, than as a network, whose vitality is depended on a collective synergy. As Deleuze and Guatari explain, whereas a tree is filiation, in which one thing stems from another, a rhizome is an alliance—not an originary verb to be conjugated, but a conjunction like "and...and...and."[33] This is because centers, such as San José, Paris, Orange County, and others do not only produce cultural objects, but also themselves depend on the circulation of these products in order to envision themselves as part of the wider cosmology of the diasporic community. It is this active affective investment into this cultural space from different points on the global diasporic map that lends to the feeling of a more democratic, if not republican, mode of political participation.

However, in applying this concept of the rhizome, which has no beginning or end, I do not suggest that the development of diasporic Vietnamese transnationalism does not have a historical precedent—it very much was a product of a particular historical condition.[34] In the same way that rhizomes themselves do not come from nothing, so too can this nationalism be accounted for, if one chooses, within a historical context. Instead, what I suggest is that diasporic transnationalism, in its current form, insofar as it is maintained and animated by movement and networks, lying underneath the surface of depoliticized cultural objects, should be observed rhizomatically, in the sense that it rejects notions of hierarchy, that Vietnamese transnationalism is indeed a multiplicity. Such thinking not only better accounts for the transitory nature of the cultural spaces and objects created by overseas Vietnamese around the globe, it also positions them on more equal terms in regards to their individual cultural production. For if a hierarchy were to be produced, by what practical measure would one organize their position in relation to one another? Would it be the amount of cultural products produced? Would it be by population size? Or would it be by how strictly they maintain some form of cultural purity? To expand on this last question, how would such notions of purity be verified? Would that not imply a certain static nature of culture? Quite differently, it is this capacity to see themselves as part of a more global, interconnected network and less as isolated enclaves of guardians of pure South Vietnameseness that sustains their political stance. For this reason, I find it useful to think of diasporic transnationality in terms of rhizomes—that is, a form of collective transnational belonging, which has no direct center, because what holds their bond is the identification with the return and not the homeland.

Going back to "Chiều Tây Đô," this idea of the return is in the first stanza:

Một đêm anh mơ mình ríu rít đưa nhau về,
Thăm quê xưa với vườn cau thề
Bàn tay anh đan dìu em bước trên cỏ khô
Đi trong hoang vắng chiều Tây Đô.[35]
One night I dreamed we happily accompany each other back,
to visit our hometown with the garden where we made our vows
My hands guiding you while we walk on the dry grass
Heading towards the deserted western capital

Here it is clear that the singing voice is coming from someone who has exiled and that this return to his lover and, more specifically, to the western capital, is only a dream. As expected for this genre, a central part to the allure of returning, is precisely the reconnection with the separated lover—a trope that has been persistent since before 1975. Just as many families were separated, relocated, or destroyed during the war, the refugee crisis that followed also broke up many families. Indeed, after the fall of Saigon, not all of those who managed to escape did so with their entire family, nor did the families that did escape manage to do so intact. One need not go over all the literature and filmic representations about the boat people to get a grasp how separation meant both a detachment with homeland and with loved ones. From this perspective, it follows that though a return might be the desired goal for some, the idea conjured by the image of hands holding each other seems to speak more to the longing of being connected to the imaginary social space than an actual return itself. In other words, the return itself is only important insofar as it is a way of reintroducing oneself back into the social fabric.

Further, although the *Tây Đô* in "Chiều Tây Đô" meant the city of Cần Thơ, the location from which the singing voice expresses itself remains unnamed. This undefined space from which the voice projects its longing makes it possible for audiences, whether they are in North America, Europe, or elsewhere, to identify themselves with the song on the basis of being diasporic. Indeed, the nonspecificity of the locus of enunciation rings as a siren emphasizing the vastness of the diasporic community and the need for a strong collective identity. As Stuart Cunningham and Tina Nguyen assert in their study of hybridity in the Vietnamese diasporic community, because *việt kiều* and the current Vietnamese government maintain a relationship based on mutual disauthentification, in which each party rejects the validity of the other, cultural production for the diasporic Vietnamese have been "centripetally organized around an officially excluded homeland."[36] It is also for this reason that Cunningham and Nguyen see the diasporic Vietnamese mediascape as being inherently different from other large diasporic communities, such as Chinese or Indian, given that they still "focus on large production centers like in the 'home' country."[37] Although I agree that this process of mutual disauthentification plays a crucial, dialectical role for the identity of each group and that for the *việt kiều* such an identity is heavily influenced by exclusion, I am less inclined to take the concept and image of homeland here as prima facie. Instead, I posit that because of this process of exclusion, which obliges cultural production to exist within a larger and more expansive international network, the notion of homeland gains its signification by way of an imagined globality. Put differently, here, rhizomatic transnationalism might be understood as the connection felt toward a collective identity, which is strengthened even further by knowing how such a song is meant to be widely distributed among the diasporic community—that part of what makes community is necessarily its transnational dimension.

RHIZOMATIC TRANSNATIONALISM, THE VIRTUAL, AND THE IMPOSSIBLE RETURN

Another salient example of this rhizomatic transnationalism can be seen in Tâm Đoan's live streamed rendition of "Chiều Tây Đô" on YouTube. Tâm Đoan, who is a well-known singer among overseas Vietnamese, begins her performance by asking audiences to like and share the video so that it would reach Vietnamese people around the world.[38] Dressed in a purple *áo dài*, a war beret, and accompanied by a guitarist in army uniform, Tâm Đoan sits on a stage decorated as a RVN military camp. Here, the song about exile and return is visibly connected to memories of the former republic by the yellow flag hung casually in the back, suggesting a causal relationship between war and exile.[39] That this video is the recording of a YouTube live stream, which is meant to be easily accessible worldwide, also speaks to the vitality and continual relevancy of the political sentiments it espouses. What was once a space dominated by recordings of live performances, then distributed manually among Vietnamese consumers around the globe, has now transformed into a demonstration of the politics in real time. Time and distance are no longer barriers to this cultural space. The digital platform transforms the notion of accessibility to the political, the previously imagined common temporality of this transnationalism no longer has to be imagined. Indeed, the virtual dimension should not go unnoticed given that it allows for forms of participatory action and community building that may not otherwise be possible.[40] At the same time, this notion of democratic participation also has resonance for those who still believe in a democratic South Vietnam.[41] What is lacking in a shared spatiality here is made up by the seeming simultaneity of the live stream. Given that Tâm Đoan's live performance of "Chiều Tây Đô" was also recorded after the stream was over, viewers can also continually rewatch, and in a certain sense continually return to the site of the common. The return thus does not need to necessarily be the expression of an individual desire, simply a collectively sustained one, shared among all those streaming from their own home, as often as they want.

Another particularly appropriate example of this shared longing of return is the song "Quê Hương Bỏ Lại" (Homeland left behind) by Tô Huyền Vân, which, as the title suggests, is about having been exiled. Starting the song with a lament of having left the homeland, the first stanza states:

Những ngày xa quê hương,
là những ngày mang đau thương
Một ngày xa quê hương
là một ngày mang đau khổ.[42]
The days I am away from the homeland
are the days that bring pain
[even] One day away from the homeland
Is a day that brings suffering.

Here, as in "Chiều Tây Đô," the crucial element is that the location of exile remains insignificant. What is emphasized, instead, is the more easily identifiable affective states of pain and suffering caused by separation from the homeland. The transition between *những ngày* (the days) to *một ngày* ([even] one day) from the first to the third line, serves to intensify the pain felt by the person in exile, where even just one day of away is an insufferable experience. Accordingly, it is because of this anguish, which makes it even more of an imperative for Vietnamese people overseas to look after another, as the song later says:

Hãy nhớ và hãy nhớ
Người Việt Nam đang lạc loài
Hãy thương và hãy quý
Tình đồng bào ta với ta
Hãy biết và hãy biết
Rằng ngày mai khi ta về
Hãy nhóm ngọn lửa hồng
Đốt sáng vạn niềm tin.[43]
Remember and remember
Vietnamese[our] people are lost
Care and cherish
The love we have for each other
Know and know
That tomorrow we might return
Let's put our pink flames together
So our faith can burn brilliantly.

From these first lines, it is evident that what motivates this collective, transnational identity and what urges diasporic Vietnamese people to care and cherish (*thương và hãy quý*) their relationships with one another, is that they are lost (*lạc loài*) in the world. The repetition of the imperative "remember" (*hãy nhớ*) and "know" (*hãy biết*), gives semblance to an echo that reverberates worldwide and serves as a reminder to the listeners of their collective vulnerability. Worth mentioning, of course, is that once again this idea of the return or journey home (*rằng ngày mai khi ta về*) appears as a common goal and offers itself as the basis of their relationality. Taking the liberty of a comparison with one of the most famous examples of the return journey, *The Odyssey*, we might say that, for Odysseus, even though the goal of arriving in Ithaca provides him and his crew a guiding telos, what substantiates his narrative and what produces his obstacles, is the journey home itself. Moreover, it is also this journey that gives the basis of their bond as men away from home.

In "Chiều Tây Đô," this return from abroad is brought up again in the last two lines of the song, that "Tàu đưa ta đi tàu sẽ đón ta hồi hương, Tây Đô sẽ sống lại yêu thương" (Boats took us away and boats will take us back home, the western capital will once more be like our memories).[44] Here, rather than deploying the pronoun *anh*, which is used elsewhere in the song, the singing voice no longer projects from the position of the exiled individual returning to their lover. Instead, the more abstract and numerically ambiguous pronoun, *ta*, which can signify both I and we, is used to suggest a more collective return. Like Odysseus's dangerous journey to Troy and back, where he and his men must sail by boat, so is the image of the return here made complete by the boat that brings the singing voice back to the homeland.

Different from Odysseus, however, what makes this concept of return powerful is that it is not embodied within a real locality but in the idea of the impossibility of the return journey itself. For this reason, Eric Henry generally characterizes this strand of music as expressing "a cosmic yearning for a homeland that is tragically inaccessible," a "cosmic for a love relationship that is tragically inaccessible," and "a cosmic yearning for a beautiful time in the past that is tragically inaccessible."[45] Thus the homeland remains in sight but perpetually out of reach, and necessarily so, which also makes it possible to identify with the notion of return whether the exile is internal or external. In this way, the return can register at different levels depending on where the audience find themselves. On the one hand, those outside Vietnam might identify with the return as a physical process, but, on the other, those inside might take the return as a temporal one to the past. In either case, ever since Đổi Mới in the 1980s, more access to cultural imports, readily available internet in Vietnam, and the physical return of many *việt kiều* has drastically changed the way *nhạc vàng* is perceived within the country. Simply looking at the popularity of YouTube channels dedicated solely to bolero music, which is simply another way to refer to *nhạc vàng* in contemporary Vietnam, says a great deal about how this rhizomatic transnationalism functions. In fact, by way of example, Sky Music Bolero and Nam Việt Bolero are two YouTube channels that have received millions of views, Sky Music Bolero boasting more than a million subscribers.[46] What is interesting about these channels is that although they are dedicated to shows produced in Vietnam, their general aesthetic is a replica of overseas productions, such as *Paris by Night* and *Asia*. Even a song like "Chiều Tây Đô," which is clearly sympathetic to RVN sentiments, has been incorporated and taken up by artists in Vietnam without changing the lyrics.[47] In these performances, the notion of return takes on new meaning—that of the reintroduction of *nhạc vàng*, albeit quite differently from how its composers would have imagined it. All this, coupled with the fact that this space has now transitioned primarily into the digital realm, means that the very idea of return requires a simultaneity between presence and absence, of a return of *nhạc vàng* and not quite.

Not without criticism, my hunch for the conditional acceptance of this type of music in Vietnam, at least in terms of censorship, has to do with the belief that such music, although politically oriented, no longer has the same political sway.[48] This view is also applicable to the party's sentiments about *việt kiều*, who, despite the antiparty politics, do not seem to represent much of a threat to the current state and therefore are allowed to return. That is, even though the music is ideologically opposed to the party, it is unlikely that the current existence of such music would be able to incite any form of viable political countermovement. Additionally, given the time that has gone by since the end of the war, it is quite possible that the younger population within the country identify this music as simply "old music" that their parents listen to, rather than as politically viable.

Although this image of *nhạc vàng* being depoliticized might explain why it is now tolerated in Vietnam, aside from the fact that it makes money, I am not convinced that it is necessarily the case that the music has no power or that the Vietnamese government welcomes it with open arms. Of course, we might say that although this music will not be the cause of the next revolution, it does remain crucial to the maintenance of transnational identification abroad. After all, *nhạc vàng* still is the living legacy of the RVN. Furthermore, even if the current "productions" of *nhạc vàng* in Vietnam tend to be more or less reproductions and reinterpretations of music from abroad, performing a performance if one wills, they still certainly contribute to the circulation and popularity of the music overall. One example is a performance of "Chiều Tây Đô" from the YouTube page GGM Bolero, where the singer is posed center stage with a live band as if it were a live performance taking place in Orange County.[49] Behind the singer are scenes of the Mekong projected onto an uneven backdrop as a woman in a white *áo dài* dances to the song.[50] Whereas overseas performances are obligated to use the stage setting because they do not have access to the actual localities, here, because the production takes place in Vietnam, the choice to implement the stage has a double reference. It is at once an attempt of the literal depictions of the song's content and simultaneously a reenactment of the overseas stage performances that gave the song its cultural imprint until this point. Yet, because the song has now been reinterpreted, where political sentiments are now aestheticized, it remains distinct from the productions abroad. As a result, one might say that the "return" of *nhạc vàng* in the form of bolero remains to be desired by those abroad and therefore reinforces the idea of the impossibility of a true return. In this way, the process of mutual disauthentification continues—neither Vietnam nor places like Orange County and elsewhere necessarily qualify as the main sources and true originator of these transnational sentiments, but rather as multiplicities of many contributors of the larger global network of rhizomatic transnationalism premised on an impossible return.

In this chapter, I argue that even though *nhạc vàng* tend to be taken as merely nostalgic or melancholic music, it is also a political force that fuels nationalist sentiments. Using Freud's distinction between mourning and melancholia to analyze the song "Chiều Tây Đô," where the former is more active process for reconciling the loss of the loved object and the latter passive process with an indeterminate cause, I argue that terms such as melancholia and nostalgia are inadequate and dismissive terms to describe the music. This is not only because they ignore the political dimensions, but also because they mirror the rhetoric of the Vietnamese Communist Party to delegitimize the cultural vestiges of the RVN. Further, I argue that this music not only represents neutral cultural objects from the diaspora, but also, due to its circulation and emphasis of the relatable idea of the return, is indeed crucial to the sustaining of a type of rhizomatic transnationalism. This is exemplified both in its popularity among overseas audiences and in its reintroduction into Vietnam, whereby the idea of the cultural center is no longer located in any fixed location. The shift from live performances in specific settings into the digital realm also complicates notions of cultural centers and what it means to form communities. What this implies, thus, is that although such music might no longer provoke political movements, as the party thought when they began to ban it, it remains a pertinent feature of Vietnamese transnationalism, which demands more critical attention.

NOTES

1. Lieu, "Performing Culture in Diaspora."
2. Although this category of music is more broadly recognized as *tân nhạc* (new music), I deliberately use the term *nhạc vàng* to refer more specifically to music produced in the RVN and in diaspora after 1975, which the communist party has historically been against.

The point is that despite being originally a negative term, *nhạc vàng* later gained value among overseas Vietnamese communities as being synonymous with memories of the RVN. For more background on Tân nhạc, see Henry, "Tân Nhạc."

3. Valverde, *Transnationalizing Viet Nam*, 50.

4. One notable example is the piece titled "Forwarding Memory through Diaporama," in which Erin Khuê Ninh takes a critical look at this form of music production positing it as a technology of memory. Here, Ninh performs a nuanced reading of a music slide show of the song "Làng Tôi," arguing it as a form of restorative nostalgia to draw out its affective capacity among second-generation Vietnamese in exile. Although I support Ninh's strategic turn toward music as an important cultural product, I differ in being content with using nostalgia as the critical frame. Despite offering a particular optic through which nostalgia could be understood, that is—distinguishing between reflective and restorative, as well as the location of fetishism through imagery, I find that the insistence on nostalgia itself still characterizes *nhạc vàng* as being passive. See Ninh, "Forwarding Memory."

5. Although nostalgia is an important aspect of this music, others have affirmed that it has strategic and culturally significant aspects that go beyond a constant reflection of past traumas. See Nguyen, "Vietnamese Sorrow."

6. By "rhizomatic," I refer to Gilles Deleuze and Félix Guattari's concept of the rhizome as a system wherein each part is a whole, which can attach itself to any other part to form a totality by way of its multiplicity rather than an ordered, hierarchical system. As they put it, "a rhizome can be connected to anything other, and must be." See introduction to *A Thousand Plateaus*, 1–26.

7. Cannon, "Virtually Audible in Diaspora," 140.

8. Although I chose to focus on Hoàng Oanh's rendition of "Chiều Tây Đô" from the thirty-second installment of *Asia*, which has almost a million views, other popular renditions include one from Asia 57 by Tuấn Vũ and Mỹ Huyền, which has almost three million views, and another by Giao Linh, which has more than thirty-five thousand views. See Asia Entertainment Official, "Chiều Tây Đô—Tuấn Vũ & Mỹ Huyền | Nhạc sĩ: Lam Phương (ASIA 57)," YouTube, 04:24, September 18, 2017, https://www.youtube.com/watch?v=zDS8LXGHMq0 (accessed February 15, 2023); Alfonso Carlson, "Chiều Tây Đô Giao Linh," YouTube, 07:47, August 16, 2016, https://www.youtube.com/watch?v=Ou7q-P96PiU (accessed February 15, 2023).

9. Asia Entertainment Official, "Chiều Tây Đô—Hoàng Oanh | Nhạc sĩ: Lam Phương | Trung Tâm Asia | ASIA 32," YouTube, 00:06, October 30, 2017, https://www.youtube.com/watch?v=1x3agFScojg (accessed February 15, 2023).

10. "Cuộc đời và sự nghiệp của ca sĩ Hoàng Oanh," Facebook, December 23, 2019, https://www.facebook.com/sbtnvoice/posts/605657186843265/.

11. "Cuộc đời và sự nghiệp."

12. "Cuộc đời và sự nghiệp."

13. Asia Entertainment, "Chuyến Đò Vĩ Tuyến—Hoàng Oanh (ASIA 12)," YouTube, 03:07, July 3, 2016, https://www.youtube.com/watch?v=JGI08Vqzb2c (accessed February 15, 2023).

14. Asia Entertainment, "Chuyến Đò Vĩ Tuyến," 03:10.

15. Báo Hải Quan Online, "Nhạc sĩ Lam Phương: Tình duyên trăm mối, một kiếp đa đoan," November 16, 2019, https://haiquanonline.com.vn/nhac-si-lam-phuong-tinh-duyen-tram-moi-mot-kiep-da-doan-115309.html (accessed February 15, 2023).

16. Báo Hải Quan Online, "Nhạc sĩ Lam Phương."
17. Taylor, "Music as a "Neocolonial Poison."
18. Taylor, "Music as a "Neocolonial Poison," 115.
19. In Taylor's article, he points out that although many people in the 1990s remember the associations with *nhạc vàng* and the prosecutions that took place, not many with whom he had spoken knew of its meaning and origin. Some of the definitions he received, then, included *yếu ớt* (weak), *lãng mạn* (romantic), *đồi trụy* (depraved), *đầu độc* (poisonous), *phản động* (reactionary), and *chống cộng* (anticommunist) ("Music as a "Neocolonial Poison," 104–105).
20. Taylor, "Music as a "Neocolonial Poison," 104–105.
21. Freud, "Mourning and Melancholia," 245.
22. Freud, "Mourning and Melancholia," 245.
23. "Mất," http://lyric.tkaraoke.com/14544/mat.html (accessed August 22, 2019).
24. Lam Phương, "Chiều Tây Đô," Lời bài hát Việt Nam, http://www.lyrics.vn/lyrics/364-chieu-tay-do.html (accessed December 26, 2019).
25. Even though melancholic patients can of course articulate things on a surface level, the lines here do not suggest a narcissistic identification with the object, which characterizes melancholia.
26. Freud, "Mourning and Melancholia," 256.
27. Lam Phương, "Chiều Tây Đô."
28. For more on these protests, see Ông and Meyer, "Protest and Political Incorporation."
29. See PBS SoCal, "Vietnamese Protest," *Social Insider with Rick Reiff*, April 15, 2014; Anh Do, "In Little Saigon, the Trump-Kim summit spurs a call for human rights in Vietnam," *Los Angeles Times*, February 26, 2019.
30. Dorais, "Politics, Kinship, and Ancestors," 94.
31. Dorais, "Politics, Kinship, and Ancestors," 96.
32. Deleuze and Guattari, *A Thousand Plateaus*, 7.
33. Deleuze and Guattari, *A Thousand Plateaus*, 25.
34. Deleuze and Guattari, *A Thousand Plateaus*, 25.
35. Lam Phương, "Chiều Tây Đô."
36. Cunningham and Nguyen, "Actually Existing Hybridity."
37. Cunningham and Nguyen, "Actually Existing Hybridity."
38. Tam Doan, "Chiều Tây Đô Live in Studio–Tam Doan (Lam Phuong)," YouTube, 05:52, May 18, 2018, https://www.youtube.com/watch?v=PY33wMI2aS0 (accessed February 15, 2023).
39. Tam Doan, "Chiều Tây Đô Live in Studio."
40. Nguyen et al., "Power Relations in Virtual Communities."
41. I do not claim that South Vietnam upheld democratic values in practice, simply that the appearance of democracy within the virtual space would be attractive for those to see the RVN as the democratic counterpoint to the current state of Vietnam.
42. Huyền Vân Tô, "Lời Bài Hát Quê Hương Bỏ Lại," https://lyric.tkaraoke.com/16145/que_huong_bo_lai.html (accessed August 24, 2019).
43. Tô, "Lời Bài Hát."
44. Lam Phương, "Chiều Tây Đô."
45. Henry, "Tân Nhạc," 137.
46. See Sky Music Bolero and Nam Việt Bolero's YouTube channels.

47. An example is Minh Luân's version posted on his YouTube channel. See "Official MV | Chiều Tây Đô—Minh Luân," YouTube, December 25, 2019, https://www.youtube.com/watch?v=J2Bjk28rB9g [private video].

48. In saying acceptance, I do not mean unconditionally accepted. In fact, many of the performances have been toned down as to appear solely aesthetic, not political. This is not to say that the aesthetic can be clearly demarked from the political, but simply that more obvious political markers such as the RVN flag can no longer be seen.

49. GGM Bolero, "Chiều Tây Đô | Tiếng Hát Hải Ngoại Nguyễn Luân | Một Cần Thơ Xưa Với Nhiều Kỷ Niệm," YouTube, May 18, 2018, https://www.youtube.com/watch?v=4nd5XY7K96U [video not available].

50. GGM Bolero, "Chiều Tây Đô."

CHAPTER 11

Ethnic Buddhism and Women in Hoa Pham's *Lady of the Realm* and Chi Vu's *Anguli Ma*

A Gothic Tale

Phạm Vũ Lan Anh

Vietnam Buddhism, religious studies scholar Alexander Soucy writes, is in his view one of the most interesting examples of ethnic Buddhism.[1] "Buddhisms become signifiers of particular 'home' cultures (e.g., as 'Vietnamese' or 'Cambodian' Buddhism)," he explains, "and therefore take on new meanings and functions in the diasporic that do not exist in the home country."[2] This statement implies one of the essential characteristics of the religion: *its syncretic feature.* In the homeland, Buddhism has had a syncretic relationship with certain elements of Taoism, Chinese spirituality, and Vietnamese folk religion.[3] The religion has become a vital intellectual force to the Vietnamese cultural makeup.[4] In the diasporic context, Vietnamese Buddhism has carried other characteristics, including legacies from regional movements of the Republic of Vietnam (RVN) and new features absorbed in the new environments. Thus Vietnamese Buddhism "can provide additional cement to bind a diasporic consciousness."[5]

The syncretic feature of Buddhism is also reflected in two novellas by Vietnamese Australian female writers, Hoa Pham's *Lady of the Realm* (2017) and Chi Vu's *Anguli Ma: A Gothic Tale* (2012). Their descriptions of Buddhism offer, in some way, a new notion of diasporic citizenship and need to be considered in a discussion of the relation between religion and gender.

This chapter argues that analyzing ethnic Buddhism in the two novellas can answer the question of how Vietnamese diasporic communities articulate and write about their relationship with both Vietnam and Australia. Buddhism becomes a medium to express diasporic predicaments of Vietnamese women, which means the religion brings a bit of peace but also recognizes suffering. In particular, the two writers offer different views about how the philosophical core of Buddhism, that "life is suffering," can reflect the traumatic events of the Vietnamese diaspora at different stages—in Vietnam, in transit, and in Australia. In turn, diasporic conditions create distances (from the homeland and its traditional folktale) and supply new materials (Gothic literature and some Indian Buddhism stories) for these diasporic writers to perceive Buddhism differently.

This chapter describes the background of the two writers and analyzes the syncretic features of Vietnamese Buddhism. It starts with Hoa Pham's *Lady of the Realm*, examining the image of the Bodhisattva of Mercy, the influence of the monk Thích Nhất Hạnh and the historical events in Vietnam. In Chi Vu's *Anguli Ma: A Gothic Tale*, I discuss two Buddhist tales, the theme of ghost story and the Gothic literary elements, to show how Vu uses darker kinds of stories to create imaginative diasporic scenarios.

HOA PHAM'S *LADY OF THE REALM*

Hoa Pham (Phạm Hồng Hoa) was born in Australia on August 3, 1972. She is a writer, a playwright, a psychologist, and also the founder of *Peril*, an Asian-Australian online art and culture magazine. She has a doctorate in creative arts and holds masters' degrees in creative writing and psychology. Pham has a successful writing career with seven books, four plays, and fourteen short stories. Pham won the Best Young Writer Awards from the *Sydney Morning Herald* for her novel *Vixen* (2000). *The Other Shore* (2014) won the Viva La Novella Prize. Her plays appeal to a wide range of readers.

Although Pham was born in Australia, Vietnam has had a profound impact on her identity and works. In her dissertation, she shares her family's stories (for example, her grandfather was a politician assassinated in Vietnam in 1975). She confirms her identity directly: "I am mostly Australian but consider myself a Vietnamese Buddhist."[6] Her perspective of a female Buddhist can be seen in *Lady of the Realm*, a result of her pilgrimage to Vietnam in 2007 with the influential monk Thích Nhất Hạnh.

Published by Spinifex in 2017, *Lady of the Realm* relates the life story of

Liên, a female clairvoyant. At the start, Liên lives in a peaceful and pretty coastal village with her family. Her tragedy begins when she discovers a disturbing ability for precognition through dream. Becoming a mouthpiece of the Lady, the female god of the village, Liên dreams about the deaths of her family and her villagers killed by Việt Minh from the North. Unfortunately, this dream comes true; the village and the Lady are destroyed. Liên is raped; her father is killed, and other female members in her family are kidnapped. Just a few people Liên led South to Saigon survive. In Saigon, the background of the second chapter, Liên seeks refuge in a large Buddhist monastery, where she decides to become a nun. She works for the School of Youth and Social Service (SYSS) founded by Thích Nhất Hạnh, studying and practicing Buddhist concepts such as meditation, consciousness, interbeing, and compassion. Here, Liên makes friends with Hương, a beautiful nun who, at the end of this chapter, burns herself to pray for peace in Vietnam. The chapter ends with an image of flames enveloping Hương and the news of Thích Nhất Hạnh being permanently exiled. In the two chapters that follow, Vietnam is reunited by the victory of the communists, but peace has not yet come because the new regime forbids Buddhism. Leaving Saigon, Liên finds a way back to her coastal village, where she discovers that many people are fleeing Vietnam by boat. It seems that Liên desires lasting peace when she meets Thích Nhất Hạnh again and joins Buddhism practices at the Prajna Monastery. The novella, however, ends when the Prajna Monastery is destroyed by the Vietnamese government.

Lady of the Realm is a miniature world of Vietnamese Buddhism. The work illustrates the basic principle of the religion, that life is suffering. Each person has suffered from different traumas, even the nuns, the monk, the monastery, and the Lady. All of them are ill fated in wartime and under the communist regime. Buddhism also affects the design of the novella. On the book cover is an image of a white, jade female Buddha, the Bodhisattva of Mercy. Titles of six chapters are named by moral standards of Buddhism and Vietnamese culture: "Hiếu, Love of family," "Upeksha, Love that goes beyond all boundaries," "Nghĩa, Love of country," "Metta, loving kindness," "Maitreya, true love," and "Karuna, compassion." Under these titles are quotes from Trịnh Minh Hà (a well-known Vietnamese female diasporic writer living in America) and the monk Thích Nhất Hạnh. Within the novella, paragraphs are divided by the stylized five-petal lotus, a Buddhism symbol of purity, enlightenment, self-regeneration, and rebirth.

Through the novella, questions fester in Liên's mind: What is peace?

And how can peace and hope come to Vietnam? Liên has found different answers for such questions through the help of the Goddesses, her grandmother (Bà), Hương, and Bình. Through Bà, Liên imagines peace as a family's connection and protection. Living with Hương, Liên understands peace as way to heal her wounds. Bình gives Liên another notion of peace when she says, "Maybe your peace is overseas, not here."[7] Under Quan Âm's halo, Liên discovers inner peace and fulfillment, which people can achieve if they have compassion, nonviolence, and an altruistic life. In other words, the writer's concerns of peace and religion reflect on the images of Bodhisattva of Mercy, the monk Thích Nhất Hạnh, and the events that took place in Vietnam over the past fifty-five years.

The Bodhisattva of Mercy

This section explores places of the Bodhisattva of Mercy and a rich tradition of literature related to the goddess in *Lady of the Realm*. In general, the Bodhisattva of Mercy (Phật bà Quan Âm or Quan Âm) has had a profound impact on Asian culture. According to Anh Tran, Quan Âm has two essential characteristics, which can be recognized in the novella.[8] First, Quan Âm is presented in many forms, several of which are explicitly female: grandmother, maiden, nun, young girl, and housewife. Second, as a personification of divine benevolence, Quan Âm is the most beloved Buddhist figure in East Asia, who embodies the virtues of compassion, mercy, and maternal love.

The image of the Lady in the novella is similar to Tran's descriptions. Like Quan Âm, the Lady has various appearances, connected closely with Vietnamese psychic life. She conjures up images of God, Goddess, Caesar, or the Mother Goddess, an indigenous religion in Vietnam.[9] In Phạm's novella, Liên has called "her name in many guises as the Lady of the Realm, as Mary, the mother of God."[10] The Lady also takes many shapes, such as "a wooden effigy kept in the center hall" of the village temple, "a giant white marble Buddha in the tree," and "the white and gold porcelain statue of Quan Am."[11]

The Bodhisattva of Mercy has inspired the writer: this goddess is a holotype of the Lady. Quan Âm and the Lady, along with other female characters, construct the women's sphere where the women share their trauma, speak up in their own voice, and express their virtues. "Quan Âm listens to the sufferings of the world, as does the Lady of the Realm."[12] The Lady is with Liên all along, beginning with a bad omen that she has sent through Liên's dream:

My dream was underwater. I could breathe, and I walked on the ocean floor, surrounded by brittle coral and bones. When I looked closer, I saw rib cages and human skulls among the debris. Fish brushed past me, indifferent to my presence. Then I saw human bodies floating by, bloated on the ocean surface. Fishermen from my village, their blood trailing in the water.[13]

Unfortunately, the nightmare comes true and changes Liên's life forever. Besides the loss of the family and the hometown, Liên is raped by a Việt Minh:

Then a Việt Minh appeared out of nowhere. Someone screamed. He grabbed me, and I struggled. He tore at my pants and grabbed my groin. Then he dropped me as his hands came away sticky with my monthly blood. I landed with a thud on the sand. He threw himself on top of me and I struggled as he forced his way inside me.[14]

This detail is quite possibly associated with Pham's real life. In "The Seed of Enlightenment," Pham shares her story:

Then I went on a pilgrimage with Thích Nhất Hạnh in Vietnam in 2007. He is a well-known Vietnamese Zen Master and he sought to heal all sufferers from the war with Great Ceremonies of Mourning. This I took to readily. The rape I had suffered from an uncle who was a refugee, I understood to be a product of the war. I too had suffered from the war.[15]

The writer and her character's experiences are different because of their circumstances and their offenders. However, they are similar to some extent in terms of the trauma and the treatment. Both suffer from sexual assaults, which is "impossible to forget but difficult to remember."[16] They are virtually identical when expecting Buddhism to provide shelter. But whereas the writer follows Thích Nhất Hạnh's practice of mediation, Liên becomes a nun in the SYSS, first to help other vulnerable people, then to rescue and enlighten herself. Through mindfulness, Liên learns forgiveness and *metta*, a form of meditation focused on the development of unconditional love for all beings. She talks about the rapist: "The Việt Minh man who raped me so long ago, was a child too once. He had been brutalised by being a soldier in the wars."[17] Interestingly, her conclusion evokes concepts such as *luật nhân quả* (cause and effect) and *sơ tâm* (beginner's mind or a child's soul, meaning the purest heart of a person). Liên is aware that the rapist is also the victim of the war in that the child's soul within the rapist is destroyed. Under the halo of Quan Âm, Liên avoids survival guilt: "I would not be killed by war and Vietnam could achieve peace."[18]

Pham creates the image of Quan Âm by reading Thích Nhất Hạnh's *The Novice: A Story of True Love*. Thích Nhất Hạnh's is based on a famous Vietnamese literary work, *The Tale of Lady Thị Kính* (*Quan Âm Thị Kính*), a well-known classic Vietnamese novel-in-verse. The *Tale of Lady Thị Kính* is about Thị Kính's intellectual journey. Respecting her father's wishes, Thị Kính marries a scholar with a promising future as a mandarin. One night, her husband asleep, Thi Kinh holds a pair of scissors she uses for sewing. She sees a hair on her husband's face and thinks it is a bad omen. She intends to cut it just as her husband wakes up, thinking that she is trying to murder him. Because of this misunderstanding, Thị Kính is thrown out of her husband's house and forced to return to her parents. Under social pressure, her family abandons her.

Failed by love, by her parents, and by the rules of society, Thị Kính turns to Buddhism. At the time only men can become monks, so Thị Kính disguises herself as a man and enters a pagoda, taking her Buddhist name Tiểu Kính Tâm. As a young and handsome monk, Tiểu Kính Tâm attracts many female villagers, including a beautiful and lustful maid Thị Mầu. After failing to win the heart of Tiểu Kính Tâm, the maid has an affair with a servant in her house and becomes pregnant. To avoid punishment from a village chief, Thị Mầu accuses Tiểu Kính Tâm of being responsible for her pregnancy. The young monk accepts the accusation and punishment from the village and is forced to leave the temple. Meanwhile, Thị Mầu abandons her newborn child under a tree. Tiểu Kính Tâm hears the child's cry and decides to raise the child. Tiểu Kính Tâm's innocence is brought back to her when she passes away. Touched by Thị Kính's selflessness, The Buddha makes her Quan Âm.

The Tale of Lady Thị Kính is significant in its religious and social meanings and in its gender-related implications. Pham captures an important detail that can express the diasporic identity: Thi Kinh, in the original work, is expelled from her village as well as from her family. In a feudal and patriarchal society, such places played an important role in determining a person's identity. To an extent, the fate of Thi Kinh also has similarities with many diasporic Vietnamese, including those who were part of "the internal migrations,"[19] a wave of refugees who came from North to South Vietnam from 1954 to 1956. To the Vietnamese boat people, Quan Âm—the afterlife of Thị Kính—is a guardian goddess, protecting them during their boat escape and their stay in the refugee camps.[20]

Thích Nhất Hạnh

Thích Nhất Hạnh is one of the main characters in *Lady of the Realm*, where he is respectfully called *thầy* (master or teacher). The novella emphasizes two salient features of Thích Nhất Hạnh: his exile status and his Engaged Buddhism. He emerges as a monk fulfilling a variety of roles in the Vietnamese Buddhist communities, living inside and outside his homeland. He becomes a witness to the Buddhist reform movement and South Vietnam's history. Writing about the real person, Pham anchors "the reader in a very specific moment in time, to comment on their societal influence (or society's influence on them), explore a mystery surrounding them, or consider a lesser-known, perhaps more human, side of an outsized public persona."[21] Thích Nhất Hạnh left Vietnam for the United States in 1966 to speak with political and religious leaders about stopping the Vietnam War. In the novel, Pham lets her protagonist narrate the monk's life: "When news of his permanent exile reached me, I wept again."[22] Because of his antiwar speeches and activities while touring North America and Europe, he was barred from returning to Vietnam, first by South Vietnam and later by the communist regime, until 2005, when he was allowed to make his first visit in thirty-nine years.[23] The monk says, "my name was banned by the government of the South, the anti-communist government, because of my activities for peace, calling for reconciliation between North and South. I became a *persona non grata*. I could not go home anymore, and I was in exile."[24] On September 30, 2018, Thích Nhất Hạnh returned to Vietnam with the wish that he could live in his "root temple," the Từ Hiếu pagoda, for the rest of his life. He passed away at the age of ninety-five on January 22, 2022.

As a diasporic writer, Pham has a special interest in the theme of exile as well as the mode of writing "between exile and diaspora."[25] Pham takes account of the nuances of internal exile through Thị Kính, the precursor of *Quan Âm Thị Kính*, and then the long external exile of Thích Nhất Hạnh. If the exilic nuance of Quan Âm is perceived in a literary context, the exile status of Thích Nhất Hạnh is more vivid, marking him a witness of a turbulent historical period. The rigid proscription of Thích Nhất Hạnh and the destruction of his monastery eventually dispel the writer's illusion of achieving peace and freedom in the homeland. Although at the end of the novella, Prajna Monastery becomes a legend, the insinuation is that Buddhism fails to heal the wounds of its followers, including the writer and her female characters. It also reminds the second-generation writer of the reasons why she becomes diasporic: the communist regime, which destroys the statue of the Lady, prohibits the development of Buddhism in a peaceful period, prevents the impact of Thích Nhất Hạnh on Vietnam religious life, and abolishes the Prajna Monastery.

Prajna Monastery represents Engaged Buddhism, a term coined by Thích Nhất Hạnh.[26] In an interview with John Malkin on July 1, 2003, the monk explained this concept:

> Engaged Buddhism is just Buddhism. When bombs begin to fall on people, you cannot stay in the meditation hall all of the time. Meditation is about the awareness of what is going on not only in your body and in your feelings, but all around you... Buddhism has to do with your daily life, with your suffering and with the suffering of the people around you. You have to learn how to help a wounded child while still practising mindful breathing. You should not allow yourself to get lost in action. Action should be meditation at the same time.[27]

As a result, Engaged Buddhism "can mean *engaging with*, or *engaging in*, as in engaging with a body of literature or an object, or in an activity; they could equally well be translated as *descending*, as in coming down from a mountain into a real world; or as *manifesting*, as in being the manifestation of a deity or a realized being; they can also mean *proceeding*, as in proceeding on a journey."[28] From this explanation, Thích Nhất Hạnh's Engaged Buddhism can be explored variously, from its practical, philosophical, and political senses to its literary ones.

Pham and her protagonist, Liên, recognize that the monk has concretized his term in practical ways. He also dedicated his life to practicing Engaged Buddhism and to making his religious ideals come true. During the war, he founded the School of Youth for Social Service, a group of ten thousand volunteers who helped both communists and anticommunists during the Vietnam War. The monk and the SYSS members led antiwar protests, rebuilt villages, resettled refugees, lobbied internationally for peace talks, and published articles and books on the crisis faced by his country and the Buddhist tradition. In exile, he founded Plum Village Monasteries (Làng Mai) for Vietnamese Buddhists living in France, Germany, America, Thailand, Hong Kong, and Australia. When he returned to Vietnam, he established Prajna Monastery to practice mediation and mindfulness, focusing on living in the here and the now.

The monk also applied Engaged Buddhism in verse and literary books. He has published more than one hundred books, including more than seventy in English. In terms of poetry, he wrote many short lines of verses, Buddhism-related traditional literature from the Lý through the Trần dynasties (1009–1400). Significantly, Pham singles out some verses as Liên's narration, reflecting her meditation and mindfulness. Some verses, such as "Present moment, wonderful moment. I am fresh as a flower"/ "I am as still as a mountain. I am like water reflecting"/ "I am arrived, I am home. In the here and in the now"/ "Breathing in, I touch my fear. Breathing out, I release my fear," appear frequently in the novella.

Engaged Buddhism not only has shaped the writer's identity, but also transferred to engaging writing. Take the topic of rape as an example. The choice of writing about this hidden trauma places Pham in a dilemma. Writing about sexual assault means facing her traumatic event. However, if they avoid mentioning the assault, Pham and her character must face the "suffering in silence," an unspoken feminine trauma.[29] Practicing mediation and mindfulness, a philosophical core of Engaged Buddhism, has become therapeutic for the survivors. Living in every present moment helps Liên escape from her painful past and achieve tolerance: "How can I continue to hate the American War veteran who cried in my arms for what he had done? The Việt Minh man who raped me so long ago, was a child too once. He had been brutalised by being a soldier in the wars."[30] Her religious belief and the inspiration from Engaged Buddhism have bolstered her courage to "describe confronting scenes and deal with difficult subject matter such as rape, suicide, violence, and of course, the Vietnam war and its casualties."[31] Consequently, both Pham and Liên successfully overcome the pain of rape and survival guilt. Engaged Buddhism changes these women's worlds and their sense of victimhood by offering them as victims an inner and spiritual strength to deal with their wounds.

In a larger sense, Thích Nhất Hạnh's Engaged Buddhism is necessary for the diaspora to escape the situation of being caught in the traumatic past. As Edward Said remarks, "the homeland inspires a never-ending mourning, a constant reminder of the past, which prevents those in exile from focusing on the future. A prolonged memory of the place they have left stops them from seeing the new place in which they now live."[32] Said's statement seems suitable to the Vietnamese women before they approach Engaged Buddhism. Focusing on the present does not mean forgetting or denying the past. It refers to reconciliation as a primary step to imagining a better future. When practicing Engaged Buddhism,

Thích Nhất Hạnh attempts to find peace, not only at the individual level but also at the national level. He believed that Engaged Buddhism is "a way to promote peace and to protest against the war in Vietnam. Based on Bodhisattva practices, it encourages members of the Inter-Being Order to engage in social services that provide comfort to people and alleviate the suffering caused by war and poverty."[33] His idea that Buddhism could be a solution for the Vietnam War crisis is one reason Thích Nhất Hạnh was exiled: both sides recognized his strength. The monk also thinks that Vietnamese Buddhism should be independent of politics. Thích Nhất Hạnh's religio-political boundary seems to conflict with the political control of a religious group. "After his second visit in 2007, he earned condemnation from the communist government by criticizing its polities on religion. The base he had set up at Bat Nha monastery in 2005 was subsequently harassed by locals, whom his followers believe were being led by undercover agents."[34]

In *Lady of the Realm*, the mentioned detail is narrated through the voice of Liên:

> The loudspeaker messages are stronger now, interrupting our meditation, denouncing Thích Nhất Hạnh and ordering us to return home. Paid by the authorities to drive us out of our home, the villagers harass the younger nuns. My breath is ragged, and I calm myself breathing in and out. It reminds me too much of when my village was taken by the Việt Minh.[35]

This eventually dispels Liên's illusion of peace in Vietnam. Thích Nhất Hạnh in the novella is reasonable when he said, "Prajna is now legend. You carry the seeds Prajna inside you to spread to the world."[36] A legend here implies the spirit of Engaged Buddhism. But the legend also reminds of the disastrous life of Thị Kính in *The Tale of Lady Thị Kính*. Both Thích Nhất Hạnh's monastery and the female character in the story are rejected by the social and historical conditions of their time.

Buddhism in Vietnam

As discussed, the novella fictionalizes historical events, including the state of Buddhism under the communist regime (1975–1986), milestones in Thích Nhất Hạnh's life (1967–2007), and the destruction of Prajna Monastery (2009). In addition, in the second chapter, titled "Upeksha, love that goes beyond all boundaries," the writer describes Hương's immolation, evoking one of the most globally shocking events in the twentieth century:

Some of the curious began to gather around her. Hương had not mediated in the street before, and this was unusual.

Then her voice rang out across the street. "I do this to wish for peace," she smiled.

Suddenly she doused herself with kerosene from the gasoline can. She produced a lighter from her robe and snapped it alight.[37]

Traced back to the place (Saigon) and the time (1963), Hương's death is a reminder of Reverend Thích Quảng Đức's immolation on June 11, 1963. The monk burns himself to protest the persecution of Buddhism in South Vietnam. His sacrificial torch was captured by the American photographer Malcolm Browne whose *The Burning Monk* won the Pulitzer Prize and led Americans to question US presence in Vietnam. In the 1960s, in addition to Thích Quảng Đức, more than six monks, nuns, and Buddhists self-immolated.[38]

These historical events are important to understanding *Lady of the Realm*, which illustrates "a dynamic interplay between novelistic invention and historical claims."[39] The self-sacrifice of Thích Quảng Đức was done in protest to the South Vietnamese pro-Catholic policies, which discriminated against Buddhists. In particular, "the Catholics were allowed to fly the Vatican Flag and parade their sacred objects, while the Buddhists (who in Hue lived under the control of Diem's younger brother Ngo Dinh Can) were forbidden to do likewise."[40] For Thích Nhất Hạnh, this event in 1963 "presented a singularity in the Buddhist struggle of the 1960s. Political opposition, spontaneously cemented in the face of ruthless government oppression, united Buddhists and non-Buddhists alike."[41] In the novella, Hương burns herself to pray for peace. Hương's death illustrates a Buddhist value called Upeksha, the love that goes beyond all boundaries.

The appearance of Vietnamese historical events in the novella shows that the writer has seriously thought about writing as a diasporic act, thinking about Vietnam as a place recreated through imagination, trauma, and distance. Moreover, it illustrates her increasing engagement with Vietnam and her desire to connect with the Vietnamese diasporic community despite her inability to speak the language.[42]

CHI VU'S *ANGULI MA*: A GOTHIC TALE

Chi Vu (Vũ Thị Mỹ Chi) was born in 1973 in Vietnam and arrived in Melbourne in 1979 as a boat person. Vu belongs to the 1.5 generation, "who experienced migration as children aged between six and sixteen years, including experiencing some of their formative socialisation, and therefore language acquisition, in the country of origin."[43] Vu is a Melbourne-based writer, dramaturge, playwright, and performance artist. She has created sixteen works. Her plays include the critically acclaimed *Coloured Aliens* (2017), *The Dead Twin* (2015), *Vietnam: A Psychic Guide* (2009), and *A Story of Soil* (2000). Her prose works have appeared in various publications, including *Joyful Strains, Growing Up Asian in Australia*, and the *Macquarie PEN Anthology of Australian Literature* (also published as *The Literature of Australia*). The novella *Anguli Ma: A Gothic Tale* was shortlisted in the NSW Premier's Literary Awards.

Anguli Ma provides an original insight into the world of Vietnamese refugees in the Western suburbs of Melbourne in the 1980s. The main character is Đào, an elderly landlady living with two female tenants, Bác and Sinh. They are boat people. Unlike Đào who came safely to Australia with her child named Trung, Bác lost her husband and her only son in the ocean. This woman is haunted by this sorrow for the rest of her life. Sinh is the youngest woman who had escaped by herself, age only sixteen, and now works as a cleaner. She is mysteriously killed at the end of the story; her fingers are found in a garage of Đào. The lives of these women become worse when Anguli Ma, an enigmatic male tenant and former North Vietnamese student, appears. He lives in the garage of Đào's house, now works in an abattoir, and gradually disturbs the lives of his housemates. He neglects to pay rent, leaves bowls of putrid offal in his room, and eats dog meat. He robs the landlady's *hụi*, "a kind of community loan scheme, where members pool money and can win it by ballot for a month or so to buy things or pay bills."[44] He also attempts to kidnap Tuyết, Đào's granddaughter. Anguli Ma may also be involved in Sinh's disappearance. Because of the loss of *hụi*, Đào is blamed, threatened, and pursued. She ends up fleeing. This is the second time Đào escapes, the first time was fleeing Vietnam by boat. No one is happy even though they live in a safer country (Australia).

The "surreal" relationship is between a mysterious monk and a brown man, who both have a vital role in the novella. "The monk in question is an enigmatic figure threaded throughout the narrative, one who appears to hang out in a local park. He interacts with no other central characters in the story save for the 'brown man' he encounters there and whom we eventually connect to the personage of Anguli Ma, the errant boarder."[45] Moreover, "the chapters titled 'the monk' and 'the brown man' provide a counter-narrative to Đào and the other realist characters and their concerns. These chapters are more surreal, providing a moment for the brown man and the monk to pause and reflect on Buddhist teachings."[46]

In writing this novella, Vu depends on various sources of inspiration. The first is a "modern tale set in Melbourne's Western suburbs in the 1980s where a Vietnamese abattoir worker becomes a murderer."[47] The second is traditional Buddhist folktales, especially Aṅgulimāla, a story that describes "a ferocious bandit or a brigand whose main occupation was to kill human beings."[48] The third is Gothic literature. "In *Angulima-a Gothic Tale*, Vu uses Western literary forms like the gothic tales and Buddhist references to create a horrific story of Vietnamese refugees."[49] Similarly, Yvette Rochelle Harvey has "read Vu's deliberate use of the Gothic as subversive in intent and practice."[50] Her works span genres such as postcolonial gothic, horror, magic-realism, and comedy. Drama is her favorite. She uses dramatic features in her novella, embracing thirty-nine stage scenarios. The characters' names are used to label the title of each scenario.

Moreover, developing a significant point of crisis is followed by a denouement and resolution of conflicts and tensions. In "Gothic Buddhist tale set in Melbourne West," a conversation between Chi Vu and Michael Cathcart of Radio National's *Book and Arts Daily*, Vu reveals some details about her writing process. Initially, the writer intended to write a play about Aṅgulimāla, the story she heard from a Zen teacher ten years ago. Afterward, she changed her mind from creating a drama to writing a novella because she found it too challenging to perform the Buddhist's meditation in the form of a drama.

The substantial contribution to this fiction is its triple hyphenation: Buddhist tradition–Gothic literature–the Vietnamese diaspora. This hyphenation examines how Buddhist factors "have cross-cut diaspora in complex ways and constitute multiple experiences of the diaspora."[51] The purpose in reviewing Buddhist factors in the hybridity is twofold, to read both backward (toward Vietnam as homeland) and forward (toward Australia as the destination). Through the triple hyphenation, Vu explores the characteristics of her diasporic community. These people "are often buoyed in their new country by new opportunities, and yet they are still haunted by their previous identity," the writer explained in an interview with Patrick McCarthy. Moreover, the women's sphere plays a vital role in exploring similarities between Buddhism and Gothic literature.[52]

Who Is Anguli Ma?

The first Buddhist folklore, which Vu borrows, is Aṅgulimāla, a life story of Ahimsaka. Ahimsaka is the scion of a well-to-do family and a brilliant student of Taxila, a well-known school in ancient India. Through wisdom and kindness, he becomes a beloved student. However, other students are jealous of him and turn the teacher against him, which ends with the teacher asking him to do something impossible: kill one thousand people. Refusing to do so, Ahimsaka is expelled from school. When he returns home, his mother is not able to protect him and he is cast out by his father. Even his fiancée's family cancels their engagement. Ahimsaka becomes an exile in his community. The young man is haunted by his teacher's curse and sets out to collect fingers by becoming a serial murderer. He strings his victims' fingers around his neck, which gives him the nickname Aṅgulimāla (finger garland or finger necklace). Buddha knows that Aṅgulimāla's final victim will be his mother. To prevent this crime, Buddha appears in front of Aṅgulimāla. With Buddha's teaching, Aṅgulimāla finds enlightenment and becomes an arhat. However,

> because of his former misdeeds, even after he was ordained as a monk and became an arhat, he still had to endure the hatred of the society he used to terrorize, sometimes suffering frightful beatings. The Buddha explained that the physical pain he suffered was a consequence of his violent past and that he should endure it with equanimity. His fate illustrates an important point in the theory of karma.[53]

Vu draws inspiration from Aṅgulimāla to create Anguli Ma. The conversation between Đào and Anguli Ma reveals his background:

> "Where is your quê?" she asked.
> "My quê gốc is in the North," he rounded out her question for her, "but my father was a teacher, so we emigrated to the South in '54."
> Đào was somewhat impressed—his people were either wealthy, intellectuals or Catholics and had been chosen to uproot from their quê gốc rather than live under the Communists. If he'd said they were '45 migrants, then she might have thought differently...
> "And what do you do now?"
> "There's a place around here in Braybrook offering work. I'm unsure if I have the kind of experience they're looking for, having only been a sinh viên [student] during the war. We just learnt how to read thick books and recite poetry, nothing of use for our new lives over here"...

Đào could see that his face was that of a Northerner, with a taller nose and high cheekbones and forehead. This son of a teacher, this former student during the war, now reduced to manual labour.[54]

Such a short dialogue recalls historical events in Vietnam, conveys the political standpoint of Đào and the writer. "They were '45 migrants" and "We emigrated to the South in '54" evoke the dark history of the Vietnamese Famine of 1945 and Operation Passage to Freedom in 1954–1955. They are the consequences of war-related policies, which led large numbers of North Vietnamese to move to South Vietnam. Đào and Anguli Ma seem more sensitive to immigration and separation between North and South Vietnam than other characters. "Others had left the North to resettle in the South in the late 1940s, either as a response to the 1944–1945 famine, or because of fears of the Việt Minh, or simply to seek employment."[55] As a result of the Geneva Accords in July 1954, "Operation Passage to Freedom, or Operation Exodus, as named by South Vietnam, saw the movement of more than 810,000 Vietnamese from north of the seventeenth parallel to the south of it."[56] According to Frankum, the Vietnamese decided to leave their homes in the North for many reasons related to policy, economics, religion, and family relations. Đào believes that Anguli Ma's family transplant themselves because they refuse to live under the communist regime.

Anguli Ma's anticommunism strongly affects Đào. She allows Anguli Ma to live in her garage not only because of her financial need but also because of the shared political standpoint that led them to leave Vietnam. As she says, "he's a Vietnamese. Everyone over here is struggling the same way. We have all lost so much already. There's no point having no tình người."[57] However, an enigmatic man like Anguli Ma living with "three women in a drafty old house without their husbands, children, siblings, fathers or mothers, without any menfolk" is problematic.[58] Eventually, these women view him "as a malevolent, volatile, threatening figure."[59] Vu gradually reveals the differences, conflicts, and problems between Anguli Ma and the other characters.

These problems come not only from gender differences but also from the writers' political views. The works of Pham and Vu present the geographical, ideological, and political differences between North and South Vietnam. Of course, "the demarcation between the North [Đàng Ngoài] and South [Đàng Trong] is a recurrent theme in Vietnamese history."[60] In the eyes of the people supporting South Vietnam, anything from North

Vietnam bears a negative meaning. In *Lady of the Realm*, the Việt Minh are called "invaders from the North."[61] In *Anguli Ma*, Anguli Ma evokes the image of the mass murderer in the Buddhism story and the image of *ông ba bị, ông kẹ*—the bugaboo who kidnaps and eats children in old Vietnamese stories.[62] In the story, Anguli Ma jokes about "yummy child's fingers" when he plays paper-rock-scissors with Tuyết, Đào's granddaughter.[63] What comes from North Vietnam becomes more and more acute in the eyes of Vietnamese refugees in Melbourne. Here, it seems that the novelist relies on her political standpoint rather than the Buddhism story to convey the image of Anguli Ma. Đào sees his transformation from a student to the menacing abattoir worker and then an evil person. Đào has assumed that "perhaps her new tenant's stubborn behavior was due to his pride: those who had a higher position in the old society must feel their decline more keenly."[64]

Vu has created a dog-meat party for Anguli Ma and his Vietnamese friends. First, the party's atmosphere reminds them of what makes people desperate enough to uproot themselves—the fall of Saigon in 1975:

> The strange night had reminded them of the old world. They shouted to each other to keep track of their progress.
> "The last time I had this much fun was..." the room was spinning so. "Hahaha."
> "Yes," someone punctuated.
> "A large group of us, post-game drinking."
> "What year?" Anguli shouted.
> "Seventy-five"...
> "The end của một cuộc đời," the workmate concluded.
> In that stillness, they avoided each other's eyes, for losing a homeland was like losing someone who knew you intimately, and whom you knew intimately. In this abyss, Anguli Ma and the workmate realised that their old life, and youth were both gone forever.[65]

Second, the party sketches Vu's conception of "repressed identity." This party is barbarous in Australia. Anguli Ma and his friends steal the injured animal on the street and kill it as if they had lived in Vietnam where "eating dog meat has long been popular," especially in the North.[66] This old habit allows characters to experience themes of repressed cultural identity viscerally. The dead animal arouses Đào's sense of being shocked and scared—an important element of Gothic horror. More important, it expresses the fear of being labeled as alien or being rejected. Đào says bitterly, "This is not our country."[67] She realizes her differences in the eyes of the local people: "everything we do is suspicious to them. They turn their noses up at our fish sauce, our green oil, our large gatherings, our tightly knit way of living."[68] Here, the "repressed identity" that Vu takes from Gothic literature has at least two meanings in the diasporic context. Repressed identity here refers to the suppression of old habits (e.g., eating dog meat) and the vague fear regarding of being uprooted, being in the margin of Australian society. Dao understands that the diasporic community is never "fully accepted by their host society and therefore feel partly alienated and insulated from it."[69]

Ghost Story

Ghost as a special character in this novella reflects ghosts in various contexts: Buddhism traditions, Vietnamese conception, diasporic writings, and Gothic fiction. In the Buddhist tradition, the trope of the hungry ghost is typically seen as one of the six stages of being human, or "six realms of existence,"[70] which includes hell, animals, hungry ghosts, humans, titans, and bodhisattvas. In the nineteenth century, under the influence of Buddhism's circle of life and death, Nguyễn Du wrote *Oration of Ten Types of Sentient Beings* (*Văn tế thập loại chúng sinh*) to express his deep compassion for ten types of homeless ghosts. These spirits are "the products of 'bad death,' painful and violent death away from home that Vietnamese call 'death in the street.' "[71] Without descendants to honor them, these wandering ghosts are stuck between this world and the next, both forgotten and feared by the living.[72] To an extent, Vu discovers that being stuck between two worlds is what the Vietnamese refugees in the 1970s and 1980s share with the wandering ghosts.

In general, ghosts "haunt individual experiences; they often become the source of a structure of feelings, the basis of the mythico-history that allows groups to analyse their collective experience and identity."[73] This view seems able to explain the theme of the ghost in Vietnamese diasporic writings such as Viet Thanh Nguyen's "Black-eyed Women" in *The Refugees* (2017) and Vu's novella. The spirit here refers to nameless graves of ill-fated Vietnamese boat people who perished at sea by disease, starvation, and dehydration, or were murdered by pirates. Thus Bác always sees her son call her "from the bottom of the ocean's body" in her dreams.[74] And intriguingly, the writer uses paronomasia, breaking Aṅgulimāla into Anguli Ma. The Vietnamese word "Ma" means "ghost." Therefore, the story about Anguli Ma implies a story about a ghost.

In the novella, Bác describes the ghost as "a presence and an absence, and they have stories waiting to be told."[75] In a conversation between Bác and Đào, Bác believes that ghosts (*ma cô hồn*) follow her during her boat journey:

> Bac tried not to sound too bitter. "None of us knew whether we were going to meet with god or the devil out there. And as we waited, we made promises to ourselves, our deities and Ancestors that if we got out, we would live our lives better. I did it too, until I lost my son"...
> The old woman remained in a dark mood. "We think we left this behind when we escaped."
> "Left what behind Bác?" she said quietly. "Women cleaning up after men?" Đào continued sweeping.
> "Left behind *ma cô hồn*, in the old world."
> Đào stopped. Wandering, hungry ghosts. Unable to be reborn as a human or animal, unable to enter heaven or hell because of their gruesome, untimely deaths.
> "We think we have a new beginning because we escaped the terror and came to a new land. But we haven't left them behind, they came with us! Can't you see it?" Bác's gaunt face and grey eyes were unwavering in the morning light.[76]

Mentioning ghosts is a way of remembering their beloved dead that "extends into public mourning."[77] Vu has transformed the ghost in Buddhist tradition into the ghost in diasporic literature, who is usually considered as "illegal migration" or "unwelcome guest."[78]

In addition to bringing Buddhist traditions to diasporic writings by using ghosts, Vu attempts to combine Buddhism and Gothic literature. The ghost relates to the popular Gothic theme having to do with the supernatural. More important, it evokes another concern occurring in the women's sphere: the female characters' powerlessness is revealed through different types of ghosts.[79]

Walter Mason suggests that Bác's character can be understood through the lens of another Buddhist folktale, *Kisa Gautami*. It narrates the story of Kisa, a woman stuck with grief because of the death of her only child.[80] Both Kisa and Bac regret not being able to protect their beloved children, and both lean on Buddhist theology to deal with their grief. However, Kisa eventually achieves spiritual enlightenment but Bác's painful past still haunts her. Kisa is aware that deaths come to human beings. In contrast, Bác relies on Buddhist concepts such as karma, the six realms of existence, to interpret her predicament: "Bác had come to the end of her days feeling she had been harassed by what she had witnessed in life. She had seen this depth of grief many times before and knew that Đào would wallow in the circle of pain for years before she would become aware of her animal situation."[81]

The women's powerlessness is also exacerbated by Anguli Ma's gender prejudice. He sneers at Đào: "Women living away from their *đại gia đình* in a foreign country, become lost, even the older women … Without obligation or direction, they become like wild beasts."[82] *Đại gia đình* means "extended family," where three or four generations live together. In this space, women play a secondary role and are almost uniformly represented as caretakers, victims or passive subjects. Anguli Ma's comment refers to the gender inequality in Vietnam as much as in Australia.

Hoa Pham's *Lady of the Realm* and Chi Vu's *Anguli Ma* show the influence of Buddhism in Vietnamese Australian literature. Hoa Pham depends on three sources to write *Lady of the Realm*. These are the Bodhisattva of Mercy, the life Thích Nhất Hạnh, and Vietnamese history. Each performs a different function in the novella. The image of the Lady is integral to "the women's sphere" in her work. Female characters share their traumas and express their virtues. *Lady of the Realm* also borrows elements from the traditional poem about Quan Âm to describe the female characters' vulnerability. In terms of the life of Thích Nhất Hạnh, the novelist focuses on his exile status, his Engaged Buddhism, and his poems to enrich her fiction. In terms of historical events, "The Burning Monk" and the destruction of Prajna Monastery are commemorated in Pham's writing. Buddhist folklore and Gothic literature complement each other in Vu's *Anguli Ma*. When Vu mentions ghosts in her writing, she presents the Vietnamese women's helplessness and engages with the boat people's trauma. In both novellas, the syncretic religious features reflect the complexity of diasporic experiences.

NOTES

1. I would like to express my great appreciation to Professors Ken Gelder and Elizabeth Anne Maxwell for their excellent supervision.
2. Soucy, "A Reappraisal."
3. Nguyen and Barber, "Vietnamese Buddhism," 132.

4. Yeager, *Vietnamese Novel in French*.
5. Cohen, *Global Diasporas*, 189.
6. Phạm, "Lingering Phantoms," 14.
7. Phạm, *Lady of the Realm*, 65.
8. Tran, "Kuan-Yin."
9. Soucy, *Contemporary Vietnamese Buddhism*.
10. Phạm, *Lady of the Realm*, 82.
11. Phạm, *Lady of the Realm*.
12. Phạm, *Lady of the Realm*, 3.
13. Phạm, *Lady of the Realm*, 3.
14. Phạm, *Lady of the Realm*, 22.
15. Phạm, "Seed of Enlightenment."
16. Nguyen, *Nothing Ever Dies*, 19.
17. Phạm, *Lady of the Realm*, 76.
18. Phạm, *Lady of the Realm*, 31.
19. Hardy, "Internal Transnationalism."
20. Nguyen, "Quan Am and Mary."
21. Rowley, "Writing Fiction About Fact."
22. Phạm, *Lady of the Realm*, 39.
23. Phạm, *Lady of the Realm*; Thich, "Vietnamese Buddhism."
24. Thich, "History of Engaged Buddhism."
25. Israel, *Outlandish*.
26. Queen, *Engaged Buddhism in the West*.
27. John Maklin, "In Engaged Buddhism, Peace Begins with You," Lion's Roar, July 1, 2003, https://www.lionsroar.com/in-engaged-buddhism-peace-begins-with-you/ (accessed February 16, 2023).
28. Garfield, *Engaging Buddhism*, xiii.
29. Nguyen, *Memory Is Another Country*.
30. Phạm, *Lady of the Ream*, 76.
31. Wauchop, "A Book Review."
32. Said, *Culture and Imperialism*, 36.
33. Thich, "Vietnamese Buddhism."
34. Soucy, *Contemporary Vietnamese Buddhism*.
35. Phạm, *Lady of the Realm*, 83.
36. Phạm, *Lady of the Realm*, 83.
37. Phạm, *Lady of the Realm*, 37–38.
38. Harris, *Buddhism and Politics*; Thich, "Vietnamese Buddhism."
39. Dalley, *Postcolonial Historical Novel*.
40. Huynh, *Where the Sea Takes Us*, 123.
41. Harris, *Buddhism and Politics*, 272.
42. Kurmann and Do, "Children on the Boat."
43. Vu, *Anguli Ma*, 130.
44. Hill, "Anguli Ma."
45. Strom, "Anguli Ma."
46. Phạm, "Lingering Phantoms."
47. Biscaia, "Anguli Ma," 1–2.
48. Brancaccio, "Angulimala," 105.

49. Pham, "Lingering Phantoms," 58.
50. Harvey, "Twitch Gothic."
51. Matsuoka and Sorenson, *Ghosts and Shadows*, 6.
52. Patrick McCarthy, "Interview with Chi Vu | Playwright The Dead Twin," August 13, 2015, https://theatreworksblog.wordpress.com/2015/08/13/interview-with-chi-vu-playwright-the-dead-twin/ (accessed February 15, 2023).
53. Buswell and Lopez, "Princeton Dictionary of Buddhism," 45.
54. Vu, *Anguli Ma*, 2–3.
55. Hansen, "Bắc Di Cư."
56. Frankum, *Operation Passage*, 14.
57. Vu, *Anguli Ma*, 12.
58. Vu, *Anguli Ma*, 4.
59. Strom, "Anguli Ma."
60. Hansen, "Bắc Di Cư," 177.
61. Pham, *Lady of the Realm*, 8.
62. Biscaia, "Anguli Ma."
63. Vu, *Anguli Ma*, 65.
64. Vu, *Anguli Ma*, 36.
65. Vu, *Anguli Ma*, 52.
66. Avieli, "Dog Meat Politics."
67. Vu, *Anguli Ma*, 55.
68. Vu, *Anguli Ma*, 55.
69. Safran, "Diasporas in Modern Societies."
70. Metzner, "Buddhist Six-Words Model."
71. Kwon, *Ghosts of War*, 20.
72. Leshkowich, "Wandering Ghosts."
73. Matsuoka and Sorenson, *Ghosts and Shadows*, 5.
74. Vu, *Anguli Ma*, 85.
75. Pham, "Lingering Phantoms," 7.
76. Vu, *Anguli Ma*, 54.
77. Livingstone, "Viet Thanh Nguyen's Ghosts."
78. Marchi, "Ghosts, Guests, Hosts."
79. Nabi, "Gender Represented."
80. Walter Mason, "Anguli Ma: A Gothic Tale," *Singapore Review of Books*, September 5, 2012, https://singaporereviewofbooks.org/2012/09/05/anguli-ma-a-gothic-tale/.
81. Vu, *Anguli Ma*, 94.
82. Vu, *Anguli Ma*, 35.

CHAPTER 12

Vietism

Human Rights, Carl Jung, and the New Vietnamese

Trinh M. Luu

After 1975, as millions of South Vietnamese were rounded up for reeducation, others slipped out to sea, took to the frontiers, or went underground, fighting to the last with weapons of whatever kind. Those who had found their way out of the country regrouped. They took to the streets in Paris, Berlin, Washington, and Melbourne to call the communist government in Vietnam to account. They fundraised to aid refugees. Many turned to the United Nations and its satellite agencies for help. Others, vowing to restore the Republic of Vietnam (RVN) in the short term, staked their fortunes on the search for strongmen.

Even as these efforts crested, a number of RVN intellectuals—among them Kim Định, then finding refuge in the United States—feared that there would be no end to the slaying. Turning their gaze to the Vietnamese abroad, then settling in different corners of the world, they saw trouble still. The militant corps that sprang up around this time had trained their weapons on one another, suspecting fellow refugees of working for the enemy. Local newsletters warned that a kind of cultural bankruptcy could impair the Vietnamese, some of whom, ethnically lost, had formed cliques to tear the communities apart.[1] Whether in Vietnam or outside it, the Vietnamese appeared to have lost their way. If this were allowed to go on, Kim Định feared, the Vietnamese would be doomed to disappear. He thus set about finding a national soul, which, he hoped, could train each Vietnamese to forsake his small vanity for the greater good.

245

It may never have occurred to anyone but Kim Định to find guidance from Carl Jung. In his freestanding volumes published in the United States, this lifelong Catholic priest drew on Jung's works to outline a program for finding that soul set adrift long ago. These works soon became the basis of Vietism (Việt Đạo), a philosophy of human rights that fuses Southeast Asian folk beliefs with German romanticism and Jungian psychology to envision a higher-man—a new Vietnamese who would arrive to lead a universal crusade for freedom.

This chapter examines how Vietism came about, what traditions it stood on, who shaped it, and when it found its way into fiction. It focuses on two scholars—Kim Định and Nguyễn Mộng Giác—both preeminent thinkers of their day. In South Vietnam before 1975, each had a towering reputation—Kim Định as a philosopher, Nguyễn Mộng Giác as a novelist and essayist. Through the books and stories they wrote, the chapter gradually brings center stage the new Vietnamese—their image for what the Vietnamese would act like, think like, and be like were they to tap into the collective unconscious that their ancestors had left for them. Kim Định and Nguyễn Mộng Giác, each in his own way, had a grand vision. The new Vietnamese, they thought, would arrive to one day overthrow communism in their homeland. But more than that, they believed that he, above men of any other race, would be the one to bring about peace and happiness to all the world over.

THE PRIMORDIAL MAN AND THE NEW VIETNAMESE

In 1977, when the Montreal-based journal *Chân Trời Mới* (New Horizon) called on all overseas forces to prepare for combat, the Vietnamese human rights campaign was already in full swing.[2] A series of coordinated actions swept the globe, bringing Vietnam's human rights abuse into the mainstream of political discourse. In Virginia, a delegation submitted petitions to US President Jimmy Carter, urging his administration not to overlook human rights when providing economic aid to Vietnam.[3] Meanwhile, a throng of protestors in Paris—thousands strong—aired their grievances as Prime Minister Phạm Văn Đồng landed in France.[4] About this time too, the Khmer-Lao-Vietnam Committee for Human Rights made its debut in Europe.[5] This organization called on the United Nations for help, counting among its supporters the literary giants Eugène Ionesco and Natalya Gorbanevskaya. The human rights theme also took hold that year in Tokyo, when Nguyễn Công Hoan, a member of Vietnam's National Congress, defected to Japan.[6] Less than two years after Saigon's fall, a network of Vietnamese activists had emerged, setting in motion a movement with human rights as its guiding spirit.

As this movement crested, quieter steps had been taken to back insurgents in Vietnam. *Chân Trời Mới* reported in 1977 that counterrevolutionaries had built up strength in the southern provinces, using guerila tactics to gain ground.[7] The monthly magazine *Hồn Việt Nam* (Vietnamese Soul) in Paris claimed that "there are already in south Vietnam people who can use guns... to take down northern Communist forces."[8] A month later, *Chân Trời Mới* printed an interview in which a refugee confirmed what then seemed speculative. Lê Kim Ngân, once a professor in South Vietnam, recounted that insurgents and possible renegades of the new regime had set off explosions in Saigon and Long Bình.[9] Not long after, the journal *Việt Đạo* (Vietism) in Japan printed a letter from defector Nguyễn Công Hoan, addressed to Lê Kim Ngân, in which he cites an attack in Saigon as proof that "our people are fighting communists in any way they can." Whereas Nguyễn Công Hoan pushed for armed resistance, Lê Kim Ngân urged the Vietnamese abroad to first develop a guiding philosophy. In a reply four days later, he introduced a doctrine to challenge what he saw as "a heterodoxy that was fundamentally foreign, out of keeping with the people, and anti-humanist." This new doctrine was given the name Vietism. Lê Kim Ngân believed that once the Vietnamese party-state dissolved, Vietism could be the basis for building "an egalitarian, humane regime to bring about happiness and prosperity for the people."[10] Political commentaries, exposés, and short stories were soon circulated across the globe, promoting Vietism as a new human rights philosophy.

Vietism sought to cultivate a Vietnamese whose every act and thought could work toward renewing the country and its people. There was then a strong belief in the perfectibility of the Vietnamese, that he could be transformed into "a being conscious of his capacity to overturn tyranny."[11] The new Vietnamese would arrive as a kind of higher-man, charged with heroic energy and a readiness to sacrifice himself for his people.[12] According to a program of "self-organization" that *Hồn Việt* published in 1980, only the Vietnamese who trains himself mentally and physically could take on the task of saving his people. He must spurn indulgences of every kind and embrace asceticism, living martially in order to change himself. The article even suggests that he should be tested, to see if "that most destructive lure"—feminine charm—could sway him still.[13]

The political commentator Nguyễn Đông-A went further, arguing that the new Vietnamese embodies the "national soul" (hồn nước). According to him, "no one is responsible for the tragedy that befell Vietnam because all of us were brought up in a culture not our own."[14] When the Vietnamese came to realize that "the soul no longer inhabits the nation, some among us carried on as xenophiles while others turned to Soviet Russia in haste, hoping to acquire the means to save our people."[15] Vietism, Nguyễn Đông-A thought, would revive the spirit in the Vietnamese, all the while letting his self-discipline and study renew that spirit in turn.[16] Vietnamese sovereignty, reset in the self, was seen as a private campaign to protect oneself from possible usurpers. As Đỗ Khiêm stated in 1980, it is not an enemy but the "loss of his soul" (vong thân, vong bản) that at every moment imperils the Vietnamese.[17]

Much of Nguyễn Đông-A's reflections echoed Kim Định's 1979 thesis, Hồn Nước Với Lễ Gia Tiên (National Soul and Ancestral Ceremony).[18] To this philosopher, his generation's mission is to transform the mass (đoàn lũ) into a kind of "federation...held together by love and compassion."[19] Kim Định saw the mass in the Jungian sense, as a force that "crushes out the insight and reflection that are still possible with the individual," possessing him, depriving him "of the moral decision as to how he should live his own life" such that he becomes a part of an obsolete, unconscious herd "ruled, clothed, fed, and educated as a social unit."[20] By adopting Carl Jung's psycho-biological view of man, Kim Định casts the contemporary Vietnamese as the product of a "psychic infection":

> [A] dissociation between consciousness and the unconscious, an unnatural and even pathological condition, a "loss of soul" such as has threatened man from the beginning of time. Again and again and in increasing measure he gets into danger of overlooking the necessary irrationalities of his psyche, and of imagining that he can control everything by will and reason alone, and thus paddle his own canoe. This can be seen most clearly in the great socio-political movements, such as Socialism and Communism.[21]

In this sense, the Vietnamese soul is the basis of moral and spiritual integrity, of breaking free from the mass. Kim Định cites the sociologist Paul Mus to suggest that the "herd mentality"[22] first took shape in Vietnam in the nineteenth century with French rule and evolved into its vilest form under socialism.[23] Often, he evokes Văn Lang, a quasimythical polity in the first millenium BCE, as the highest point of humanism that ancestors of the Vietnamese had achieved.[24] In effect, the spiritual autonomy symbolized by Văn Lang had proliferated under agrarian societies before "the arrival of western culture," fading quickly thereafter to just a "faint presence in the south."[25] By the twentieth century, the Vietnamese had effectively become a parable for the modern man, plagued so deeply by a "psychic epidemic" that they stood defenseless against the mass.[26] Western psychoanalysis had opened to Kim Định a view of Vietnamese modern history, and the violence that it wrought, as the consequence of either overlooking the human psyche or negating it, as did the socialist state, which drew its strength from the "greatest possible accumulation of depotentiated social units."[27]

Jung appears to have cast a shadow over Kim Định as he reflected on how to turn the Vietnamese into "a whole being" (con người toàn diện).[28] Like the Swiss psychiatrist, Kim Định found the West all too vulnerable to fanatical ideology, that the freedoms it offers the modern man would lead to "one goal which is practically indistinguishable from the Marxist ideal."[29] His pursuit was as psychological as it was political, and it involved finding "a mode of emancipation that would leave society intact."[30] With that resolve, Kim Định adopted the idea of the collective unconscious (tiềm thức cộng thông or vô thức cộng thông),[31] which, according to Jung, "comprises in itself the psychic life of our ancestors right back to the earliest beginnings."[32] Archetypes, or "primordial images" (sơ nguyên tượng), make up this collective psychology.[33] They are "symbols which are older than historic man, which are inborn in him from the earliest times, and, eternally living, outlasting all generations."[34] This repository of symbols, biologically inherited and existing in "the dark hinterland of the psyche," lies "in the unconscious of every man."[35] Kim Định likened this notion of the collective unconscious to "what the Vietnamese customarily refer to as the soul of rivers and mountains" (hồn sông núi)—the national soul.[36]

Inspired still more by Jung, Kim Định found in rituals the possibility of raising the Vietnamese out of the mass and bringing him closer to an "authentic existence."[37] If for Jung, myths "*are* the mental life of the primitive tribe, which immediately falls to pieces and decays when it loses its mythological heritage," Vietnamese rites are to Kim Định key to the collective unconscious.[38] He believed that rites could "reactivate the powers slumbering in the psyche."[39] When Kim Định claims that "the highest purpose of rituals is to bring one closer to the Primordial Man (thủy tổ cội gốc),"[40] he is drawing on Jung's assertion that religious experience "enables the conscious mind to preserve its link with the unconscious."[41] When Kim Định further claims that "contact with the Primordial Man would forge the fullest image of self,"[42] he appears to accept the Jungian premise that self-realization is possible when projected symbols are assimilated into consciousness.

Like Jung, moreover, Kim Định saw the individual as bearer of the psyche. Kim Định did not promote the concept of an autonomous being in search of pure spirituality—the creature of libertarian philosophy that is often considered the subject of human rights.[43] He instead defined the self as a reflection of the cosmos (*vũ trụ chi tâm*).[44] As Curtis Smith explains, "at the farthest reaches of the psyche, its individuality merges into the materiality of the world. At some point the boundaries between psyche and world blurs to the point of extinction."[45] Kim Định reinterprets this cosmic allusion as "the perfect unity of heaven, earth and man,"[46] allowing him to achieve "total humanity" (*nhân bản toàn diện*)—when an individual is linked to the larger life of his race.[47] *Hồn Việt* similarly defined "humanism" (Đạo Người) as an ethical order in which "myriad things resonate harmoniously," and the cultivated self achieves an "interactive relationship ... with the transcendent substance of the cosmos."[48] According to Trần Văn Ân, the newspaper's main advisor, this homo-cosmic continuum is key to renewing the Vietnamese community abroad. This community would consist of men who, by their own will, open themselves to the world and "become one with the cosmos, living fully with its many splendors."[49]

Like Kim Định, Trần Văn Ân turned to Western science to rethink the character of the Vietnamese. The unpublished personal papers of this "gladiator," as he called himself, show him to have been an erudite thinker and an influential political strategist. While in France from 1975 onward, he channeled his energy into reviving Vietnamese culture. If Jung had provided some conceptual basis for Kim Định to imagine a new Vietnamese, the ethologist Konrad Lorenz plays a similar though less visible role in Trần Văn Ân's reflections.[50] Late twentieth-century Europe was home to a lively debate on social biology. Lorenz was at the center of it, not least for the analogy he drew between the evolution of instincts in animals and the development of social rites in man.[51] According to the Austrian scientist, although rituals evolve to such an extent that they become unrecognizable, and although it may be impossible to trace the present form of rituals to their origin, "some intermediate steps on the same line of development are accessible to be studied."[52]

This definition of cultural heritage fascinated Trần Văn Ân.[53] He found hope in the possibility of retracing Vietnamese cultural evolution to "recover essences" and to have them serve as the basis for cultural renewal.[54] His aim was to return the Vietnamese man to an "ethnic being" (*con người dân tộc*) that he once was, defined by his "ethnic identity" (*dân tộc tánh*) and held together by an "ethnic unconscious" (*Đại ngã dân tộc*). If Vietnamese Confucianism were his heritage (*vốn* Việt Nho), it had altogether disappeared and left him as "man without tradition," without ground under his feet—a mass man. Trần Văn Ân thought that Vietnamese culture, once revived, could function as the sacred link uniting all Vietnamese, guiding their development as ethnic beings, as men "who evolve to still higher selves with his community."[55]

Where Kim Định's and Trần Văn Ân's ideas overlap most is their belief in the transmission of racial attributes. By calling into use the concept of the archetype, which Jung defines as "the deposits of all our ancestral experiences," accumulated across millennia and leaving their mark on "the inherited brain-structure," Kim Định reinforces the idea that the collective unconscious is biologically passed on.[56] But whereas Jung, for the better part of his career, argued that "all human races have a common collective psyche," in Kim Định's philosophy, the collective unconscious appears to be limited by race and culturally determined.[57] It is the experience of their forebears, and no other, that the Vietnamese inherits.[58] In one sense, stressing the hereditary nature of the collective unconscious allows Kim Định to project a transcendent reality to which all Vietnamese are linked by a psycho-biological kinship. Though geographically dispersed, they remain connected to what Sharon Kim calls "the larger body of [their] race, and its transhistorical memory in culture."[59] This collective unconscious would give the Vietnamese everyman, not just a selected few, the potential to cultivate a larger personality. In another sense, by figuring the collective unconscious as an "adaptive acquisition," Kim Định takes the experience of exile beyond the drama of the self, giving it a far greater significance—an evolutionary significance.[60] If 1975 spawned for the first time the figure of the Vietnamese refugee, to Kim Định and Trần Văn Ân, this figure stands as part of an unbroken lineage. Physiologically linked to his ancestors, the Vietnamese refugee inherits the collective unconscious, transforms it in some small way through experience and self-cultivation, before passing it on to future generations through not only the cultural artifacts that he creates, but also biologically, through the very inherited brain-structure.

Whether in Canada, Japan, the United States, or France, these exiled intellectuals believed that the reinvented Vietnamese would rise from a personality training initiative to become his people's only saving grace.[61] The pursuit of this figure shows just how wide the range of discourse that these intellectuals—as much at home in French, English, and

Chinese as they are in Vietnamese—drew on to reimagine Vietnamese humanism. Their ideas took shape just as "the last utopia" was coming to the fore, when human rights emerged in the last quarter century as the "best defense against the communist threat."[62] Vietnamese activists continue to see human rights as "the only generally intelligible way in modern political ethics"[63] to challenge the Socialist Republic of Vietnam (SRV), but Kim Định and his contemporaries found little guidance from the creed. They shifted the discourse from politics to that "something inside which one cannot realize, but one can know."[64] If human rights figure the state as an "essential crucible,"[65] Kim Định attempted to recover a model of humanity that foregrounds man as a "citizen of the cosmos" (công dân vũ trụ),[66] intellectually free to cultivate his identity.[67] And if the Enlightenment heritage of human rights takes reason as the condition for "autocracy of the mind,"[68] Kim Định's contempt for the mass man reveals his deep skepticism for the type of human that is left "when intellect breaks away from instinct."[69] Set apart from the herd, the new Vietnamese would arrive as a unique kind of man, bearing a unique heritage that he slowly but ceaselessly unlocks through self-cultivation to reach "the Primordial Man."[70] This is the ancestor who embodies what Lydia Liu calls "the originary plurality of humanity" and who represents eternal creation and self-creation.[71] If the Primordial Man points to a lost humanity, the new Vietnamese, belonging to the future, was a novel political invention, and the product of an effort to rethink the vision of "free and full personality development."[72]

NGUYỄN MỘNG GIÁC AND VIETNAMESE HUMANISM

But such a man who stands above the herd could not be willed into being as soon as need presented itself. Whereas the militant organizations that sprang up at around this time looked to strongmen,[73] Kim Định wanted to search for "the right man." Man-of-the-future had set his development on this prophet. At the 1984 World Conference in Chinese Philosophy, Kim Định beseeched representatives of fifty nations to "discover the Ju man whom we badly need." Now as ever, he stressed, "activities aiming at perfecting man like poetry, rites, dance, game and above all, music" are key to unlocking the right man.[74]

At about this time, Kim Định's vision had inspired some Vietnamese to forge a "cultural front" (mặt trận văn hóa).[75] The initial spadework unfolded in the early 1980s, just as the Vietnamese began to shake off the nightmare of their flight and take stock of their life in exile. An essay in a 1983 issue of *Dân Quyền* (Civil Rights) may have made the strongest push for this front.[76] Việt Thường, the author and a Kim Định partisan, saw this front as all the more important in the 1980s, when factionalism had deepened divides within Vietnamese communities. The sense of unity was evidently shaken as groups regarded one another with suspicion, unsure "if they are failing nationalists or operating incognito for the enemy."[77] Still more, the SRV's campaigns to destroy "poisonous cultural vestiges" of South Vietnam fanned the fear that Vietnamese culture was quickly disappearing.[78] Thus, between the 1970s and 1980s there resounded the call to grow and preserve a culture that was being torn up by the SRV.[79]

Pushed by this impulse to treasure and preserve, the Vietnamese founded cultural institutions to isolate and grow Vietnamese arts, free of Western influence.[80] Academies emerged, tasked with training Vietnamese youth in the martial and literary tradition of their predecessors.[81] To raise the general esteem for the arts and humanities, cultural journals appeared in greater numbers, some choosing to stay above politics in order to showcase the creative genius of the Vietnamese.[82] Such journals became the meeting place of learned men who volunteered their time to translate Vietnamese literature and poetry into Western languages. A cultural renaissance was then unfolding.[83] In the heartland of southern California,[84] the fear of being a people without culture spurred the lay writer to put into prose what he remembered, channeling the belief that the cultural front was "within the reach of every refugee the world over."[85] By the early 1980s, anthologies of Vietnamese fiction slowly showed up on local bookshelves, bookended by self-published memoirs.[86] "Vietnamese culture" underwent a modest redefinition. It was now seen as "a way of being and thinking" unique to the Vietnamese refugee.[87] "Four millennia of Vietnamese art" being kept alive, and the new forms created by a people creating themselves, made up the cultural estate of the Vietnamese diaspora.

In this context, literature was put in the service of fostering an "ethnic consciousness" (*ý thức Việt tộc*).[88] When the renowned artist Võ Đình wrote in 1981 that a certain Vietnamese spirit (*tính Việt*) resides within him, urging him to move under the surface of everyday life to discover "Vietnam as an ever-present reality," he was giving the impression of the poet as an avatar of early Vietnamese life.[89] According to Võ Đình, the Vietnamese "maker of culture" must live in constant awareness of this reality, never yielding to the temptation of practicing "Western art" and never letting the cultural front drop out of sight. Echoing Kim Định and Trần Văn Ân, who, through unraveling the defeat of the ethnic Vietnamese, saw cultural revival as the first step to reinstating him, Võ Đình found in literature an analog to the kind of vision that his contemporaries had held on to. He quotes the Polish American poet Czeslaw Milosz to suggest that it is in the imagination that the poet can be the maker and redeemer of man. The wonder and majesty of a child's world appeals to him, as it did to Milosz, because it is there that the poet, in his true vocation, sees both past and future, both the Primordial Man and man hereafter.[90] Literature is cast in this way as the domain for renewing Vietnamese civilization on new frontiers.[91] The writer-poet, forming a segment of Vietnamese refugees whose intuitive power has not been blunted but perhaps sharpened by exile, becomes the builder of a higher standard of genius, out of which the higher-man—the new Vietnamese—would emerge.

Whether this ideal type existed is not a question the evidence could settle, but an ostensible image of him is given in "Mẹ Trong Lòng Người Đi" (The Émigré's Mother). He appears in this short story as a wayward child on his way to being "a mover and shaker of the world" (*tay chọc trời quấy nước*).[92] An omniscient narrator in fact imagines this child climbing to a rooftop. In the narrator's mind, the rash and unreflecting child would fall prey to "his desire to wipe out all the stars, and replace them with his own." It quickly becomes clear that this child is the narrator's fancy, his story showing a quality of fairytale. All the same, the narrator speaks to this imaginary child, advising him to spare in his game the one star he calls "Mother's" (Vì Sao Mẹ). He warns the child that his future would fall into darkness, "pitiful and forlorn," if this single star is forsaken.[93] Not much else happens before the story ends with the narrator urging the child to become, above all, a poet.[94]

Given little plot to push it forward, the story trades in details. Within the space of some fifteen pages are folk ballads, poetry, and autobiographical bits. Images of prison camps, escape, and the eager manhunt, compressed into a paragraph, precede a tragic description of a man locked up and broken, trusting to his fate. A brief reference to "a band of men mad with reason" (*bọn đàn ông mê lý trí*) may be the most outwardly political element of the piece. As he speaks to the child, the narrator often steps back to reflect on the mother as something more than "a metaphor for the homeland."[95] At the level of detail then, this seemingly trivial story bears the spirit of its age, making itself read as a meditation on the Vietnamese-to-be, rising from the devolved state of his kin.

"Mẹ Trong Lòng Người Đi" was published in 1984 as part of the short story collection *Ngựa Nản Chân Bon* (Surrender).[96] Although printed in California, Nguyễn Mộng Giác first wrote the stories that would later make up this collection in Indonesia, at the Kuku Refugee Camp, where he stayed from December 6, 1981, to February 9, 1982. He reached America on November 23, 1982.[97] Before the end of the war, Nguyễn Mộng Giác dabbled in fiction but did not hit the literary scene until very late. The journal *Bách Khoa* (Encyclopedic) first featured his writings in 1971, and effectively launched his career as a novelist and an essayist. Some three years later, when his novel won the Vietnamese PEN Club award (Văn Bút Việt Nam), this Bình Định native was in a flush of celebrity and circulated among the most esteemed writers of South Vietnam.[98] His creativity did not seem stifled when the South folded. From 1975 to his lucky escape, Nguyễn Mộng Giác eked out a living by selling used books and working in a noodle factory. He was imprisoned twice in this period—first in October 1979, when the police arrested the factory owners and those associated with their business for suspected espionage, and, second, when he was caught trying to flee the country.[99] He wrote on the sly all the while, nearly completing *Sông Côn mùa lũ* (The River Floods), a saga chronicling the fortunes of eighteenth-century warriors, before his fifth and successful exit.[100]

Nguyễn Mộng Giác's fiction gives the sense that he was a writer deeply affected by the turbulence of his time. At the Kuku Refugee Camp, he began drafting *Mùa biển động* (Swelling Sea), another saga that would define him as the main pillar of Vietnamese diasporic literature. This five-volume novel recreates South Vietnam as it moves from the 1968 Huế Massacre to the 1980s, when "men lose themselves in a glut of misery and vice."[101] While carrying forward this novel from the first volume to its last, completed in 1989, Nguyễn Mộng Giác also managed the journal *Văn Học* (Literary Studies), one of the first of its kind to appear in the United States.[102] These efforts give credence to his conviction that "great literature...counters the forces that suppress divine human rights."[103] Nguyễn Mộng Giác's statement, like an authorial credo, echoing Kim Định, captures the ideals that Vietnamese intellectuals then ascribed to letters and the arts. As one of his contemporaries and longtime contributor to *Văn Học* stated, "national salvation" is the office of Vietnamese literature.[104] Phạm Kinh Vinh, in homage to Kim Định, evokes the yet-to-arrive "ideal Vietnamese" (*con người lý tưởng Việt tộc*) as the final reach of Vietnamese history. He vows to "bring to life the ethnic Vietnamese on all continents where Vietnamese refugees reside, and ensure that he prevails for eternity."[105] Literature was seen as the medium. First quickened to guard against cultural extinction, Vietnamese diasporic literature became by the early 1980s the keeper of this vision of future man.

SOCIALIST EUGENICS: THE NEW VIETNAMESE IN "VỀ NGUỒN"

The new Vietnamese in "Mẹ Trong Lòng Người Đi" comes into sharper relief when placed alongside his counterpart in "Về Nguồn" (Return to the Source), another story in the collection that seeds, more than others, the fear that the Vietnamese were doomed to disappear under communist rule. Different as the two stories are in language and style, both give a sense of the conflicting utopianisms that Nguyễn Mộng Giác found himself confronting after 1975. In "Về Nguồn," Tân heads a college admissions committee under the SRV. The new academic year is about to start, and he has yet to check the political backgrounds of the applicants to keep "descendants of the enemy from higher education." Under pressure, Tân sends a letter to the director of the Planning Institute, seeking his advice on how to weed out those with poor pedigrees. It so happens that the director is vexed by a different set of problems. A kind of defiant sluggishness has set in among the people and, with the flight of the Vietnamese causing a brain drain, national productivity continues to drop. Incidentally, the director recalls Hồ Chí Minh's motto that "building socialism requires socialist men." At his wife's urging, he drafts a proposal suggesting that "artificial insemination" could be used to produce a stock of thoroughbreds. This proposal soon makes its way to the secretary general, who launches a program that brings together "human and technological prowess to fulfill the mission."

Before leaving the country in 1981, Nguyễn Mộng Giác had witnessed the most forceful attempt to bring the Vietnamese closer in image to the socialist man. Scores of articles, written by the most influential cultural figures, fostered the belief that "it is the duty of every sector and every person to build the new man from birth, training him to ... possess the right thoughts and sentiments, the intellect and physical fitness for mastery over society, nature, and himself."[106] Chế Lan Viên, a leading member of the Writer's Union, wrote in 1979 that "we, Vietnamese socialists, have our own breed."[107] Like the director in "Về Nguồn," he cites Hồ Chí Minh's slogan to call for the creation of "a new Vietnamese" (*con người Việt Nam mới*). This is the Vietnamese socialist man, one whose commitment to proletarian internationalism would bring him nearer to the total man. Drawing from the world of horticulture, Chế Lan Viên likens the making of the new Vietnamese to "growing trees, though we must first sow seeds to cultivate the best of them."

It has been said that "cultivation is a form of reason" because human triumph over nature manifests in the ability to control production.[108] In this sense and through such a metaphor, it would seem that Chế Lan Viên is endorsing scientific intervention to "master the very raw materials of the subject, neutralizing all negative physical and psychological aspects inherited from the [feudal] past at the level of the germ plasm."[109] He goes on urging that as a condition for creating the new man, Vietnam must have "a nest of advanced science and technology for the phoenix to lay eggs." The symbolism of the phoenix—its premise of self-generation and eternal life—would not have been lost on this poet. Yet, by pairing this image with scientific and technological progress, he recasts the bird as a symbol of secular immortality gained through applied science. The new socialist Vietnamese is by extension what Peter Frizsche and Jochen Hellbeck call "a defiantly secular figure, one who [is] no longer concerned with religious or moral purification."[110]

This insistence—that the Vietnamese socialist man is the scientific negation of all "chaotic and ineffectual psychological impulses"[111]—is a signature of any political writing from the period. Lê Sĩ Thắng, one of Chế Lan Viên's contemporaries, argued in 1978 that the Vietnamese have always displayed a "dispassionate skepticism towards spirits," though they only truly broke free from their sway in 1930, under the guidance of the Vietnamese communist party.[112] To illustrate the development of the Vietnamese into a rational being, Lê Sĩ Thắng evokes Thánh Gióng. This is a character from folk mythology who, under the pen of nationalist poets, acquires the guise of a three-year-old child transforming himself into a giant after eating rice and with his iron horse defeats an army of invaders before ascending to heaven.[113] It is fitting that Tháng Gióng should be a metaphor for the Vietnamese who, according to the author, "knows to grow himself, rising above deities" through his strength and sharp wit.[114] By 1980, when the astronaut Phạm Tuân took his maiden flight on the Soviet Union's Soyuz 37 spacecraft and newspapers headlined his journey as the triumph of human intelligence, it would seem that Vietnam, having "turned its back on spirits"[115] to keep in step with its Soviet patron, was finally brought into the age of technology.[116]

"Về Nguồn" is notable for the way it reinscribes such rationalist discourse to suggest that a certain eugenicist sentiment had in fact taken hold in Vietnam, providing a "scientific gloss" on class politics.[117] Despite its modest length, the story is broken into four smaller fragments, closely interwoven to tie agricultural to human engineering. This specific structure gradually expands the focus from husbandry to eugenics, drawing a connection between the biotechnological solution to low productivity, on the one hand, and the regressive evolution of the Vietnamese, on the other. When compared with documents from the same period that openly set out to create a Vietnamese socialist man, "Về Nguồn" reveals just how this biological fantasy would fail in its own right.

The biosocial rhetoric of the late 1970s comes through quite early on in the first section. As Tân investigates the applicants' family history, his superior describes the process of selecting college students as "refining the Vietnamese stock." Guided by this ethos, Tân ranks the applicants according to their political past. He writes "traitor" on most files, on some, "child of feudal colonialists and should be sent to labor camp." These prospective students are identified all the same as "enemies of the people" who, owing to their fathers' background, are set apart from the socialists. For good measure, Tân would only grant "children of communist officials or of former guerilla fighters" the coveted tittle of being "the nation's future," thus protecting it from the undesirable, pre-socialist class.

The story takes place in a time of war—the 1979 conflict between China and Vietnam—when national newspapers took to labeling the Chinese, the Americans, Vietnamese émigrés, and those fleeing the country as the enemy. The tendency then was to represent these groups as what Joanne Woiak calls "hereditary paupers."[118] Trần Bạch Đằng, for example, published an article in which he portrays "the enemy's arrogance" as a kind of "hereditary disease."[119] Others, such as Nghị Đoàn and Nguyễn Hữu Thái, wrote that "reactionary forces had used the bloodline doctrine" (*thuyết huyết thống*) to stir up unrest among the Chinese population in Vietnam.[120] At a time when the political and the biological are blurred, a play sharing the name of Nguyễn Mộng Giác's story—"Về Nguồn"—was staged to bring into focus an image of the ideal revolutionary. It is set in the Republic of Vietnam, where the love affair between Vân, a teacher, and Hưng, a steel plant worker, unfolds despite opposition from Vân's father. In small moves, the play reveals the father to be a capitalist who owns the steel mill. Phạm Vũ Thư, in a review published in 1979, suggested that the play had its most powerful hold on him when Vân defies her father, choosing to "stand with the downtrodden." He evokes a kind of hereditarian argument to explain the protagonist's defiance: Vân "carries within her the heritable qualities of a poor family," adding, almost as an afterthought, that she is the daughter of "a peasant woman."[121]

If these articles, for their time, show that ideology often shaded over to biology to assign moral fitness to some Vietnamese, in Nguyễn Mộng

Giác's story, experimental biology is taken out of the agricultural context and put to test in human genetics. At various moments in the second section, the director of the Planning Institute takes advice from his helpmate, a cadre at the Institute of Animal Husbandry (Viện nghiên cứu chăn nuôi). She has just returned from Ba Vì's cattle breeding farm, where livestock imported from India, Cuba, and the Soviet Union are kept for mating. According to the director's wife, humans "obey the same laws of heredity." In a certain technocratic spirit, she recalls that Nazi Germany, "though without the scientific expertise that Vietnam now commands," had conducted experiments to improve the quality of its population. Within a technical discourse of husbandry, she presents the Nazi pursuit of racial purity as a search for biological perfection. It is at this moment that the director's proposal comes at last into focus: "We will use the sperm of communists who have proven themselves,... and select mothers who champion the 'three responsibilities'—as producers, household caregivers, and national defenders—and exceptional girl-soldiers" to produce a new generation of revolutionaries.[122]

Taking up barely a page of the story, the character of the director's wife is built around details that point to the larger reality of biological experimentation undertaken in Vietnam. The Institute of Animal Husbandry, Ba Vì's farmstead, as well as the imported animals housed there are details that Nguyễn Mộng Giác may have lifted from period literature on husbandry. Ba Vì in the 1970s was held up as a laboratory where foreign seeds were nursed into plants stronger and more productive than native stock. According to a 1978 article, Ba Vì horticulturalists had grown "grass seedlings from abroad" into a lush crop, feeding livestock species across the country.[123] Scientists there reportedly cross-bred foreign and domestic animals to create "superior offspring" that could bring about economic abundance.[124] In these texts, the practice of husbandry is allied with the conventions of diplomacy—hybrid species are presented as symbols of socialist fraternity and the "collective human transformation" of nature.[125] Husbandry became a way of demonstrating the fruitfulness of human industry and collaboration, on which the future of socialism depended. But whereas period articles use husbandry as a metaphor for human agency, "Về Nguồn" recasts it as a peril to the Vietnamese. By making the director's wife an expert on animal breeding who specializes in the introduction of foreign strains into native species, permanently changing their physiology, Nguyễn Mộng Giác alludes to the inevitable dissolution of the Vietnamese racial identity when the same industrial techniques are used on humans.

The program to create socialist men through artificial insemination passes the politburo, and hits its stride in the fourth, and last, section. To build a welfare system for the fittest, the Central Women's Union sets about selecting fourteen "ideal mothers"; the Health Ministry joins the Society for the Protection of Mothers and Children to care for them; and the Ministry of Education drafts special curricula for the coming eugenic children, "the perfected product of socialist reproduction." According to Christina Kiaer, the eugenic baby is "the ultimate socialist object." He belongs to the collective, "existing in public nurseries and kindergartens rather than in the materially and emotionally cluttered lap of the family."[126] In the final moment, when cadres from the Institute of Animal Husbandry arrive in Hanoi to collect sperm, the story takes a surprising turn. It reveals that selected donors, their belief in "this absurd trial" lapsing, have secretly asked subordinates to provide sperm in their stead. The story ends with a slight to the vision of socialism, stating that future Vietnamese socialists are descendants of the chiefs of commerce, the petroleum custodians, the economic policemen—those who, "already with immense wealth, will only conspire to grow their fortune."

In her analysis of a Soviet play where Milda—"her body a well-equipped factory"—propositions Iakov—the perfect specimen of proletarian masculinity—to father her child, Kiaer suggests that Iakov's participation is a "metaphor of alienated labor." By contract, he is asked to "produce a product and then give it up, to be alienated from it forever." The eugenic child, the proof of Milda and Iakov's reproductive labor, is then "expropriated by the state, which 'represents' [them]."[127] In "Về Nguồn," neither the women nor men selected for the experiment initiates, as Milda does, the contract of procreation. The mothers are asked to offer themselves to the collective without their husbands knowing. If the husbands by chance find out, the labor union's secretariat is swiftly sent in to "set them at ease." In contrast, men selected for their immaculate pedigrees could, through their own cunning, free themselves from the obligation. Yet, the new breed of Vietnamese emerging from this experiment inherits only the fathers' hereditary materials, not the mothers'. The final line of the story—"from father to son" (*cha truyền con nối*)—sums up the outcome of this trial.

MOTHER RIGHT: THE NEW VIETNAMESE IN "MẸ TRONG LÒNG NGƯỜI ĐI"

This peculiar ending can only be understood in relation to "Mẹ Trong Lòng Người Đi." If the fragments of "Về Nguồn" add up to only a loose plot, "Mẹ Trong Lòng Người Đi" shows no semblance of one. It takes on a scarcely definable form, narrated in the first person though it is unclear whether the "I" refers to a fictional persona or the author. Its central image is the child, its text mainly strewn with folk verses, and though the few autobiographical details seem to give it some frame, a striking hollowness still runs through it. This unusual structure may reflect a scene of loss that is central to the story. In creating the fantastical world through which his imaginary child moves, the narrator also calls up "the despair of having lost a mother" (*nỗi khổ xa mẹ, mất mẹ*). The remainder of the story figures this maternal loss as key to the development of the child, who represents the new Vietnamese.

Structurally, the mother's death "opens up a series of representational possibilities." According to Carolyn Dever, "in the space of the missing mother, novelists... are free to reinscribe the form and function of maternity." In Nguyễn Mộng Giác's fiction, the mother's absence not only evokes "the specter of the motherless and vulnerable child," but also allows the story to take a "backward-looking quest" for originary trauma—the moment the mother disappears.[128] As a structural device, maternal death creates "a crisis in which self-understanding, represented as the ability to craft a coherent life story or autobiography," depends entirely on reviving the dead mother.[129] Nguyễn Mộng Giác appears to arrange poetry and folk verses as symbols through which the story steps backward in time to reveal an original way of life ruled, according to Kim Định, by the mother.

Thematically, the phrase "*mất mẹ*" resonates with the belief that Vietnamese civilization was once matriarchal—peaceful, benevolent, when "life had not yet broken away from the harmony of nature"[130]—long before it gave way to patriarchal rule.[131] This notion of a matriarchal heritage was to underlie much of Kim Định's philosophy. In a 1982 publication, Kim Định outlines two cultural stages that he thought defined Vietnamese history: one presided over by women (*văn hóa còn mẹ*), the other dominated by statesmen and hence "motherless" (*văn hóa mất mẹ*).[132] Here and elsewhere, he constructs an early Vietnamese society based on the religious and civic primacy of the mother. The Vietnamese in this matriarchal state is said to have achieved a noble agricultural life; held together by a sense of fraternity, they were self-reliant and free from strife.[133] Kim Định suggested that as a general course of cultural evolution, this society at last yielded to paternal rule to protect itself from foreign aggression. Although peaceful, the shift to father-rule gradually displaced the original mode of life such that by the twentieth century, descendants of the Vietnamese could no longer sense the divinity of the Mother. They thus "ushered in a western culture full of masculine drive" (*rước văn minh Thái Tây đầy nam tính về*),[134] which quickly took hold and gave rise to an imperium governed through law and reason.[135] This view of Vietnamese history defines the communist state not as the logical end, as is often claimed,[136] but as the consequence of a certain decline in the psychological health of its people. Kim Định goes so far as to suggest that as a "foreign system trying to take its place on the Vietnamese scene,"[137] communism is indication that a civilizational "schizophreny [sic]" had seized the Vietnamese long ago.[138]

Hardly his own, Kim Định's concept of a mother-centric order was derived from Johann Jacob Bachofen's pioneering though largely discredited theory of "Mother Right." In 1861, this Swiss anthropologist drew on myth, classical literature, and material artifacts to argue that a primitive state of matriarchy had flourished before Greek polities. This epoch saw the development of agriculture and sedentary life, and descent was traced through women—"the repository of all culture, of all benevolence, of all devotion." Before the shift to a paternal system, "the relationship which stands at the origin of all culture, of every virtue, of every nobler aspect of existence, is that between mother and child."[139] Kim Định glossed this notion of Mother Right as "the mother principle" (*nguyên lý mẹ*) and less often as "matriarchy" (*mẫu quyền*). Echoing Bachofen, Kim Định claimed that traces of this primordial world are still present in myth, which when studied could reveal something about "our culturally structured souls."[140]

But unlike Bachofen who examined myth "to come a little closer to the eternal meaning of things," Kim Định wanted to redeem the mother principle to one day recover the harmony that defined this lost culture.[141] In his view, the ancient world was something of a utopia of human communion where man and nature, consciousness and the unconscious, spirituality and sensuality had not yet separated. This represented to Kim Định a supreme harmony in which the early Vietnamese had lived. Although he freely translated long passages from "Mother Right," Kim Định also revised the Swiss scholar's theory along the way. Whereas Bachofen evoked the age of the mothers as a cultural stage that has passed, Kim Định saw Vietnamese antiquity as both historical and eternal: a world that is forever out of reach to Bachofen is to Kim Định a part of the collective unconscious, which is always present as a resource to transform human personality.[142] Merging Bachofen with Jung, Kim Định saw the Vietnamese primordial mother as an image laid down in the collective unconscious of every man and as a force for self-development and redemption. If through Jung Kim Định had detected a psychological disorder in the modern Vietnamese, it was then in Bachofen that he found an ethnohistorical vocabulary to prescribe a cure.

"Mẹ Trong Lòng Người Đi" evokes the same set of symbols to capture the essence of this prehistory. In the first few pages is a scene set in some remote past, where a grandmother, mother, and daughter are brought together. They are shown moving past each other as if "every woman extends backwards into her mother and forwards into her daughter."[143] In this self-contained world, mother and daughter share what Nguyễn Mộng Giác describes as "lessons on being a mother." Before long, he merges these three figures into the singular "Vietnamese mother" (*bà mẹ Việt Nam*), the central archetype symbolizing the totality of the Vietnamese psyche. Within the political climate of the 1980s, "Mẹ Trong Lòng Người Đi" does not so much construct a "feminist family romance"[144] as call up the archetypal image that could give direction to a people afflicted by a "split personality."[145] This condition, which Kim Định describes as "a rupture between intelligence and feeling" (*chẻ đôi tâm trí*), first presses in on the individual, causing him to act "incoherently." At the level of the family, when the elements of pathology are so deeply rooted, such psychosis breeds disorder, setting the ground for "despotism" when it crosses into national politics.[146]

"Mẹ Trong Lòng Người Đi" throws into relief the effects of this psychological disorder. Apart from the scene of maternal unity, the story is very much about specific people and events. A naval officer is sent time and again to labor camps; a former pilot, recently released from camp, tries to flee the country, is caught, escapes, only to be hounded out of society. Another, also failing to take flight, has to go into hiding. And then there is what feels like the core of the story—a description of the narrator's state of mind when he is held in a dark cell. These images, recurring often throughout the stories in the collection, convey a sense of terror that Nguyễn Mộng Giác associates with a society run by "men mad with reason." The author depicts this society unfolding as a result of having "repudiated the mother."[147] Kim Định, in much the same way, saw postwar Vietnam casting aside "the mother kingdom" (*Vương quốc của mẹ*)[148] to make way for a doctrine that "leaves no place for religion."[149] Here, Kim Định is using religion in the Jungian sense, as a "conscientious regard for the irrational factors of the psyche," or "as the careful observations and taking account of certain invisible and uncontrollable factors, [which] is an *instinctive attitude* peculiar to man" (emphasis in the original). By this measure, religion is a "natural function" that does not cease to exist with scientific rationality, but "reappears—evilly distorted—in the deification of the State." The Vietnamese seized by psychosis—"man mad with reason"—is the Jungian mass man who has "deliver[ed] himself up to [the state] psychologically as well as morally."[150]

If the communist state increases its power by "cut[ting] the ground from under his [mass man] feet psychically," Kim Định and Nguyễn Mộng Giác believed that the only way forward for the Vietnamese is to find the archetypal mother. This, they thought, would restore a kind of psychological unity and help the Vietnamese cut loose the state's hold on them. Although images of the mother appear here and there in "Mẹ Trong Lòng Người Đi," often in faraway places, they come to the fore in the final moment when the narrator is in solitary confinement. Adjusting to the darkness of the cell at last, he finds marks of graffiti and some writing on the walls. There are dates and names. In the corner are prayers to the Virgin Mary and the Bodhisattva Quán Thế Âm—"two portraits of maternal compassion that have found their place in this prisonhouse." "I root about," the narrator confides, "but could not find the name of a leader, of a hero, or a slogan. In despair, we are each reduced to a child who only knows to call on his mother."[151]

The narrator has been speaking all this while to his young listener—the imaginary child. According to Jung, the child motif, much like the mother, arises during "an agonizing situation of conflict from which there seems to be no way out."[152] Such a conflict comes to pass because "the inevitable one-sidedness and extravagances of the conscious mind" build up a "debt which has to be paid off from time to time in the form of hideous catastrophes."[153] It was in 1980, not long before Nguyễn Mộng Giác's short stories hit local bookstands, that Kim Định alerted his readers to this moment of danger: "Now, more than fifty thousand descendants of Lạc Hồng, not least those held in re-education camps, feel at the depth of their being what it is like to be 'motherless.'"[154]

"Mẹ Trong Lòng Người Đi" evokes both the mother and the child as symbols of redemption, showing how crises may be a creative force for the Vietnamese to rediscover himself. This is because in crisis, the child archetype has a compensatory relation to consciousness and manifests, sometimes with the mother, to signify "a higher stage of self-realization."[155] Always and everywhere, it "represents the strongest, most ineluctable urge in every being, namely the urge to realize itself."[156] The child motif does not therefore refer to a real child, but man's instinctive drive to create from within a superior self. In "Mẹ Trong Lòng Người Đi," the character of the child is the narrator's unconscious other, in a moment, crossing over to consciousness. It is a literary image of the new Vietnamese in that "the child is a potential future":

> Hence the occurrence of the child motif in the psychology of the individual signifies as a rule an anticipation of future developments, even though at first sight it may seem like a retrospective configuration.... [T]he "child" paves the way for a future change of personality. In the individuation process, it anticipates the figure that comes from the synthesis of conscious and unconscious elements in the personality.[157]

What the imaginary child in "Mẹ Trong Lòng Người Đi" shares with the new Vietnamese is its futurity. Both point to an end state of personality cultivation, when Vietnamese "all over the world" will have become "the ideal beings that their ancestors had tried to bring about" (*con người lý tưởng của tổ tiên Lạc Việt đã cố thực hiện*).[158]

Nguyễn Mộng Giác's fiction has brought into view two conceptions of Vietnamese humanism that were in conflict with each other: on one side, the socialist man, a specimen of biotechnological ingenuity, and on the other, the new Vietnamese, cultivated with "the intelligence that comes from afar."[159] Each side reaches for a higher level of humanity, for a class of supermen that would outlive any single being. Each stood for a certain conception of the ideal human, and through him, an ideal future for the Vietnamese. The eugenic child in "Về Nguồn" is thought to inherit the biological fitness of his revolutionary father. His genetic signature will be a template for the Vietnamese "ten or twenty generations" down the line.[160] In his own way, the new socialist Vietnamese embodies the belief in rationality and self-transcendence, so much so that he is given the name "Man of Great Mind."[161] He represents the promise of social biology, which won over Vietnamese bureaucrats in the 1970s and 1980s. It was in this spirit that high school students were asked as part of their graduate exam to "discuss the function of labor in man's evolution from gibbons."[162] Lamarckian inheritance had its appeal, as it did in Soviet Russia in the 1920s, when experiments to change the biological makeup of the Russian population were undertaken with great zeal.[163] That fervor soon died down when Soviet geneticists found that "if acquired characters are inherited, then, obviously, all representatives of the proletariat bear in themselves the traces of all the unfavorable influences."[164] The Vietnamese eugenic child is the product of one idea—human agency at the forefront—taken to its logical end.

Opposite him stands the new Vietnamese, self-cultivated according to the pattern of ideas already there before him. He was brought into being by a population keenly aware of its fall, and afraid that one day "exiled Vietnamese would vanish among the masses of men, unnamed and without a history, drifting about with no roots."[165] His inventors provided a descriptive psychology to tie him to a collective unconscious. Their effort grew out of "a resilience founded on the very embrace of defeat," as Jing Tsu might say, and he was their only guarantee of Vietnamese survival.[166] They believed that if he dug deep enough, every Vietnamese would recover a link to the primordial mother he once shunned. She would guide him in his development so that he could move closer to the sacred goal of self-rule to one day, when brought together with those like him, overturn communism in his homeland.

To Kim Định and Nguyễn Mộng Giác, the mother is the collective unconscious, the mythopoetic source of consciousness, the Vietnamese inner character. She came to represent the very ideals of natural rights, which went against the SRV's state-centered definition of human rights. As early as 1977, representatives of the SRV defended the claim that human rights only work in the long term when they are backed by a government. They tied human rights to national self-determination and in that way dismissed the kind of "human rights diplomacy" that Jimmy Carter had tested.[167] Instead, keepers of the party-state reiterated the Soviet Union's view that only the socialist state can enable every man to be all he can.[168] But, just as the socialist man must be created gradually, human rights can only be developmental. The very measures condemned by the international community as human rights abuse—persecution, reeducation, new economic zones—were explained away as part and parcel of building an eventual utopia. Just as occurred in mid-twentieth-century Europe, difference in class and biological makeup often showed up as justifications to include some and keep out others.

In the 1970s and 1980s, some intellectuals in the diaspora rejected this conception of human rights as at odds with Vietnamese tradition. This community placed faith neither in a state nor in the human rights documents that proclaim natural equality of all mankind. Following Kim Định, they found in the Vietnamese past a loftier model of human fellowship based on the culture of the mother and a notion of psycho-biological kinship. In due time, they presented this higher ideal—Vietism—as a model not only for their kin, but also for people of the third world to "establish peace on which all races could flourish." The Vietnamese believed they were poised to lead this universal crusade for freedom, and in that belief, they opened the way for something approaching "messianic universalism."[169]

NOTES

1. Thượng Văn, "Những biểu hiện lệch lạc trong đấu tranh bây giờ," *Nhân Văn*, no. 13 (April 1983), 39–45; Frizsche and Hellbeck, "The New Man," in Geyer and Fitzpatrick, *Beyond Totalitarianism*, 339.
2. "Quan Điểm," *Chân Trời Mới*, nos. 22 and 23 (1977), 1; "Việt kiều tại Canada biểu tình nhân gày quốc tế nhân quyền 10-12-77," *Chân Trời Mới*, no. 24 (1977), 6.
3. "Vietnamese protested against human rights violations in VN," *Tiên Rồng* I, no. 4 (April 1977), 1.
4. Vo Van Ai, "Lettre ouverte à m. Phan Van Dong, premier ministre de la république socialiste du Viet Nam à l'occasion de sa visite officielle en France le 25 Avril 1977," *Quê Mẹ* (May 7, 1977), 2, 3.
5. Comité Khmer-Lao-Vietnamien pour la défense des Droits de l'homme was jointly founded by Prince Sisowath Thomico of Cambodia, Prince Mangkra Souvannaphouma of Laos, and Võ Văn Ái. "Ủy ban bảo vệ quyền làm người Cambốt-Lào-Việt Nam tố cáo sự vi phạm nhân quyền của chính quyền cộng sản tại ba nước," *Quê Mẹ* (July 14, 1977).
6. "Tin chấn động thế giới," *Việt Đạo* (April 6, 1977).
7. "Kháng chiến Việt Nam và đấu tranh hải ngoại," *Chân Trời Mới*, no. 24 (1977), 6.
8. Phạm Hữu, "Thời gian đã chín mùi ngày nhân dân miền nam đứng dậy ngày đổi mới," *Hồn Việt* (November 15–30, 1977), 4–5, 15.
9. Pierre Saint-Germain, "Le Vietnam résiste au Communiste...," *La Presse* (June 12, 1977).
10. "Thư dân biểu Nguyễn Công Hoan gửi GS Lê Kim Ngân," *Việt Đạo* (May 1977), 4–5.
11. Võ Văn Ai, "Ý thức quốc kháng," 27.
12. Trần Văn Ân, "Nói về lãnh đạo."
13. "Dọn mình làm người đấu tranh ái quốc," *Hồn Việt*, no. 5 (1980).
14. Nguyễn Đông-A, "Có hồn nước hay không có hồn nước," *Hồn Việt*, no. 1 (July 1980), 1.
15. Nguyễn Đông-A, "Lập chí lập mạng," *Hồn Việt*, no. 2 (August 1980), 9, 3.
16. "Phục Việt: khai thác và phát huy tinh hoa Việt," *Hồn Việt*, no. 2 (1980).
17. Đỗ Khiêm, "Chính và Tà, Tà và Địch," *Hồn Việt*, no. 1 (July 1980).
18. Kim Định, *Hồn Nước*, 32.
19. Kim Định, *Hồn Nước*, 23.
20. Jung, *Undiscovered Self*, 2, 8.
21. Jung, *Collected Works*, 429.
22. Kim Định, *Hồn Nước*, 32.
23. Kim Định, *Hồn Nước*, 24–25.
24. Kim Định, *Kinh Hùng*, 90.
25. Kim Định, "Triết lý tả nhậm," 50.
26. Jung, "Religion as the Counterbalance."
27. Jung, *Undiscovered Self*, 74.
28. Kim Định, *Hồn Nước*, 33.
29. Jung, *Undiscovered Self*, 28; Kim Định, *Hồn Nước*, 32.
30. Kim Định, *Hồn Nước*, 35.
31. Kim Định, *Hồn Nước*, 33, 42.
32. Jung, *Collected Works*, 112.
33. Kim Định, *Hồn Nước*, 76.
34. Jung, *Collected Works*, 402.

35. Jung, *Collected Works*, 154, 69.
36. Kim Định, *Hồn Nước*, 42.
37. Kim Định, *Hồn Nước*, 38.
38. Jung, *Collected Works*, 154. Italics in the original.
39. Kim Định, *Hồn Nước*, 38.
40. Kim Định, *Hồn Nước*. Kim uses the term "Primordial Man" in his English essay "The Role and Conditions."
41. Jung, *Collected Works*, 122–123.
42. Kim Định, *Hồn Nước*, 38.
43. Slaughter, *Human Rights, Inc.*, 19–20.
44. Kim Định, *Hồn Nước*, 45.
45. Smith, *Jung's Quest for Wholeness*, 98.
46. Kim Định, *Hồn Nước*, 38.
47. Kim Định, *Tâm Tư*, 2–3.
48. Chun-chieh Huang, *Humanism*, 23; "Đạo Trời," *HV*, no. 4 (November 1980), 1; "Từ đạo người," *Hồn Việt*, no.7 (April 1981), 1; "Học người xưa: Tìm tự do trong giáo lý Nhà Phật và trong Nho học," *Hồn Việt*, no. 5 (December 1980), 7.
49. Trần Văn Ân, "Tại sao Cộng."
50. Trần Văn Ân, personal correspondence with Nguyễn Hoài Vân (Rennes, June 15, 1990).
51. Since the end of World War II, Konrad Lorenz has been under attack for the way his works biologically substantiated Nazi extermination policies. See, for example, Deichmann, *Biologists Under Hitler*; Burkhardt, *Patterns of Behavior*.
52. Lorenz, *On Aggression*, 74.
53. Trần Văn Ân, personal correspondence. See also Kim Định, "Vietnamese Cultural Heritage."
54. Trần Văn Ân, *Hồi ký Trần Văn Ân*, 706.
55. Trần Văn Ân, "Chung quanh vấn đề Việt học," 409–411.
56. Rensma, "Analytical Psycholgy," 259.
57. Jung, *Collected Works*, 275.
58. Kim Định, *Vấn đề Nguồn Gốc Văn*; Kim Định, *Kinh Hùng*, 72.
59. Kim, "Lamarckism," 206.
60. Percival, *Jung's Theory of Archetype*, 470.
61. Kim Định, *Hồn Nước*, 41.
62. Moyn, *Last Utopia*, 76.
63. Williams, "Religious Faith and Human Rights," in Douzinas and Gearty, *Meanings of Rights*, 71–82, 72.
64. Kim Định, "Role and Conditions."
65. Moyn, "Plural Cosmopolitanisms," in Douzinas and Gearty, *Meanings of Rights*, 193–211, 211.
66. Việt Thương, "Sự cần thiết của mặt trận văn hóa trong công cuộc cứu quốc và kiến quốc," *Dân Quyền*, no. 69 (November 1983), 12–20, 14.
67. Kim Định, *Cửa Khổng*.
68. Marwah, "Bridging Nature and Freedom?" 405.
69. Việt Thương, "Sự cần thiết," 14.
70. Kim Định, "The Role and the Conditions," 2.
71. Liu, "Shadows of Universalism," 411.

72. Kim Định, *Hồn Nước*, 89.
73. Mặt trận quốc gia thống, *Tuyển Tập Chuyện Kháng Chiến*.
74. Kim Định, "Role and Conditions."
75. Việt Thường, "Sự cần thiết của mặt trận văn hóa trong công cuộc cứu quốc và kiến quốc," *Dân Quyền*, no. 69 (November 1983), 12–20, 14; Kim Định, "Triết Việt trên đất Mỹ," *Văn học Nghệ thuật*, no. 2 (May 1978), 3–7.
76. Việt Thường, "Sự cần thiết," 12; Hoàng Văn Chí, "Nghiên cứu văn hóa," *Dân Quyền*, no. 72 (February 1984), 16–18.
77. "Những hoạt động gián điệp của cộng sản ở vài vùng trên đất Mỹ," *Việt Nam Hải Ngoại*, no. 21 (January 4, 1978), 41.
78. "Tổ chức văn hóa Việt ra mắt trên thủ đô Canada," *Dân Quyền*, no. 69 (November 1983), 21; Lê Tất Điều, "Lập viện văn hóa Việt Nam," *Dân Quyền*, no. 69 (November 1983), 29.
79. Võ Đình, "Bàn về làm văn-nghệ ở hải-ngoại," *Tập San Văn Hóa* 1, no.1 (December 1981), 72–75, 73.
80. "Kiện toàn mặt trận văn hóa," *Dân Quyền*, no. 72 (February 1984), 3.
81. Đỗ Quý Toàn, "Góp ý kiến về các lớp học văn, sử Việt Nam," *Dân Quyền*, no. 72 (February 1984), 40–42.
82. Thụy Khuê, "Thử tìm một lối tiếp cận văn sử học về: Hai mươi nhăm năm văn học Việt Nam hải ngoại 1975–2000," *Hợp Lưu* (Confluence) 89, November 8, 2010, http://hopluu.net/a826/thu-tim-mot-loi-tiep-can-van-su-hoc-ve-hai-muoi-nham-nam-van-hoc-viet-nam-hai-ngoai-1975-2000.
83. Dư Tử Lê and Võ Văn Hà, *Quê Hương*, 3–4.
84. Vĩnh Phúc, *Đối Thoại*, 68.
85. Phạm Kim Vinh, *Văn Hóa Dân Tộc*, 147.
86. Nguyen Ngoc Bich, *War and Exile*; Hoang, "Reeducation Camps."
87. Hoàng Văn Chí, "Văn hóa và dân tộc," *Nguyệt Báo Độc Lập* (January 1984).
88. Võ Đình, "Bàn về làm văn-nghệ ở hải-ngoại," *Tập San Văn Hóa* 1, no. 1 (December 1981), 72–75.
89. Võ Đình, "Bàn về làm," 73–74.
90. Võ Đình, "Bàn về làm."
91. Jing Tsu, "Extinction and Adventures."
92. Nguyễn Mộng Giác, "Mẹ Trong Lòng Người Đi" [Mother in Your Heart], in *Ngựa Nản Chân Bon*.
93. Nguyễn Mộng Giác, "Mẹ Trong Lòng Người Đi."
94. Nguyễn Mộng Giác, "Mẹ Trong Lòng Người Đi."
95. Nam Dao, "hình như có điều gì . . . ," *Da Màu*, March 28, 2009, https://damau.org/4956/hinh-nhu-co-dieu-gi.
96. Nguyễn Mộng Giác, *Ngựa nản chân bon*.
97. Nguyễn Mộng Giác, "Sống và viết tại hải ngoại," *Việt*, no. 2 (1998), http://nguyenmonggiac.com/tieu-luan-tuy-but/73-song-va-viet-tai-hai-ngoai.html.
98. Mac Lam, Pham Phu Minh, and Tran Doan Nho, "Nguyễn Mộng Giác với Phạm Phú Minh và Trần Doãn Nho," *Nguyễn Mộng Giác*, March 23, 2009, https://nguyenmonggiac.com/phong-van/219-nguyen-mong-giac-voi-pham-phu-minh-va-tran-doan-nho.html.
99. Nguyễn Mộng Giác, "Nghĩ về văn học hải ngoại," 199; "Nguyễn Mộng Giác: Trò chuyện với sinh viên," *talawas*, March 14, 2006, http://www.talawas.org/talaDB/showFile.php?res=6667&rb=0102 (website discontinued).
100. Luân Hoán, "Nguyễn Mộng Giác, dòng văn bên dòng sông Côn," *luanhoan.net*,

n.d., http://luanhoan.net/tacpham/DuaHoiBeban2/web/9_NguyenMongGiac.htm (accessed September 9, 2016).

101. Thụy Khuê, "*Mùa biển động* của Nguyễn Mộng Giác," *thuykhue.free.fr*, May 2001, http://thuykhue.free.fr/tk06/muabiendong.html (accessed June 2016).

102. Nguyễn Mộng Giác, "Nghĩ về văn học hải ngoại," 150–151.

103. Nguyễn Mộng Giác, "Nghĩ về văn học hải ngoại," 157.

104. Phạm Kim Vinh, *Văn Hóa Dân Tộc*, 28.

105. Phạm Kim Vinh, *Văn Hóa Dân Tộc*, 252.

106. "Phát triển và nâng cao chất lượtng nhà trẻ," *Hà Nội Mới*, January 7, 1979.

107. Chế Lan Viên, "Làm chủ con người. Con người làm chủ," *Nhân Dân*, January 7, 1979.

108. Scott, *Shakespeare's Nature*, 4.

109. Kiaer, *Everyday Life*, 185.

110. Frizsche and Hellbeck, "New Man," 305.

111. Frizsche and Hellbeck, "New Man," 316.

112. Lê Sĩ Thắng, "Vài nét," in Phạm Như Cương, *Về vấn đề xây*, 83–315, 292, 315.

113. Trần Quốc Vượng, "The Legend of Ông Dóng," in Taylor and Whitmore, *Essays into Vietnamese Pasts*, 16.

114. Lê Sĩ Thắng, "Vài nét," 293.

115. Lê Sĩ Thắng, "Vài nét," 191.

116. Thép Mới, "Việt Nam-Vũ Trụ," *Sài Gòn Giải Phóng*, July 25, 1980.

117. Paul, "Eugenics and the Left," 569.

118. Woiak, "Designing a Brave New World," 122.

119. Trần Bạch Đằng, "Lịch sử tái hiện," *Sài Gòn Giải Phóng*, February 22, 1979.

120. Nghị Đoàn, "Chung quanh vấn đề người Hoa," *Nhân Dân*, January 5, 1979; Nguyễn Hữu Thái, "Hiểm họa thường trực của châu Á," *Tuổi Trẻ*, March 22, 1979. For a discussion of the bloodline theory in China, see Wu, *Cultural Revolution*.

121. Phạm Vũ Thư, "Về Nguồn: một con đường mới," *Tuổi trẻ*, March 22, 1979.

122. Pettus, *Sacrifice and Desire*.

123. G. L., "Từ 12 hạt giống," *Lao Động*, January 25, 1979.

124. Nhật Ninh, "Người kỹ sư và con F3," *Nhân Dân*, January 12, 1979.

125. Scott, *Shakespeare's Nature*, 30.

126. Kiaer, *Everyday Life*, 205.

127. Kiaer, *Everyday Life*, 195, 198.

128. Dever, *Death and the Mother*, 2.

129. Dever, *Death and the Mother*, 7.

130. Bachofen, *Myth, Religion*, 76.

131. On the cult of the mother in Vietnam, see Dror, *Cult, Culture, and Authority*; Gadkar-Wilcox, "Women and Mythology."

132. Kim Định, *Kinh Hùng*, 100.

133. See Trần Văn Đoàn, "Mẫu Tính Trong Văn Hóa Việt: The Metaphysical Principle of Maternity in Vietnamese Culture," November 7, 2002, http://www.simonhoadalat.com/HOCHOI/TRIETHOC/MautinhVHViet.htm#_ftnref13 (accessed December 10, 2016).

134. Kim Định, *Kinh Hùng*.

135. Kim Định, *Thái Bình Minh Triết*, 21.

136. For a discussion of the "continuity thesis," see Marr, *Vietnamese Tradition*; Ninh, *World Transformed*.

137. Whitmore, "Communism and History," in *Vietnamese Communism*, ed. Turley, 11.
138. Kim Định, *Thái Bình*, 19.
139. Bachofen, *Myth, Religion*, 79.
140. Campbell, introduction to *Myth Religion and Mother Right*, lvi.
141. Kim Định, *Kinh Hùng*.
142. See Gossman, "Orpheus Philologus Bachofen"; Neumann, *Great Mothers*.
143. Jung and Kerényi, *Science of Mythology*, 191.
144. Hirsch, *Mother-Daughter Plot*, 130.
145. Kim Định, *Thái Bình*, 19.
146. Kim Định, *Thái Bình*, 19–20.
147. Nguyễn Mộng Giác, *Ngựa Nản Chân Bon*.
148. Kim Định, *Thái Bình*, 35.
149. Kim Định, *Thái Bình*, 20.
150. Jung, *Undiscovered Self*, 18–20 (emphasis in the original); Odajnyk, *Jung and Politics*.
151. On the significance of the Virgin Mary and the Bodhisattva Quán Thế Âm for Vietnamese refugees, seer Soucy, "A Reappraisal."
152. Jung and Kerényi, *Science of Mythology*, 103.
153. Jung and Kerényi, *Science of Mythology*, 97.
154. Kim Định, *Kinh Hùng*, 41.
155. Jung and Kerényi, *Science of Mythology*, 103.
156. Jung and Kerényi, *Science of Mythology*, 89.
157. Jung and Kerényi, *Science of Mythology*, 83.
158. Phạm Kim Vinh, *Văn Hóa Dân Tộc*, 251.
159. Donoghue, *We Irish*, 143.
160. Nguyễn Mộng Giác, *Ngựa Nản Chân Bon*.
161. Lê Sĩ Thắng, "Vài nét," 293.
162. "Học sinh lớp 10 tiếp tục thi tốt nghiệp phổ thông," *Hà Nội Mới* (June 8, 1975).
163. See Spektorowski, "Eugenic Temptation"; Adams, "Politics of Human Heredity."
164. Quoted in Adams, "Politics of Human Heredity," 881.
165. Phạm Kim Vinh, *Văn Hóa Dân Tộc*, 253.
166. Tsu, *Failure, Nationalism, and Literature*, 223.
167. Ngô Bá Thành, "'Bảo vệ nhân quyền' hay chính sách can thiệp vào công việc nội bộ các nước của Carter?" *Luật Học*, no. 4 (1979): 67–74.
168. Nguyễn Ngọc Minh, "Hội nghị khoa học về nhân quyền: Chủ nghĩa xã hội là chế độ ưu việt nhất để bảo vệ phát triển các quyền con người," *Luật Học*, no. 4 (1979): 61–66.
169. Hunt, *University of Nike*, 183.

Bibliography

ARCHIVES AND RESEARCH LIBRARIES

A. S. Cook Library, Towson State University, Baltimore, MD
Central Intelligence Agency-Electronic Reading Room, Langley, VA, US
Gerald Ford Library, Ann Arbor, MI, US
Library and Archives of Canada, Ottawa, CAN
Lyndon B. Johnson Presidential Library, Austin, TX, US
National Archives II, College Park, MD, US
National Archives of Australia, Canberra, AUS
Public Records Office, Kew, England, UK
Richard Nixon Presidential Library and Museum, Yorba Linda, CA, US
Vietnam Center and Archive at Texas Tech University, Lubbock, TX, US
Vietnam National Archives Center II, Hồ Chí Minh City, Vietnam
Vietnam National Archives Center III, Hanoi, Vietnam

Newspapers

American Prospect
Bách Khoa
Baltimore Sun
Bình Minh
Chân Trời Mới
Chính Luận
Dân Chúa
Dân Quyền
Đối Diện
Dòng Việt
Globe and Mail
Giữ Thơm Quê Mẹ
Hậu Phương
Hartford Courant
Hà Nội Mới
Hồn Việt
Lao Động
Le Monde
Liên Đoàn

Luật Học
La Presse
Los Angeles Times
New York Review of Books
New York Times
Nguyệt Báo Độc Lập
Nhân Dân
Phật Giáo Việt Nam
Quê Mẹ
Sài Gòn Giải Phóng
Saigon Post
Singapore Review of Books
Sóng Thần
South China Morning Post
Star Gazette
Tập San Văn Hóa
Thế giới nghệ sĩ
The Guardian
Tiếng gọi miền Tây
Tiếng Nói Dân Tộc
Trái Tim Đức Mẹ
Tricycle: The Buddhist Review
Tuổi trẻ
Tư Tưởng
U.S. News & World Report
Vấn Đề
Van Hanh Bulletin
Van Hanh Newsletter
Văn hóa Nghệ thuật
Việt Đạo
Viet Nam Bulletin
Việt Nam Hải Ngoại
Vietnam Guardian
Washington Post

Books, Periodicals, Theses, and Blogs

Adams, Mark B. "The Politics of Human Heredity in the USSR, 1920–1940." *Genome* 31, no. 2 (1989): 879–884.

Anderson, David. *Vietnamization: Politics, Strategy, Legacy*. Lanham, MD: Rowman & Littlefield, 2019.

Asselin, Pierre. *A Bitter Peace: Washington, Hanoi, and the Making of the Paris Agreement*. Chapel Hill: University of North Carolina Press, 2002.

———. *Vietnam's American War*. New York: Cambridge University Press, 2018.

Athreya, Venkatesh. "Perestroika and the Third World: The Changing Status of the Concept of 'Neocolonialism.'" *Social Scientist* 17, no. 7/8 (1989): 28–36.

Avieli, Nir. "Dog Meat Politics in a Vietnamese Town. Ethnology." *An International Journal of Cultural and Social Anthropology* 50, no. 1 (2012): 58–78.
Bachofen, Johann Jakob. *Myth, Religion and Mother Right*. Princeton, NJ: Princeton University Press, 1992.
Batchelor, Stephen, trans. *Verses from the Center: A Buddhist Version of the Sublime*. New York: Riverhead Books, 2000.
Berman, Larry. *Lyndon Johnson's War: The Road to Stalemate in Vietnam*. New York: W. W. Norton, 1989.
———. *No Peace, No Honor: Nixon, Kissinger, and Betrayal in Vietnam*. New York: The Free Press, 2001.
Berrigan, Daniel, and Thích Nhất Hạnh. *The Raft Is Not the Shore: Conversations Toward a Buddhist/Christian Awareness*. Boston, MA: Beacon Press, 1975.
Bhikkhu Thich Minh Chau. *Milindapanha and Nagasenabhiksusūtra: A Comparative Study*. Patna: Kalika Press, 1963.
Bhiksu Thich Minh Chau. *The Chinese Madhyama Āgama and the Pāli Majjhima Nikāya: A Comparative Study*. Saigon: Saigon Institute of Higher Buddhist Studies Publication Department, 1964.
Bhiksu Minh Chau. *Xuanzang: The Pilgrim and Scholar*. Ho Chi Minh City: Phật học viện quốc tế xuất bản, 1988.
Biscaia, Maria Sofia Pimentel. "Anguli Ma: A Gothic Tale." *Bedford Park* 5, no. 2 (2013): 1–2.
Bộ Kinh tế Quốc gia. *Việt Nam niên giám thống kê, quyển thứ năm, 1954-1955*. Saigon: Viện Quốc gia thống kê, 1957.
———. *Việt Nam niên giám thống kê, quyển thứ chín, 1960-1961*. Saigon: Viện Quốc gia thống kê, 1962.
Boylan, Kevin. "The Red Queen's Race: Operation Washington Green and Pacification in Binh Dinh Province, 1969–70." *Journal of Military History* 73, no. 4 (October 2009): 1195–1230.
Brancaccio, Pia. "Angulimala or the Taming of the Forest." *East and West* 49, no. 1/4 (1999): 105–18.
Brigham, Robert. *Reckless: Henry Kissinger and the Tragedy of Vietnam*. New York: Public Affairs, 2018.
Bùi Diễm, with David Chanoff. *In the Jaws of History*. Bloomington: Indiana University Press, 1989.
Bui, Long T. *Returns of War: South Vietnam and the Price of Refugee Memory*. New York: New York University Press, 2018.
Burkhardt, Richard W., Jr. *Patterns of Behavior: Konrad Lorenz, Niko Tinbergen, and the Founding of Ethology*. Chicago: University of Chicago Press, 2005.
Buswell, Robert, and Donald Lopez. *The Princeton Dictionary of Buddhism*. Princeton, NJ: Princeton University Press, 2014.
Callison, Charles Stuart. *The Land-to-the-Tiller Program and Rural Resource Mobilization in the Mekong Delta of South Vietnam*. Athens: Ohio University, 1974.
Cannon, Alexander M. "Virtually Audible in Diaspora: The Transnational Negotiation of Vietnamese Traditional Music." *Journal of Vietnamese Studies* 7, no. 3 (2012): 122–156.
Cao Văn Luận. *Bên giòng lịch sử, Hồi ký 1940-1965* [In the course of history, memoir 1940–1965]. Saigon: Trí Dũng, 1972.
Cao Văn Thân, "Land Reform and Agricultural Development, 1968–1975." In Vu and Fear, *Republic of Vietnam*, 47–56.

Carter, James. *Inventing Vietnam*. New York: Cambridge University Press, 2012.
Chandola, Harish. "New Economic Zones." *Economic and Political Weekly* 12, no. 4 (January 22, 1977): 83–85.
———. "Saigon Today." *Economic and Political Weekly* 12, no. 3 (January 15, 1977): 48–49.
Chân Không. *Con Đường Mở Rộng* [A Pathway Opens]. Nắng Mới, 2011. Kindle.
Chan Khong. *Learning True Love: Practicing Buddhism in a Time of War*. Berkeley, CA: Parallax Press, 2007.
Chapman, Jessica M. *Cauldron of Resistance: Ngo Dinh Diem, the United States, and 1950s Southern Vietnam*. Ithaca, NY: Cornell University Press, 2013.
Chapman, John. "Return to Vietnam of Exiled Zen Master Thich Nhat Hanh." In Taylor, *Modernity and Re-enchantment*, 294–341.
Chi, Paul Van. *Catholic Choral Music in Vietnam 1945-1975*. Portland, OR: Self-published, 2002.
Christians, Clifford G., Theodore Glasser, Denis McQuail, Kaarle Nordenstrengh, and Robert A. White. *Normative Theories of the Media: Journalism in Democratic Societies*. Urbana: University of Illinois Press, 2009.
Chung, Vu Van. "Foreign Capital Inflows and Economic Growth: Does Foreign Capital Inflows Promote the Host Country's Economic Growth?" Tokyo: Policy Research Institute, Ministry of Finance, 2015.
Chung, Young Iob. *South Korea in the Fast Lane: Economic Development and Capital Formation*. New York: Oxford University Press, 2007.
Clarke, Jeffrey. *Advice and Support: The Final Years, 1965-1973*. Washington, DC: Government Printing Office, 1988.
Clemis, Martin. *The Control War: The Struggle for South Vietnam, 1968-1975*. Norman: University of Oklahoma Press, 2018.
Cohen, Robin. *Global Diasporas: An Introduction*. London: Routledge, 2001.
Collet, Christian, and Hiroko Furuya. "Enclave, Place, or Nation?: Defining Little Saigon in the Midst of Incorporation, Transnationalism, and Long Distance Activism." *Amerasia Journal* 36, no. 3 (2010): 1–27.
———, and Pei-Te Lien. *The Transnational Politics of Asian Americans*. Philadelphia, PA: Temple University Press, 2009.
Congregation of The Mother Coredemptrix, *Biểu Chứng Đức Tin và Tình Yêu: Testimony of Faith and Love*. Carthage, MO: CMC Brothers, 1986.
Cunningham, Stuart D., and Tina Nguyen. "Actually Existing Hybridity: Vietnamese Diasporic Video." In *The Media of Diaspora: Mapping the Globe*, edited by Karim H. Karim. London: Routledge, 2003.
Dacy, Douglas. *Foreign Aid, War and Economic Development South Viet Nam 1955-1975*. New York: Cambridge University Press, 1986.
Dalley, Hamish. *The Postcolonial Historical Novel: Realism, Allegory, and the Representation of Contested Pasts*. Basingstoke, UK: Palgrave Macmillan, 2014.
Đặng Phong. *Lịch sử kinh tế Việt nam 1945-2000* [History of the Vietnamese Economy 1945–2000], vol. 2. Hanoi: Khoa học xã hội, 2005.
———. *Kinh tế miền Nam Việt Nam thời kỳ 1955-1975* [The Economy of South Vietnam 1955–1975]. Hanoi: Khoa Hoc Xa Hoi, 2004.
Deichmann, Ute. *Biologists under Hitler*. Cambridge, MA: Harvard University Press, 1996.
Deleuze, Gilles, and Félix Guattari. *A Thousand Plateaus: Capitalism and Schizophrenia*. Minneapolis: University of Minnesota Press, 1987.

Dever, Carolyn. *Death and the Mother from Dickens to Freud: Victorian Fiction and the Anxiety of Origins*. New York: Cambridge University Press, 1998.
DeVido, Elise Anne. " 'Buddhism for this World': The Buddhist Revival in Vietnam, 1920–1951, and Its Legacy." In Taylor, *Modernity and Re-enchantment*, 256–262.
Đinh Văn Chấp. "Dịch thơ đời Lý và Trần" [Translating Poetry from Ly and Tran Times], *Nam Phong* 115 (March 1927): 238–244.
Đỗ Mậu. *Việt Nam: Máu Lửa Quê Hương Tôi* [Vietnam: War in My Native Land]. Self-published, 1986.
Đỗ Nhuận. *Âm thanh cuộc đời*. Hà Nội: Âm nhạc, 2003.
Đoàn Độc Thư, and Xuân Huy. *Giám Mục Lê Hữu Từ & Phát Diệm 1945-1954* [Bishop Le Huu Tu and Phat Diem, 1945–1954]. N.p.: Sử Liệu Hiện Đại, 1973.
Donnell, John. "Prospects for Political Cohesion and Electoral Competition." In Donnell and Joiner, *Electoral Politics,* 151–172.
———, and Charles Joiner, eds. *Electoral Politics in South Vietnam*. Lexington, MA: Lexington Books, 1974.
Donoghue, Denis. *We Irish: Essays on Irish Literature and Society*. Berkeley: University of California Press, 1988.
Dorais, Louis-Jacques. "Politics, Kinship, and Ancestors: Some Diasporic Dimensions of the Vietnamese Experience in North America." *Journal of Vietnamese Studies* 5, no. 2 (Summer 2010): 91–132.
Douzinas, Costas, and C. A. Gearty. *The Meanings of Rights: The Philosophy and Social Theory of Human Rights*. Cambridge: Cambridge University Press, 2014.
Dror, Olga. "Translator's Introduction." In *Mourning Headband for Hue: An Account of the Battle for Hue, Vietnam 1968*, by Nhã Ca. Bloomington: Indiana University Press, 2014.
———. *Making Two Vietnams: War and Youth Identities, 1965–1975*. New York: Cambridge University Press, 2018.
———. *Cult, Culture, and Authority: Princess Liễu Hạnh in Vietnamese History*. Honolulu: University of Hawai'i Press, 2007.
Du Tử Lê, and Võ Văn Hà. *Quê Hương: Tuyển Tập Văn Chương Việt Nam* [Hometown: An anthology of Vietnamese literature]. n.p.: Gìn Vàng Giữ Ngọc, 1977.
"Education in the Republic of Vietnam." *Bulletin 1972 of the UNESCO Regional Office for Education in Asia* 6, no. 2, March 1972.
Elliott, David. *Changing Worlds: Vietnam's Transition from Cold War to Globalization*. New York: Oxford University Press, 2012.
Emerson, Ralph Waldo. "Education," in Emerson, *Lectures and Biographical Sketches*. Boston, MA: Houghton Mifflin, 1883.
Espiritu, Yen Le. "Toward a Critical Refugee Study: The Vietnamese Refugee Subject in US Scholarship." *Journal of Vietnamese Studies* 1, no. 1–2 (2006): 410–433.
———. *Body Counts: The Vietnam War and Militarized Refuge(es)*. Berkeley: University of California Press, 2014.
Fear, Sean. "The 1971 Presidential Election and the Twilight of the Republican Vietnam." Paper presented at the Workshop "Studying Republican Vietnam: Issues, Challenges, and Prospects," University of Oregon, Eugene, OR, October 2019.
———. "Saigon Goes Global: South Vietnam's Quest for International Legitimacy in the Age of Détente." *Diplomatic History* 42, no. 3 (June 2018): 428–455.
Fear, Sean. "The Ambiguous Legacy of Ngo Dinh Diem in South Vietnam's Second Republic (1967–1975)." *Journal of Vietnamese Studies* 11, no. 1 (2016): 1–75.

Forest, James H. *The Unified Buddhist Church of Vietnam: Fifteen Years for Reconciliation.* Alkmaar, NL: International Fellowship of Reconciliation, 1978.
Frankum, Ronald Bruce. *Operation Passage to Freedom: The United States Navy in Vietnam, 1954-1955.* Lubbock: Texas Tech University Press, 2007.
Fredrick, Cynthia Kay. "The South Vietnamese Constitution of April 1, 1967: The Institutionalization of Politics in the Second Republic." PhD diss., University of London, 1969.
Freud, Sigmund. "Mourning and Melancholia." In *The Standard Edition of the Complete Psychological Works of Sigmund Freud, Volume XIV (1914-1916): On the History of the Psycho-Analytic Movement, Papers on Metapsychology and Other Works.* London: Hogarth Press, 1957.
Frizsche, Peter, and Jochen Hellbeck. "The New Man in Stalinist Russia and Nazi Germany." In *Beyond Totalitarianism: Stalinism and Nazism Compared*, edited by Michael Geyer and Sheila Fitzpatrick. New York: Cambridge University Press, 2009.
Fromm, Eric. *May Man Prevail? An Inquiry into the Facts and Fictions of Foreign Policy.* Garden City, NY: Doubleday, 1964.
Gadkar-Wilcox, Wynn. "Existentialism and Intellectual Culture in South Vietnam." *Journal of Asian Studies* 73, no. 2 (2014): 377-395.
———. "Women and Mythology in Vietnamese History: Le Ngoc Han, Ho Xuan Huong, and the Production of Historical Continuity in Vietnam." *Positions: East Asia Cultures Critique* 13, no. 2 (2005): 411-439.
Garfield, Jay. *Engaging Buddhism: Why It Matters to Philosophy.* New York: Oxford University Press, 2015.
Gawthorpe, Andrew. *To Build as Well as Destroy: American Nation Building in South Vietnam.* Ithaca, NY: Cornell University Press, 2018.
Gethin, Rupert. *The Foundations of Buddhism.* Oxford: Oxford University Press, 1998.
Gibbs, Jason. "Capitalist Music Brings Jail: Love Songs in Ha Noi during Viet Nam's American War." Paper presented at the Beyond Dichotomies Conference, Seattle, May 2008.
———. "How Does Hanoi Rock? The Way to Rock and Roll in Vietnam." *Asian Music*, 39/1 (2008).
———. "A Missing Legacy: Evidence of Recorded Sound in Pre-1945 Vietnam." In *Formations of Phonographic Modernity in East and Southeast Asia: Exploring the Gramophone Industry and Music Genres*, edited by Yamauchi Fumika and Ying-fen Wang. Urbana: University of Illinois Press, forthcoming.
———. "Phượng Hoàng và thời phôi thai của nền nhạc rock Việt." In *Ban nhạc Phượng Hoàng—The Beatles của Sài Gòn*, 17-32. Hồ Chí Minh City: Domino Books, 2020.
———. *Rock Hà Nội và Rumba Cửu Long.* Translated by Nguyễn Trương Quý. Hà Nội: Tri thức, 2008.
———. "Songs of Night's Intimacy: The Bolero of Vietnam." Paper presented at the conference "Engaging with Vietnam," Honolulu, HI, October 6, 2016.
Goodman, Allan. *Politics in War: The Bases of Political Community in South Vietnam.* Cambridge, MA: Harvard University Press, 1973.
Gossman, Lionel. "Orpheus Philologus Bachofen versus Mommsen on the Study of Antiquity." *Transactions of the American Philosophical Society*, 73, no. 5 (1983): 1-89.
Guimary, Donald. "The Press of South Vietnam: A Recent Perspective." *Gazette* 21, no. 3 (1975): 163-169.
Hansen, Peter. "Bắc Di Cư: Catholic Refugees from the North of Vietnam, and Their Role

in the Southern Republic, 1954–1959." *Journal of Vietnamese Studies* 4, no. 3 (October 2009): 173–211.
Hardy, Andrew. "Internal Transnationalism and the Formation of the Vietnamese Diaspora." In *State/Nation/Transnation—Perspectives on Transnationalism in the Asia-Pacific*, edited by Katie Willis and Brenda Yeoh. New York: Routledge, 2014.
Harris, Ian. *Buddhism and Politics in Twentieth Century Asia*. London: Bloomsbury, 2010.
Harvey, Yvette Rochelle. "Twitch Gothic: An Exploration of the Female Protagonist in Contemporary Australian Gothic Short Fiction." Melbourne, AU: RMIT University, 2018.
Hassler, Alfred. *Saigon, USA*. New York: Richard M. Baron, 1970.
Heidegger, Martin. "Letter on Humanism." In *Pathmarks*, edited by William McNeill. New York: Cambridge University Press, 1998.
Henry, Eric. "Tân Nhac: Notes toward a Social History of Vietnamese Music in the Twentieth Century." *Michigan Quarterly Review* 44, no. 1 (2005): 135–147.
Herring, George. *America's Longest War: The United States and Vietnam, 1950-1975*, 2nd ed. New York: John Wiley & Sons, 1979.
Hill, Lisa. "Anguli Ma: A Gothic Tale, by Chi Vu." *ANZ LitLovers LitBlog* (blog), 2012.
Hirsch, Marianne. *The Mother-Daughter Plot: Narrative, Psychoanalysis, Feminism*. Bloomington: Indiana University Press, 1993.
Hồ Thới Sang. *Kinh Tế Việt Nam* [The Economy of Vietnam]. Saigon: Đại Học Saigon, 1971.
Hoàng Đức Nhã, "Striving for a Lasting Peace: The Paris Accords and Aftermath." In Vu and Fear, *Republic of Vietnam*, 57–70.
Hoàng Hà et al., eds. *Trui Rèn Trong Lửa Đỏ* [Steeled by Fire]. Ho Chi Minh City: Thành Đoàn Thanh Niên Cộng Sản and Văn Nghệ, 1985.
Hoàng Thị Hồng Nga. "Giáo dục Đại học dưới chế độ Việt Nam Cộng hoà (1956–1975)" [University Education under the Republic of Vietnam, 1956–1975]. PhD diss., Vietnam National University–Hanoi, 2016.
Hoang, Tuan. "'Our Lady's Immaculate Heart Will Prevail': Vietnamese Marianism and Anticommunism, 1940–1975." *Journal of Vietnamese Studies* 17, no. 2-3 (Spring-Summer 2002): 126–157.
———. "From Reeducation Camps to Little Saigons: Historicizing Vietnamese Diasporic Anticommunism." *Journal of Vietnamese Studies* 11, no. 2 (Spring 2016): 43–95.
———. "Ideology in Urban South Vietnam, 1950–1975." PhD diss., University of Notre Dame, 2013.
———. "Political, Military, and Cultural Memoirs in Vietnamese." In Vu and Fear, *Republic of Vietnam*, 179–189.
———. "Ultramontanism, Nationalism, and the Fall of Saigon: Historicizing the Vietnamese American Catholic Experience." *American Catholic Studies* 130, no. 1 (Spring 2019): 1–36.
Hope, Marjorie and James Young. *The Struggle for Humanity: Agents of Nonviolent Change in a Violent World*. Maryknoll, NY: Orbis Books, 1977.
Hopkins, George. "Historians and the Vietnam War: The Conflict over Interpretations Continues." *Studies in Popular Culture* 23, no. 2 (October 2000): 99–108.
Hoskins, Janet Alison, and Thien-Huong T. Ninh. "Globalizing Vietnamese Religions." *Journal of Vietnamese Studies* 12, no. 2 (2017): 1–19.
Hosmer, Stephen, Konrad Kellen, and Brian Jenkins. *The Fall of South Vietnam: Statements by Vietnamese Military and Civilian Leaders*. New York: Crane, Russak, 1980.

Houtart, François. "International Responsibility for the Reconstruction of Vietnam." *Cross Currents* 25, no. 3 (Fall 1975): 269–282.
———. "Vietnam: A City Struggling to Be Born." *Economic and Political Weekly* 12, no. 45/46 (November 5–12, 1977): 1885–1886.
Huang, Chun-chieh. *Humanism in East Asian Confucian Contexts*. New Brunswick, NJ: Transaction Publishers, 2010.
Hunt, Joshua. *University of Nike: How Corporate Cash bought American Higher Education* Brooklyn, NY: Melville House, 2018.
Huy Đức. *Bên Thắng Cuộc Quyển I: Giải phóng* [The Winning Side Volume 1: Liberation]. CreateSpace Independent Publishing Platform, 2013.
Huynh, Kim. *Where the Sea Takes Us: A Vietnamese-Australian Story*. New York: Fourth Estate, 2007.
Huỳnh, Sanh Thông. *To Be Made Over: Tales of Socialist Reeducation in Vietnam*. New Haven, CT: Council on Southeast Asia Studies, 1988.
Israel, Nico. *Outlandish: Writing between Exile and Diaspora*. Stanford, CA: Stanford University Press, 2000.
Jamieson, Neil. *Understanding Vietnam*. Berkeley: University of California Press, 1995.
Jaspers, Karl. "Kant's 'Perpetual Peace.'" In *Philosophy and the World: Selected Essays and Lectures*, translated by E. B. Ashton, 88–91. Chicago: Regnery, 1963.
Johnson, Robert David. *Congress and the Cold War*. New York: Cambridge University Press, 2006.
Joiner, Charles. "Elections and Building Political Institutions in South Vietnam: An Assessment." In Donnell and Joiner, *Electoral Politics*.
———. "South Vietnam: Political, Military, and Constitutional Arenas in Nation-Building," *Asian Survey* 8(1): 58–71.
———. *The Politics of Massacre: Political Processes in South Vietnam*. Philadelphia, PA: Temple University Press, 1974.
Jones, Howard. *My Lai: Vietnam, 1968, and the Descent into Darkness*. New York: Oxford University Press, 2017.
Jung, Carl G. "The Undiscovered Self." New York: American Library, 1959.
———. *The Collected Works of C. G. Jung: West and East*. Princeton, NJ: Princeton University Press, 1969.
———. *The Collected Works of C. G. Jung: The Development of Personality*. London: Routledge & Kegan, 1977.
———, and C. Kerényi. *Science of Mythology: Essays on the Myth of the Divine Child and the Mysteries of Eleusis*. Translated by R. F. C. Hull. New York: Psychology Press, 2002.
———. *The Collected Works of C. G. Jung: Complete Digital Edition*. Princeton, NJ: Princeton University Press, 2014.
Kadura, Johannes. *The War after the War: The Struggle for Credibility during America's Exit from Vietnam*. Ithaca, NY: Cornell University Press, 2016.
Kahin, George. *Intervention: How America Became Involved in Vietnam*. New York: Alfred A. Knopf, 1986.
Kant, Immanuel. *Kant's Critique of Practical Reason and Other Works on the Theory of Ethics*. Translated by Thomas Kingsmill Abbot. London: Longmans, Green & Co., 1889.
———. *Principles of Politics: Including his Essay on Perpetual Peace: A Contribution to Political Science*. Translated by W. Hastie. Edinburgh: T & T Clark, 1891.
Karnow, Stanley. *Vietnam: A History*. New York: Penguin, 1983.

Kanesa-Thasan, S. "Stabilizing an Economy: A Study of the Republic of Korea." *Staff Papers (International Monetary Fund)* 16, no. 1 (March 1969): 19.
Keith, Charles. *Catholic Vietnam: A Church from Empire to Nation.* Berkeley: University of California Press, 2012.
Kiaer, Christina. *Everyday Life in Early Soviet Russia: Taking the Revolution Inside.* Bloomington: Indiana University Press, 2006.
Kiều Chinh, "The Cinema Industry." In Vu and Fear, *Republic of Vietnam,* 165–172.
Kim Định. *Cửa Khổng: Nho giáo nguyên thủy.* Sài Gòn: Nguyễn bá Tòng, 1965.
———. *Hồn Nước Với Lễ Gia Tiên.* Sunnyvale: H. T. Kelton, 1980.
———. *Kinh Hùng Khải Triết.* San Jose, CA: Thanh Niên Quốc Gia, 1982.
———. "The Role and the Conditions of 'JU' in Our Present Age." Presentation at the First World Conference in Chinese Philosophy, Taichung, Taiwan, August 19–25, 1984. https://vntaiwan.catholic.org.tw/kimdinh/therole.htm.
———. *Thái Bình Minh Triết.* Thời Điểm, 1997.
———. *Vấn đề Nguồn Gốc Văn Hóa Việt Nam.* Sài Gòn: Nguồn Sáng, 1973.
———. "The Vietnamese Cultural Heritage towards Contemporary Life." *Vietnam Missionaries in Asia,* April 17, 1997. http://www.catholic.org.tw/vntaiwan/kimdinh/culture.htm.
Kim, Sharon. "Lamarckism and the Construction of Transcendence in 'The House of Mirth.'" *Studies in the Novel,* 38, no. 2 (Summer 2006): 187–210.
Kim, Taekyoon. "Translating Foreign Aid Policy Locally: South Korea's Modernization Process Revisited." *Asian Perspective* 37, no. 3 (2013): 409–436.
Kimball, Jeffery. *The Vietnam War Files: Uncovering the Secret History of Nixon-Era Strategy.* Lawrence: University Press of Kansas, 2003.
———. *Nixon's Vietnam War.* Lawrence: University Press of Kansas, 1998.
King, Sallie B. "Thich Nhat Hanh and the Unified Buddhist Church of Vietnam: Nondualism in Action." In *Engaged Buddhism: Buddhist Liberation Movements in Asia,* edited by Christopher S. Queen and Sallie B. King, 329–334. Albany, NY: SUNY Press, 1996.
Kissinger, Henry. *Ending the Vietnam War: A History of America's Involvement in and Extraction from the Vietnam War.* New York: Simon and Schuster, 2003.
Koo, Youngnok. *Korea and the United States: A Century of Cooperation.* Honolulu: University of Hawai'i Press, 1984.
Koshy, Susan. "From Cold War to Trade War: Neocolonialism-Colonialism and Human Rights." *Social Text* 58, no. 1 (1999): 1–32.
Krueger, Anne. *The Development Role of the Foreign Sector and Aid.* Cambridge, MA: Harvard University Press, 1979.
Kumin, Judith. "Orderly Departure from Vietnam: Cold War Anomaly or Humanitarian Innovation?" *Refugee Survey Quarterly* 27, no. 1 (2008): 104–117.
Kurmann, Alexandra, and Tess Do. "Children on the Boat: The Recuperative Work of Postmemory in Short Fiction of the Vietnamese Diaspora." *Comparative Literature* 70, no. 2 (June 2018): 218–234.
Kwon, Heonik. *Ghosts of War in Vietnam.* New York: Cambridge University Press, 2008.
Kỷ niệm về nhạc sĩ Anh Bằng. Houston, TX: Văn Đàn Đồng Tâm, 2009.
Kỷ Yếu Giáo Phận Thái Bình: 80 Năm Thành Lập, 1936–2016 [Commemoration of the Diocese of Thái Bình: Eighty Years since Its Founding, 1936–2016]. Hà Nội: Hồng Đức, 2016.
Kỷ Yếu Giáo Xứ Đức Mẹ La Vang: Hành Trình Đức Tin 30 Năm [Commemoration of the Our Lady of La Vang Parish: A Journey of Faith over 30 Years]. Portland, OR: Our Lady of La Vang Parish, 2015.

Lâm, Vĩnh-Thế. *The History of South Vietnam: The Quest for Legitimacy and Stability, 1963–1967.* New York: Routledge, 2021.

———. "The Assasination of Deputy Trần Văn Văn on December 7, 1966." Eugene: University of Oregon, US Vietnam Research Center, March 15, 2022. https://usvietnam.uoregon.edu/en/the-assasination-of-deputy-tran-van-van-on-december-7-1966-part-1.02

Lê Khoa. *Tình Hình Kinh Tế Miền Nam Việt Nam (1955–1975) Qua Các Số Liệu Thống Kê* [The Economic Situation of South Vietnam through Statistics]. Ho Chi Minh City: Vien Khoa Hoc Xa Hoi, 1979.

Lê, Linda. *Héroïnes: un rêve éveillé*. Paris: Christian Bourgois éditeur, 2017.

Lê Mạnh Hùng. *Nhìn Lại Sử Việt: Thời Cận Hiện Đại 1945–1975* [Re-examining Vietnamese History, Modern Era 1945–1975]. Arlington, VA: Tổ Hợp Xuất Bản Miền Đông Hoa Kỳ, 2015.

Lê Sĩ Thắng. "Vài nét về con người Việt Nam truyền thống." In *Về vấn đề xây dựng con người mới*, edited by Phạm Như Cương. Hà Nội: Khoa học xã hội, 1978.

Lê Tấn Tài. "Nhận Xét Về Một Số Biện Pháp Kinh Tế Tài Chính Căn Bản Của Chính Phủ Từ Năm 1966 Đến Nay" [Comments on Some Basic Financial and Economic Measures of the Government from 1966 to the Present]. MA thesis, Saigon National Academy of Administration, 1970.

Lê Thương. *Nhạc tiền chiến* [Antebellum Music], edited by Đỗ Kim Bảng. Sài Gòn: Kẻ sĩ, 1970.

Lee, Eun Ho. "The Role of the Military in Nation-Building: A Comparative Study of South Vietnam and South Korea." PhD diss., Southern Illinois University, 1971.

Leshkowich, Ann Marie. "Wandering Ghosts of Late Socialism: Conflict, Metaphor, and Memory in a Southern Vietnamese Marketplace." *Journal of Asian Studies* 67, no. 1 (February 2008): 5–41.

Lieu, Nhi T. "Performing Culture in Diaspora: Assimilation and Hybridity in Paris by Night Videos and Vietnamese American Niche Media." In *Alien Encounters: Popular Culture in Asian America*, edited by Thuy Linh Nguyen Tu and Mimi Thi Nguyen. Durham, NC: Duke University Press, 2007.

Lipman, Jana K. *In Camps: Vietnamese Refugees, Asylum Seekers, and Repatriates*. Berkeley: University of California Press, 2020.

Liu, Lydia. "Shadows of Universalism: The Untold Story of Human Rights around 1948." *Critical Inquiry* 40 (Summer 2014).

Livingston, Jo. "Viet Thanh Nguyen's Ghosts." *New Republic*, July 25, 2019. https://newrepublic.com/article/144016/viet-thanh-nguyens-ghosts.

Logevall, Fredrik. *The Origins of the Vietnam War*. New York: Taylor & Francis, 2014.

Lorenz, Konrad. *On Aggression*. New York: Routledge, 1966.

Luân Hoán. *Tác giả Việt Nam: Vietnamese Authors*. Gardena, CA: Songvan, 2005.

Lưu Văn Lợi and Nguyễn Anh Vũ. *Le Duc Tho-Kissinger Negotiations in Paris*. Hanoi: The Gioi Publishers, 1996.

Lý Ngọc Lương, "Viện Đại học Cần Thơ tại miền Tây Nam phần." M.A. thesis, Saigon, Học viện Hành chính quốc gia, 1974.

Lý Quí Chung. *Hồi Ký Không Tên* [Memoir with No Name]. Ho Chi Minh City: Trẻ.

Mã Thiện Đồng. *Biệt Động Sài Gòn: Chuyện Bây Giờ Mới Kể* [Saigon Commandos: Now It Can Be Told]. Ho Chi Minh City: Tổng Hợp, 2013.

Magdoff, Harry. *The Age of Imperialism: The Economics of U.S Foreign Policy*. New York: Monthly Review Press, 1969.

Manuel, Peter. *Cassette Culture: Popular Music and Technology in North India*. Chicago: University of Chicago Press, 1993.

Marcel, Gabriel. *Paix sur la terre: 2 discours, 1 tragédie*. Paris: Aubier, 1965.

Marchi, Lisa. "Ghosts, Guests, Hosts: Rethinking 'Illegal' Migration and Hospitality through Arab Diasporic Literature." *Comparative Literature Studies* 51, no. 4 (2014): 603–26.

Marwah, Inder. "Bridging Nature and Freedom? Kant, Culture, and Cultivation." *Social Theory and Practice* 38, no. 3 (July 2012): 385–406.

Marr, David G. *Vietnamese Tradition on Trial: 1920-1945*. Berkeley: University of California Press, 1984.

Matsuoka, Atsuko Karin, and John Sorenson. *Ghosts and Shadows: Construction of Identity and Community in an African Diaspora*. Toronto: University of Toronto Press, 2001.

Mặt trận quốc gia thống nhất giải phóng Việt Nam [National Unified Front]. *Tuyển Tập Chuyện Kháng Chiến*. San Jose, CA: Đông Tiến, 1985.

Mazumdar, Sanjoy. "Creating a Sense of Place: The Vietnamese-Americans and Little Saigon." *Journal of Environmental Psychology* 20 (2000): 319–333.

McAllister, James. "'Only Religions Count in Vietnam': Thich Tri Quang and the Vietnam War," *Modern Asian Studies* 42, no. 4 (July 2008): 751–782.

McCormick, Thomas. *America's Half-Century: United States Foreign Policy in the Cold War*. Baltimore, MD: Johns Hopkins University Press, 1989.

McKelvey, Robert S. *A Gift of Barbed Wire: America's Allies Abandoned in South Vietnam*. Seattle: University of Washington Press, 2002.

McLaughlin, Colette Marie, and Paul Jesilow. "Conveying a Sense of Community along Bolsa Avenue: Little Saigon as a Model of Ethnic Commercial Belts." *International Migration* 36, no. 1 (2002): 49–65.

McLellan, Janet. *Many Petals of the Lotus: Five Asian Buddhist Communities in Toronto*. Toronto: University of Toronto Press, 1999.

Metzner, Ralph. "The Buddhist Six- Words Model of Consciousness and Reality." *Journal of Transpersonal Psychology* 28, no. 2 (1996).

Miller, Edward. "Development, Space, and Counterinsurgency in South Vietnam's Bến Tre Province, 1954–1960." In *Development in a Decolonizing World: Between Local and Global*, edited by Stephen Macekura and Erez Manela, 150–172. New York: Cambridge University Press, 2018.

———. *Misalliance: Ngô Đình Diệm, the United States, and the Fate of South Vietnam*. Cambridge, MA: Harvard University Press, 2013.

———. "Religious Revival and the Politics of Nation Building: Reinterpreting the 1963 'Buddhist Crisis' in South Vietnam." *Modern Asian Studies* 49, no. 6 (2015): 1903–1962.

Miller, Terry E. "Music and Theater in Saigon—1970: An American Soldier's Observations Revisited." In *New Perspectives on Vietnamese Music: Six Essays*, edited by Phong T. Nguyen, 20–35. New Haven, CT: Yale Center for International and Area Studies, 1991.

Moody, Dale Lindner. "The Manufacturing Sector in the Republic of Vietnam: Its Structure, Productivity, and Development." PhD diss., University of Florida, 1975.

Moyar, Mark. "Political Monks: The Militant Buddhist Movement during the Vietnam War." *Modern Asian Studies* 38, no. 4 (2004): 749–84.

———. *Triumph Forsaken: The Vietnam War, 1954–1965*. New York: Cambridge University Press, 2006.

Moyn, Samuel. *The Last Utopia*. Cambridge, MA: Harvard University Press, 2021.

Moyne, Samuel. "Plural Cosmopolitanisms and the Origins of Human Rights." In *The Meanings of Rights*, edited by Costas Douzinas and Conor Gearty. New York: Cambridge University Press, 2014.
Nabi, Asmat. "Gender Represented in the Gothic Novel." *IOSR Journal of Humanities and Social Science* 22, no. 11 (2017): 73–77.
Nagarjuna, *Verses from the Center: A Buddhist Version of the Sublime*, trans. Stephen Batchelor. New York: Riverhead Books, 2000.
Nan, Han-chen. *Resolutely Struggle against Imperialism*. Peking: Foreign Language Press, 1965.
Neumann, Erich. *The Great Mothers: An Analysis of the Archetype*. Princeton, NJ: Princeton University Press, 2015.
Ngô Bảo Châu et al., eds. *Kỷ yếu Đại học Humboldt 200 năm (1810-2010), kinh nghiệm thế giới và Việt Nam* [In commemoration of 200 years of Humboldt University, world and Vietnamese experiences]. Ho Chi Minh City: Trí Thức, 2011.
Ngô Thế Vinh. "Những năm ảo vọng: Giáo sư Phạm Hoàng Hộ và bộ sách Cây cỏ Việt nam" [The Years of Illusion, Professor Phạm Hoàng Hộ and his book '*Vietnam's flora*']. Blog, February 5, 2017. http://blackhorseva.blogspot.com/2017/02/267-ngo-vinh-nhung-nam-ao-vong-giao-su.html.
Nguyen Anh Tuan. *South Vietnam Trial and Experience, A Challenge for Development*. Athens: Ohio University Center for International Studies, 1987.
Nguyễn Bằng. "Ngoại Thương Miền Nam Và Viện trợ Thương Mại Hoá Của Mỹ" [The Foreign Trade in South Vietnam and Commercial Import Program of US]. *Tạp Chí Nghiên Cứu Kinh tế* [Journal of Economic Studies], no. 9 (1962): 39–44.
Nguyễn Cao Kỳ. *Buddha's Child: My Fight to Save Vietnam*. New York: St. Martin's Press, 2001.
———. *Twenty Years and Twenty Days: How and Why the United States Lost Its First War with China and the Soviet Union*. New York: Stein and Day, 1976.
Nguyễn Công Luận. *Nationalist in the Viet Nam Wars: Memoirs of a Victim Turned Soldier*. Bloomington: Indiana University Press, 2012.
Nguyen, Cuong Tu, and A. W. Barber. "Vietnamese Buddhism in North America: Tradition and Acculturation." In *The Faces of Buddhism in America*, edited by Charles S. Prebish and Kenneth K. Tanaka. Berkeley: University of California Press, 1998.
Nguyễn Đức Cường. "Building a Market Economy during Wartime." In Taylor, *Voices from the Second Republic*, 89–16.
———. "Coping with Changes and War, Building a Foundation for Growth." In Vu and Fear, *Republic of Vietnam*, 13–14.
Nguyễn Lang (Thích Nhất Hạnh). *Việt Nam Phật Giáo Sử Luận* [Essays on the History of Vietnamese Buddhism]. Hanoi: Văn Học, 1994.
Nguyen, Lemai, Luba Torlina, Konrad Peszynski, and Brian Corbitt. "Power Relations in Virtual Communities: An Ethnographic Study." *Electronic Commerce Research: New York* 6, no. 1 (January 2006): 21–37.
Nguyen, Lien-Hang T. *Hanoi's War: An International History of the War for Peace in Vietnam*. Chapel Hill: University of North Carolina Press, 2012.
Nguyễn Long. *Ký ức của một người Việt, 1934–1994* [Memories of a Vietnamese, 1934-1994]. Westminster, CA: Nguyễn Long, 1994.
Nguyen Manh Hung. "'Vietnam: A Television History': A Case Study in Perceptual Conflict

between the American Media and the Vietnamese Expatriates." *World Affairs* 147, no. 2 (Fall 1984): 71–84.

———. "Refugee Scholars and Vietnamese Studies in the United States, 1975–1982." *Amerasia* 11, no. 1 (1984): 89–99.

Nguyen, Marguerite. "Vietnamese American New Orleans." *Minnesota Review*, no. 84 (2015): 114–128.

———, and Catherine Fung. "Refugee Cultures: Forty Years after the Vietnam War." *MELUS: Multi-Ethnic Literature of the United States* 41, no. 3 (Fall 2016): 1–7.

Nguyen, Mimi Thi. *The Gift of Freedom: War, Debt, and Other Refugee Passages*. Durham, NC: Duke University Press, 2012.

Nguyen, Minh. "Vietnamese Sorrow: A Study of Literary Discourse in Popular Music Life." PhD diss., University of California, Riverside, 2018.

Nguyễn Mộng Giác. *Ngựa nản chân bon*. Westminster, CA: Người Việt, 1984.

———. "Nghĩ về văn học hải ngoại: tiểu luận." Gardena, CA: Văn Mới, 2004.

Nguyen, Nathalie Huynh Chau. *Memory Is Another Country: Women of the Vietnamese Diaspora*. Santa Barbara, CA: Praeger, 2009.

Nguyen Ngoc Bich. *War and Exile: A Vietnamese Anthology*. Springfield, MA: Vietnamese PEN, 1989.

Nguyễn Phú Đức, with Arthur Dommen. *The Viet-Nam Peace Negotiations: Saigon's Side of the Story*. Christiansburg, VA: Dalley Book Service, 2005.

Nguyen, Thao. "Quan Am and Mary: Vietnamese Religious, Cultural, and Spiritual Phenomena." *Buddhist-Christian Studies* 37, no. 1 (2017): 191–208.

Nguyen Tien Hung, and Jerrold Schecter. *The Palace File*. New York: Harper & Row, 1986.

Nguyễn, Tuấn Cường. "The Promotion of Confucianism in South Vietnam (1955–1975) and the Role of Nguyễn Đăng Thục as a New Confucian Scholar." *Journal of Vietnamese Studies* 10, no. 4 (Fall 2015): 30–81.

Nguyễn Văn Cung and Nguyễn Văn Thắng. "Giới thiệu lịch sử đại cương Luật Khoa Đại học đường Sài Gòn" [General History of Law Faculty of Saigon University]. Houston, November 4, 2002. https://ongvove.wordpress.com/2015/08/03/gioi-thieu-lich-su-dai-cuong-luat-khoa-dai-hoc-duong-sai-gon/.

Nguyễn Văn Noãn. "Kiểm duyệt báo chí ở Việt nam." *Báo Chí Tập San* 2, no. 1 (Summer 1968): 210–224.

Nguyễn Văn Ngọc. *Linh Địa Lavang* [Holy Site of La Vang]. Carthage, MO: Nguyệt San Trái Tim Đức Mẹ, 1978. Reprint, Saigon, 1970.

Nguyễn Văn Ngôn. *Kinh Tế Việt Nam Cộng hòa* [The Economy of the Republic of Vietnam]. Saigon: Tien Bo, 1972.

Nguyễn Văn Thuỳ. "Proposal for a Model Core Curriculum for the First Two Undergarduate Years in Institutions of Higher Education in Vietnam," PhD diss., Michigan State University, 1971.

Nguyễn, Việt Chước. *Lược Sử Báo Chí Việt Nam* [An Overview of the History of the Press in Vietnam]. Saigon: Nam Sơn, 1974.

Nguyen, Viet Thanh. *Nothing Ever Dies: Vietnam and the Memory of War*. Cambridge, MA: Harvard University Press, 2016.

Nguyen-Marshall, Van. "Appeasing the Spirits along the 'Highway of Horror': Civic Life in Wartime South Vietnam." *War and Society* 35, no. 3 (2018): 206–222.

———. "Student Activism in Time of War: Youth in the Republic of Vietnam, 1960s–1970s." *Journal of Vietnamese Studies* 10, no. 2 (2015): 43–81.

———. "Tools of Empire? Vietnamese Catholics in South Vietnam." *Journal of the Canadian Historical Association* 20, no. 2 (2009): 138–159.

———. "Associational Life of the Middle Classes in Saigon (1950s–1970s)." In *The Reinvention of Distinction*, vol. 2, edited by Van Nguyen-Marshall, Lisa B. Welch Drummond, and Danièle Bélanger. Dordrecht: Springer, 2012. https://doi.org/10.1007/978-94-007-2306-1_4.

Ngy Thanh. *Đại Lộ Kinh Hoàng* [Highway of horror]. Self-published, 2022.

Nhã Ca. "Writers of the Republic of Vietnam." Translated by Trùng Dương. In Vu and Fear, *Republic of Vietnam*, 155–164.

Nha Tổng giám đốc Kế hoạch, Phủ Thủ tướng. *Niên giám thống kê Việt Nam 1967–1968*, vol. 14. Saigon: Viện Quốc gia thống kê, 1968.

Ninh, Erin Khuê. "Forwarding Memory through Diaporama: The Passing-on of Việt Kiều Nostalgia." *Amerasia Journal* 35, no. 2 (January 1, 2009): 146–167.

Ninh, Kim. *A World Transformed: The Politics of Culture in Revolutionary Vietnam, 1945–1965*. Ann Arbor: University of Michigan Press, 2002.

———. "Renovating in Transition?" *Southeast Asian Affairs* (1990): 383–395.

Nkrumah, Kwame. *Neo-Colonialism the Last Stage of Imperialism*. New York: International Publishers, 1965.

Odajnyk, Volodymyr Walter. *Jung and Politics: The Political and Social Ideas of C. G. Jung*. New York: iUniverse, 2007.

Ông, Như-Ngọc T., and David S. Meyer. "Protest and Political Incorporation: Vietnamese American Protests in Orange County, California, 1975–2001." *Journal of Vietnamese Studies* 3, no. 1 (2008): 78–107.

Park, Kisung. *Military Authoritarian Regimes and Economic Development: the ROK's Economic Takeoff under Park Chung Hee*. Monterey, CA: Naval Postgraduate School, 2008.

Paul, Diane. "Eugenics and the Left." *Journal of the History of Ideas* 45, no. 4 (October–December 1984): 567–590.

Penniman, Howard. *Elections in South Vietnam*. Washington, DC: American Enterprise Institute, 1972.

Percival, R. S. "Is Jung's Theory of Archetypes Compatible with Neo-Darwinism and Sociobiology?" *Journal of Social and Evolutionary Systems* 16, no. 4 (1993): 459–487.

Pettus, Ashley. *Between Sacrifice and Desire: National Identity and the Governing of Femininity in Vietnam*. New York: Routledge, 2004.

Phạm Công Luận. *Sài Gòn: Chuyện đời của phố*. Hà Nội: Hội Nhà Văn, 2013.

Phạm Duy. *Hồi ký thời phân chia Quốc-Cộng*. Midway City, CA: Phạm Duy Cường Productions, 1991.

Pham, Hoa. "Finding a Place in the World—Vietnamese-Australian Diasporic Writing." *Long Paddock Modern Mobilities: Australian-Transnational Writing* 71, no. 1 (2011).

———. "The Seed of Enlightenment." *Peril*, October 14, 2012.

———. "Lingering Phantoms: Haunted Literature and Counter Memories from Vietnam/American War." Sydney, AU: University of Western Sydney, 2016.

———. *Lady of the Realm*. Mission Beach, AU: Spinifex Press, 2017.

———. "We Are Vietnamese. A Reflection on Being Vietnamese-Australian." *PORTAL Journal of Multidisciplinary International Studies* 15, no. 1–2 (June 26, 2018).

———, and Scott Brook. "Generation V—Searching for Vietnamese Australia." In *Australian*

Made: A Multicultural Reader, edited by Sonia Mycak and Amit Sarwal. Sydney: Sydney University Press, 2011.

Phạm Kim Ngọc, "Reform or Collapse: Economic Challenges during Vietnamization." In Vu and Fear, *Republic of Vietnam*, 35–46.

Phạm Kim Vinh. *Văn Hóa Dân Tộc và Văn Hóa Lưu Vong*. Westminster, CA: PKV, 1986.

Phạm Phú Minh. "Công việc xuất bản và phát hành tại miền Nam trước năm 1975." Paper presented at the conference "20 năm Văn học miền Nam 1954–1975" [20 years of South Vietnamese literature, 1954–1975], California, December 6, 2014. http://www.tienve .org/home/literature/viewLiterature.do;jsessionid=3FBC8FD753C926C2391446850F DE6D2C?action=viewArtwork&artworkId=18467.

Phạm Thị Phương. *Lịch sử hình thành và phát triển Viện Đại học Cần Thơ (1966–1975)* [The history of the University of Cần Thơ]. MA thesis, Vietnam National University, Hồ Chí Minh City, 2010.

Phạm Trần, "Life and Work of a Journalist." In Vu and Fear, *Republic of Vietnam*, 117–128.

Phan Đắc Lực. *Vị Trí Của Tư bản Lũng Đoạn Nước Ngoài Trong Nền Kinh Tế Miền Nam Việt Nam* [The Role of Foreign Capitalism in the Economy of South Vietnam]. Hanoi: Khoa Hoc Xa Hoi, 1964.

Phan Phát Huồn. *Việt Nam Giáo Sử*, quyển II (1933–1960) [The Church History of Vietnam]. Saigon: Cứu Thế Tùng Thư, 1962.

Phan Quang Dan. *The Republic of Vietnam's Environment and People*. Unpublished manuscript. Saigon, 1975.

Phan Thiện Giới. "Chính Sách Quan Thuế Và Công Cuộc Khuếch Trương Kinh Tế Tại Việt Nam" [Tax Policy and Economic Expansion in Vietnam]. PhD diss., Saigon University, 1960.

Pho, Helen Nguyen. "'These Goodies Haunt Your Mind': Consumer Culture and Resistance to American Nation-Building in South Vietnam, 1963–1975." MA thesis, University of Texas at Austin, 2012.

Picard, Jason. "'Renegades': The Story of South Vietnam's First National Opposition Newspaper, 1955–1958." *Journal of Vietnamese Studies* 10, no. 4 (2015): 1–29.

———. "'They Eat the Flesh of Children': Migration, Resettlement, and Sectionalism in South Vietnam, 1954–1957." In Tran and Vu, *Building a Republican Nation*.

Pike, Douglas, ed. *The Bunker Papers*. Berkeley, CA: Asian Foundation, 1990.

Popkin, Samuel. *The Rational Peasant: The Political Economy of Rural Society in Vietnam*. Berkeley: University of California Press, 1979.

Prentice, David. "Choosing 'the Long Road': Henry Kissinger, Melvin Laird, Vietnamization, and the War over Nixon's Vietnam Strategy." *Diplomatic History* 40, no. 3 (June 2016): 445–474.

Price, David H. *Cold War Anthropology: The CIA, the Pentagon, and the Growth of Dual Use Anthropology*. Durham, NC: Duke University Press, 2016.

Queen, Christopher, ed. *Engaged Buddhism in the West*. Boston, MA: Wisdom Publications, 2000.

Quinn-Judge, Sophie. *The Third Force in the Vietnam War: The Elusive Search for Peace, 1954–75*. London: I. B. Tauris, 2017.

Reich, Thomas Charles. "Higher Education in Vietnam: United States Agency for International Development Contract in Education, Wisconsin State University—Steven Point and Republic of Vietnam." MA thesis, University of Wisconsin-Stevens Point, 2003.

Rensma, Ritske. "Analytical Psychology and the Ghost of Lamarck: Did Jung Believe in the Inheritance of Acquired Characteristics?" *Journal of Analytical Psychology* (2013): 258–277.

Republic of Vietnam. *The New Press Law of Vietnam*, with an introduction by Nguyễn Ngọc Phách. Washington, DC: Vietnamese Embassy, 1970.

Reyes, Adelaida. *Songs of the Caged, Songs of the Free: Music and the Vietnamese Refugee Experience*. Philadelphia, PA: Temple University Press, 1999.

Riley, Myrne R. "Report on the School of Mechanical Engineering National Technical Center Saigon, South Vietnam." University of Missouri-Rolla, January 1971. https://scholarsmine.mst.edu/civarc_enveng_facwork/546/.

Roberts, Mervin Edwin. *The Psychological War for Vietnam, 1960–1968*. Lawrence: University Press of Kansas, 2018.

Robinson, Courtland. "The Comprehensive Plan of Action for Indochinese Refugees, 1989–1997: Sharing the Burden and Passing the Buck." *Journal of Refugee Studies* 17, no. 3 (September 2004): 319–333.

———. *Terms of Refuge: The Indochinese Exodus and the International Response*. London: Zed Books, 1998.

Rowley, Steven. "Writing Fiction About Fact: Using Historical Figures as Characters on Michael Cunningham, George Saunders, and Other 'Literary Grave-Robbers.'" April 18, 2019. https://lithub.com/writing-fiction-about-fact-using-historical-figures-as-characters/.

Ruether, Rosemary Radford. *Christianity and Social Systems, Historical Constructions and Ethical Challenges*. Lanham, MD: Rowman & Littlefield, 2009.

Sachs, Dana. *Life We Were Given: Operation Babylift, International Adoption, and the Children of War in Vietnam*. Boston, MA: Beacon Press, 2010.

Safran, William. "Diasporas in Modern Societies: Myths of Homeland and Return." *Diaspora: A Journal of Transnational Studies* 1, no. 1 (1991): 83–99.

Sahlins, Marshall. *Confucius Institutes: Academic Malware*. Chicago: Prickly Paradigm Press, 2015.

Said, Edward. *Culture and Imperialism*. New York: Vintage Books, 1994.

Sansom, Robert. *The Economics of Insurgency in the Mekong Delta of Vietnam*. Cambridge, MA: MIT Press, 1970.

Sartre, Jean-Paul. *Colonialism and Neocolonialism*. New York: Routledge, 2001.

Schafer, John. "Death, Buddhism, and Existentialism in the Songs of Trịnh Công Sơn." *Journal of Vietnamese Studies* 2, no. 1 (2007): 144–186.

Scott, Charlotte. *Shakespeare's Nature: From Cultivation to Culture*. Oxford: Oxford University Press, 2014.

Scruton, Roger. *How to Think Seriously about the Planet: The Case for an Environmental Conservatism*. Oxford: Oxford University Press, 2012.

Sheehan, Neil, Henrick Smith, E. W. Kenworthy, and Fox Butterfield. *The Pentagon Papers: The Secret History of the Vietnam War*. New York: Bantam Books, 1971.

Sherry, Vincent. "The Evolution of the Legal System of the Republic of Vietnam." PhD diss., University of Southern Mississippi, 1974.

Slaughter, Joseph. *Human Rights Inc.: The World Novel, Narrative Form, and International Law*. New York: Fordham University Press, 2007.

Small, Ivan V. "'Over There': Imaginative Displacements in Vietnamese Remittance Gift Economies." *Journal of Vietnamese Studies* 7, no. 3 (2012): 157–183.

Smith, Curtis D. *Jung's Quest for Wholeness: A Religious and Historical Perspective.* New York: SUNY Press, 1990.
Smith, Harvey H., et al. *Area Handbook for South Vietnam.* Washington, DC: U.S. Government Printing Office, 1967.
Smith, Jeffrey A. *War and Press Freedom: The Problem of Prerogative Power.* New York: Oxford University Press, 1999.
Sorley, Lewis, ed. *The Vietnam War: An Assessment by South Vietnam's Generals.* Lubbock: Texas Tech University Press, 2010.
Soucy, Alexander. "A Reappraisal of Vietnamese Buddhism's Status as 'Ethnic.'" *Journal of Vietnamese Studies* 12, no. 2 (2017): 20–48.
———. "Thích Nhất Hạnh in the Context of the Modern Development of Vietnamese Buddhism." In *Oxford Research Encyclopedia of Buddhism*, edited by Richard K. Payne and Georgios T. Halkias. https://oxfordre.com/religion/view/10.1093/acrefore/9780199340378.001.0001/acrefore-9780199340378-e-944.
———. "Contemporary Vietnamese Buddhism." In *Oxford Handbook of Contemporary Buddhism*, vol. 1, edited by Michael Jerryson, 177–195. Oxford: Oxford University Press, 2016.
Spektorowski, Alberto. "The Eugenic Temptation in Socialism: Sweden, Germany, and the Soviet Union." *Comparative Studies in Society and History* 42, no. 1 (2004): 84–106.
Stewart, Geoffrey. *Vietnam's Lost Revolution: Ngô Đình Diệm's Failure to Build an Independent Nation, 1955–1963.* New York: Cambridge University Press, 2017.
Strom, Dao. "Anguli Ma: A Gothic Tale (by Chi Vu): A Review." *DiaCRITICS* (blog), February 18, 2013. https://dvan.org/2013/02/anguli-ma-a-gothic-tale-by-chi-vu-can-we-transcend-our-violent-being.
Stur, Heather. *Saigon at War: South Vietnam and the Global Sixties.* New York: Cambridge University Press, 2020.
Szabo, Daniel, and Kenichi G. Kuwabara. "Market for US Products in Vietnam." *World Trade Information Service: Economic Report*, Part 1, no. 62–76 (1961).
Tăng Thân Làng Mai. *Đi Gặp Mùa Xuân: Hành trạng thiền sư Thích Nhất Hạnh.* Hanoi: Thế Giới, 2022.
Taylor, K. W. *A History of the Vietnamese.* New York: Cambridge University Press, 2013.
———, and John K. Whitmore. *Essays into Vietnamese Pasts.* Ithaca, NY: Cornell University Press, 2018.
———, ed. *Voices from the Second Republic of South Vietnam (1967–1975).* Ithaca, NY: Cornell Southeast Asia Program Publications, 2014.
Taylor, Philip. "Music as a 'Neocolonial Poison' in Postwar Southern Vietnam." *Crossroads: An Interdisciplinary Journal of Southeast Asian Studies* 14, no. 1 (2000): 99–131.
———, ed. *Modernity and Re-enchantment: Religion in Post-Revolutionary Vietnam.* Singapore: Institute of Southeast Asian Studies, 2007.
Tetsusaburo, Kimura. *The Vietnamese Economy, 1979–86.* Tokyo: Institute of Development Economies, 1989.
Thế Nhân. "Tương Quan Giữa Ngoại Thương, Hối Đoái Và Ngân Hàng" [Correlation between Foreign Trade, Foreign Exchange and Banking]. *Tạp Chí Chấn Hưng Kinh Tế* [Journal of Economic Development] no. 658 (1969): 11–13.
Thích Đôn Hậu. *Muốn hết khổ* [Wanting to End Suffering]. Translated by Đinh Văn Chấp. Hanoi: Impr. Đuốc Tuệ, 1942.
Thích Minh Châu. *Trước sự nô lệ của con người* [On the Cusp of Human Slavery]. Saigon: Viện Đại Học Vạn Hạnh, 1970.

Thích Nhất Hạnh, *Vietnam: Lotus in a Sea of Fire*. New York: Hill and Wang, 1967.
———. "History of Engaged Buddhism: A Dharma Talk by Thich Nhat Hanh." *Human Architecture* 6, no. 3 (Summer 2008): 29–36.
———. "The Struggle for Peace in Vietnam." In *Religion and International Affairs*, edited by Jeffrey Rose and Michael Ignatieff. Toronto: House of Amans, 1968.
———. *Nẻo Về Của Ý*. Hà Nội: Hồng Đức, 2017.
Thich, Nhat Hanh. "History of Engaged Buddhism: A Dhrama Talk by Thich Nhat Hanh, Ha Noi, Vietnam, May 6–7, 2008." *Human Architecture: Journal of Sociology of Self-Knowledge* 6, no. 3 (2008).
Thích Thiện-Hòa, ed. *50 Năm Chấn Hưng Phật Giáo*. Saigon: Viện Hóa-Đạo, 1970.
Thich, Quang Minh. "Vietnamese Buddhism in America." PhD diss., Florida State University, 2007.
Tôn Thất Đính. *20 Năm Binh Nghiệp* [My Twenty-Year Military Career]. San Jose, CA: Chanh Da, 1998.
Toner, Simon. "Imagining Taiwan: The Nixon Administration, the Developmental States, and South Vietnam's Search for Economic Viability, 1969–1975." *Diplomatic History* 41, no. 4 (September 2017): 772–798.
Topmiller, Robert. *The Lotus Unleashed: The Buddhist Peace Movement in South Vietnam, 1964–1966*. Lexington: University Press of Kentucky, 2002.
Trần Đại. "Nhân vụ tăng giá giấy báo vừa qua thử nhìn lại tương quan giữa chính quyền và báo chí ở những nước chậm tiến." *Bách Khoa*, no. 318 (April 1, 1970): 35–44.
Trần Đình. "Vốn Lãi Và Bộ Mặt Đế Quốc Của Viện Trợ (Interest and the Imperialist Nature of Aid)." *Đối Diện: Hải Ngoại*, no. 43–44 (1973): 42–52.
Trần Quang Minh. "A Decade of Public Service: Nation-Building during the Interregnum and Second Republic (1964–75)." In Taylor, *Voices from the Second Republic*, 39–88.
Trần Văn Ân. "Tại sao Cộng sản cũng nói nhân bản mà giết người? Con người Việt nên như thế nào?" In *Con người Mác-xít: Vật chất sống-biết suy tư* [Matière vivante et pensante]. Unpublished papers. Rennes, June 1986.
——— and Văn Lang. "Chung quanh vấn đề Việt học." In *Đấu sĩ Cách mạng-Văn hóa, Chính trị-Ngoại giao, Viết báo-ngồi tù III*. Unpublished papers. Rennes: Tủ sách Gia Đình, 1989.
———. "Nói về lãnh đạo." In *Hồi ký Trần Văn Ân: Đấu sĩ, cách mạng-văn hóa, chánh trị-ngoại giao, viết báo-ngồi tù III*. Unpublished memoir. Paris.
Trần Văn Chánh. "Chương trình Giáo dục và sách giáo khoa thời Việt Nam Cộng hoà" [Curricula and Textbooks under the RVN]. *Tạp chí Nghiên cứu và Phát triển* [Research and Development Journal] no. 7–8 (2014): 184–241.
Trần Văn Đôn. *Our Endless War: Inside Vietnam*. San Rafael, CA: Presidio Press, 1978.
Tran, Anh Q. "Kuan-Yin: A Case of Inculturation in Chinese Buddhism." *The Journal of Asian American Theological Forum (AATF)* 4, no. 1 (May 2017): 59–63.
Trần, Claire Thị Liên. "*Thanh-Lao-Công* (Young Christian Workers) in Tonkin, 1935–1945: From Social to Political Activism." *Journal of Vietnamese Studies* 17, no. 2-3 (Spring-Summer 2022): 93–125.
Trần, Đình Trụ. *Ship of Fate: Memoir of a Vietnamese Repatriate*. Honolulu: University of Hawai'i Press, 2017.
Tran, Nu-Anh. "South Vietnamese Identity, American Intervention, and the Newspaper *Chính Luận* [Political Discussion], 1965–1969." *Journal of Vietnamese Studies* 1, no. 1–2 (February/August 2006): 169–209.

---, and Tuong Vu, eds. *Building a Republican Nation in Vietnam, 1920-1963*. Honolulu: University of Hawai'i Press, 2022.
Tran, Quan. "Remembering the Boat Exodus: A Tale of Two Memorials." *Journal of Vietnamese Studies* 7, no. 3 (2012): 80–121.
Tran, Tri Vu. *Lost Years: My 1,632 Days in Vietnamese Reeducation Camps*. Berkeley, CA: Institute of East Asian Studies, 1988.
Trùng Dương. "*Sóng Thần*'s Campaign for Press Freedom." In Vu and Fear, *Republic of Vietnam*, 139–154.
Truong Hoang Lem. "A Test of Survival—The Case of South Vietnam." PhD diss., University of Southern California, 1971.
Trường Kỳ. *Một thời nhạc trẻ*. Montreal: Trường Kỳ, 2002.
Truong Nhu Tang. *A Viet Cong Memoir: An Inside Account of the Vietnam War and its Aftermath*. New York: Vintage, 1986.
Tsu, Jing. "Extinction and Adventures on the Chinese Diasporic Frontier." *Journal of Chinese Overseas* 2, no. 2 (November 2006), 247–268.
---. *Failure, Nationalism, and Literature: The Making of Modern Chinese Identity, 1895-1937*. Stanford, CA: Stanford University Press, 2006.
Tùng Giang. *Hồi ký nhạc sĩ Tùng Giang: Âm nhạc, tình yêu, tình bằng hữu*. Westminster, CA: Thúy Nga, 2005.
Turley, William. *Vietnamese Communism in Comparative Perspective*. Boulder, CO: Westview Press, 1980.
United Nations Statistical Office. *Statistical Yearbook*. New York: United Nations, 1970.
US Department of State. *Foreign Relations of the United States [FRUS], 1955-1957*. Vol. 1, *Vietnam*, edited by Edward C. Keefer, David W. Mabon, and John P. Glennon. Washington: Government Printing Office, 1985.
---. *FRUS, 1958-1960*. Vol. 1, *Vietnam*, edited by Edward C. Keefer, David W. Mabon, and John P. Glennon. Washington: Government Printing Office, 2000.
---. *FRUS, 1964-1968*. Vol. 3, *Vietnam, June-December 1965*, edited by David C. Humphrey, Edward C. Keefer, and Louis J. Smith. Washington: Government Printing Office, 1996.
---. *FRUS, 1964-1968*. Vol. 6, *Vietnam, January-August 1968*, edited by Kent Sieg and David S. Patterson. Washington: Government Printing Office, 2002.
---. *FRUS, 1964-1968*. Vol. 7, *Vietnam, September 1968-January 1969*, edited by Kent Sieg and Edward C. Keefer. Washington: Government Printing Office, 2003.
---. *FRUS, 1964-1968*. Vol. 29, Part 1, *Korea*, edited by Karen L. Gatz. Washington: Government Printing Office, 2000.
---. *FRUS, 1969-1976*. Vol. 6, *Vietnam, January 1969-July 1970*, edited by Edward C. Keefer and Carolyn Yee. Washington: Government Printing Office, 2006.
---. *FRUS, 1969-1976*. Vol. 10, *Vietnam, January 1973-July 1975*, edited by Bradley Lynn Coleman and Edward C. Keefer. Washington: Government Printing Office, 2010.
Valverde, Caroline Kieu Linh. "Making Transnational Viet Nam: Vietnamese American Community, Viet Nam Linkages through Money, Music, and Modems." *American Quarterly* 55, no. 4 (2003): 820–21.
Valverde, Kieu-Linh Caroline. *Transnationalizing Viet Nam: Community, Culture, and Politics in the Diaspora*. Philadelphia, PA: Temple University Press, 2012.
van der Kroef, Justus M. "The Vietnamese Refugee Problem." *World Affairs* 142, no. 1 (Summer 1979): 3–16.

Veith, George. *Black April: The Fall of South Vietnam, 1973-75*. New York: Encounter Books, 2012.
———. *Drawn Swords in a Distant Land: South Vietnam's Shattered Dreams*. New York: Encounter, 2021.
Vennema, Alje. *The Viet Cong Massacre at Hue*. New York: Vantage Press, 1976.
Vietnam Courier. *Those Who Leave*. Houston, TX: U.S.-Vietnam Friendship Association, 1979.
———. *Vietnam, Which Human Rights*. Ann Arbor: University of Michigan, 1980.
Vĩnh Phúc. *Đối Thoại: 13 văn thi sĩ nói về mình và văn học*. Văn Nghệ, 2001.
Vo Dang, Thanh Thuy. "Anticommunism as Cultural Praxis: South Vietnam, War, and Refugee Memories in the Vietnamese American Community." PhD diss., University of San Diego, 2008.
Võ Đoàn Ba. "Ngoại Viện Hoa Kỳ Tại Việt Nam 1960—1970 (US Assistance to Vietnam 1960–1970)." MA thesis, Saigon National Academy of Administration, 1972.
Vo Kim Son. "Personal Reflections on the Educational System," in Vu and Fear, *Republic of Vietnam*, 105–116.
Võ Nhân Trí. "Sự Xâm Nhập Kinh Tế của Mỹ Vào Các Nước Đang Phát Triển ở Châu Á" [America's Economic Penetration into Developing Countries in Asia]. *Tạp Chí Nghiên Cứu Kinh Tế* [Journal of Economic Studies] no. 80 (1974): 69–75.
Võ Văn Sen. *Sự Phát Triển Chủ Nghĩa Tư Bản Ở Miền Nam Việt Nam 1954-1975* [Development of Capitalism in South Vietnam 1954–1975]. Ho Chi Minh City: Ho Chi Minh City Press, 2005.
Vu, Chi. *Anguli Ma: A Gothic Tale*. Artarmon, NSW, AU: Giramondo Publishing, 2012.
Vũ Quang Hùng. "Tôi ám sát người sắp làm Thủ tướng Sài Gòn." *Minh Đức* (blog), April 30, 2011. Accessed April 21, 2022. http://minhduc7.blogspot.com/2012/03/toi-am-sat-nguoi-sap-lam-thu-tuong-sai.html.
Vũ Tài Mạnh. "Nhìn Qua Tình Hình Ngân Hàng Thương Mại Trong Năm 1974" [Looking Through the Situation of Commercial Banks in 1974]. *Tập San Quốc Phòng* [Journal of Defense] no. 56 (1975): 101–108.
Vu, Tuong. *Vietnam's Communist Revolution: The Power and Limits of Ideology*. New York: Cambridge University Press, 2017.
———, and Sean Fear, eds. *The Republic of Vietnam, 1955-1975: Vietnamese Perspectives on Nation Building*. Ithaca, NY: Cornell Southeast Asian Publications, 2020.
Vultee, Fred. "The Second Casualty: Effects of Interstate Conflict and Civil War on Press Freedom." *Media, War, and Conflict* 2, no. 2 (August 2009): 111–127.
Vương Pen Liêm. *Những Vụ Án Tối Tâm*. Saigon: Nguyên Hà, 1967.
Wauchop, Angela. "A Book Review of Hoa Pham's 'Lady of the Realm.'" *Backstory* (blog), June 8, 2018. Accessed February 15, 2023. https://www.backstoryjournal.com.au/2018/06/08/book-review-hoa-phams-lady-realm/.
Whitmore, John K. "Communism and History." In *Vietnamese Communism in Comparative Perspective*, edited by William Turley, 11–44. Boulder, CO: Westview Press, 1980
Whorf, Benjamin Lee. *Language, Thought, and Reality: Selected Writings of Benjamin Lee Whorf*. Cambridge, MA: MIT Press, 1964.
Wiest, Andrew. *Vietnam's Forgotten Army: Heroism and Betrayal in the ARVN*. New York: New York University Press, 2008.
Willbanks, James. *Abandoning Vietnam: How America Left and South Vietnam Lost Its War*. Lawrence: University Press of Kansas, 2004.

Williams, Rowan. "Religious Faith and Human Rights." In *The Meanings of Rights*, edited by Costas Douzinas and Conor Gearty, 71–82. New York: Cambridge University Press, 2014.
Woiak, Joanne. "Designing a Brave New World: Eugenics, Politics, and Fiction." *The Public Historian* 29, no. 3 (Summer 2007): 105–129.
Wong, Deborah Anne. *Speak It Louder: Asian Americans Making Music*. New York: Routledge, 2004.
Woodside, Alexander. *Community and Revolution in Modern Vietnam*. Boston, MA: Houghton Mifflin, 1976.
Wu, Yiching. *The Cultural Revolution at the Margins: Chinese Socialism in Crisis*. Cambridge, MA: Harvard University Press, 2014.
Yeager, Jack Andrew. *The Vietnamese Novel in French: A Literary Response to Colonialism*. Hanover, NH: University Press of New England, 1987.
Young, Marilyn. *The Vietnam Wars, 1945–1990*. New York: HarperCollins, 1991.
Zinoman, Peter. "A Republican Moment in the Study of Modern Vietnam." In Tran and Vu, *Building a Republican Nation*.

Contributors

Wynn Gadkar-Wilcox is professor of History at Western Connecticut State University. He studies the intellectual history and historiography of modern Vietnam. He has published *Allegories of the Vietnamese Past* (2010), *East Asia and the West* (with Xiaobing Li and Yi Sun) (2019), and *Vietnam and the West* (ed., 2010).

Jason Gibbs is the author of *Rock Hà Nội & Rumba Cửu Long* (2008). He wrote the entry for Vietnam in the *Continuum Encyclopedia of Popular Music of the World* and has published articles in *Asian Music, Journal of Vietnamese Studies, Southeast Asian Research* and *BBC* Tiếng Việt.

Thanh Hoang is a lecturer in the Faculty of International Relations of the University of Social Sciences and Humanities, Vietnam National University, Ho Chi Minh City. She obtained her PhD in International Relations at the University of Social Sciences and Humanities, Hanoi. Her dissertation explains why the defense relations of Vietnam and the United States depend on American interests in the region. She is the co-author (with Cuong Nguyen) of a chapter titled "Mediatized Infra-Politics and Government Accountability in Vietnam," in Nhu Truong and Tuong Vu, *The Dragon's Underbelly: Dynamics and Dilemmas of Vietnam's Economy and Politics*.

Tuan Hoang is Blanche E. Seaver Professor of Humanities and Teacher Education and associate professor at Pepperdine University, teaching in the Great Books and History programs. Among his publications are "Ultramontanism, Nationalism, and the Fall of Saigon: Historicizing the Vietnamese American Catholic Experience," *American Catholic Studies* 130, no. 1 (Spring 2019); and "'Our Lady's Immaculate Heart Will Prevail': Vietnamese Marianism and Anticommunism, 1940–1975," *Journal of Vietnamese Studies* 17, nos. 2–3 (Summer 2022).

Adrienne Minh-Châu Lê is a PhD candidate at Columbia University focusing on twentieth-century Vietnamese and United States history. Her research interests include the South Vietnamese Buddhist antiwar movement, South Vietnamese civil society, postwar migration, and the Vietnamese diaspora.

Trinh M. Luu earned her PhD in comparative literature from the University of California, Berkeley, where she served as managing editor of the *Journal of Vietnamese Studies*. From 2020 to 2021, she was a research fellow at the University of Oregon's Global Studies Institute. Her works examine Vietnamese law and literature, human rights, postwar migration, and the Vietnamese diaspora.

Phạm Thị Hồng Hà is a senior research fellow at Institute of History, Vietnam Academy of Social Sciences. Her works focus on the economy and society of the Republic of Vietnam (RVN). Her dissertation studies the banking system in southern Vietnam before 1975. Her first book on US aid for RVN (1955–1975) was published in 2017.

Vinh Phu Pham is a literary scholar with a background in Vietnamese Francophone and nineteenth-century Spanish peninsular literature. He received his BA and MA in Spanish language and literature from Florida Atlantic University, and his Ph.D. in comparative literature from Cornell University. Vinh has published articles on José Martí, José Rizal, Spanish contemporary politics, and other works relating to Vietnamese literature and culture. Currently he is a visiting lecturer at Fulbright University Vietnam and the English editor of the *US-Vietnam Review*.

Phạm Vũ Lan Anh received her PhD in English and Theater Studies from the University of Melbourne. From 2010 to 2017, she was a lecturer in the Literary Studies Department of Da Lat University, where she taught comparative literature, Chinese literature, and reception theories.

David L. Prentice received his PhD from Ohio University and is an award-winning instructor at the Osher Lifelong Learning Institute at Oklahoma State University. His work has appeared in *Diplomatic History*, the *Journal of Military History*, and several edited volumes. His first book (University Press of Kentucky) examines America's exit strategy from Vietnam.

Trương Thùy Dung is a researcher at the Institute of History Academy of Social Sciences, Hanoi, Vietnam. She earned her PhD from the University of Hamburg, Germany, in 2020. Her research interests focus on but are not limited to the educational and cultural developments of the Republic of Vietnam, the Vietnamese wars in the twentieth century, Vietnamese literature and linguistics, and Southeast Asian history.

George J. Veith earned his PhD in history from Monash University and is the author of four books on the Vietnam War. They include *Code-Name Bright Light: The Untold Story of U.S. POW Rescue Efforts during the Vietnam War*, *Leave No Man Behind: Bill Bell and the Search for American POW/MIAs from the Vietnam War*, *Black April: The Fall of South Vietnam, 1973–1975*, and, most recently, *Drawn Swords in a Distant Land: South Vietnam's Shattered Dreams.* He also published an e-book with the Cold War International History Project titled "The Return to War: North Vietnamese Decision-Making, 1973–1975."

Tuong Vu is professor and head of the Political Science Department and director of the US-Vietnam Research Center at the University of Oregon. His research has focused on the modern history and politics of East and Southeast Asia, with a particular focus on Vietnam. Vu is the author or editor of eight books, including, most recently, *Building a Republican Nation in Vietnam, 1920–1963* (with Nu-Anh Tran); *Toward a Framework for Vietnamese American Studies: History, Community, and Memory* (with Linda Ho Peche and Alex-Thai Vo); *The Republic of Vietnam, 1955–1975: Vietnamese Perspectives on Nation-Building* (with Sean Fear); and *Vietnam's Communist Revolution: The Power and Limits of Ideology*.

Index

Abrams, Creighton, 29
academic freedom, 158–163
agency: Commercial Import Program and, 89–97; of Vietnamese refugees, 13–14
American Medical Association, 117
Anguli Ma: A Gothic Tale (Vu), 234–242
Aṅgulimāla, 236–237
Anh Bằng, 179, 204, 206
An Phú, 178
anticommunism: Catholic Church and, 193–194, 196, 199–201; Commercial Import Program as tool of, 84–89; peace negotiations and influence of, 44–49, 57–59; political and intellectual culture in RVN and, 4–5, 22, 105–121; postwar Vietnam, 247; refugee Vietnamese communities and, 14, 190, 210–211, 238–239; Vietnam war and, 7
antiwar movement: Buddhist activism in RVN and, 126–129; music production and, 172–173; Nhất Hạnh's work with, 147–149; in US, 24, 29–30, 33–35, 72
Armed Forces of the RVN (RVNAF): recruitment statistics for, 18n40; scholarly reassessment of, 5; Thiệu in, 22; Vietnamization strategy and, 25–30; war and devastation of, 5, 23, 33–35
Army of the RVN (ARVN), 72–73
arts, 14
Asia, 203–205, 212, 218
Asia Foundation, 128–129, 142n27, 146, 148–149, 162, 164n16

Asian Pacific policies, 13–14
Asia Records, 179–180
Asia Sóng Nhạc, 180
Aśoka (emperor), 155
Asselin, Pierre, 42
associational culture: Catholic Vietnamese Americans and, 189–201; in South Vietnam, 194–198
Association of Former Military Police, 14
Association of Newspaper Publishers (Hội Chủ Báo), 75
Association of Our Lady (Hội Đức Bà), 191
August Revolution (1945), 193
authoritarianism, 2

Bách Khoa, 71, 255
Bachofen, Johan Jacob, 262–263
Bac II certificate, 108–109
Bài Ca Hay, 178
ballroom dance, 169, 714
banking industry (Vietnam), 93–97
Bảo Đại, 1
Battle of Saigon, 1
Berman, Larry, 42
Bình, Nguyễn Thị, 55, 57
Bình Xuyên, 1
Blue Army of Our Lady of Fatima, 7, 196–197
Bodhisattva of Mercy, 227–230, 242, 264–265
bolero music, 218–219
bootleg recordings, 182–183
broadcast industry (RVN), 175–177
Browne, Malcolm, 234
Buddhist crisis, 147–149

299

Buddhist thought and activism: academic freedom and, 145–163; communist suppression of, 140–141, 141n2; existentialism and, 154–158; in literature of Vietnamese refugees, 16, 224–242; Thích Nhất Hạnh and, 15, 124–141, 145–149, 165n4, 230–234; peace initiatives and, 42–44, 48, 52–54; revival movement and, 15–16; RVN and, 4–5, 64; syncretism, in Vietnamese Buddhism, 224; Thích Minh Châu's scholarship on, 150–154, 230–234; Vietnam War and, 2, 6–8, 23, 124–141
Bùi Diễm, 25, 36n16, 43
Building a Republican Nation in Vietnam, 1920-1963, 1–2
Bunker, Ellsworth, 49–53, 55
Burning Monk, The, 234
Bút Thần, 75

cải lương, 169–170, 172, 175–177, 180–181, 205
Cambodia: North Vietnamese invasion of, 34–35, 54; Vietnamese-Chinese conflict with, 10, 12; Vietnamese exports to, 96–97
Cần Lao Party, 22
Cannon, Alexander, 204
Cao Đài, 6–7
Cao Văn Luận (Father), 106–107, 118–119
Capitol, 180
Carter, Jimmy, 246, 266
cassette technology, 181–182
Cathcart, Michael, 236
Catholic Action groups, 7, 192–201
Catholic Church: associational culture of, 16, 189–201; Buddhist and, 234; in colonial-era Vietnam, 190–194; newspapers in Vietnam and, 70–71, 74, 77; in RVN, 194–198; Second Republic scholarship on, 4–5; Thiệu's conversion to, 22–24; Vietnamese Americans and, 189–190, 198–201; war in South Vietnam and, 6–8
censorship: of Buddhist activism, 138–139; of music, 169–173, 182–185, 188n81, 204, 219–220; press in South Vietnam and, 61, 65–69, 74–79, 80n2
Center of Educational Material (Trung tâm học liệu), 114
Central Intelligence Agency (CIA), 22, 128–129, 146, 149, 162, 164n16
Chân Không (sister), 141, 148–149
Chân Tín (father), 70, 74, 79
Chân Trời Mới (New Horizon), 246–247
Châu Kỳ, 178, 205
Chế Lan Viên, 256–257
Chennault, Anna, 25
"Chiều Tây Đô" (Lam Phương's song), 204–207, 209–211, 214–220, 221n8
Chí Hòa Prison, 129
Children of Mary (Hội Con Đức Bà), 191
China: North Vietnam supported by, 1, 5, 12, 34, 39n70, 100n9; postwar economic investment in Vietnam by, 189; Vietnamese-Cambodia conflict with, 10, 12, 258
Chính Luận, 67–68, 71–73, 75
Chomsky, Noam, 212
Christians, Clifford, 69
Chu Tử (Ao Thả Vịt, A Duck Pond, ATV), 75–76
citizenship, 14
civil society: Buddhist movement and, 125; public universities and, 117–121, 121n1; in Second Republic, 64–65; Thích Minh Châu's analysis of, 149–150; Vietnam War impact on, 6–8
class warfare, 12
Clifford, Clark, 25
Colgan, Harold (father), 196–197
colonial era: censorship in, 65–66; education policy in, 105–106; French rule in, 25, 105; music production in, 179–180, 184; nationalism in, 64–65
Commercial Import Program, 15, 30–31, 83–99
Committee for Government Operations, 86
Committee for Peace, 44
communist government of Vietnam: music censorship by, 182–185,

Index 301

188n81, 204, 219–220; postwar establishment of, 140–141; refugees and, 9
community, 13–14
Conference of the Economic Aspect of Printing, Publishing, and Distributing Books, 114
Congregation of the Mother Co-Redemptrix (CMC), 194, 199–200
constitution, 4–5, 48, 65, 79
consumer markets, 83–99
Continental Records, 181
corruption, 95–97
Counterpart Fund, 84, 86
critical refugee studies (CRS), 12–14
Critique of Practical Reason (Kant), 156–157
cultural heritage and production: as propaganda, 169; by refugee communities and, 203–220; Vietist cultural front and, 246, 250–253; by Vietnamese diaspora, 16; during Vietnam War, 182–184
Cunningham, Stuart, 215
currency exchange rate, 92–97, 102n42

Đại Dân Tộc (Great Nation), 68
Đại Hội Nhạc Trẻ Taberd (Taberd Youth Music Festival), 175
Đại Hội Văn Hóa Dân Tộc (National Culture Congress), 186n23
đại nhạc hội, 175
Đài Phát Thanh Quân Đội (Armed Forces Radio), 176
Đại Việt Party, 22, 71
Đài Vô Tuyến Việt Nam (Vietnam Radio; VTVN), 176
Đà Lạt University, 106–107
dân ca mambo, 169–170, 180
dancehalls, 174–175
Dân Chủ (Democracy), 76
Đặng Văn Sung, 71
Dân Quyền (Civil Rights), 253
de-Americanization, 25–30
Decree 007-TT/SLU, 68, 74–76, 79
Decree No.2661/GD/PC/ND, 111
Deleuze, Gilles, 212–213
democratic institutions in South Vietnam, 70–71, 78–79

Democratic Republic of Vietnam (North Vietnam): Catholic Church and, 193–195, 201n12; economic aid for China and Soviet Union to, 100n9; media images of, 10–11; music production in, 169, 182–185, 188n81; peace negotiations with, 41–49; Thiệu's strategies concerning, 23, 25–30; US bombing of, 25–26, 29–30, 50–51, 58; US negotiations with, 33–35, 49–54
Dever, Carolyn, 261
Dhammapada, 154–155
diasporic Vietnamese. *See* refugees from South Vietnam
Diệm, Ngô Đình: authoritarianism of, 7–8, 64–66; Battle of Saigon and, 1; Catholic Church and, 196; coup against, 23, 42, 64; music production under, 169; peace initiatives of, 42–43, 44; political reforms of, 2, 22, 63–65, 69; press criticism of, 65–66; rural development under, 42, 132
Điện Biên Phủ: fall of, 25
Diên Hồng, 178
Điện Tín (Telegraph), 67, 76
Đinh Văn Chấp, 150
Doãn Quốc Sỹ, 12
Đối Diện (Face-to-Face), 70, 73–77
Đỗ Khiêm, 248
Đôn, Trần Văn, 21, 44–46, 55
Đỗ Quý Toàn, 12
Dorais, Louis-Jacques, 211–212
Dreyfus, Lee Sherman, 119
Dror, Olga, 183
Dư Âm, 180
Đuốc Nhà Nam, 75
Dương Quảng Hàm, 114
Dương Văn Minh, 22–23, 32, 42, 56
Duy Khánh, 178, 205
Dzu, Trương Đình, 48–49, 55, 56

Easter Offensive (1972), 34
East-West Center, 162
economic conditions: Commercial Import Program and, 83–99; music industry and, 182–184; in postwar Vietnam,

13–14, 19n74; in wartime South Vietnam, 6–8, 28–35
education policy in Republic of Vietnam, 105–121
Eisenhower, Dwight D., 1
elections: peace negotiations and, 48, 56–59; Second Republic establishment of, 4–5; in wartime South Vietnam, 32–35
elite politics: higher education policy in RVN and, 117, 121n1; in South Vietnam, 4–5, 63–65, 69
Emerson, Ralph Waldo, 160–161
employment, in wartime South Vietnam, 6–8
engaged Buddhism, 231–234
Espiritu, Yen Le, 12
Essay on Perpetual Peace (Kant), 156–157
ethnic identity, 252–254
eugenics, 256–260
existentialism, 154–158
exports to Vietnam, 85–99

Falk, Charles, 111–112
Famine of 1945, 238
Federation of South Vietnamese Journalists, 68
Fellowship of Reconciliation, 128, 147
First Indochina War, 117, 168–169; Catholic Action and, 193, 200
First National City Bank (Vietnam), 91
First Republic (Vietnam), 2; fall of, 6–7, 64; music industry in, 168–171; press censorship during, 61, 65; republicanism during, 7
foreign markets, 83–99
"Forwarding Memory through Diaporama" (Ninh), 221n4
Four No's policy, 56–57
France: decline in exports to Vietnam from, 88; Indochina War and, 25; peace negotiations and, 44–45; Vietnamese refugee activism in, 246–247, 251–252
French Indochina, 25, 64–66, 105–106, 179–180; Catholicism in, 190–194; herd mentality in, 248
French Revolution, 191

Freud, Sigmund, 207–210
Fromm, Erich, 157

Gaddis, John Lewis, 35n6
Gagnon, Gerárd, 194
Gandhi, Mohandas, 165n34
General Mobilization Law, 7, 18n40
Geneva Accords (1954), 9, 25, 43–46, 106, 195, 238
Geneva agreement (1979), 9
German romanticism, 246
Germany, 119–120, 123n51
GGM Bolero, 219
ghosts, 240–242
Giải Phóng Nam Bộ (Southern Liberation), 176
Gödel, Kurt, 159
Goodman, Allan, 4, 49
Gorbanevskaya, Natalya, 246
Gothic literature, 236–242
Guattari, Félix, 212–213
Gươm Thiêng Ái Quốc (Sacred Patriotic Sword), 176

Harriman, W. Averell, 26, 51
Harvey, Yvette Rochelle, 236
Hà Văn Đính, 136
Henry, Eric, 218
Heschel, Abraham, 147
higher education: in Republic of Vietnam, 15, 18n32; RVN policies for, 104–121; student enrollment statistics for, 110–111; Thích Minh Châu on, 158–163; in Vietnamese refugee literature, 256–260. *See also* public universities
"Hippies à go go," 175
Hoạch, Lê Văn, 43
Hoà Hảo religious group, 6–7
Hoàng Đức Nhã, 24
Hoàng Ngọc Lung, 35n7
Hoàng Oanh, 205–206
Hoàng Thi Thơ, 178, 206
Hoành Sơn record label, 180
Hồ Chí Minh, 256; loyalty to, 8; nationalism of, 63; Vietnamese refugees' denunciation of, 14
Hồng Hoa, 180

Hồ Ngọc Tuấn, 136
Hồng Sơn Đông, 76
Hồn Nước Với Lễ Gia Tiên (National Soul and Ancestral Ceremony) (Kim Định), 248
Hồn Việt Nam (Vietnamese Soul), 247, 250
Hồ Thị Minh, 135
humanism, 252–256
human rights: in postwar Vietnam, 10–14; Vietism and campaign for, 246–266
Humphrey, Hubert, 25
Hùng Cường, 172
Hương, Thanh, 133–134
Huỳnh, Sanh Thông, 11
Hy, Nguyễn, 136

Import Committee (Vietnam National Bank), 86
imports, 83–86, 94–97, 101n26, 102n28
Indochinese University, 106, 112
Institute for Higher Buddhist Studies (Saigon Buddhist Studies College), 145
Institute for Historic Cao Dai Religion, 14
Institute of Animal Husbandry (SVN), 258–260
Institute of Exchange Rate, 92
Institute of Secular Affairs (Viện Hóa Đạo), 147
intellectual community (RVN): academic freedom and, 145–163; Buddhist revival movement and, 15–16; culture of, 105–106, 120–121; music production and, 184; republicanism and, 2; Thích Minh Châu and, 155–158; Vietism in refugee community and, 245–246, 251–256, 266
International Control Commission, 44
International Monetary Fund (IMF), 91
International Outdoor Youth Music Festival, 175
Ionesco, Eugène, 246

Japan: imports to South Vietnam from, 84–90, 101n26; Vietnamese refugees in, 246–247, 251–252
Jaspers, Karl, 157

Johnson, Alexis, 44
Johnson, Lyndon Baines, 24–26, 37n33, 41, 47–52
Joiner, Charles, 4
Jung, Carl, 246, 248–251, 262–263

Kahin, George T., 147
Kant, Immanuel, 149, 156–157
Kennedy, John F., 64
Kennedy, Robert, 25
Khánh, Nguyễn, 66–67, 79
Khmer-Lao-Vietnam Committee for Human Rights, 246
Kiaer, Christina, 260
kích động nhạc (action music), 172, 179, 186n43
"Kiếp nghèo" (Lam Phương's song), 206
Kim, Sharon, 251
Kimball, Jeffery, 42
Kim Định, 245–246, 248–253, 255, 261–266
Kim Ngân, Lê, 247
King, Martin Luther Jr., 128, 147
Kisa Gautami (Buddhist folktale), 241–242
Kissinger, Henry, 33, 45, 57–58
Kokua Van Hanh, 162
Korean War, 98–99
Koster, Alter, 119
Krainick, Horst Gunther, 119

Lady of the Realm (Hoa Pham), 225–234, 242
LaFollette, Robert Russell, 117–118
Laird, Melvin, 21, 33
Lam Phương (Lâm Đình Phùng), 204–206, 209
Lam Son, 180
Land to the Tiller legislation (Vietnam), 32
Laos, 25–26, 33–35, 54
League of the Sacred Heart (Liên Minh Thánh Tâm), 194, 199–200
Lê Bá Kông, 114
Lê Dinh, 179
Lê Đức Thọ, 50–51, 57–58
Legion of Mary, 194
Lê Minh Bằng, 179, 180
Lê Ngọc Liên (cô Sáu Liên), 180
Lê Sĩ Thắng, 257

Lê Thế Lành, 136
Lê Văn Tài, 180
Lipman, Jana, 13
literature: Bodhisattva of Mercy in, 227–230; Buddhist syncretism in, 224–242; by Thích Nhất Hạnh, 232–234; publishing in RVN, 114–115; of Vietnamese refugees, 11–13, 16, 253–260
Liu, Lyu, 252
Lodge, Henry Cabot, 47
Lorenz, Konrad, 250, 268n51
Love and Understanding (Hiểu và Thương), 140
Lửa Thiêng, 114–115
Lý Quí Chung, 70, 75, 79
Ly Tao, 178

Madhyama Agama/Zhōng Āhánjīng, 150
Mahayana canon, 150
Mai, Nhất Chi, 137–139
Mai Lệ Huyền, 172
Mai Thảo, 12
Majjhima Nikāya, 150
Malkin, John, 231
Mạnh Cương, 104
manufacturers, 83–99, 102n28
Many Flags, 117–118
Marcel, Gabriel, 157
Marcuse, Herbert, 165n36
Marian devotionalism in Vietnam, 16, 191–196, 264–265
martyrs, 190–194
Mason, Walter, 241–242
"Mất" (loss/lost) (Lam Phương's song), 209
May Man Prevail (Fromm), 157
McArthur, George, 78
McCarthy, Eugene, 25
McCarthy, Patrick, 236
McNamara, Robert, 128, 142n20, 147
media: music broadcasts, 175–177; and refugee radio and television programs, 10–12; during Vietnam War, 8. *See also* print media; radio; Radiodiffusion-Télévision Française; Radio-France-Asie
melancholia, 205–211, 222n25

Menander (Greek King), 150–151
"Mẹ Trong Lòng Người Đi" (The Émigré's Mother) (Nguyễn Mộng Giác), 254–256, 260–266
Mẹ Việt Nam (Mother Vietnam), 176
military elites: music for, 169–171; public education in RVN and, 117; South Vietnam nation-building and, 4–5, 63–66, 69
Miller, Arthur, 147
Milosz, Czeslaw, 254
Minh Kỳ, 179
Minh Phát, 178
Mookerjee, Satkari, 145
"Mother Right" theory, 261–266
"Mourning and Melancholia" (Freud), 207, 209–210
Movement for the Reparation to the Immaculate Heart of Mary (Phong Trào Đền Tạ Trái Tim Vô Nhiệm Đức Mẹ), 194, 199
Mùa biển động (Swelling Sea) (Nguyễn Mộng Giác), 255
Mùa hè đỏ lửa (Summer of Red Flames), 175
Mus, Paul, 248
music: broadcasting of, 175–177; in the marketplace, 173–175; publishers, 177–183; nostalgia and melancholia in refugee, 205–211; refugee communities and, 13–14, 203–220; RVN-era production of, 16, 168–169, 171–173; security forces and, 170–171, 173–175; sheet music publishers of, 177–179; smuggling of to postwar SVN, 206–207; sound recordings of, 179–182
Mỹ Hạnh, 179

Nagarjuna (Buddhist philosopher), 155
Nam Việt Bolero, 218
National Bank of Vietnam: Commercial Import Program and, 91–97; Import Committee of, 86
national church, 192–194
National Cursillo Movement, 7, 189, 197, 199–200

nationalism: in colonial era, 63; peace negotiations and influence of, 50–56; in refugee communities, 190, 204–220; Vietist concept of, 247–248, 250–251; Vietnam war and, 7, 12. *See also* transnationalism
National Liberation Front (NLF): peace negotiations and, 41–46, 48, 50–59; Vietnam war and, 23, 25–28, 38n41, 134, 136
National Security Council (NSC), 51
National Self-Determination Movement, 44
National Technical Center (Saigon), 113
National University (*Quốc Tử Giám*), 159
nation-building in South Vietnam, 61–69
Nava Nalanda Mahivara University, 145, 149
neocolonialism: Commercial Import Program and, 83–84; refugee music and, 206–207
Newspaper Editors Association, 68
newspapers: music coverage in, 171–173, 176, 178; role in RVN of, 61–79. *See also* media; press in RVN
New Vietnamese, 250–266
Ngày Giải phóng miền Nam (April 30, 1975), 208–209
Ngày mất Nước (April 30, 1975), 208–209
Nghị Đoàn, 259
Nghiệm, Phạm Việt, 133–134
Nghiêm Xuân Thiện, 66
Ngọc Chánh, 179
Ngô Đình Thục (Bishop), 107, 196
Ngô Thị Kha, 180
Ngô Văn Mạnh (Năm Mạnh), 179
Ngô Văn Tri, 179
Ngựa Nản Chân Bon (Surrender) (Nguyễn Mộng Giác), 255–256
Nguyen, Lien-Hang, 4
Nguyen, Marguerite, 13
Nguyen, Tina, 215
Nguyen, Viet Thanh, 241
Nguyễn Cao Kỳ, 21, 23, 35, 36n14, 46–48, 50, 52–53, 55–56, 64–65, 203
Nguyễn Cao Kỳ Duyên, 203
Nguyễn Công Hoan, 246–247

Nguyễn Công Luận, 72, 73
Nguyễn Đăng Minh, 178
Nguyễn Đông-A, 247–248
Nguyễn Hữu Hanh, 93–94
Nguyễn Hữu Thái, 259
Nguyễn Khánh, 4–5, 42–43
Nguyễn Khuyến (Bảo Thu), 178
Nguyễn Mộng Giác, 246, 252–266
Nguyễn Ngọc Bích, 11
Nguyễn Ngọc Lan (father), 70, 77
Nguyễn Ngọc Ngạn, 203
Nguyễn Ngọc Phách, 67–68
Nguyễn Ngọc Thơ, 42
Nguyễn Phú Đức, 25, 38n46
Nguyễn Quang Trình, 106
Nguyễn Tấn Linh, 72
Nguyễn Tất Oanh (Tám Oanh), 180
Nguyễn Văn Cung, 116
Nguyễn Văn Đông, 178–179, 181
Nguyễn Văn Hinh, 22
Nguyễn Văn Thắng, 116
Nguyễn Văn Thiệu, 7
Nhạc Hay Của Bạn, 178
Nhạc Mới, 179
Nhạc Ngày Xanh, 180
nhạc tiền chiến, 169
nhạc trẻ, 173–175, 177, 179, 182, 186n43
Nhạc Tuyển Vô Tuyến, 180
nhạc vàng, 183–184, 204–220, 220n2, 222n19
Nhật Ngân, 206
Nho giáo, 114
Nietzsche, Friedrich, 159
Ninh, Erin Khuê, 221n4
Nixon, Richard, 21, 25, 27–29, 33, 40n76, 41, 45, 52–53, 57–58, 70
North Vietnam. *See* Democratic Republic of Vietnam
North Vietnamese Army (NVA), 28–29, 34
nostalgia, 205–211
Novice: A Story of True Love, The (Thích Nhất Hạnh), 229

Odyssey, The (Homer), 217–218
Operation Passage to Freedom (1954–1955), 238
Orderly Departure Program (ODP), 9

Our Lady of Fatima, 192–194, 196–199
Our Lady of La Vang, 190–194, 196
Our Lady of Lourdes, 191–192

Paris by Night, 203–204, 212, 218
Paris Peace talks, 24–26, 33, 41, 49–52, 58–59, 152–153, 156–158; music as response to, 172
Paul VI (pope), 147
Peace Committee, 55
Pentalateral Agreement (1950), 88
Performing Arts Department (Phòng Văn Nghệ), 171
Peril, 225
petroleum industry, 87–88
Phạm, Hoa, 225–234, 242
Phạm Duy, 204, 206
Phạm Hoàng Hộ, 115
Phạm Kim Ngọc, 91
Phạm Kim Vinh, 255
Phạm Mạnh Cương, 182
Phạm Ngọc Chi, 192–193
Phạm Tuân, 257
Phạm Văn Đồng, 246
Phan Huy Quát, 43–46
Phan Quang Đán, 66
pharmaceutical industry, 87–88
Phật Giáo Việt Nam (Vietnamese Buddhism), 126
Philippines, 9–10
philosophy: Thích Minh Châu on, 149–150, 154–158; and Vietism of refugees, 16, 246–266
Phó Quốc Lân, 205
Phượng Hoàng Band, 173
Picard, Jason, 65
Pius XI (pope), 192
Plato, 160
Plum Village Monasteries (Làng Mai), 231
politics: philology of Thích Minh Châu and, 150–154; press role in, 69–71; in RVN, 3–5, 62–69; Vietnam war and growth of, 7–8
Prajna Monastery, 230–234
press and newspapers: content analysis of, 69–71; defense of press freedom, 74–79; nation-building and rise of, 63–69; in RVN, 61–79; in SVN, 258–260; Vietnamization criticism in, 71–74; during Vietnam War, 8, 15. *See also* media
Press Law 019/1969, 67, 79
Primordial Man, 252–254
property rights, 10
Provisional Revolutionary Government (PRG), 55–59
psychoanalysis: refugee music production and, 206–208; Vietism and, 248–250, 263–266
Psychological Warfare Bureau, 170–171, 176, 185n15
public universities: academic development of, 107–116; admissions requirements, 108–109; examinations and accreditation, 114–116; postcolonial transformation of, 105–107; research and publishing at, 113–115; in RVN, 104–121; teacher training and hiring and, 107–113; Vietnam War and, 117–121
publishing, 113–115. *See also* individual publishing house; media; press. *See also under* music; public universities

Quan Tue Tran, 13
"Quê Hương Bỏ Lại" (Homeland left behind) (Tô Huyền Vân), 216–217
Questions of Milinda, 150–151

racial identity, 251–252
radio, 175–177. *See also* media
Radiodiffusion-Télévision Française (French Radio and Television Broadcasting), 175–176
Radio-France-Asie, 175–176, 205
recording industry: bootlegs in, 182–183; Vietnamese music and, 179–182
record labels. *See under* individual company name
reexport practices, 96–97
refugees, South Vietnamese (*việt kiều*): agency of, 13–14; Buddhism in literature of, 224–242; Catholic associational culture and, 189–190, 198–201;

diasporic images and historiography of, 8–14; literature by, 4–5, 11–12, 224–242; music of RVN and, 184–185; popular images and historiography on, 5–14; recreational activities of, 16; republicanism and, 16, 203–220; smuggling of music to postwar SVN, 206–207; statistics on, 18n29; transnationalism of, 211–220; Vietism and, 245–266

Reich, Thomas, 119

religion: Catholic Church in South Vietnam and, 6–8, 63–65; Thích Minh Châu's analysis of, 151–154; Vietnamese refugees and, 14. *See also* Buddhist thought and activism

relocation camps: media images of, 10–11; memoirs by refugees of, 12–14

republicanism in Vietnam: diaspora and survival of, 16; history of, 1–3; postwar suppression of, 10; refugee communities and, 203–220; Second Republic scholarship and, 3–5; Vietnamese refugee culture and politics and, 13–14; Vietnam War's impact on, 7–8

Republic of Vietnam (RVN): Buddhist activism and, 124–141; Catholicism in, 194–198; Commercial Import Program and government agency in, 89–97; diasporic images and historiography on, 8–14; economic development in, 28–32; founding of, 1–2; geographic boundaries of, 17n6; higher education in, 15, 18n32, 104–121; music industry in, 168–185; peace negotiations with North Vietnam, 15, 41–49, 53–59; population statistics for, 18n31; press coverage in, 61–79; refugee identification with, 204–220, 245; scholarship on, 3–5, 17n8; South Korea compared with, 97–99, 103n68; tax reforms and modernization in, 30–32; Thích Minh Châu's analysis of, 151–154; US economic aid to, 7–8, 15, 28–35, 40n76, 45, 83–99; Vietnamization strategy and, 14–15, 21–35, 70–74

Reyes, Adelaida, 204

rhizome metaphor, 211–220, 221n6

Riley, Myrne, 113

rituals, 249–250

rock music, 173–175, 177

rural development: Buddhist movement and, 125–126, 130–141; foreign aid and, 85, 93–96; higher education and, 107, 110–117; politics and, 3, 23, 28, 30, 32, 131–132

Said, Edward, 232

Sansom, Robert, 3

School of Mechanical Engineering, 113

School of Youth for Social Service (SYSS) (Trường Thanh Niên Phụng Sự Xã Hội), 125–141, 146–148, 162, 226, 231

Second Indochina War, 117, 147, 151

Second Republic. *See* Republic of Vietnam (RVN)

Second Vatican Council, 197–198

security forces, musicians in, 170–171

"Seed of Enlightenment, The" (Phạm), 228

self-help villages, 130–132

self-immolation, 137–139, 233–234

sheet music, 177–179

Sisters of Vincent de Paul, 191

Sky Music Bolero, 218

Smith, Curtis, 250

socialist ideology, 10–14, 256–260

Socialist Republic of Vietnam (SRV): China and, 14; counterrevolutionary movement in, 247; music censorship in, 183–185, 188n81, 204, 219–220; New Vietnamese ideology in, 256–260; Vietist activism and, 16, 245–266

sodality associations, 191–192, 194, 199–200

Sơn Ca, 181

Sông Côn mùa lũ (The River Floods) (Nguyễn Mộng Giác), 255

Song Ngọc, 178

Sóng Nhạc, 179–180

Songs of the Caged, Songs of the Free (Reyes), 204
Sóng Thần (Tsunami), 68–71, 75–76
Soucy, Alexander, 224
Southeast Asian Development Advisory Group (SEADAG), 118–119
South Korea, 97–99, 103n68
South Vietnam. *See* Republic of Vietnam (RVN)
Soviet Union, 1, 5, 12, 34, 39n70, 100n9
"Speaking to Youth" (Nói Với Tuổi Hai Mươi), 130
Speak It Louder (Wong), 204
Sponge Cake operation, 91
state: Diệm's creation of, 63–64; press coverage of, 61–69, 74–76; Vietnam War impact on, 5–8
Strategic Hamlets Campaign, 42, 132
Struggle Movement (1966), 7–8
Stur, Heather, 7
syncretism, in Vietnamese Buddhism, 224
Syndicate of Publishers, 68

Taberd Lycée, 191
Tale of Lady Thị Kính, The (Quan Âm Thị Kính), 229–230
Tâm Đoan, 215–216
tân cổ giao duyên, 170, 180
tân nhạc, 169–170, 176–177, 180–181, 206, 220n2
Tân Thanh (New Sound), 180
Tạ Văn Tài, 73
taxation, 92
Taylor, Maxwell, 45
Taylor, Philip, 206, 222n19
teacher training and hiring, 107–113
tea rooms (*phòng trà*), 174–175
television, 177. *See also* media
Tết Offensive, 7–8, 25, 41, 49–50, 52, 58, 65, 173–177
Thailand, 10, 96–97
Thánh Gióng, 257
Thich, Quảng Liên, 43–44
Thích Đôn Hậu, 150
Thích Minh Châu: on academic freedom, 158–163; Buddhist activism and, 15–16, 127–128; Buddhist crisis and, 147–149, 164n4; defense of work by, 149–150; on philosophy, 154–158; political philology of, 150–154
Thích Nhất Hạnh: Buddhist activism and, 15, 124–141, 145–149, 165n4, 230–234; in Pham's *Lady of the Realm*, 225–226, 228–234, 242; Vietnam War and, 6–7
Thích Quảng Đức, 234
Thích Thanh Văn, 128, 133
Thích Thiện Minh, 53, 55
Thien-Huong Ninh, 13
Thiên Thai, 180
Thiệu, Nguyễn Văn: coup against Diệm and, 23; de-Americanization strategy of, 25–30; early life and career of, 22–24; economic reforms of, 30–32; peace negotiations and, 46–59; press coverage of, 65, 67–69, 76–77; Second Republic and, 49–50, 65; strategic failures of, 32–35; US relations with, 24–26, 45; Vietnamization strategy and, 14–15, 21–35, 71, 74
Third Force initiative, 42, 55
Thời Luận (Current Commentary), 65–66
Those Who Leave, 10
Thousand Plateaus, A (Guattari), 212–213
303 Committee, 149
Thủ, Trần Đình, 194
Thuận Giao, 73
Thùy Dương Nhạc Tuyển, 178
Thuy Vo Dang, 14
Tiếng K Thời Đại, 178
Tiếng Nói Dân Tộc (National Voice), 70, 72–73
Tiếng Nói Tự Do (Voice of Freedom), 176
Tillich, Paul, 159
Tình Ca 20 company, 178
Tình Ca Quê Hương, 180
Tinh Hoa Miền Hoa, 178
Tin Sáng (Morning News), 77
tobacco industry, 87–88
Tô Huyền Vân, 216–217
Tôn, Nguyễn, 135
Tôn Thất Thiện, 6

Topmiller, Robert, 149, 164n16
trade relations, 84–89, 94–97
Trăm Hoa Miền Nam (One hundred flowers of the south), 179, 181
Trầm Tử Thiêng, 206
Tran, Nu-Anh, 67, 227
Trần Bạch Đằng, 259
Trần Cam, 73
Trắng Đen (Black & White), 67
Trần Lục (father), 191
transnationalism: in music of Vietnamese refugees, 211–220; Vietism human rights campaign and, 246–266; Vietnamese refugees and, 13–14, 19n74
Transnationalizing Viet Nam (Valverde), 204
Trần Thái Thủy, 73
Trần Thiện Thanh (Nhật Trường), 178
Trần Trọng Kim, 114
Trần Văn Ân, 250–251, 254
Trần Văn Đôn, 21
Trần Văn Thọ (father), 74
Trần Văn Tuyên, 72
Tri, Nguyễn Chí, 134–135
Triệu Việt, 72
Trình Bầy (Presentation), 71
Trịnh Công Sơn, 204
Trịnh Quan, 182–183
Trí Quang, Thích, 127
Trọng Phú, 77
Trùng Dương (Nguyễn Thị Thái), 70–71
Trương Bá Cần, 77
Trường Kỳ, 175
Trương Như Tảng, 44
Truth Operation, 91
Tsu, Jing, 266
Tư Tưởng (Thought), 145–146

ultramontanism, 191–194
Unified Buddhist Church, 129, 133, 135, 140, 147, 162
Union of Journalists, 68
United Nations High Commissioner for Refugees (UNHCR), 9
United States: antiwar movement in, 24, 29–30, 33–35, 72; bombing of North Vietnam by, 25–26, 29–30, 50–51, 58; broadcasting industry in RVN and, 176–177; buffer strategy in Vietnam and, 63, 83; Diệm and, 23, 42; economic aid to Vietnam and, 15, 28–35, 40n76, 45, 83–99; higher education in Vietnam and, 111, 117–121; military forces in Vietnam from, 2–5, 6–8, 12, 43–47, 63, 83; Thích Nhất Hạnh's work in, 147–149; peace negotiations and, 33–35, 41–42, 45–54, 56–59; refugee communities in, 9–14, 189–190, 198–201, 251–253; South Korea and, 97–99, 103n689; Thiệu and, 22–30, 33–35, 49–54; Vietnamese press coverage of, 72–74, 77–78; Vietnamization strategy and, 21–35
universities, public. See public universities
University of Cần Thơ, 106–110, 112, 115–116, 122n22
University of Florida, 117
University of Huế, 106–108, 112–113, 118–119
University of Missouri-Rolla, 117
University of Saigon, 106–109, 111, 112
US Agency for International Development (USAID), 84–86, 88, 93, 101n17, 117
USG-GVN Economic Agreement, 88

Valverde, Kieu-Linh Caroline, 204
Vấn Đề (Issues), 71
Vạn Hạnh Buddhist University: founding of, 106–107, 126, 128, 131, 139–140; Thích Minh Châu and, 145–149, 152–154, 158–163
Vạn Hạnh Institute, 162
Van Hanh Newsletter/Van Hanh Bulletin, 145–146, 148–149, 162
Văn Học (Literary Studies), 255
Văn Lang, 248–249
"Về Nguồn" (Return to the Source) (Nguyễn Mộng Giác), 256–260
videos, 204–220
Việt, Trần Thanh, 73–74
Việt Anh, 72

Viet Cong, 3–5
Việt Đạo (Vietism), 247
Việt Hải, 180
Vietism: humanism and, 252–256; and mothers, 260–266; New Vietnamese and Primordial Man theory and, 246–252; postwar emergence of, 16, 245–246; socialist eugenics and, 256–260
Việt Khang, 209
Việt Minh, 22, 28, 169, 193–194, 235–242
Vietnam: Chinese-Cambodian conflict with, 10, 12; postwar resettlement in, 10
Vietnam: A Television History, 11
Vietnamese American studies (VAS), 11–14
Vietnamese Environmental Protection Society, 14
Vietnamese General Buddhist Association, 126
Vietnamese-language archive, 11–13
Vietnamese National Army, 22
Vietnamese PEN Club, 255
Vietnamization strategy, 14–15, 21–35, 35n7, 70–74
Vietnam: Lotus in a Sea of Fire (Thích Nhất Hạnh), 128, 149
Vietnam National Army, 1
Việt Nam Nhạc Tuyển, 179
Việtnam (Hãng Dĩa Việt Nam), 179–180
Vietnam Studies, 11–12
Việt Nam Sử lược (A Brief History of Vietnam) (Trần Trọng Kim), 114
Việt Nam thi văn hợp tuyển (Selected Vietnamese Verses and Prose), 114
"Việt Nam Tôi Đâu" (Where Is My Vietnam?), 209
Việt Nam Văn học sử yếu (History of Vietnamese Literary Works), 114
Vietnam War: de-Americanization of, 27–30; music about, 206–220; public universities and, 117–121; state and society during, 5–8; Thích Minh Châu's analysis of, 149–150, 160–161
Vietnam: Which Human Rights?, 10
Việt Thường, 253
village economy: Land to the Tiller legislation and, 32; in Second Republic era, 3–5
Vinh, Lê Văn, 135
Võ Đình, 253–254
Voice of America, 176
vọng cổ (longing for the past), 170, 172, 180
Võ Văn Thơ, 136
Vu, Chi (Vũ Thị Mỹ Chi), 234–242

Watergate scandal, 33
Whorf, Benjamin Lee, 152
Wiest, Andrew, 5
Willbanks, James, 35
Woiak, Joanne, 259
women refugee writers, 224–242
Wong, Deborah, 204
World Conference in Chinese Philosophy, 252
Wulff, Erich, 119–120

Young Turks, 23
youth groups, 15, 125–141

Studies of the Weatherhead East Asian Institute

Columbia University

Selected Titles

(Complete list at https://weai.columbia.edu/content/publications)

Confluence and Conflict: Reading Transwar Japanese Literature and Thought, by Brian Hurley. Harvard East Asian Monographs, 2022.

Inglorious, Illegal Bastards: Japan's Self-Defense Force During the Cold War, by Aaron Skabelund. Cornell University Press, 2022.

Madness in the Family: Women Care, and Illness in Japan, by H. Yumi Kim. Oxford University Press, 2022.

Uncertainty in the Empire of Routine: The Administrative Revolution of the Eighteenth-Century Qing State, by Maura Dykstra. Harvard University Press, 2022.

Outsourcing Repression: Everyday State Power in Contemporary China, by Lynette H. Ong. Oxford University Press, 2022.

Diasporic Cold Warriors: Nationalist China, Anticommunism, and the Philippine Chinese, 1930s–1970s, by Chien-Wen Kung. Cornell University Press, 2022.

Dream Super-Express: A Cultural History of the World's First Bullet Train, by Jessamyn Abel. Stanford University Press, 2022.

The Sound of Salvation: Voice, Gender, and the Sufi Mediascape in China, by Guangtian Ha. Columbia University Press, 2022.

Carbon Technocracy: Energy Regimes in Modern East Asia, by Victor Seow. University of Chicago Press, 2022.

Disunion: Anticommunist Nationalism and the Making of the Republic of Vietnam, by Nu-Anh Tran. University of Hawai'i Press, 2022.

Learning to Rule: Court Education and the Remaking of the Qing State, 1861–1912, by Daniel Barish. Columbia University Press, 2022.

Art Across Borders: Japanese Artists in the United States Before World War II, by Ramona Handel-Bajema. Merwin Asia, 2021.